Zenescope Entertainment Presents.

Grimm Fairy Tales

Different Seasons Volume 3

zenescope

GRIMM FAIRY TALES
DIFFERENT SEASONS

VOLUME THREE

CREATED AND STORY
JOE BRUSHA
RALPH TEDESCO

ART DIRECTOR
ANTHONY SPAY

TRADE DESIGN
CHRISTOPHER COTE

EDITOR
RALPH TEDESCO

THIS VOLUME REPRINTS THE
FOLLOWING COMIC BOOK
ISSUES GRIMM FAIRY TALES 2010
HALLOWEEN SPECIAL, 2010 HOLIDAY
EDITION, VALENTINE'S DAY
SPECIAL 2013, ST. PATRICK'S DAY
SPECIAL 2013, AND 2012 SWIMSUIT
SPECIAL PUBLISHED BY ZENESCOPE
ENTERTAINMENT

WWW.ZENESCOPE.COM

FIRST EDITION, DECEMBER 2013
ISBN: 978-1-939683-03-8

WWW.ZENESCOPE.COM
FACEBOOK.COM/ZENESCOPE

ZENESCOPE ENTERTAINMENT, INC.

Joe Brusha • President & Chief Creative Officer
Ralph Tedesco • Editor-in-Chief
Jennifer Bermel • Director of Licensing & Business Development
Raven Gregory • Executive Editor
Anthony Spay • Art Director
Christopher Cote • Senior Designer & Production Manager
Dave Franchini • Direct Market Sales & Customer Service
Stephen Haberman • Marketing Manager

GRIMM FAIRY TALES CREATED BY JOE BRUSHA AND RALPH TEDESCO

Grimm Fairy Tales™

Different Seasons Volume 3

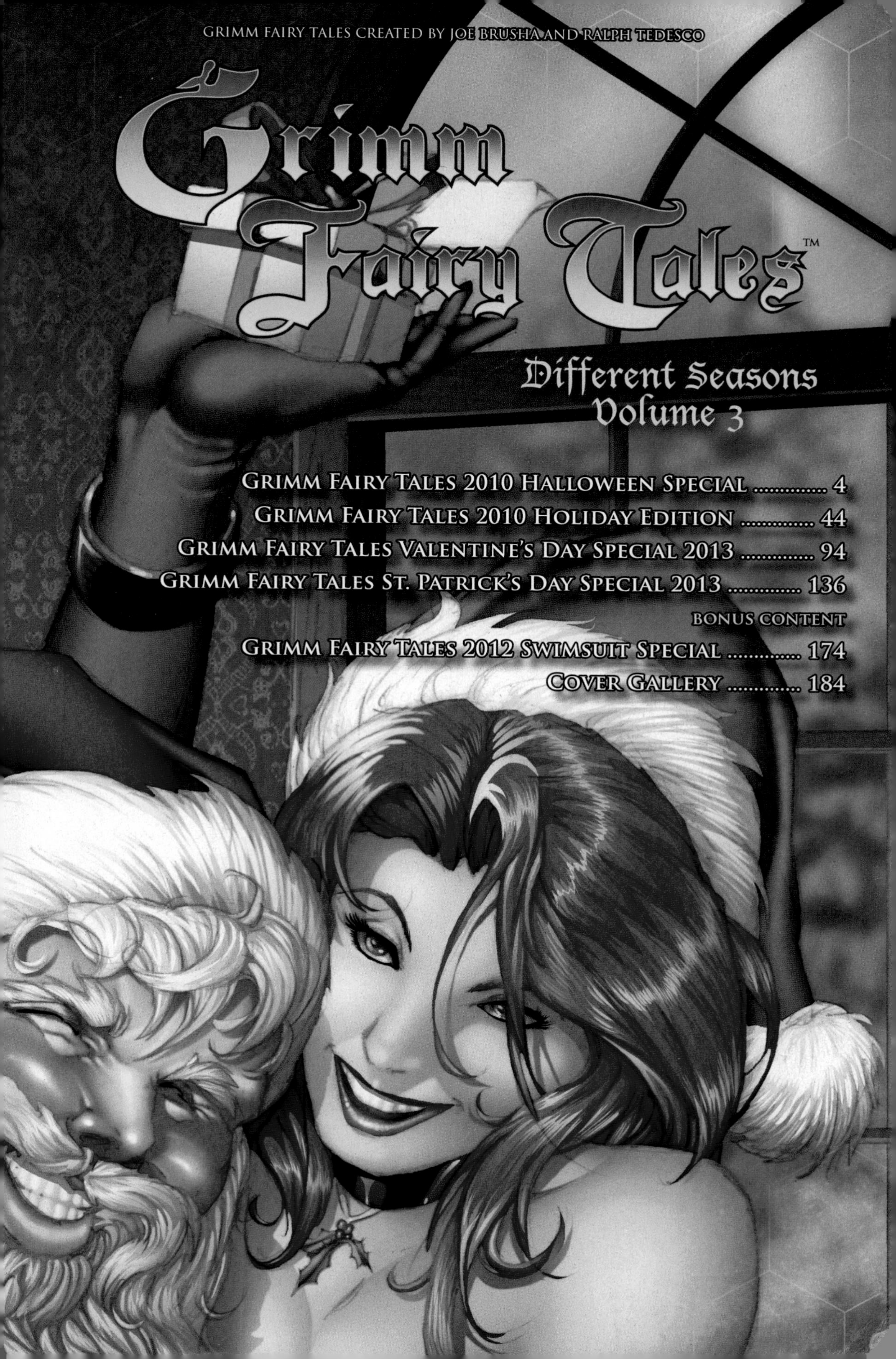

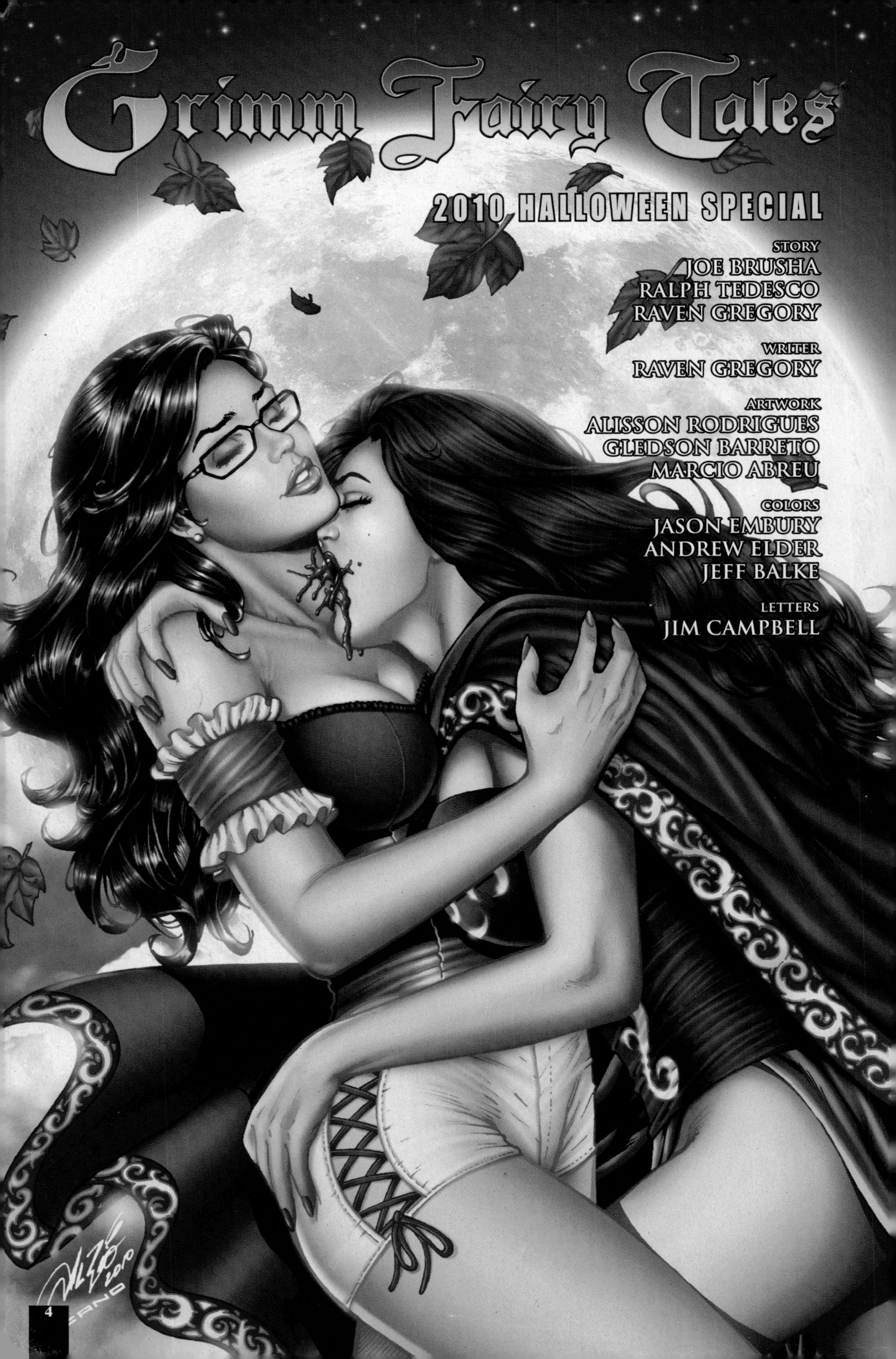
Grimm Fairy Tales
2010 HALLOWEEN SPECIAL
STORY
JOE BRUSHA
RALPH TEDESCO
RAVEN GREGORY
WRITER
RAVEN GREGORY
ARTWORK
ALISSON RODRIGUES
GLEDSON BARRETO
MARCIO ABREU
COLORS
JASON EMBURY
ANDREW ELDER
JEFF BALKE
LETTERS
JIM CAMPBELL

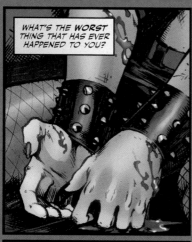

WHAT'S THE WORST THING THAT HAS EVER HAPPENED TO YOU?

BREAK UP WITH YOUR BOYFRIEND OR GIRLFRIEND? FLAT TIRE ON THE FREEWAY?

GET MUGGED? GET IN A CAR ACCIDENT? PARENTS GET DIVORCED?

MAYBE SOMEBODY DIED? SOMEBODY CLOSE TO YOU? SOMEONE YOU LOVED?

SOMEBODY DIE IN FRONT OF YOU?

CHECK.

THAT KIND OF HORROR... IT CHANGES YOU.

IN MORE WAYS THAN ONE.

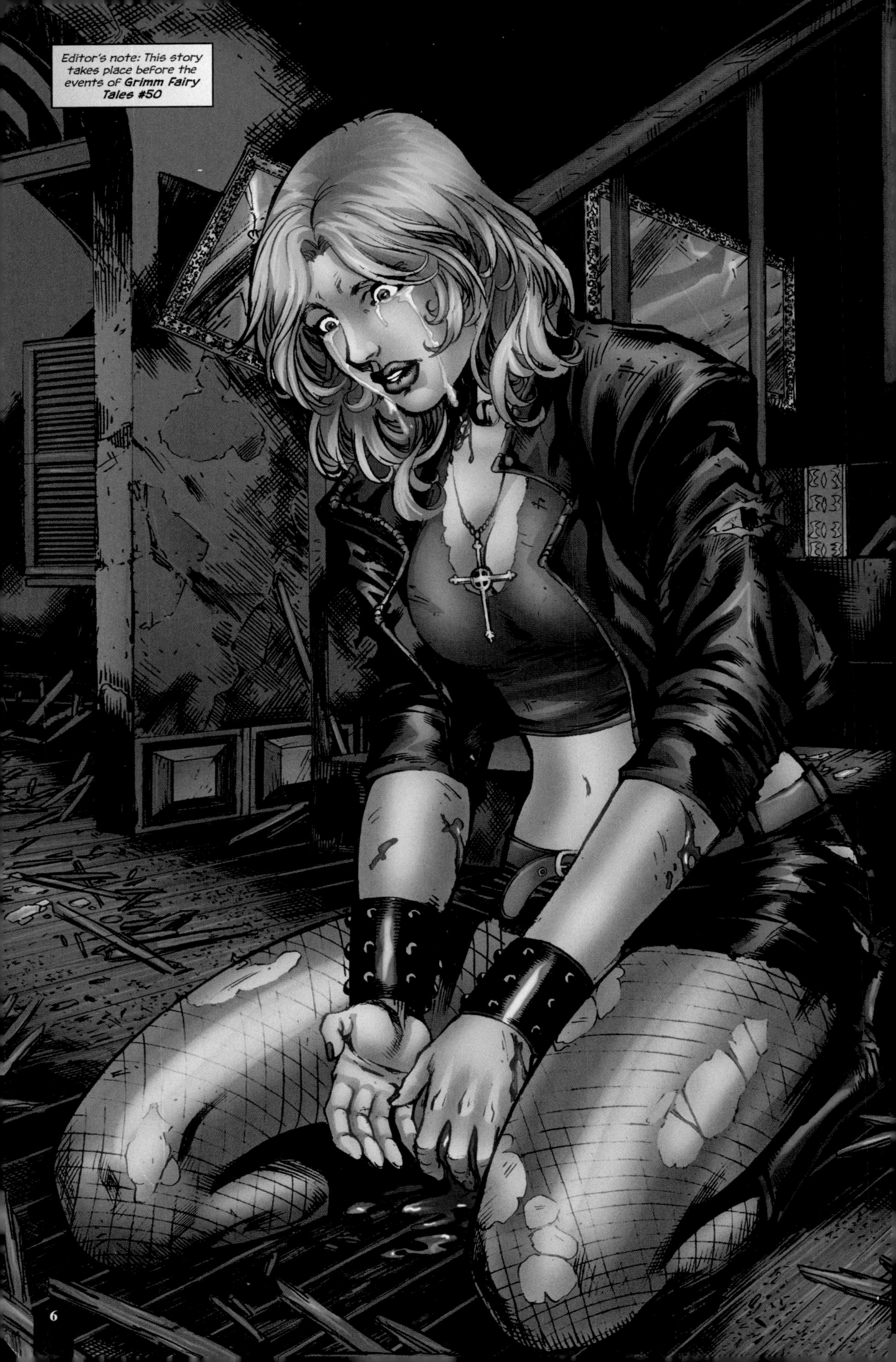
Editor's note: This story takes place before the events of Grimm Fairy Tales #50

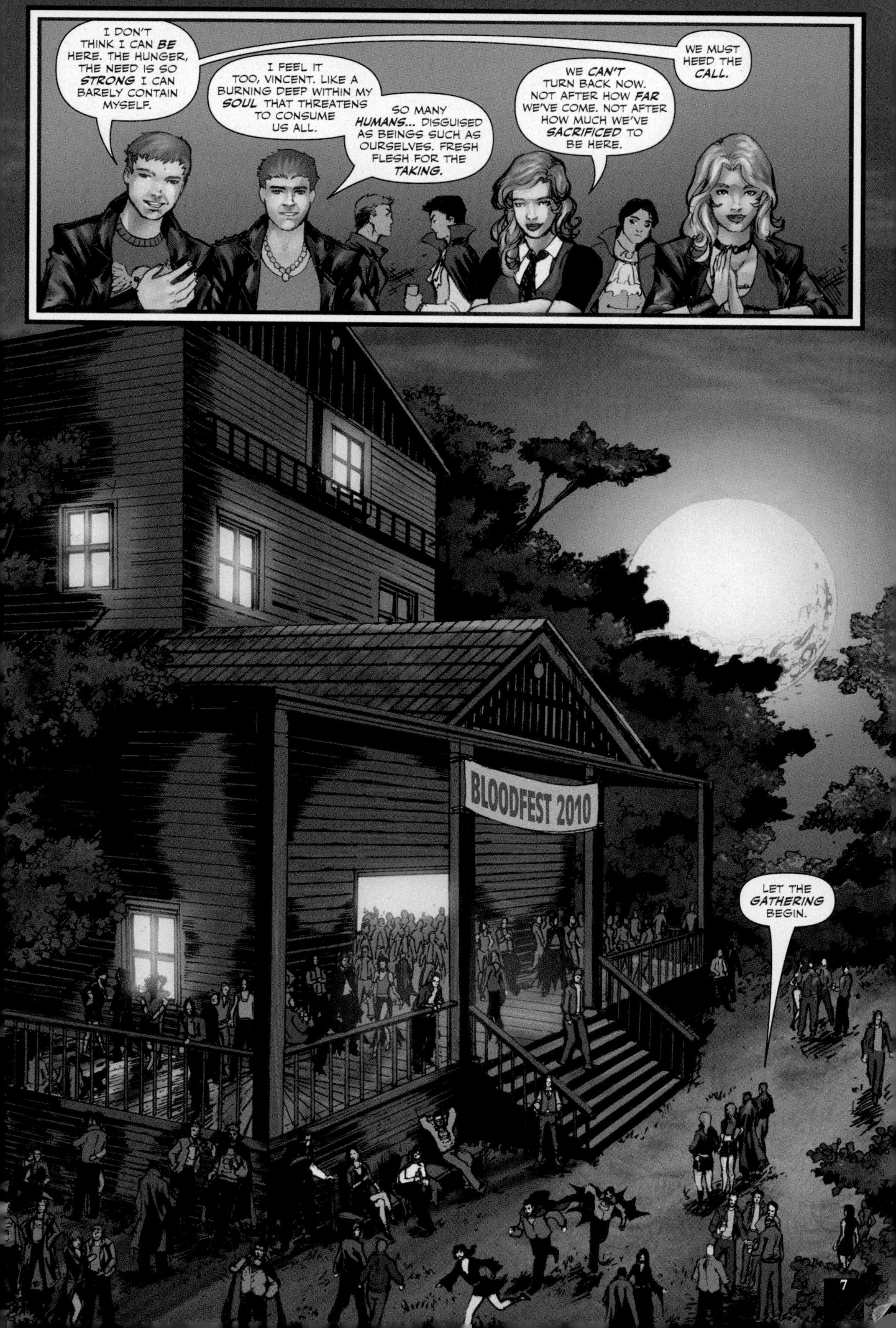
I DON'T THINK I CAN *BE* HERE. THE HUNGER, THE NEED IS SO *STRONG* I CAN BARELY CONTAIN MYSELF.
WE MUST HEED THE *CALL.*
I FEEL IT TOO, VINCENT. LIKE A BURNING DEEP WITHIN MY *SOUL* THAT THREATENS TO CONSUME US ALL.
SO MANY *HUMANS...* DISGUISED AS BEINGS SUCH AS OURSELVES. FRESH FLESH FOR THE *TAKING.*
WE *CAN'T* TURN BACK NOW. NOT AFTER HOW *FAR* WE'VE COME. NOT AFTER HOW MUCH WE'VE *SACRIFICED* TO BE HERE.
BLOODFEST 2010
LET THE *GATHERING* BEGIN.

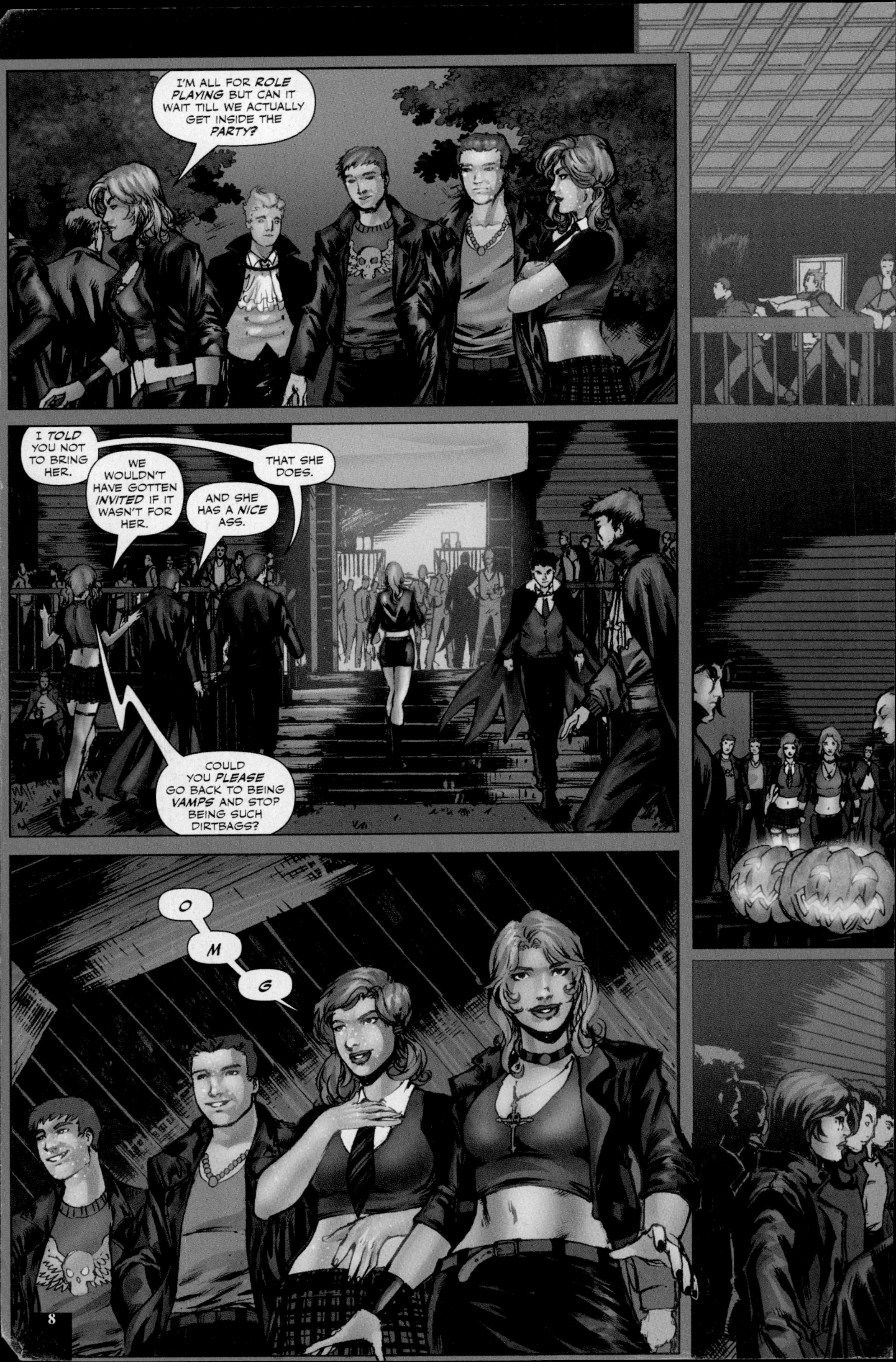
I'M ALL FOR ROLE PLAYING BUT CAN IT WAIT TILL WE ACTUALLY GET INSIDE THE PARTY?
I TOLD YOU NOT TO BRING HER.
WE WOULDN'T HAVE GOTTEN INVITED IF IT WASN'T FOR HER.
AND SHE HAS A NICE ASS.
THAT SHE DOES.
COULD YOU PLEASE GO BACK TO BEING VAMPS AND STOP BEING SUCH DIRTBAGS?
O
M
G

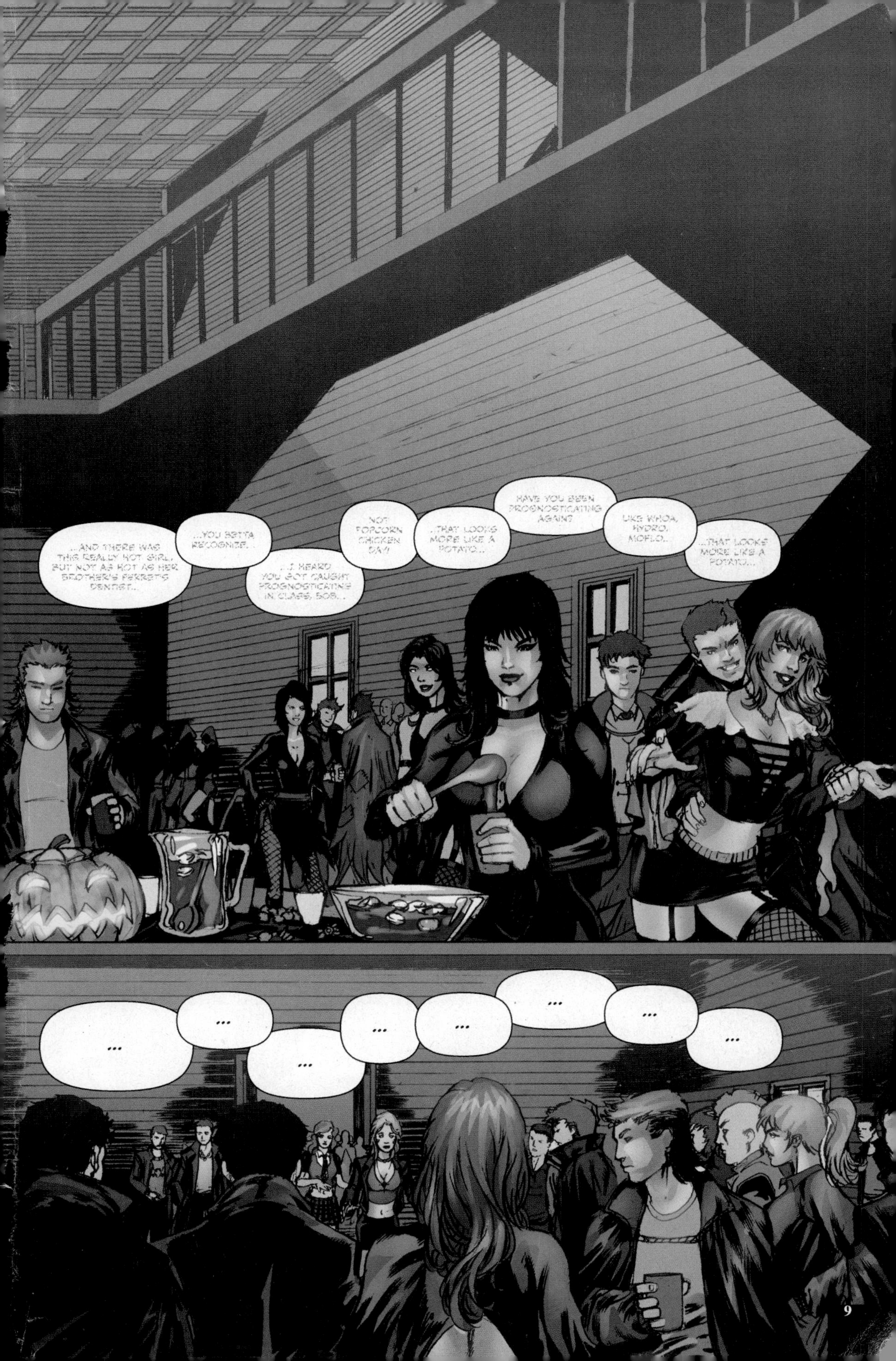
...AND THERE WAS THIS REALLY HOT GIRL, BUT NOT AS HOT AS HER BROTHER'S FERRET'S DENTIST...
...YOU BETTA RECOGNIZE...
...I HEARD YOU GOT CAUGHT PROGNOSTICATING IN CLASS, BOB...
NOT POPCORN CHICKEN DAY!
..THAT LOOKS MORE LIKE A POTATO...
HAVE YOU BEEN PROGNOSTICATING AGAIN?
LIKE WHOA, HYDRO, MOFLO...
...THAT LOOKS MORE LIKE A POTATO...
...
...
...
...
...
...
...
...

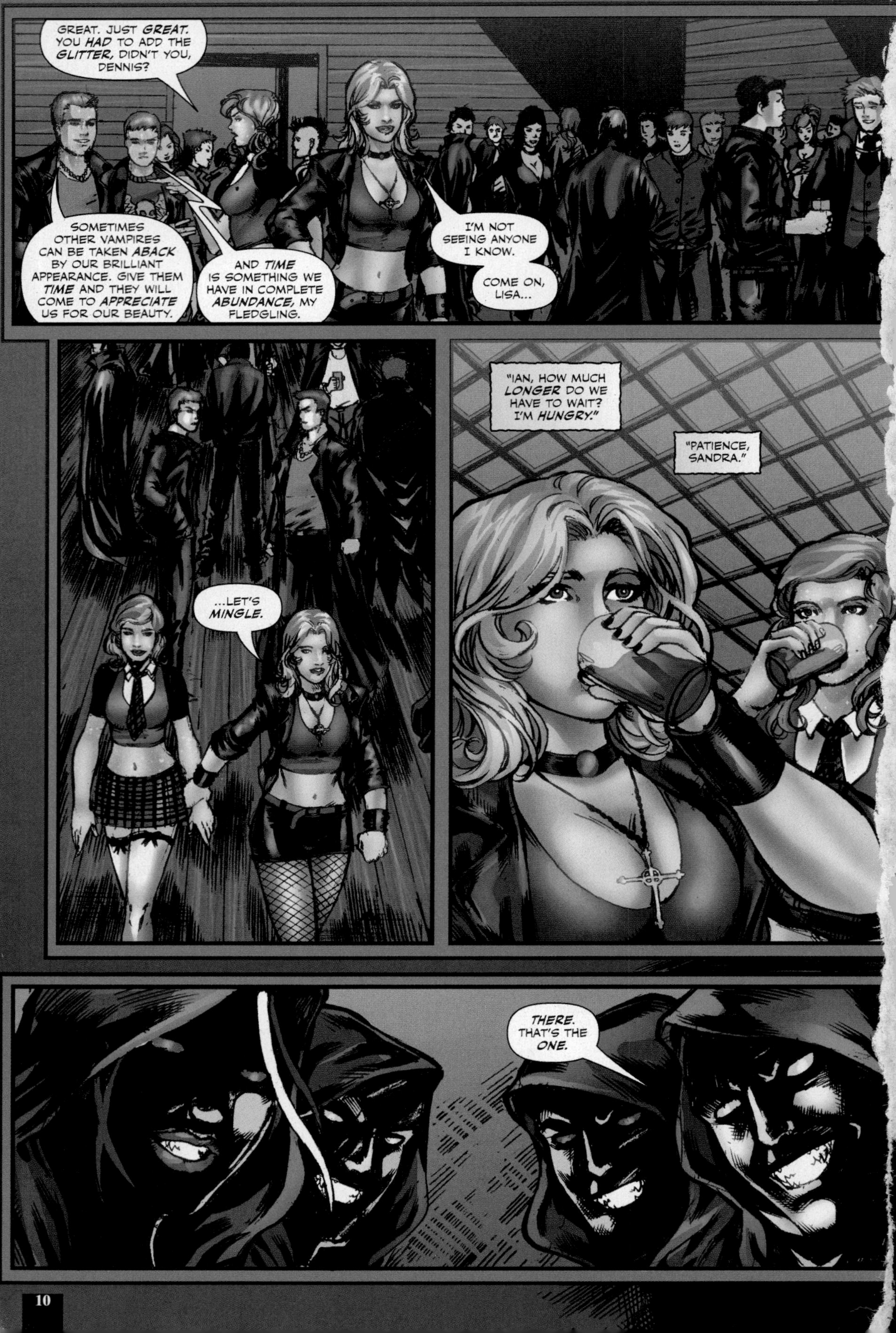
GREAT. JUST GREAT. YOU HAD TO ADD THE GLITTER, DIDN'T YOU, DENNIS?
SOMETIMES OTHER VAMPIRES CAN BE TAKEN ABACK BY OUR BRILLIANT APPEARANCE. GIVE THEM TIME AND THEY WILL COME TO APPRECIATE US FOR OUR BEAUTY.
AND TIME IS SOMETHING WE HAVE IN COMPLETE ABUNDANCE, MY FLEDGLING.
I'M NOT SEEING ANYONE I KNOW.
COME ON, LISA...
...LET'S MINGLE.
"IAN, HOW MUCH LONGER DO WE HAVE TO WAIT? I'M HUNGRY."
"PATIENCE, SANDRA."
THERE. THAT'S THE ONE.

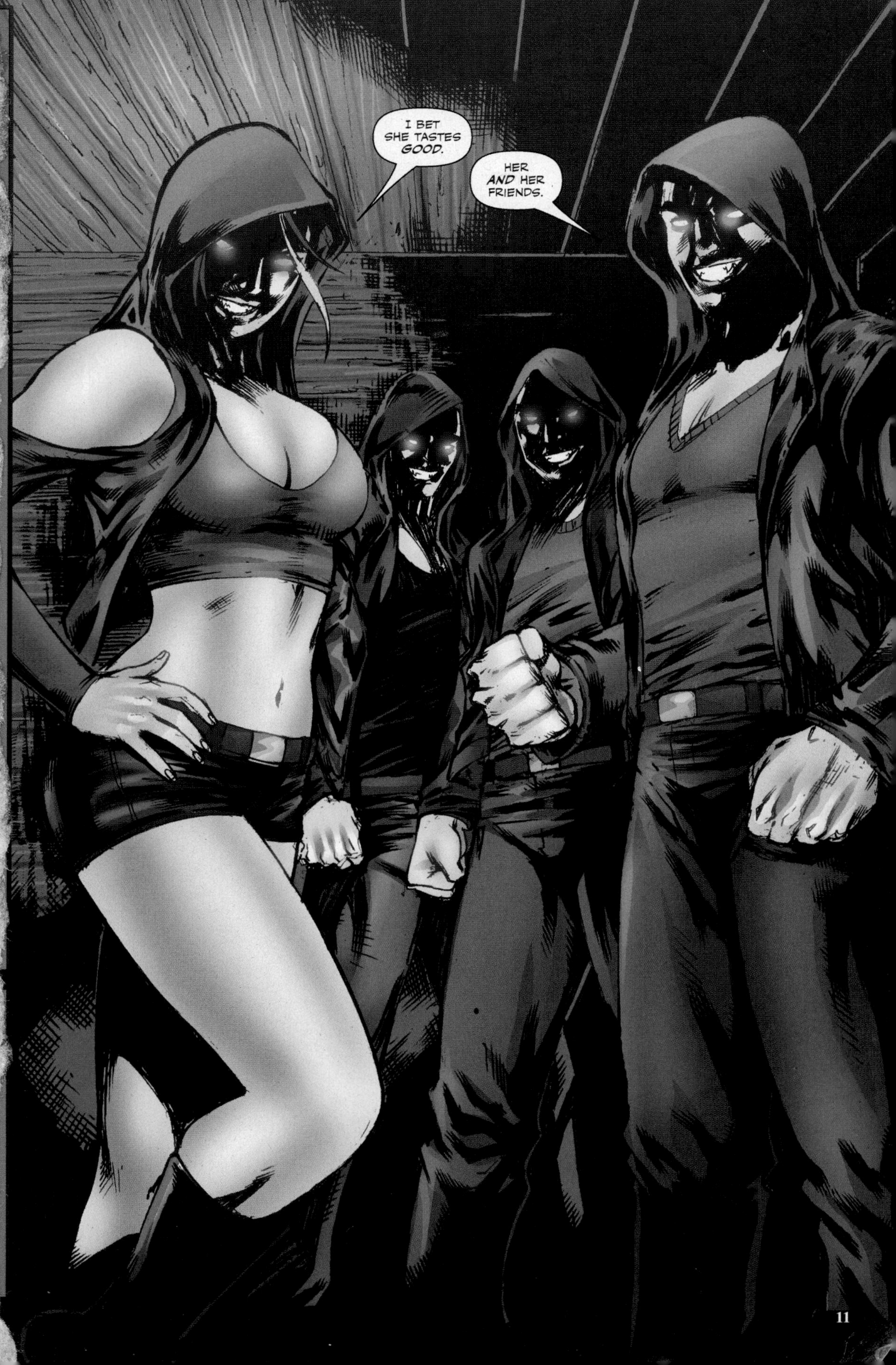
I BET SHE TASTES GOOD.
HER AND HER FRIENDS.

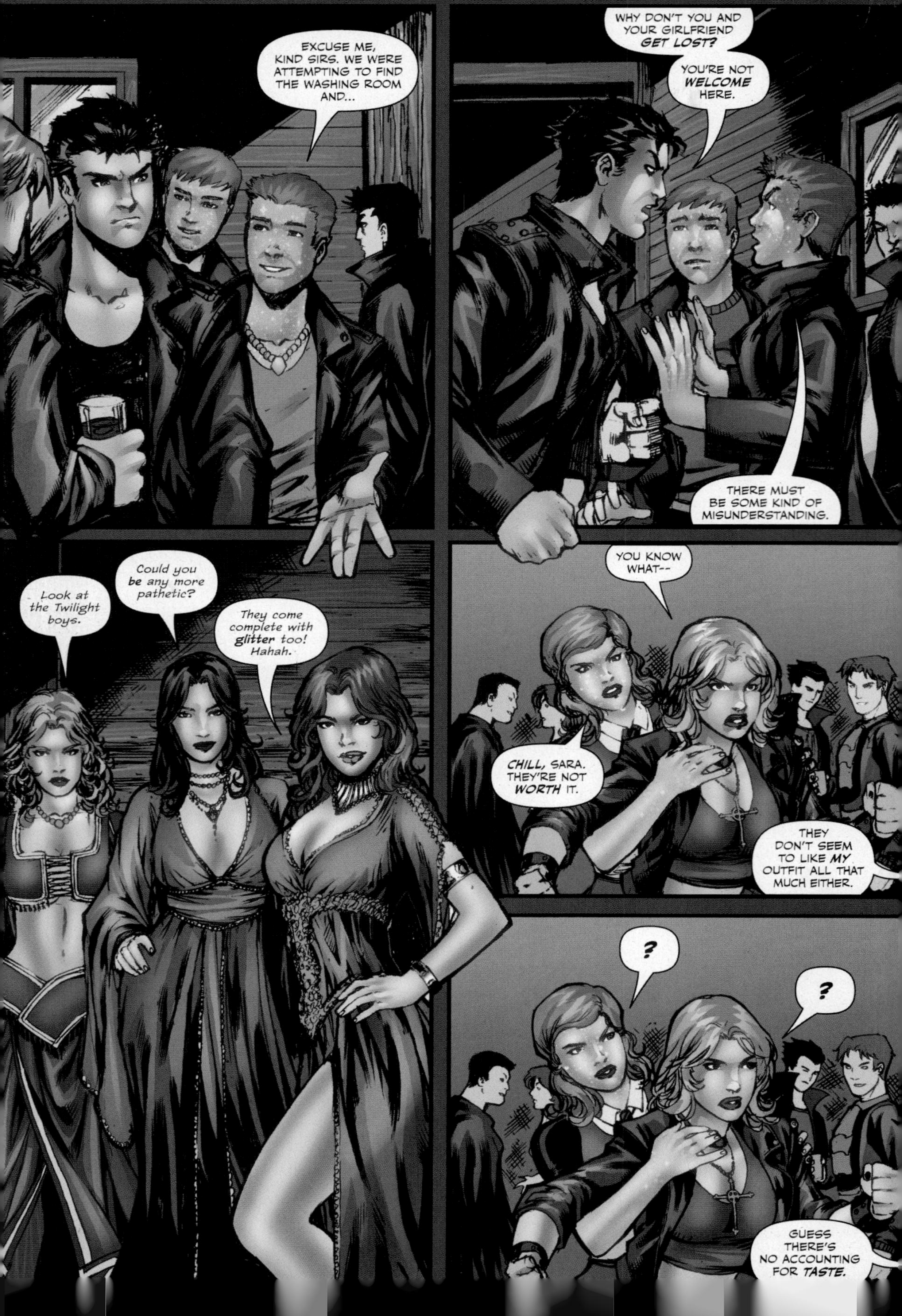
EXCUSE ME, KIND SIRS. WE WERE ATTEMPTING TO FIND THE WASHING ROOM AND...
WHY DON'T YOU AND YOUR GIRLFRIEND GET LOST?
YOU'RE NOT WELCOME HERE.
THERE MUST BE SOME KIND OF MISUNDERSTANDING.
Look at the Twilight boys.
Could you be any more pathetic?
They come complete with glitter too! Hahah.
YOU KNOW WHAT--
CHILL, SARA. THEY'RE NOT WORTH IT.
THEY DON'T SEEM TO LIKE MY OUTFIT ALL THAT MUCH EITHER.
?
?
GUESS THERE'S NO ACCOUNTING FOR TASTE.

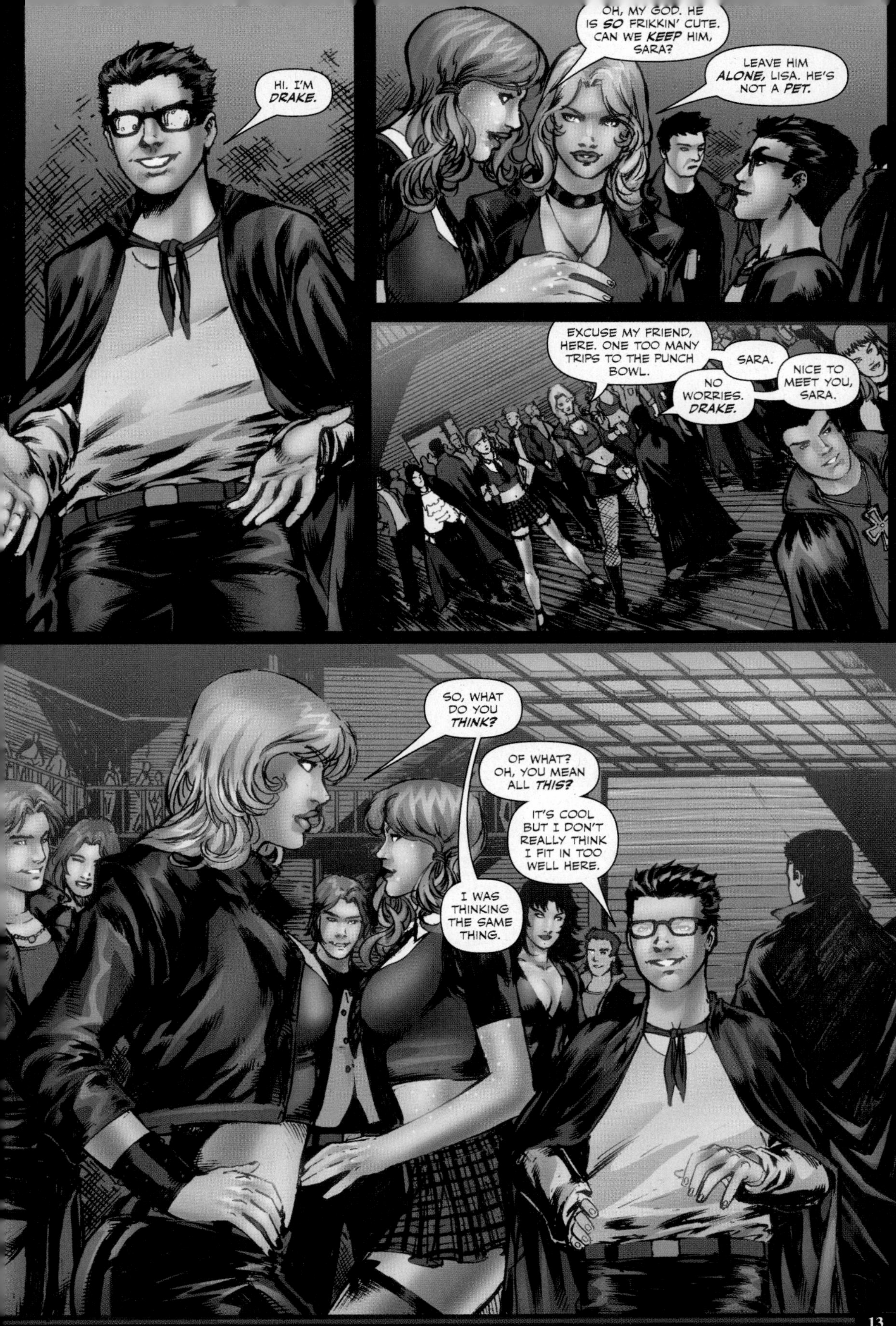
HI. I'M DRAKE.
OH, MY GOD. HE IS SO FRIKKIN' CUTE. CAN WE KEEP HIM, SARA?
LEAVE HIM ALONE, LISA. HE'S NOT A PET.
EXCUSE MY FRIEND, HERE. ONE TOO MANY TRIPS TO THE PUNCH BOWL.
SARA.
NO WORRIES. DRAKE.
NICE TO MEET YOU, SARA.
SO, WHAT DO YOU THINK?
OF WHAT? OH, YOU MEAN ALL THIS?
IT'S COOL BUT I DON'T REALLY THINK I FIT IN TOO WELL HERE.
I WAS THINKING THE SAME THING.

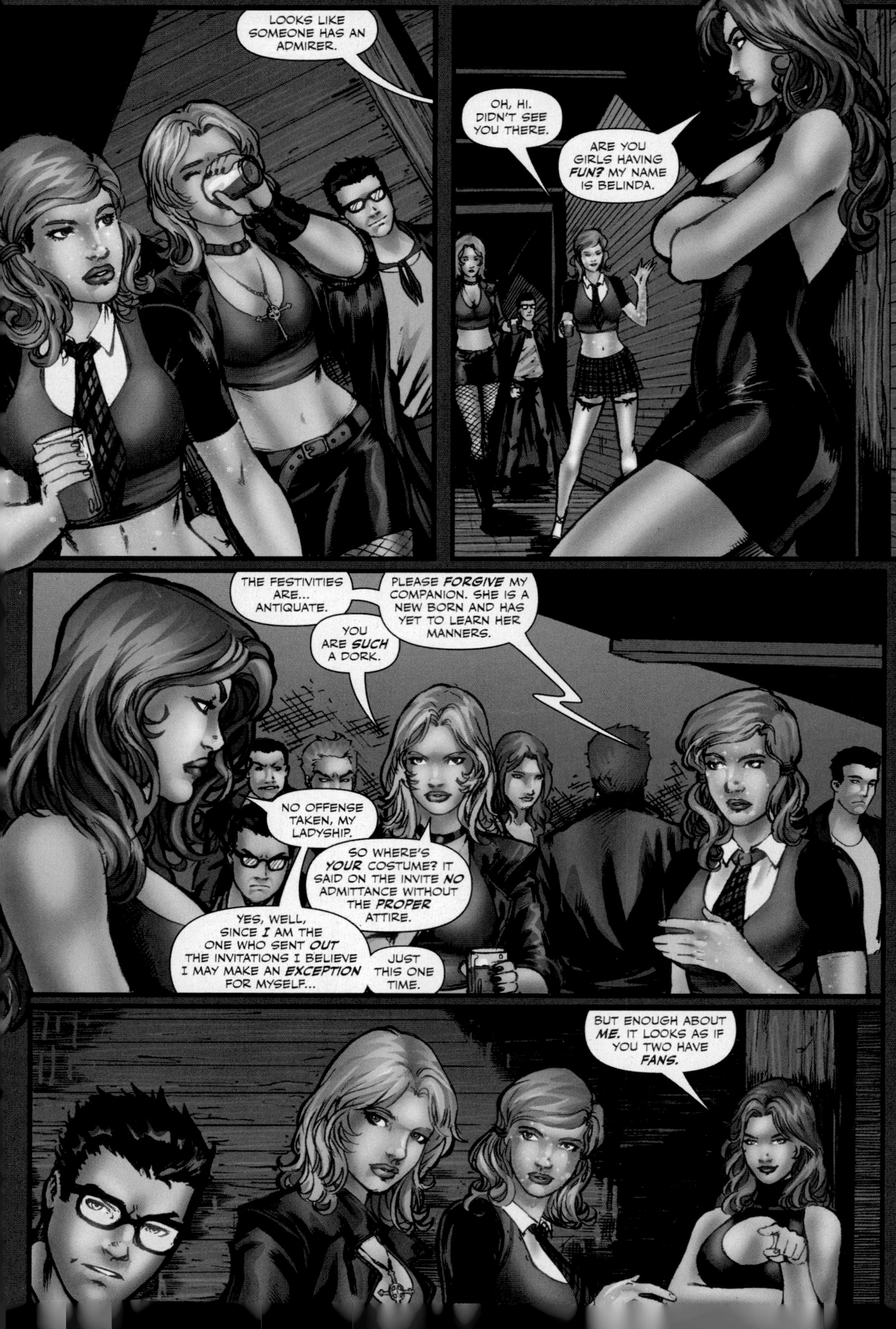
LOOKS LIKE SOMEONE HAS AN ADMIRER.
OH, HI. DIDN'T SEE YOU THERE.
ARE YOU GIRLS HAVING FUN? MY NAME IS BELINDA.
THE FESTIVITIES ARE... ANTIQUATE.
PLEASE FORGIVE MY COMPANION. SHE IS A NEW BORN AND HAS YET TO LEARN HER MANNERS.
YOU ARE SUCH A DORK.
NO OFFENSE TAKEN, MY LADYSHIP.
SO WHERE'S YOUR COSTUME? IT SAID ON THE INVITE NO ADMITTANCE WITHOUT THE PROPER ATTIRE.
YES, WELL, SINCE I AM THE ONE WHO SENT OUT THE INVITATIONS I BELIEVE I MAY MAKE AN EXCEPTION FOR MYSELF...
JUST THIS ONE TIME.
BUT ENOUGH ABOUT ME. IT LOOKS AS IF YOU TWO HAVE FANS.

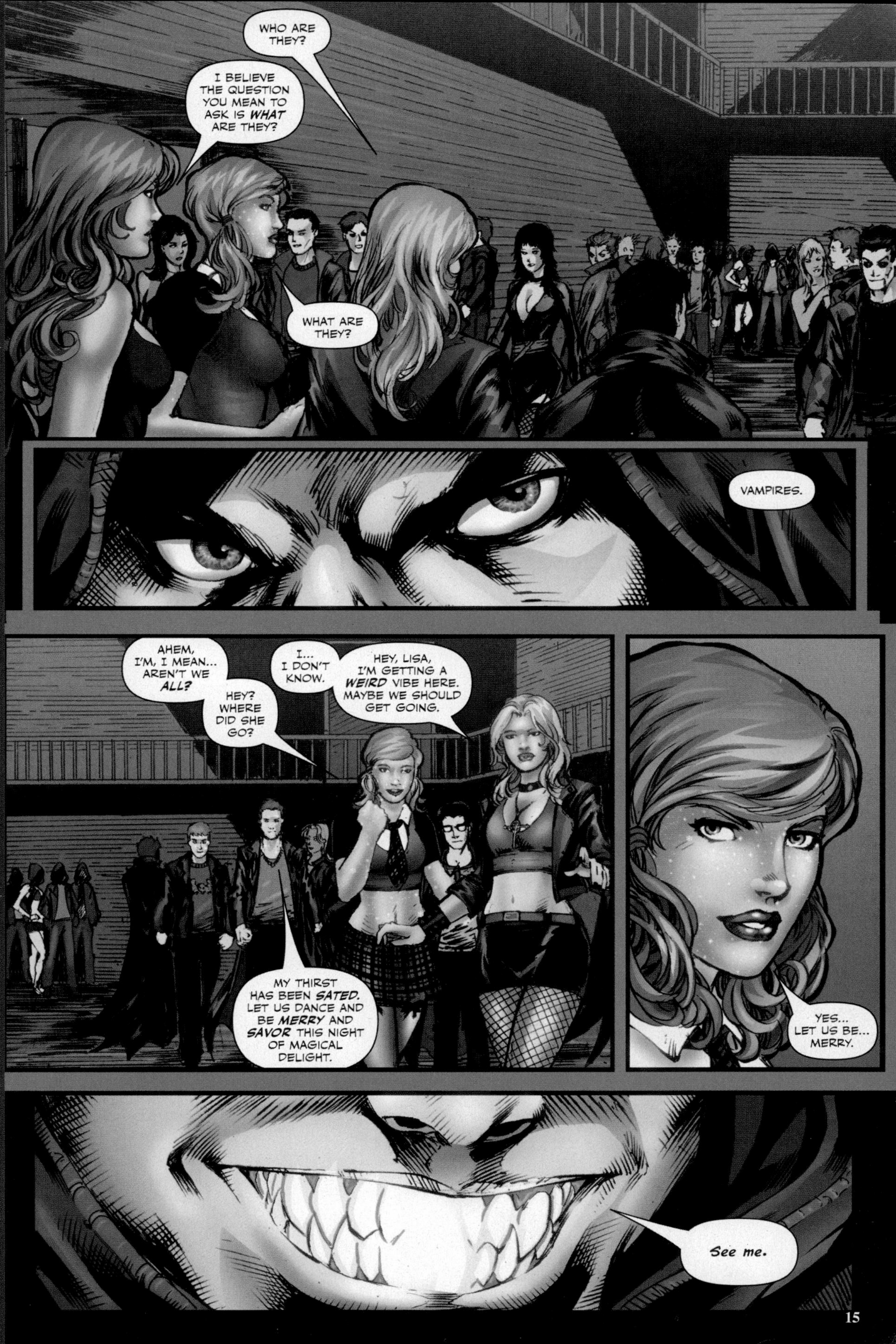
WHO ARE THEY?
I BELIEVE THE QUESTION YOU MEAN TO ASK IS *WHAT* ARE THEY?
WHAT ARE THEY?
VAMPIRES.
AHEM, I'M, I MEAN... AREN'T WE *ALL?*
HEY? WHERE DID SHE GO?
I... I DON'T KNOW.
HEY, LISA, I'M GETTING A *WEIRD* VIBE HERE. MAYBE WE SHOULD GET GOING.
MY THIRST HAS BEEN *SATED.* LET US DANCE AND BE *MERRY* AND *SAVOR* THIS NIGHT OF MAGICAL DELIGHT.
YES... LET US BE... MERRY.
See me.

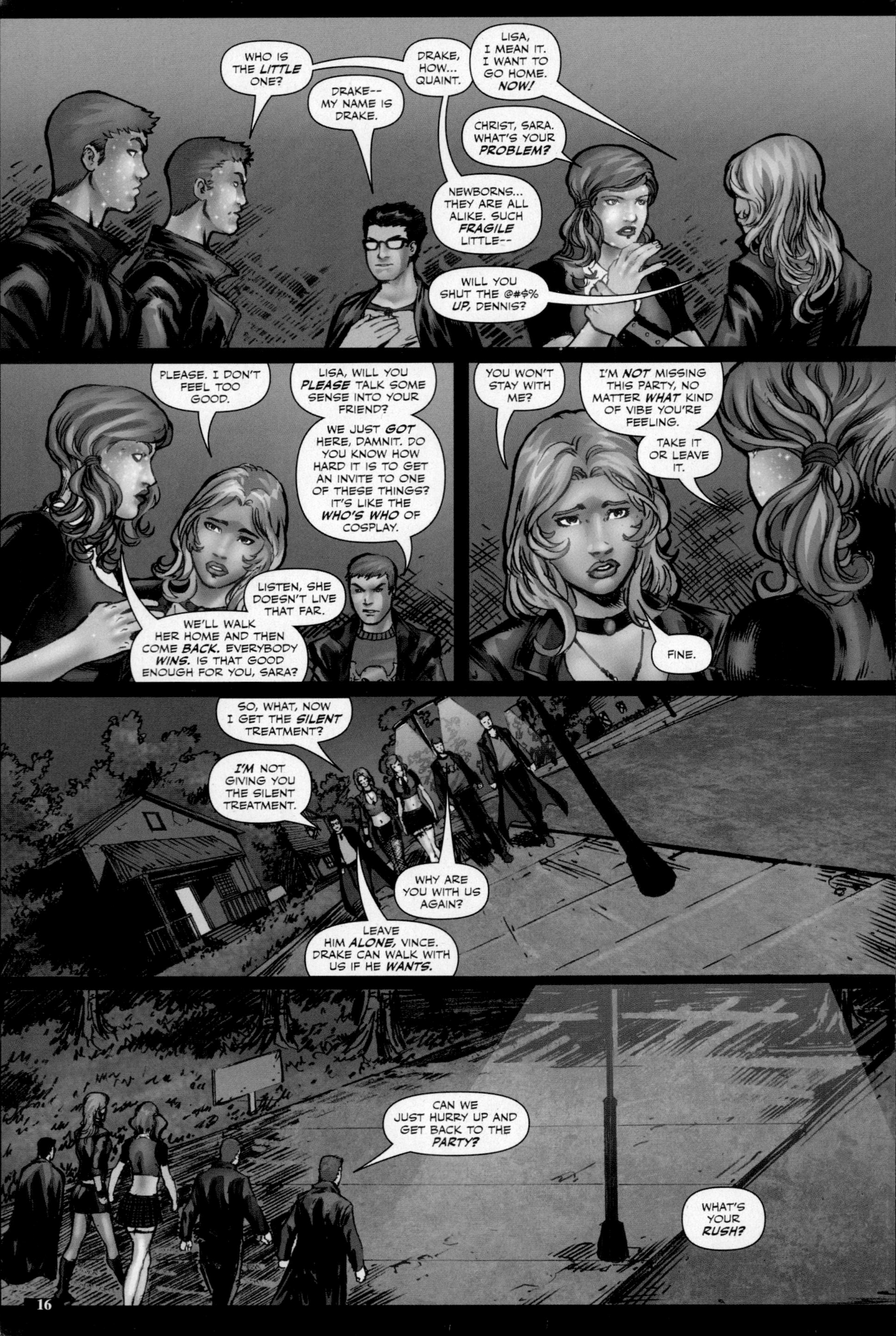
WHO IS THE LITTLE ONE?
DRAKE-- MY NAME IS DRAKE.
DRAKE, HOW... QUAINT.
NEWBORNS... THEY ARE ALL ALIKE. SUCH FRAGILE LITTLE--
LISA, I MEAN IT. I WANT TO GO HOME. NOW!
CHRIST, SARA. WHAT'S YOUR PROBLEM?
WILL YOU SHUT THE @#$% UP, DENNIS?
PLEASE. I DON'T FEEL TOO GOOD.
LISA, WILL YOU PLEASE TALK SOME SENSE INTO YOUR FRIEND?
WE JUST GOT HERE, DAMNIT. DO YOU KNOW HOW HARD IT IS TO GET AN INVITE TO ONE OF THESE THINGS? IT'S LIKE THE WHO'S WHO OF COSPLAY.
LISTEN, SHE DOESN'T LIVE THAT FAR.
WE'LL WALK HER HOME AND THEN COME BACK. EVERYBODY WINS. IS THAT GOOD ENOUGH FOR YOU, SARA?
YOU WON'T STAY WITH ME?
I'M NOT MISSING THIS PARTY, NO MATTER WHAT KIND OF VIBE YOU'RE FEELING.
TAKE IT OR LEAVE IT.
FINE.
SO, WHAT, NOW I GET THE SILENT TREATMENT?
I'M NOT GIVING YOU THE SILENT TREATMENT.
WHY ARE YOU WITH US AGAIN?
LEAVE HIM ALONE, VINCE. DRAKE CAN WALK WITH US IF HE WANTS.
CAN WE JUST HURRY UP AND GET BACK TO THE PARTY?
WHAT'S YOUR RUSH?

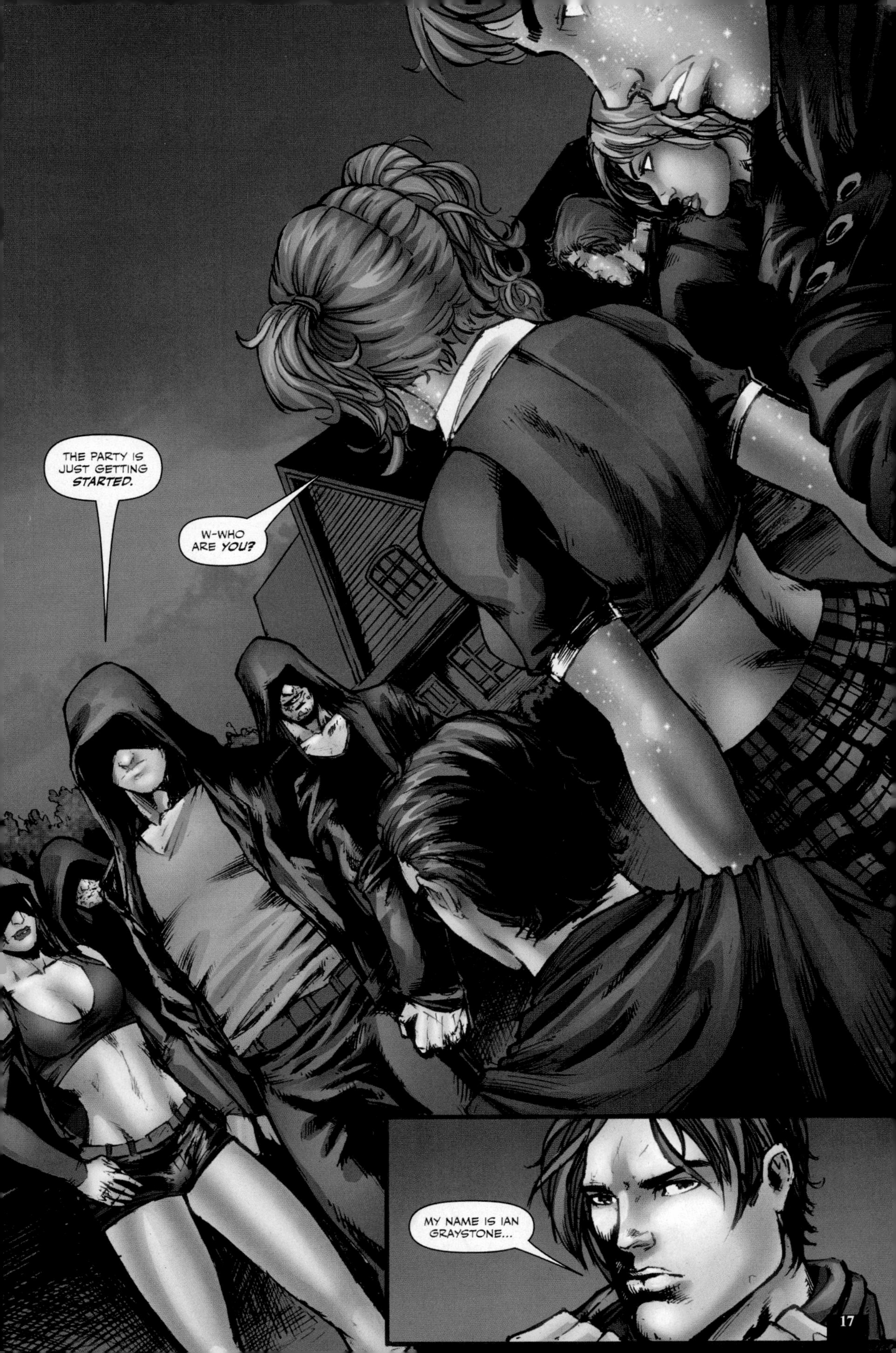
THE PARTY IS JUST GETTING STARTED.
W-WHO ARE YOU?
MY NAME IS IAN GRAYSTONE...

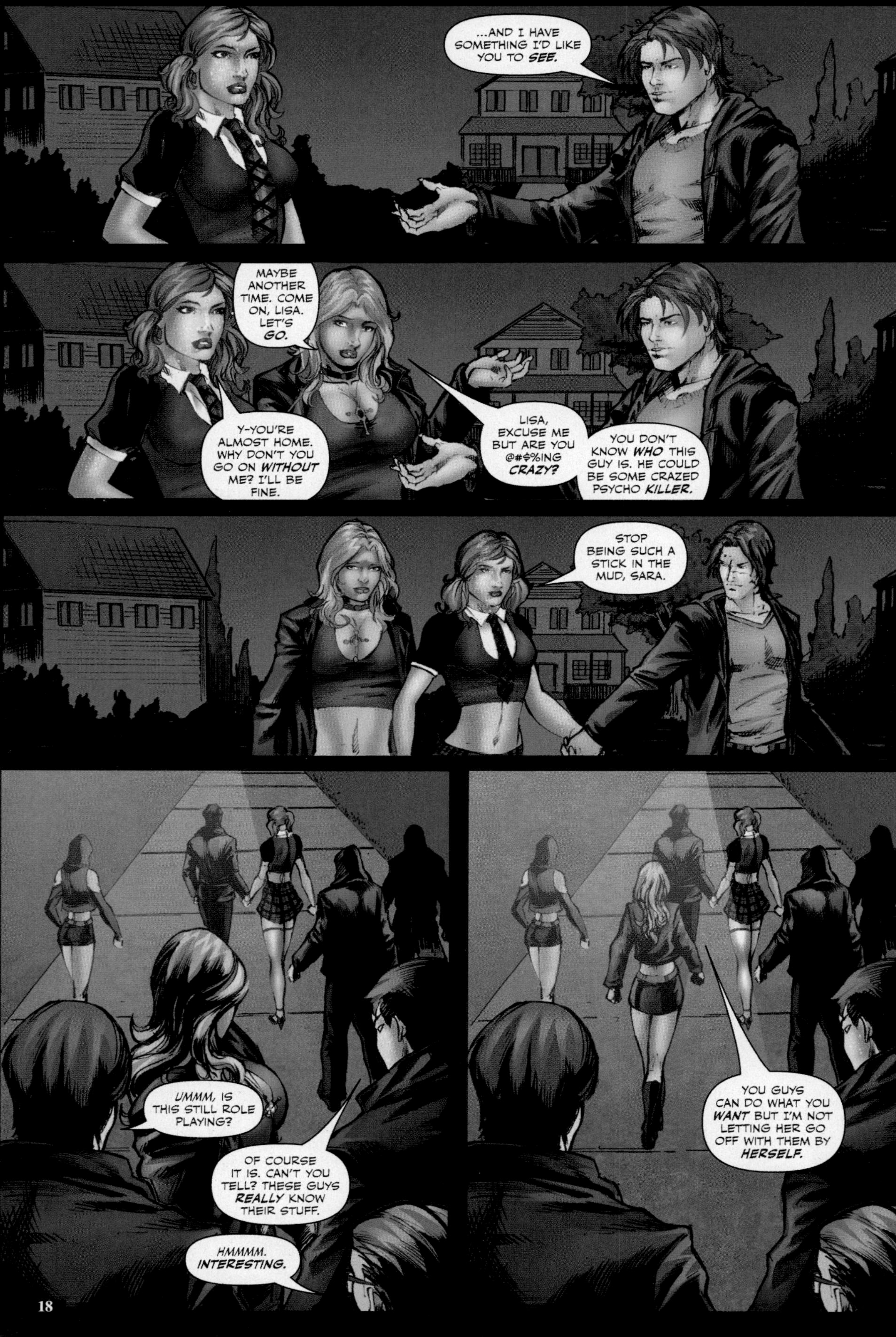
...AND I HAVE SOMETHING I'D LIKE YOU TO SEE.
MAYBE ANOTHER TIME. COME ON, LISA. LET'S GO.
Y-YOU'RE ALMOST HOME. WHY DON'T YOU GO ON WITHOUT ME? I'LL BE FINE.
LISA, EXCUSE ME BUT ARE YOU @#$%ING CRAZY?
YOU DON'T KNOW WHO THIS GUY IS. HE COULD BE SOME CRAZED PSYCHO KILLER.
STOP BEING SUCH A STICK IN THE MUD, SARA.
UMMM, IS THIS STILL ROLE PLAYING?
OF COURSE IT IS. CAN'T YOU TELL? THESE GUYS REALLY KNOW THEIR STUFF.
HMMMM. INTERESTING.
YOU GUYS CAN DO WHAT YOU WANT BUT I'M NOT LETTING HER GO OFF WITH THEM BY HERSELF.

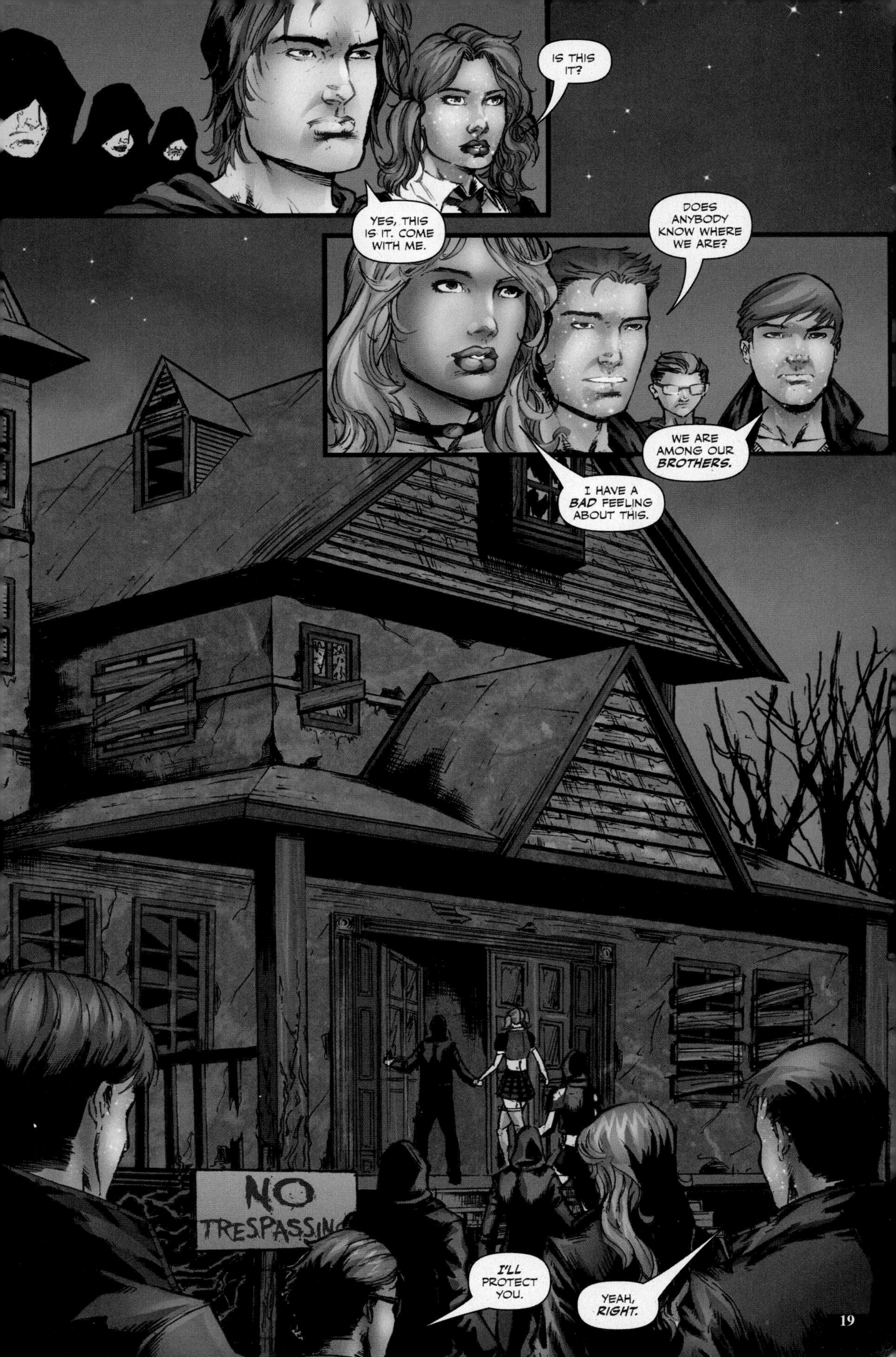
IS THIS IT?
YES, THIS IS IT. COME WITH ME.
DOES ANYBODY KNOW WHERE WE ARE?
WE ARE AMONG OUR BROTHERS.
I HAVE A BAD FEELING ABOUT THIS.
NO TRESPASSING
I'LL PROTECT YOU.
YEAH, RIGHT.

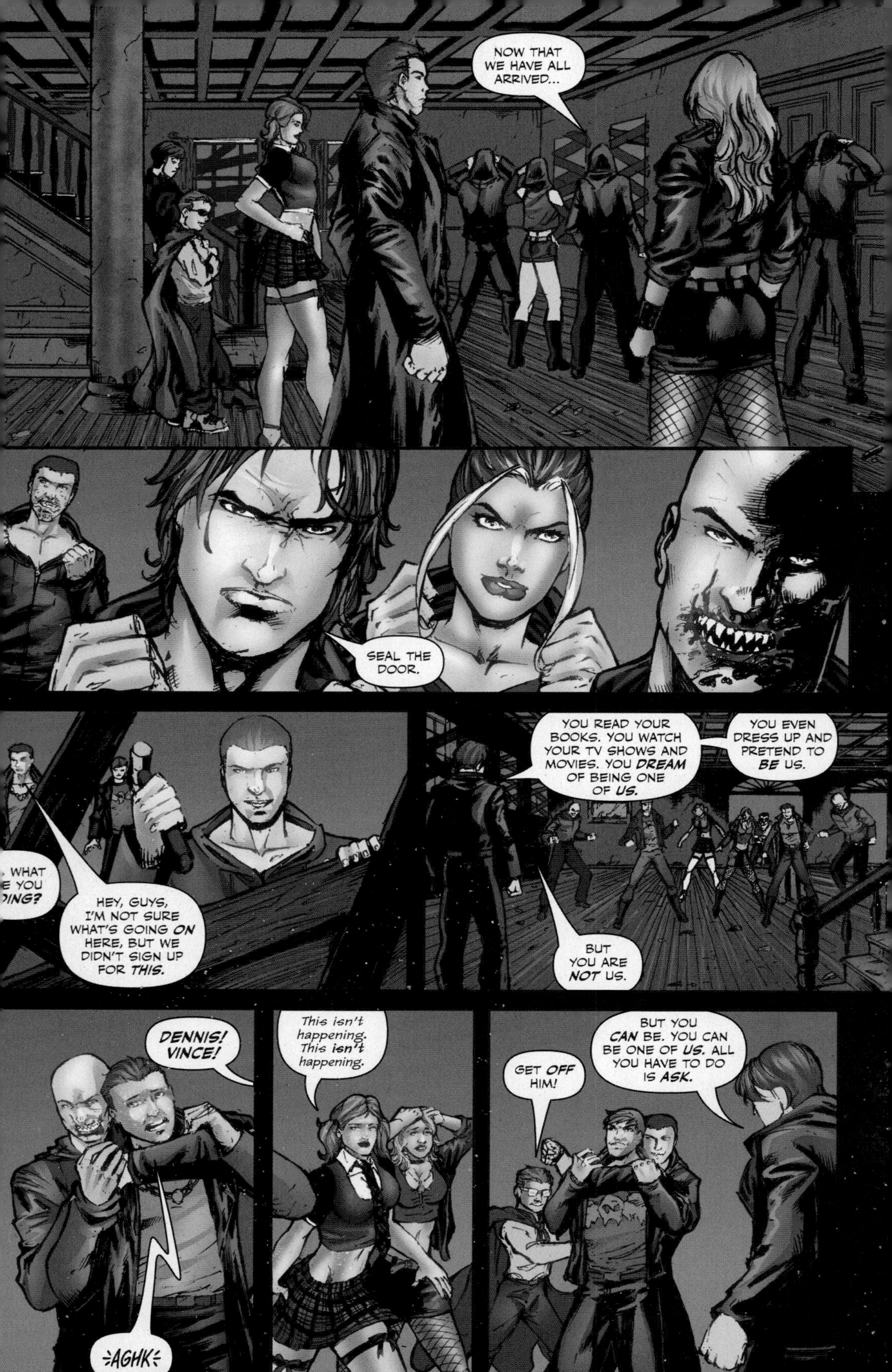
NOW THAT WE HAVE ALL ARRIVED...
SEAL THE DOOR.
WHAT
HEY, GUYS, I'M NOT SURE WHAT'S GOING *ON* HERE, BUT WE DIDN'T SIGN UP FOR *THIS*.
YOU READ YOUR BOOKS. YOU WATCH YOUR TV SHOWS AND MOVIES. YOU *DREAM* OF BEING ONE OF *US*.
YOU EVEN DRESS UP AND PRETEND TO *BE* US.
BUT YOU ARE *NOT* US.
DENNIS! VINCE!
AGHK
This isn't happening. This isn't happening.
GET *OFF* HIM!
BUT YOU *CAN* BE. YOU CAN BE ONE OF *US*. ALL YOU HAVE TO DO IS *ASK*.

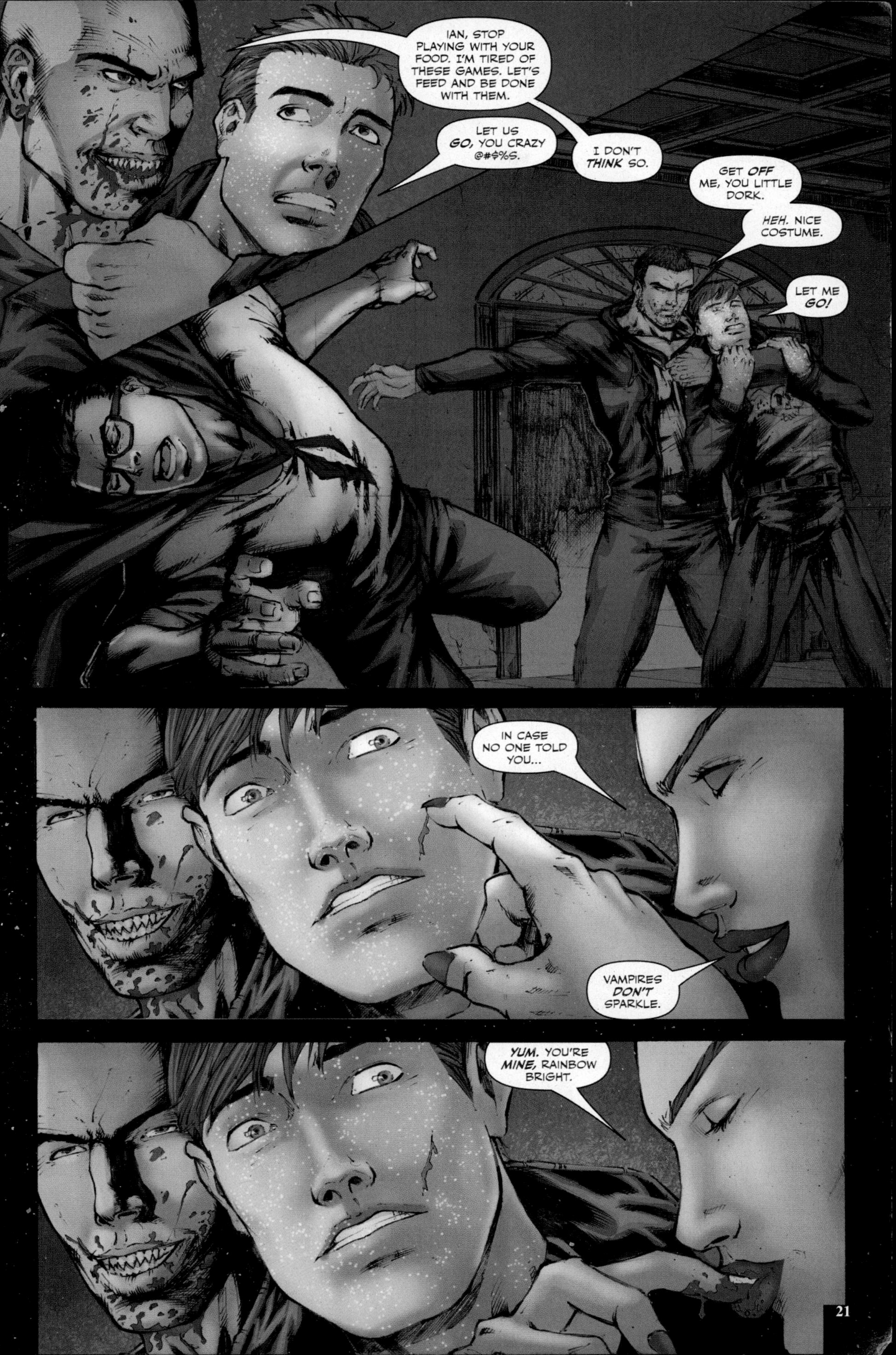
IAN, STOP PLAYING WITH YOUR FOOD. I'M TIRED OF THESE GAMES. LET'S FEED AND BE DONE WITH THEM.
LET US *GO,* YOU CRAZY @#$%S.
I DON'T *THINK* SO.
GET *OFF* ME, YOU LITTLE DORK.
HEH. NICE COSTUME.
LET ME *GO!*
IN CASE NO ONE TOLD YOU...
VAMPIRES *DON'T* SPARKLE.
YUM. YOU'RE *MINE,* RAINBOW BRIGHT.

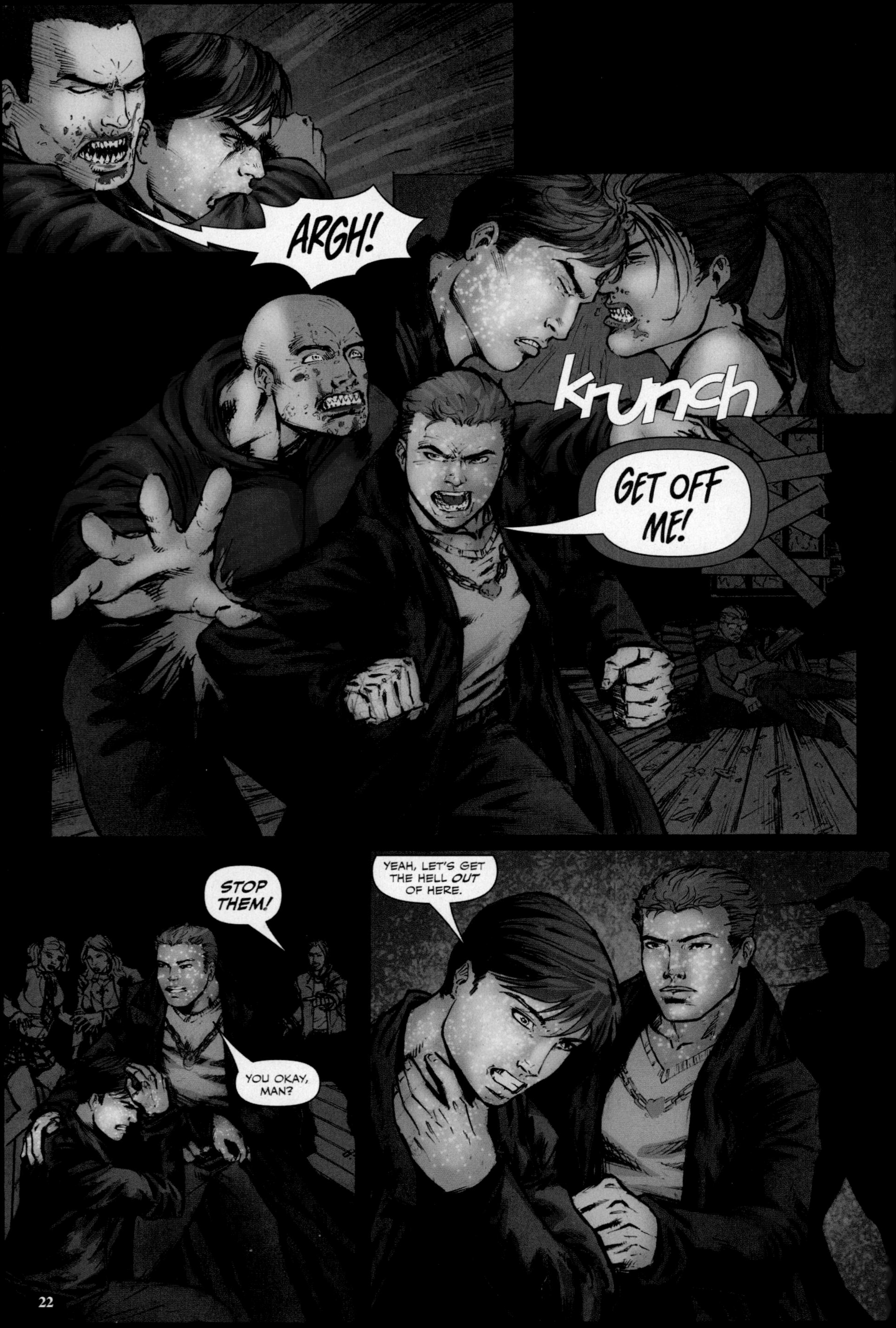
ARGH!
krunch
GET OFF ME!
STOP THEM!
YOU OKAY, MAN?
YEAH, LET'S GET THE HELL OUT OF HERE.

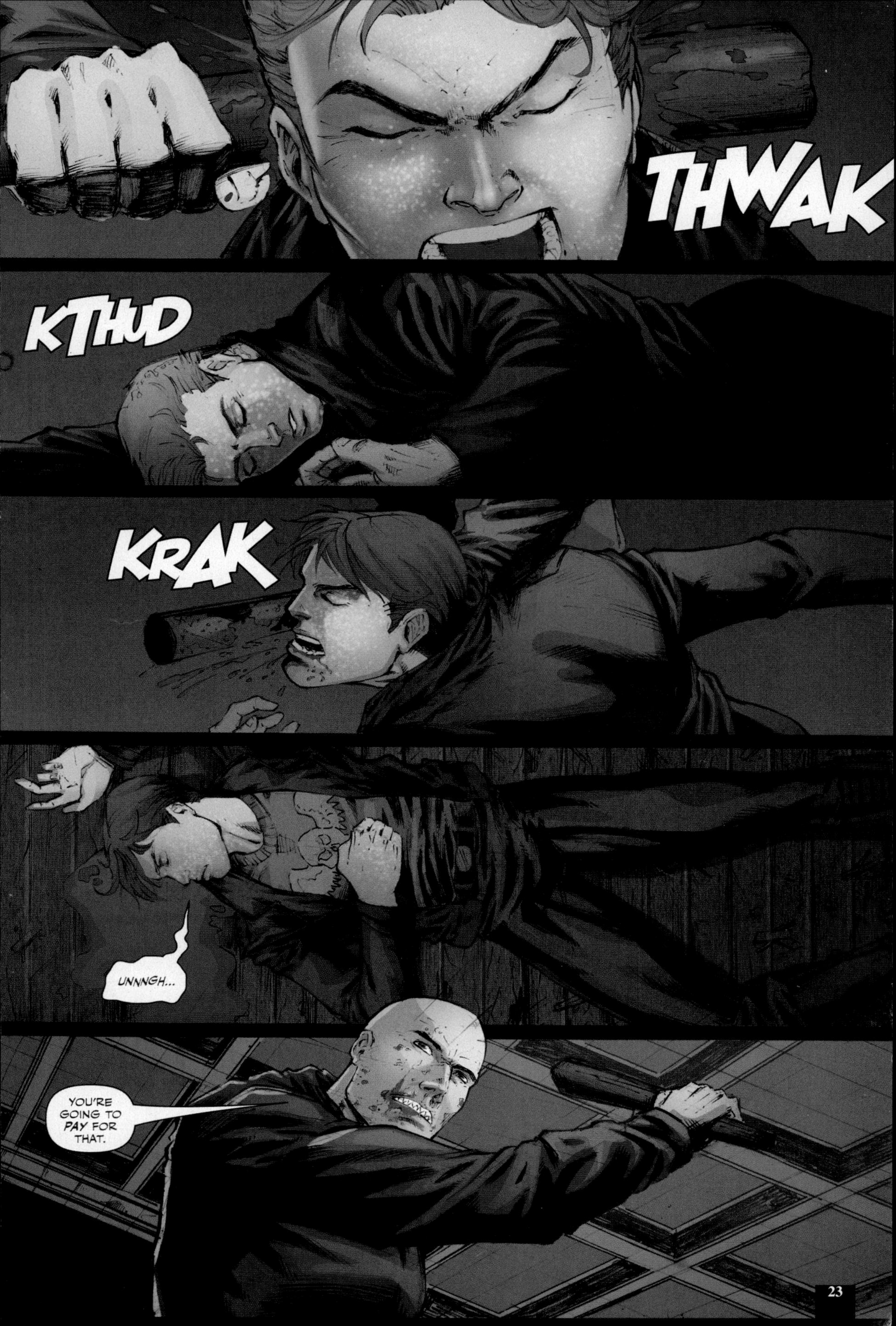
THWAK
KTHUD
KRAK
UNNNGH...
YOU'RE GOING TO PAY FOR THAT.

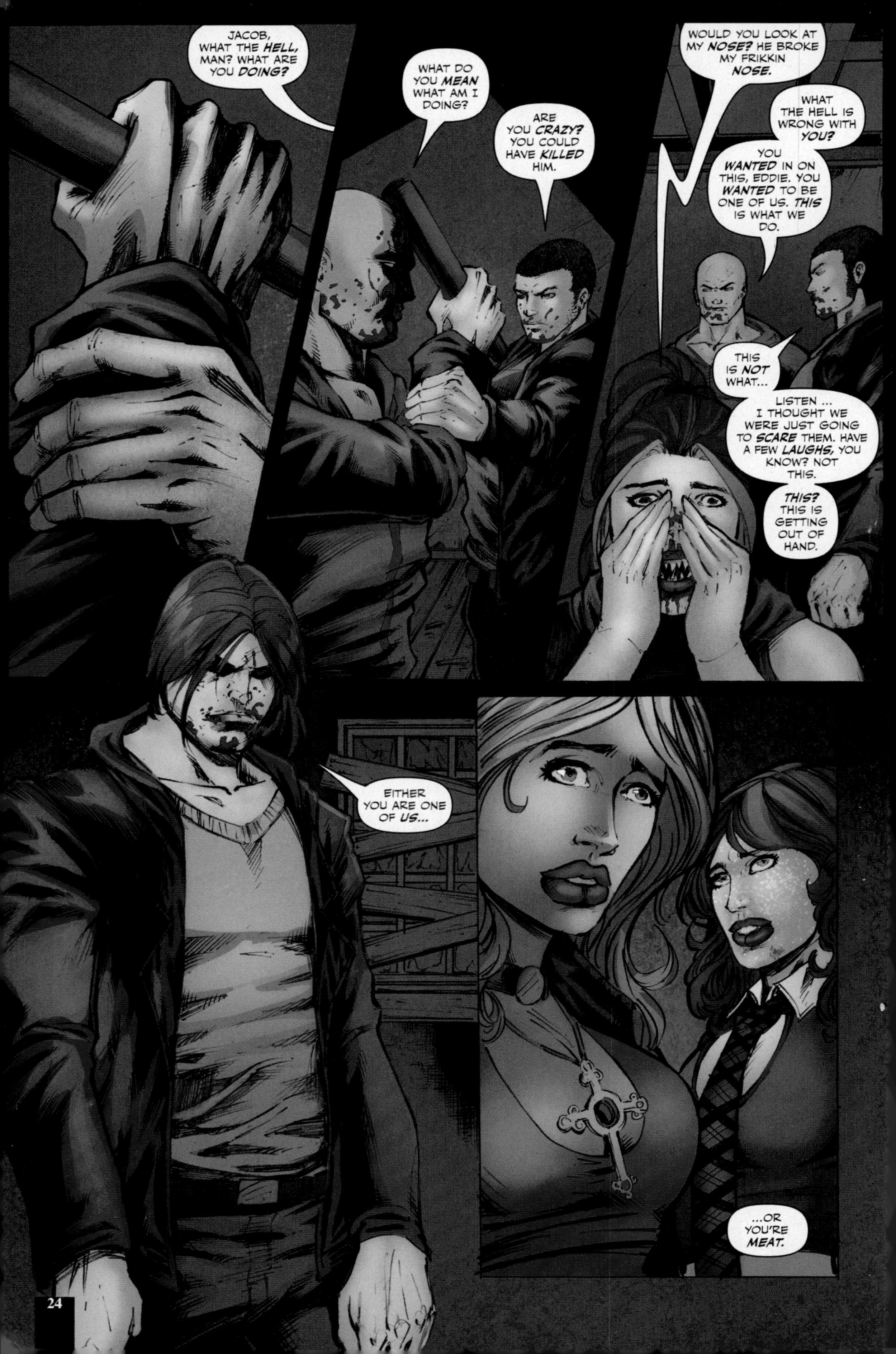
JACOB, WHAT THE HELL, MAN? WHAT ARE YOU DOING?
WHAT DO YOU MEAN WHAT AM I DOING?
ARE YOU CRAZY? YOU COULD HAVE KILLED HIM.
WOULD YOU LOOK AT MY NOSE? HE BROKE MY FRIKKIN NOSE.
WHAT THE HELL IS WRONG WITH YOU?
YOU WANTED IN ON THIS, EDDIE. YOU WANTED TO BE ONE OF US. THIS IS WHAT WE DO.
THIS IS NOT WHAT...
LISTEN ... I THOUGHT WE WERE JUST GOING TO SCARE THEM. HAVE A FEW LAUGHS, YOU KNOW? NOT THIS.
THIS? THIS IS GETTING OUT OF HAND.
EITHER YOU ARE ONE OF US...
...OR YOU'RE MEAT.

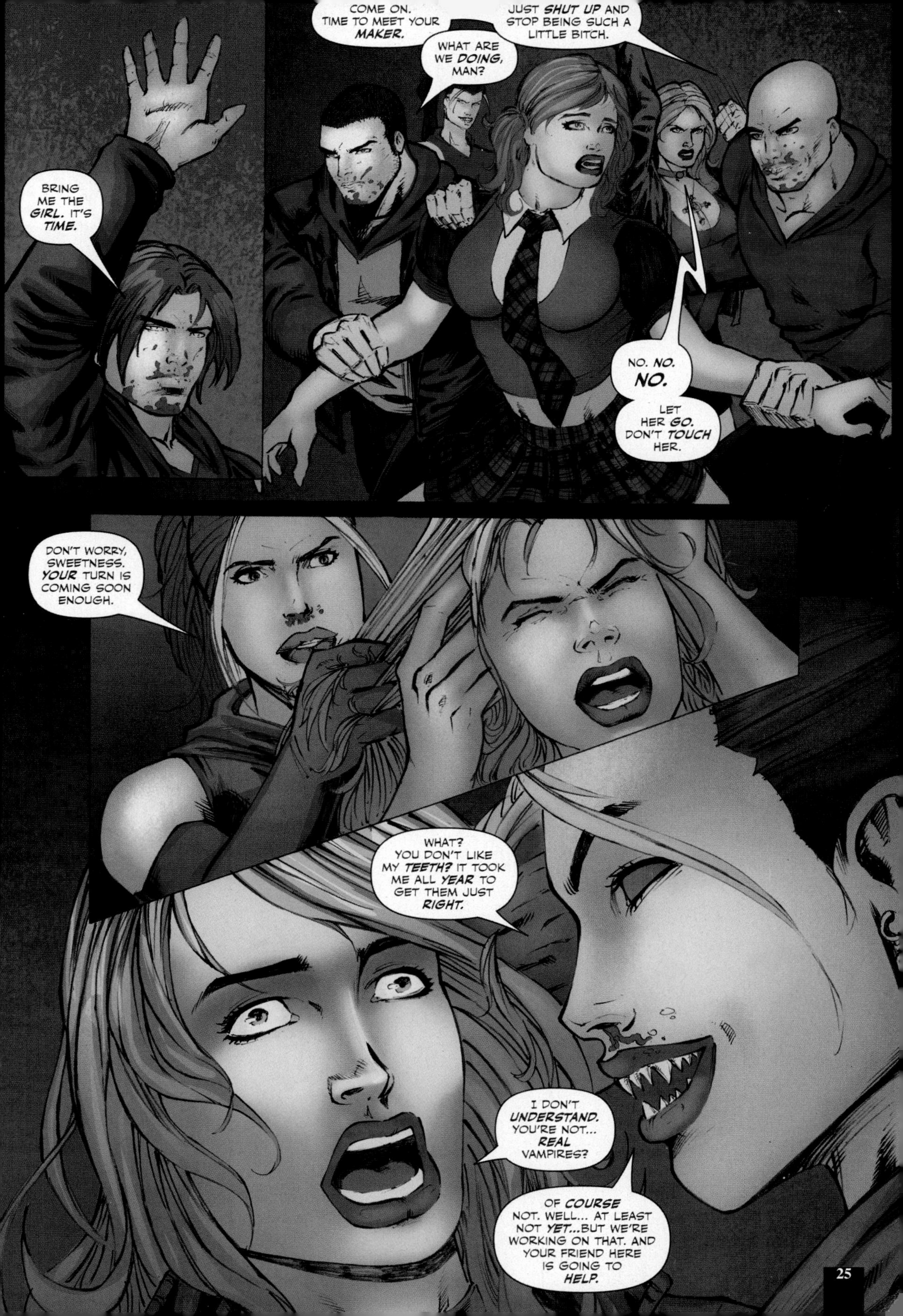
BRING ME THE GIRL. IT'S TIME.
COME ON. TIME TO MEET YOUR MAKER.
WHAT ARE WE DOING, MAN?
JUST SHUT UP AND STOP BEING SUCH A LITTLE BITCH.
NO. NO. NO.
LET HER GO. DON'T TOUCH HER.
DON'T WORRY, SWEETNESS. YOUR TURN IS COMING SOON ENOUGH.
WHAT? YOU DON'T LIKE MY TEETH? IT TOOK ME ALL YEAR TO GET THEM JUST RIGHT.
I DON'T UNDERSTAND. YOU'RE NOT... REAL VAMPIRES?
OF COURSE NOT. WELL... AT LEAST NOT YET...BUT WE'RE WORKING ON THAT. AND YOUR FRIEND HERE IS GOING TO HELP.

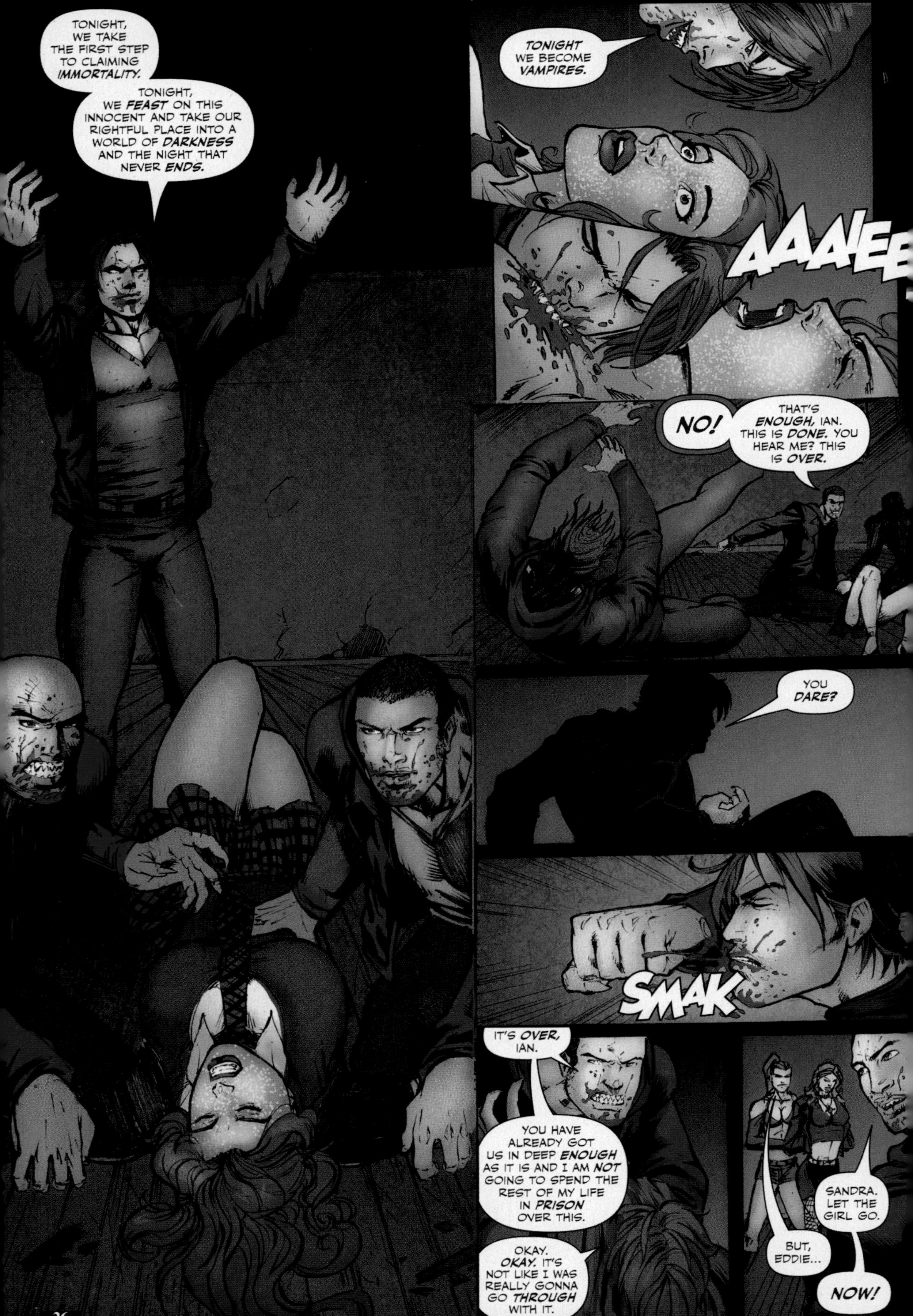

TONIGHT, WE TAKE THE FIRST STEP TO CLAIMING IMMORTALITY.
TONIGHT, WE FEAST ON THIS INNOCENT AND TAKE OUR RIGHTFUL PLACE INTO A WORLD OF DARKNESS AND THE NIGHT THAT NEVER ENDS.
TONIGHT WE BECOME VAMPIRES.
AAAIEE
NO!
THAT'S ENOUGH, IAN. THIS IS DONE. YOU HEAR ME? THIS IS OVER.
YOU DARE?
SMAK
IT'S OVER, IAN.
YOU HAVE ALREADY GOT US IN DEEP ENOUGH AS IT IS AND I AM NOT GOING TO SPEND THE REST OF MY LIFE IN PRISON OVER THIS.
OKAY. OKAY. IT'S NOT LIKE I WAS REALLY GONNA GO THROUGH WITH IT.
SANDRA. LET THE GIRL GO.
BUT, EDDIE...
NOW!

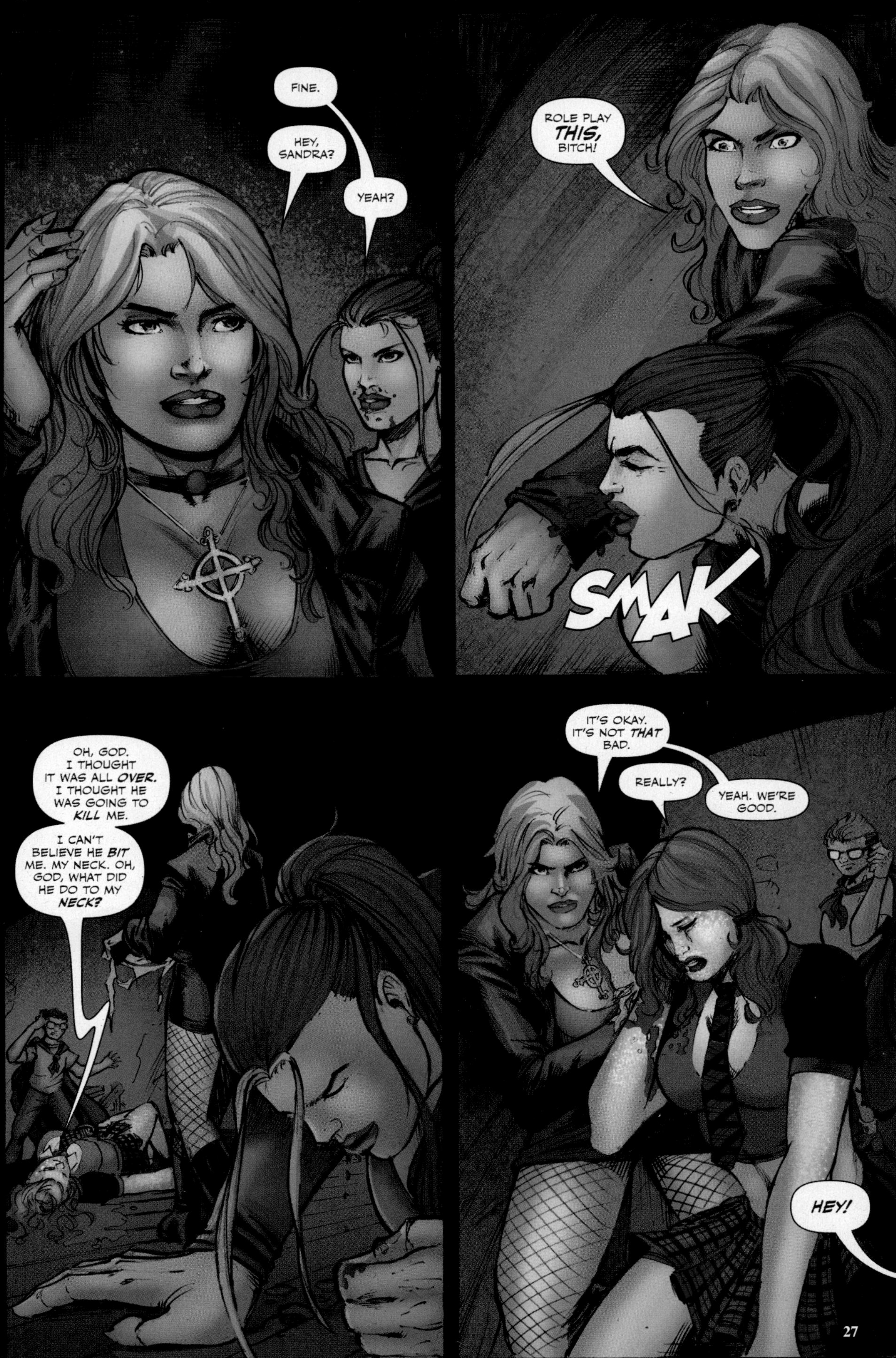
FINE.
HEY, SANDRA?
YEAH?
ROLE PLAY THIS, BITCH!
SMAK
OH, GOD. I THOUGHT IT WAS ALL OVER. I THOUGHT HE WAS GOING TO KILL ME.
I CAN'T BELIEVE HE BIT ME. MY NECK. OH, GOD, WHAT DID HE DO TO MY NECK?
IT'S OKAY. IT'S NOT THAT BAD.
REALLY?
YEAH. WE'RE GOOD.
HEY!

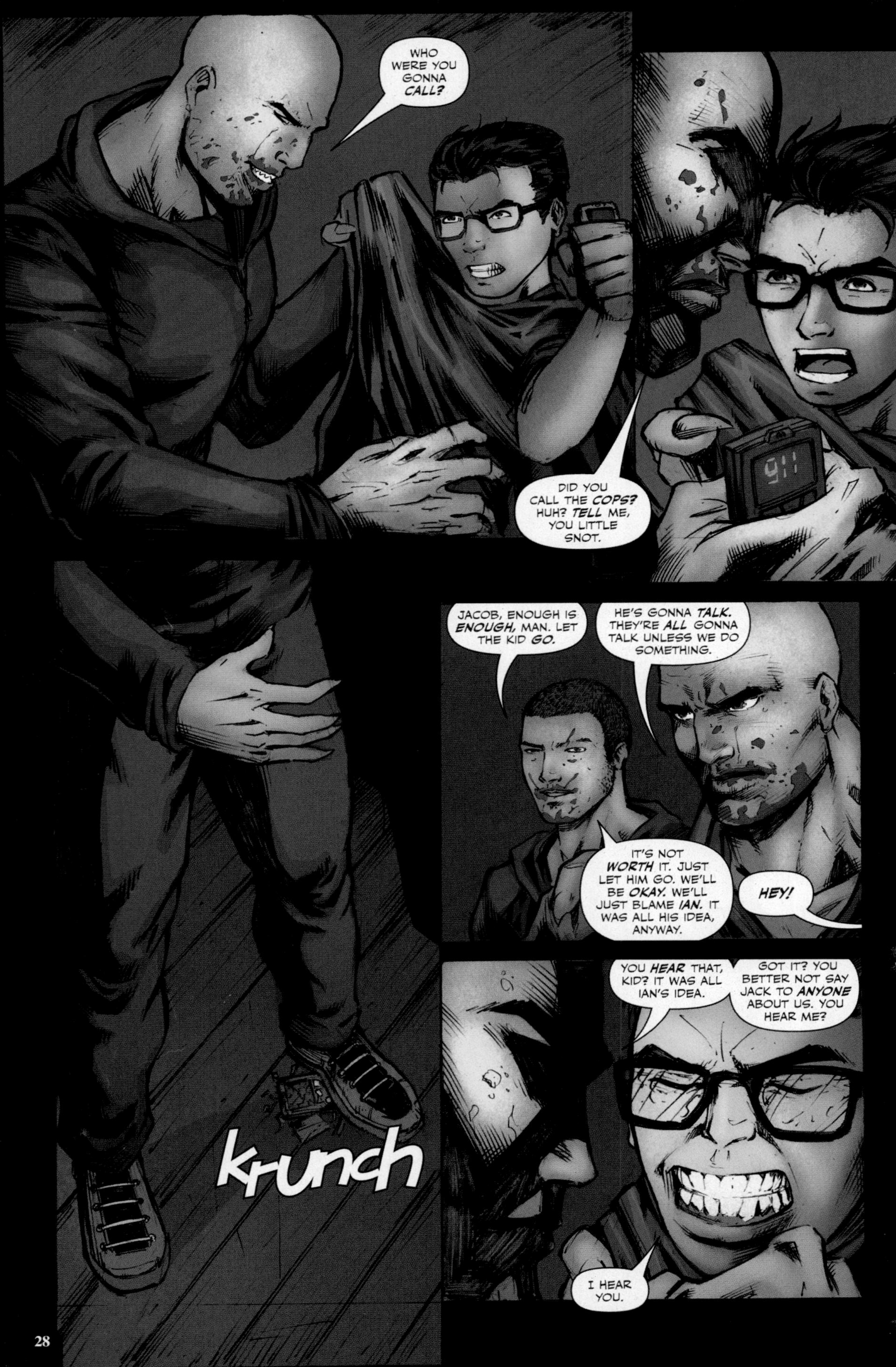
WHO WERE YOU GONNA CALL?
911
DID YOU CALL THE COPS? HUH? TELL ME, YOU LITTLE SNOT.
krunch
JACOB, ENOUGH IS ENOUGH, MAN. LET THE KID GO.
HE'S GONNA TALK. THEY'RE ALL GONNA TALK UNLESS WE DO SOMETHING.
IT'S NOT WORTH IT. JUST LET HIM GO. WE'LL BE OKAY. WE'LL JUST BLAME IAN. IT WAS ALL HIS IDEA, ANYWAY.
HEY!
YOU HEAR THAT, KID? IT WAS ALL IAN'S IDEA.
GOT IT? YOU BETTER NOT SAY JACK TO ANYONE ABOUT US. YOU HEAR ME?
I HEAR YOU.

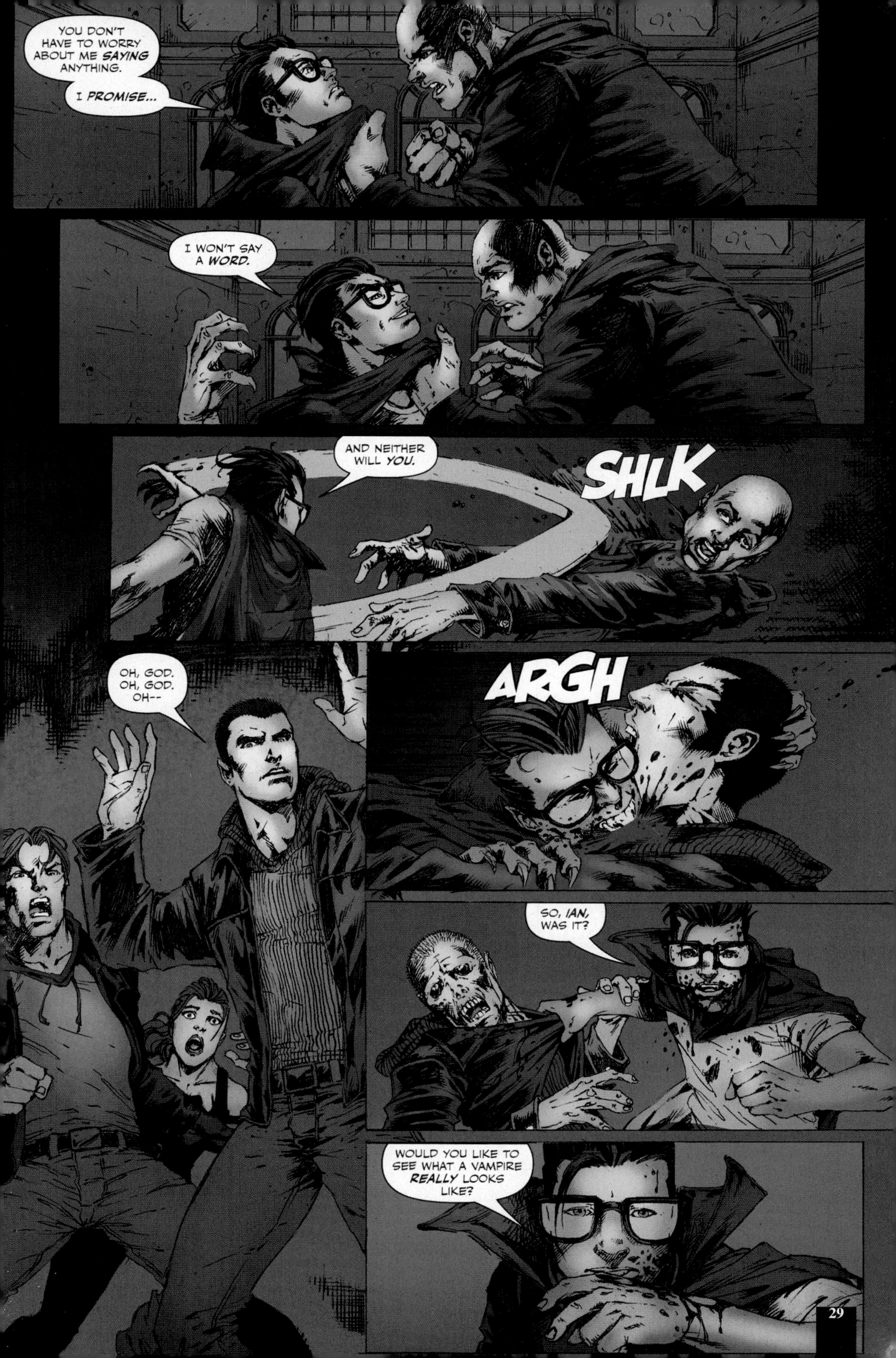
YOU DON'T HAVE TO WORRY ABOUT ME SAYING ANYTHING.
I PROMISE...
I WON'T SAY A WORD.
AND NEITHER WILL YOU.
SHLK
OH, GOD. OH, GOD. OH--
ARGH
SO, IAN, WAS IT?
WOULD YOU LIKE TO SEE WHAT A VAMPIRE REALLY LOOKS LIKE?

I HAD PLANNED ON LETTING YOU AND YOUR FRIENDS GO.
skrkkk
IF ONLY YOU HAD ALLOWED ME TO CALL THE POLICE.
sklttch
shlkkk
I COULD HAVE GONE ABOUT MY MEAL COMPLETELY UNINTERRUPTED.
BUT I'M AFRAID THAT IS NO LONGER AN OPTION.

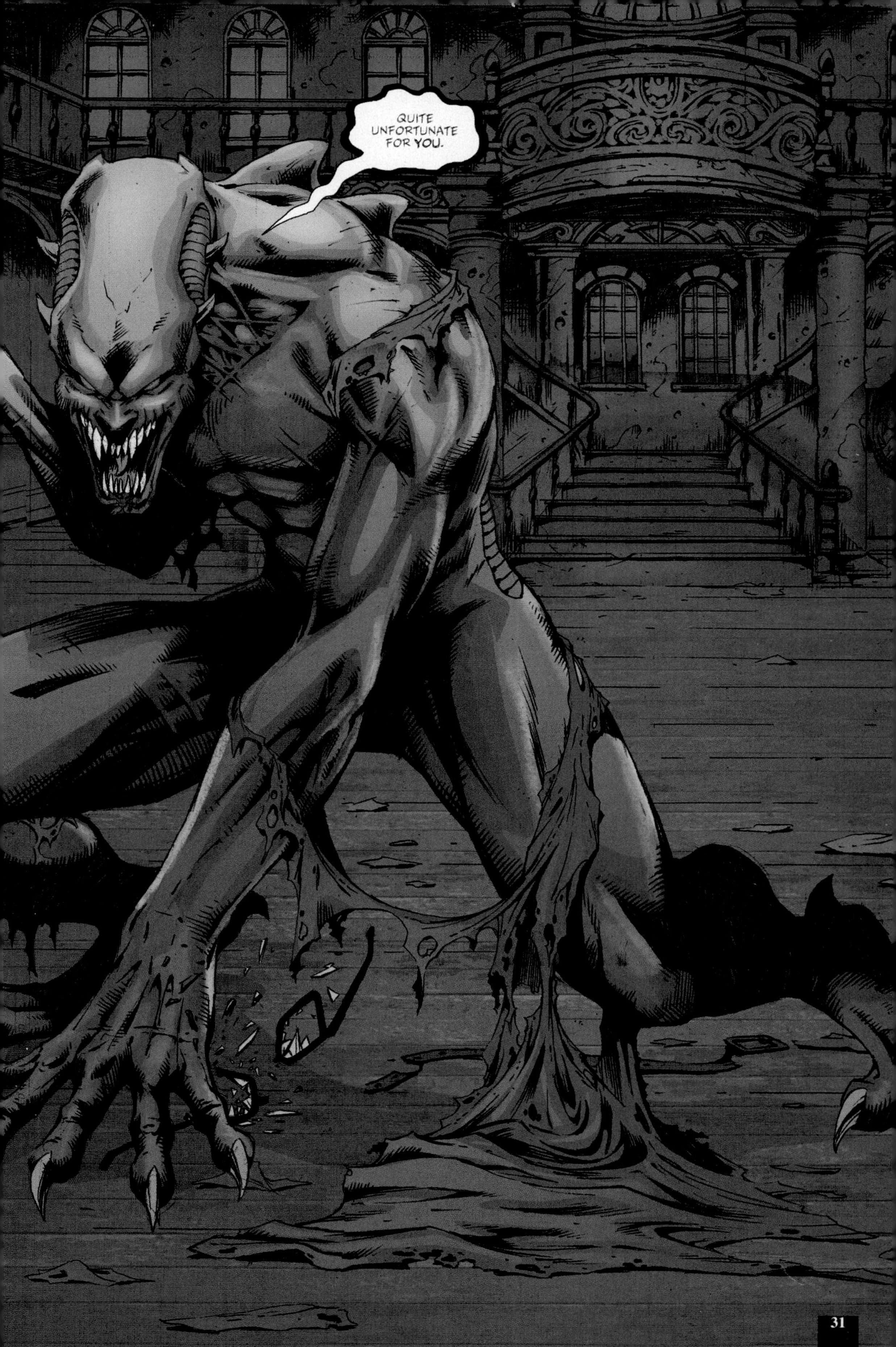
QUITE UNFORTUNATE FOR YOU.

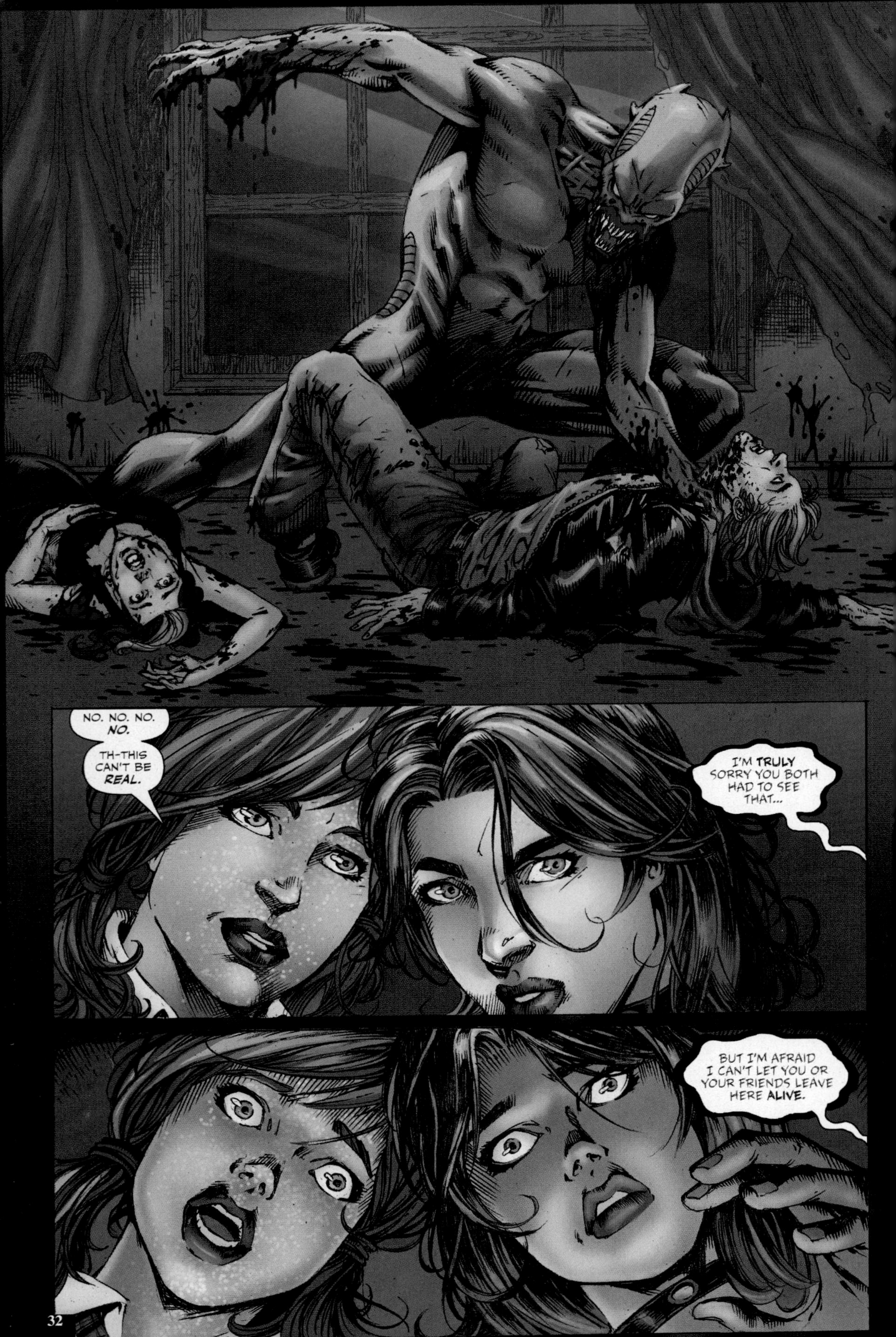
NO. NO. NO. NO.
TH-THIS CAN'T BE REAL.
I'M TRULY SORRY YOU BOTH HAD TO SEE THAT...
BUT I'M AFRAID I CAN'T LET YOU OR YOUR FRIENDS LEAVE HERE ALIVE.

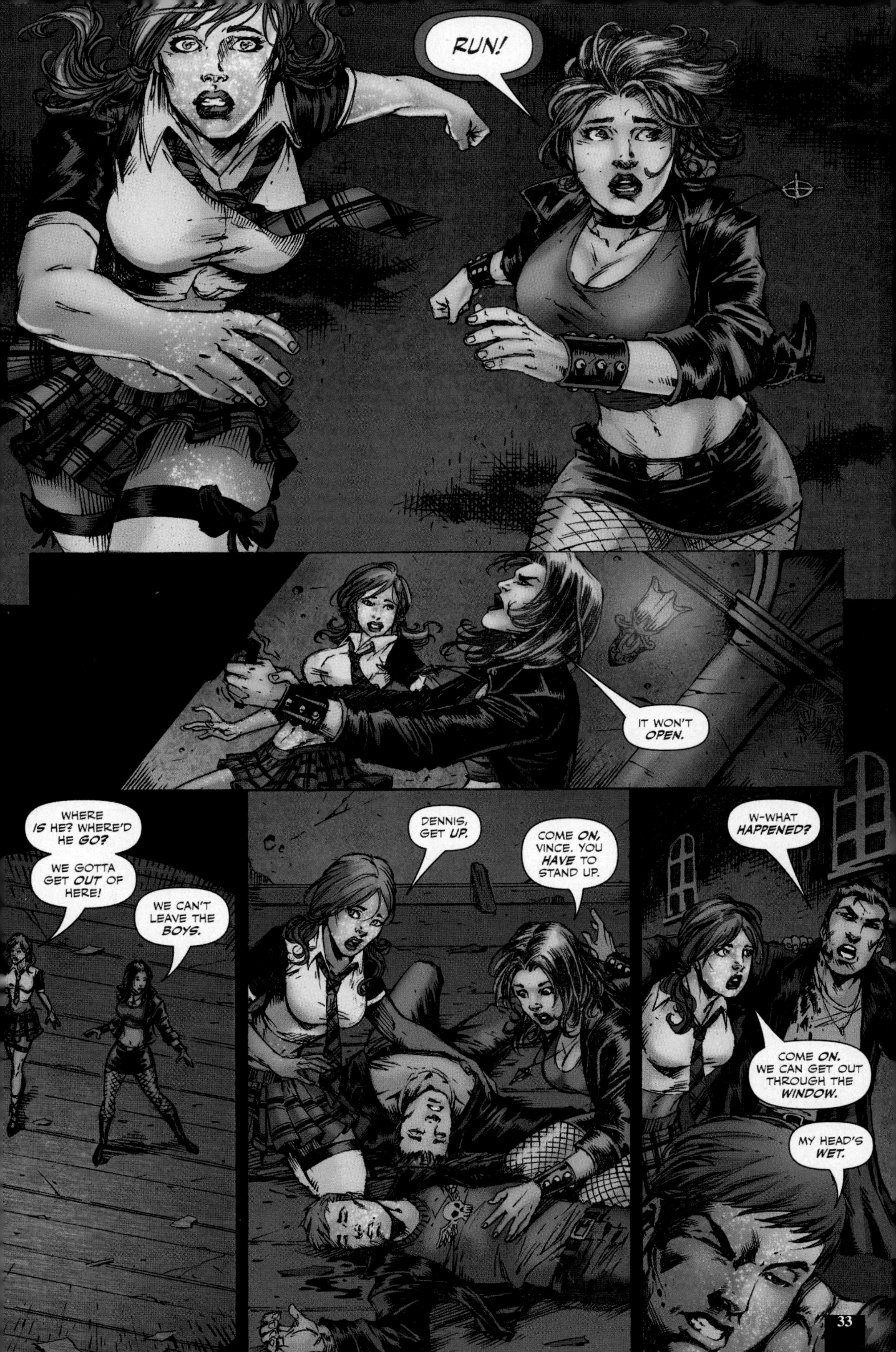
RUN!
IT WON'T OPEN.
WHERE IS HE? WHERE'D HE GO?
WE GOTTA GET OUT OF HERE!
WE CAN'T LEAVE THE BOYS.
DENNIS, GET UP.
COME ON, VINCE. YOU HAVE TO STAND UP.
W-WHAT HAPPENED?
COME ON. WE CAN GET OUT THROUGH THE WINDOW.
MY HEAD'S WET.

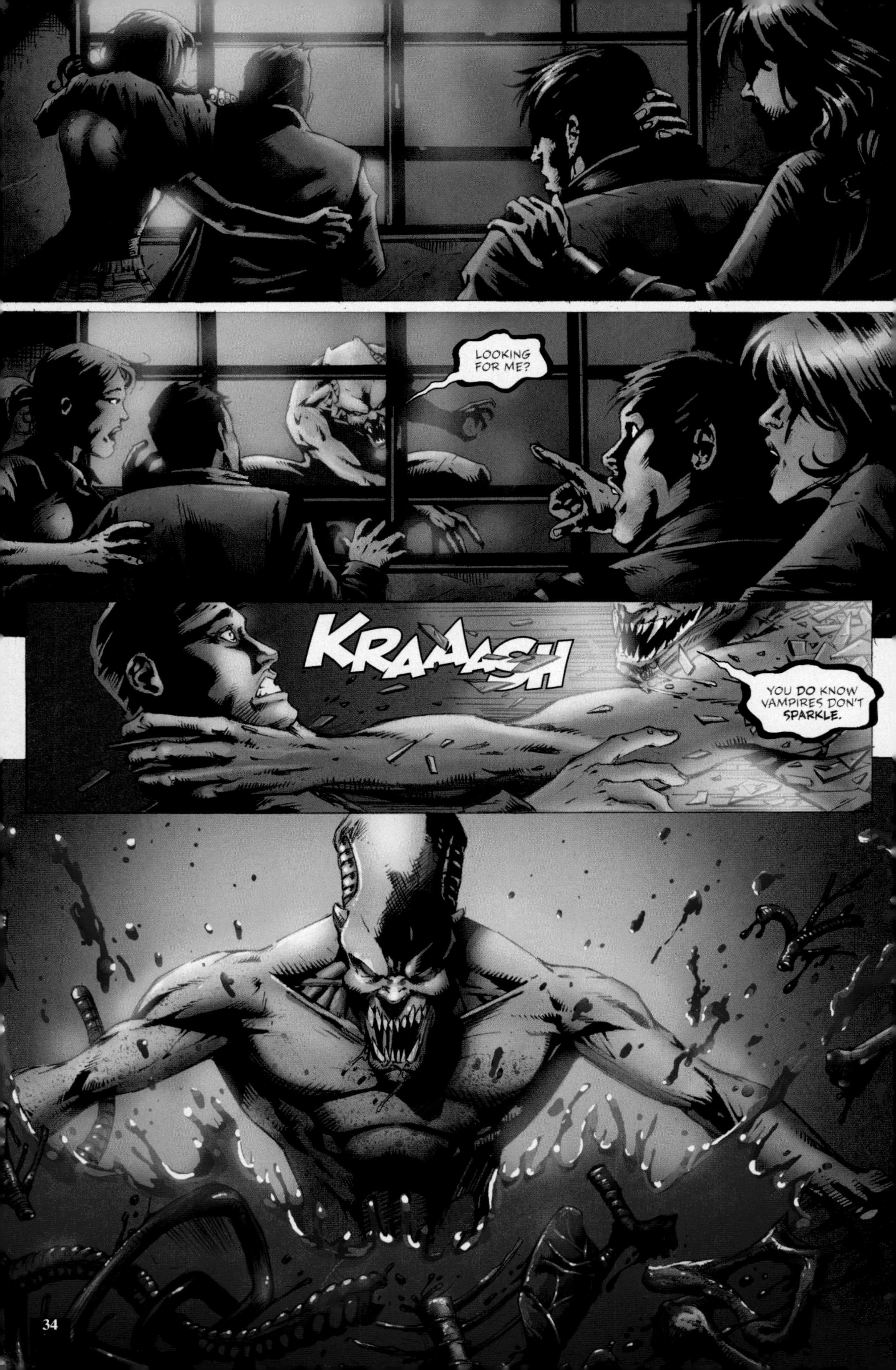
LOOKING FOR ME?
KRAAASH
YOU DO KNOW VAMPIRES DON'T SPARKLE.

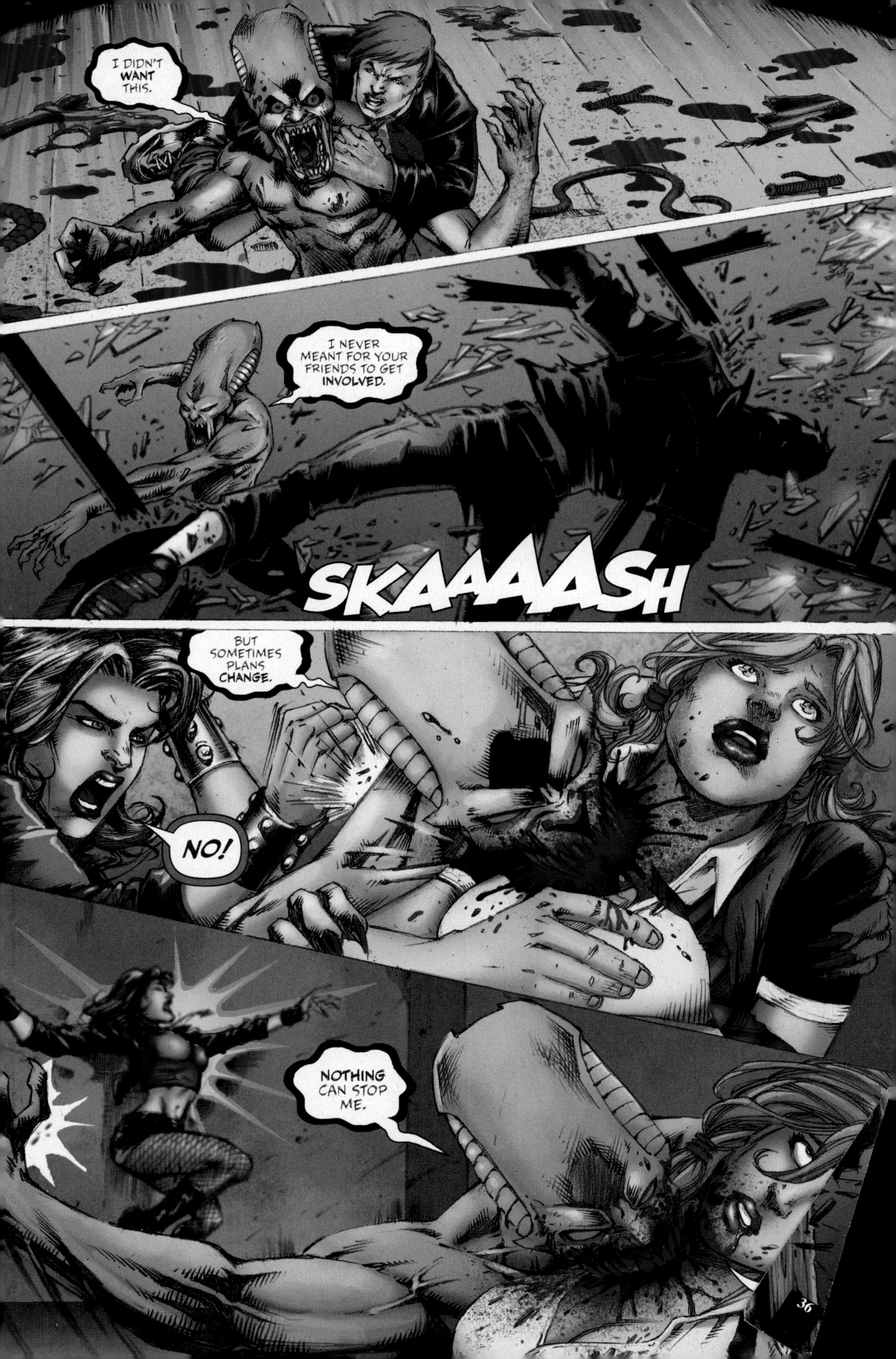
I DIDN'T WANT THIS.
I NEVER MEANT FOR YOUR FRIENDS TO GET INVOLVED.
SKAAAASH
BUT SOMETIMES PLANS CHANGE.
NO!
NOTHING CAN STOP ME.

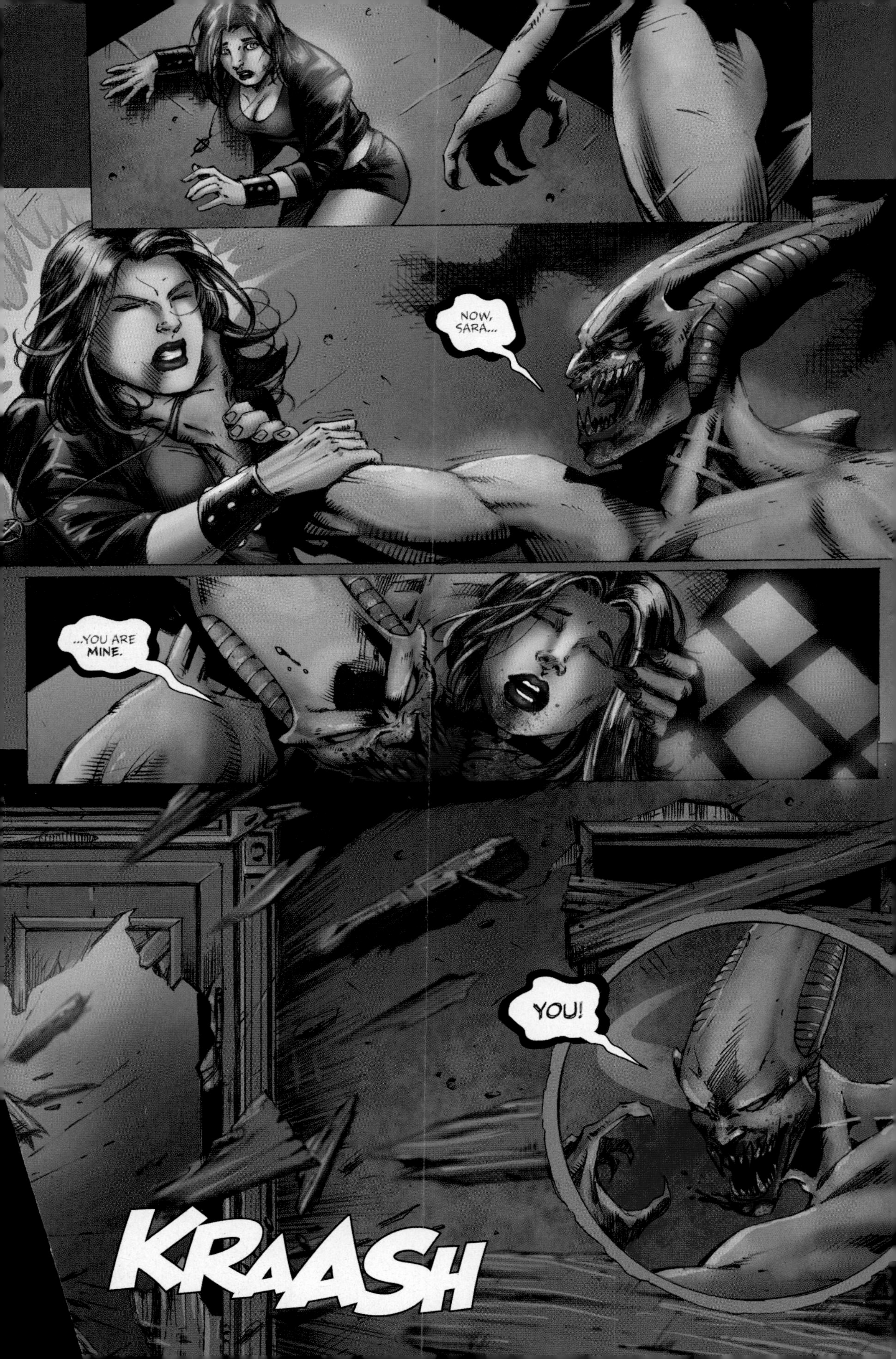
NOW, SARA...
...YOU ARE MINE.
YOU!
KRAASH

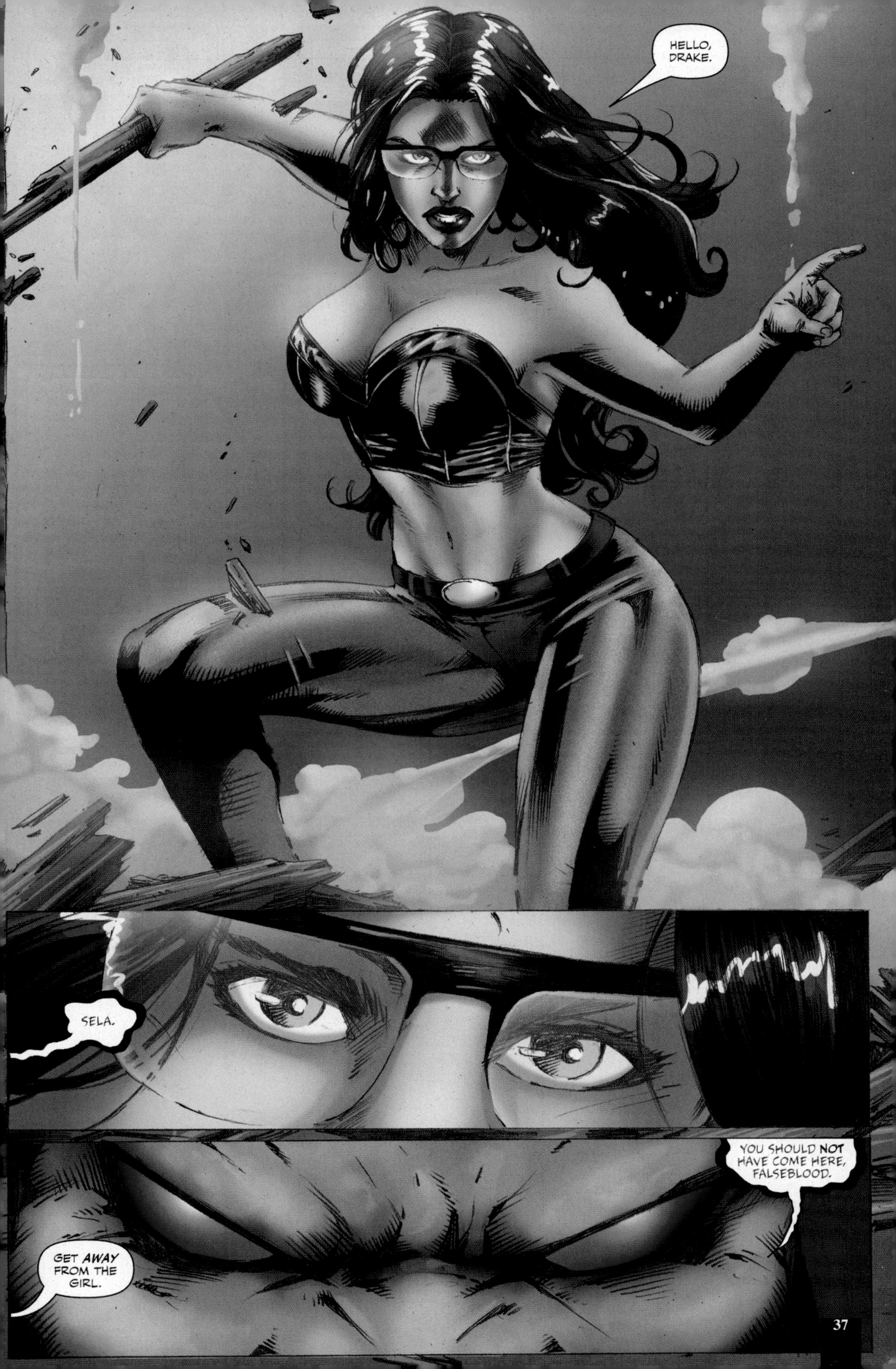
HELLO, DRAKE.
SELA.
YOU SHOULD NOT HAVE COME HERE, FALSEBLOOD.
GET AWAY FROM THE GIRL.

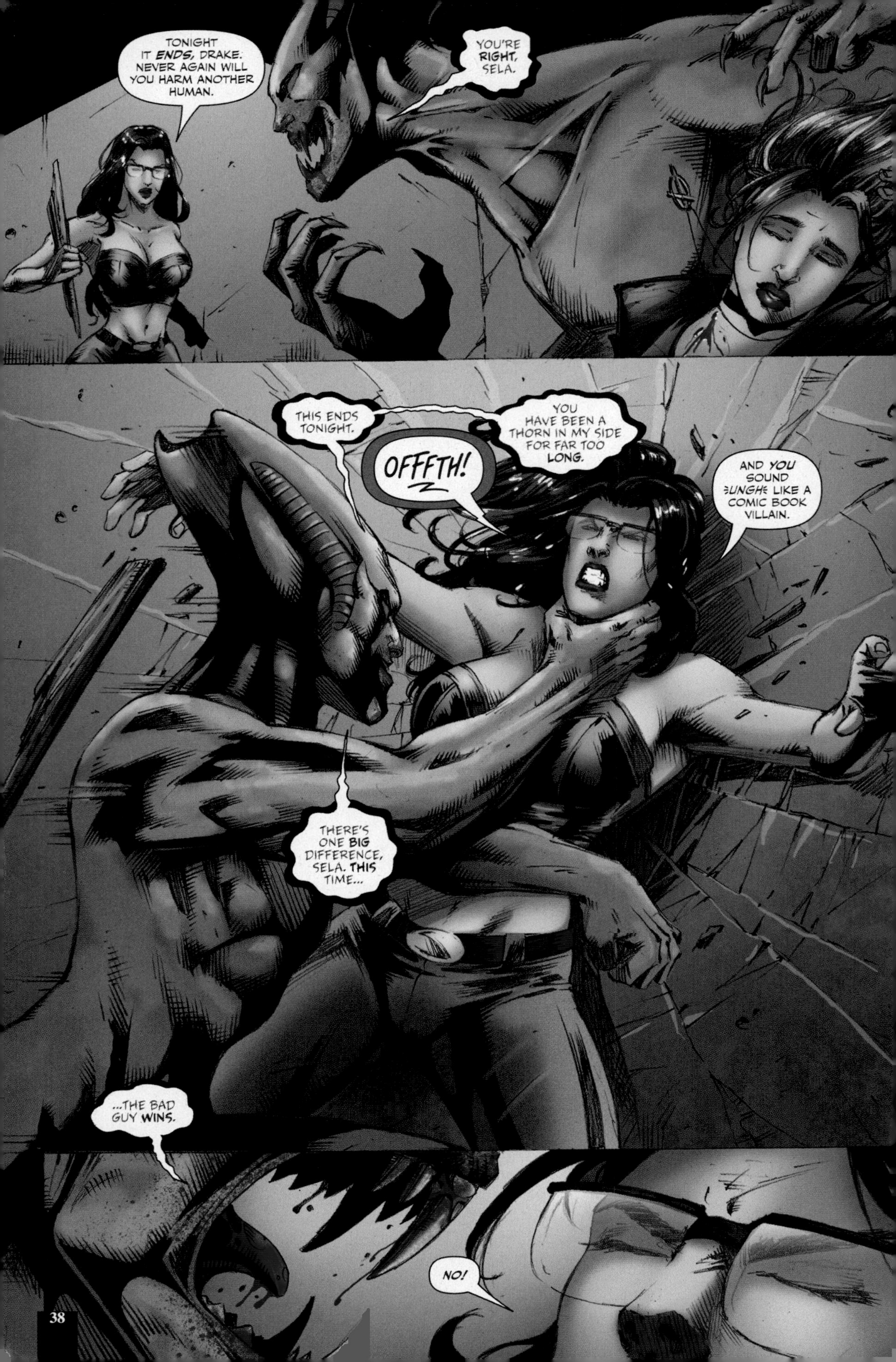
TONIGHT IT ENDS, DRAKE. NEVER AGAIN WILL YOU HARM ANOTHER HUMAN.
YOU'RE RIGHT, SELA.
THIS ENDS TONIGHT.
YOU HAVE BEEN A THORN IN MY SIDE FOR FAR TOO LONG.
OFFFTH!
AND YOU SOUND =UNGH= LIKE A COMIC BOOK VILLAIN.
THERE'S ONE BIG DIFFERENCE, SELA. THIS TIME...
...THE BAD GUY WINS.
NO!

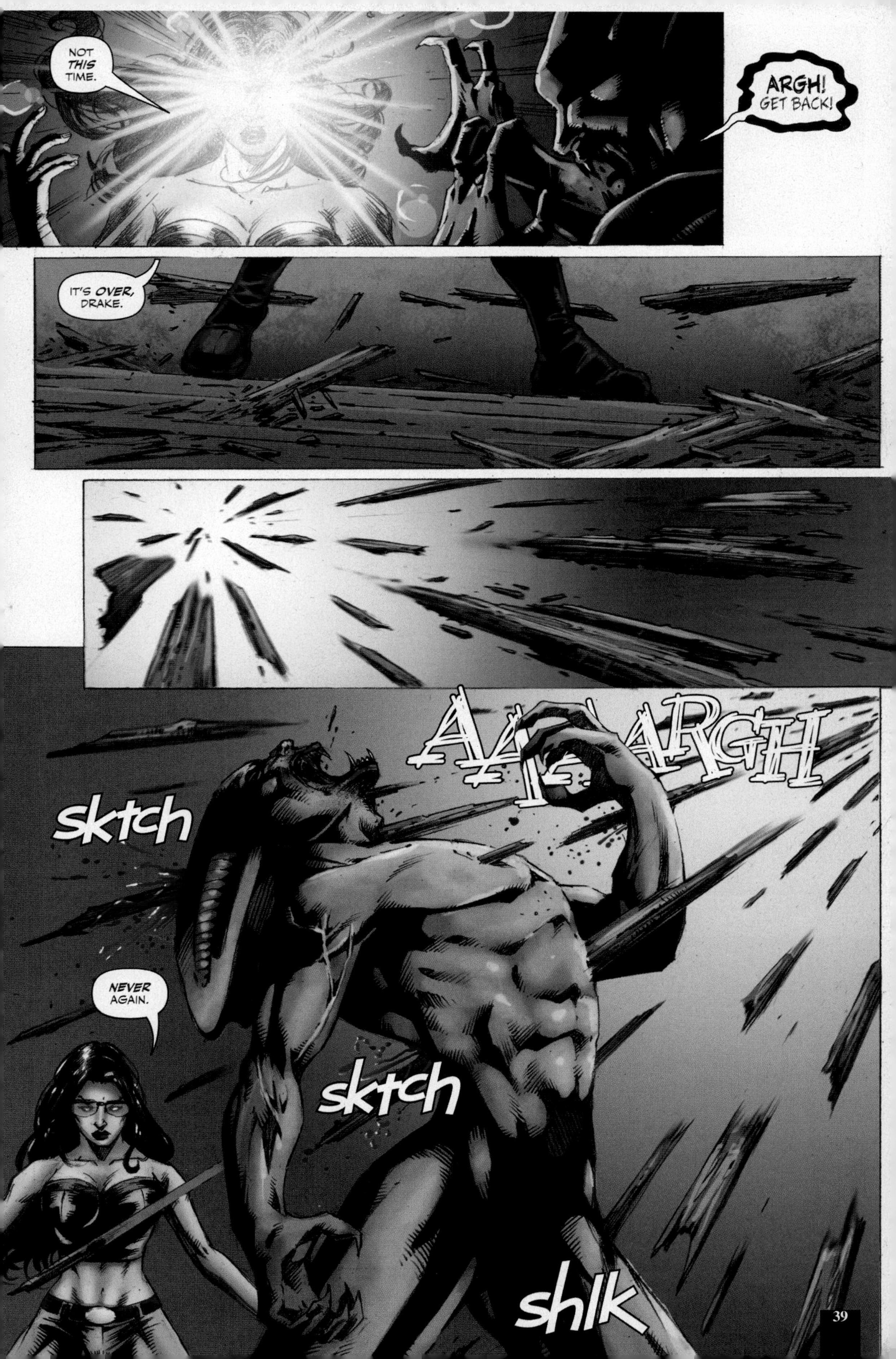
NOT THIS TIME.
ARGH! GET BACK!
IT'S OVER, DRAKE.
AAAARGH
sktch
NEVER AGAIN.
sktch
shlk

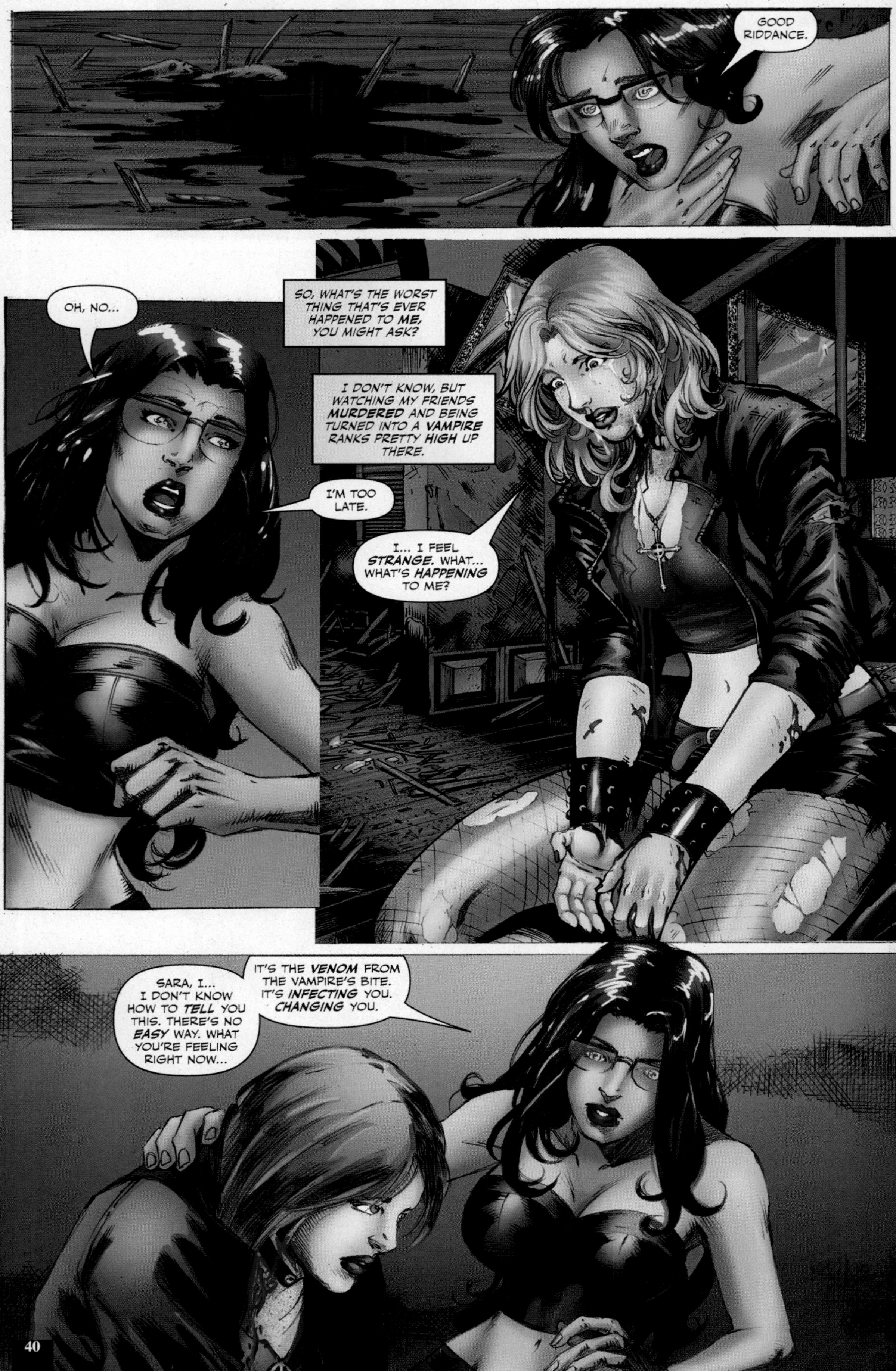
GOOD RIDDANCE.
OH, NO...
SO, WHAT'S THE WORST THING THAT'S EVER HAPPENED TO ME, YOU MIGHT ASK?
I DON'T KNOW, BUT WATCHING MY FRIENDS MURDERED AND BEING TURNED INTO A VAMPIRE RANKS PRETTY HIGH UP THERE.
I'M TOO LATE.
I... I FEEL STRANGE. WHAT... WHAT'S HAPPENING TO ME?
SARA, I... I DON'T KNOW HOW TO TELL YOU THIS. THERE'S NO EASY WAY. WHAT YOU'RE FEELING RIGHT NOW...
IT'S THE VENOM FROM THE VAMPIRE'S BITE. IT'S INFECTING YOU. CHANGING YOU.

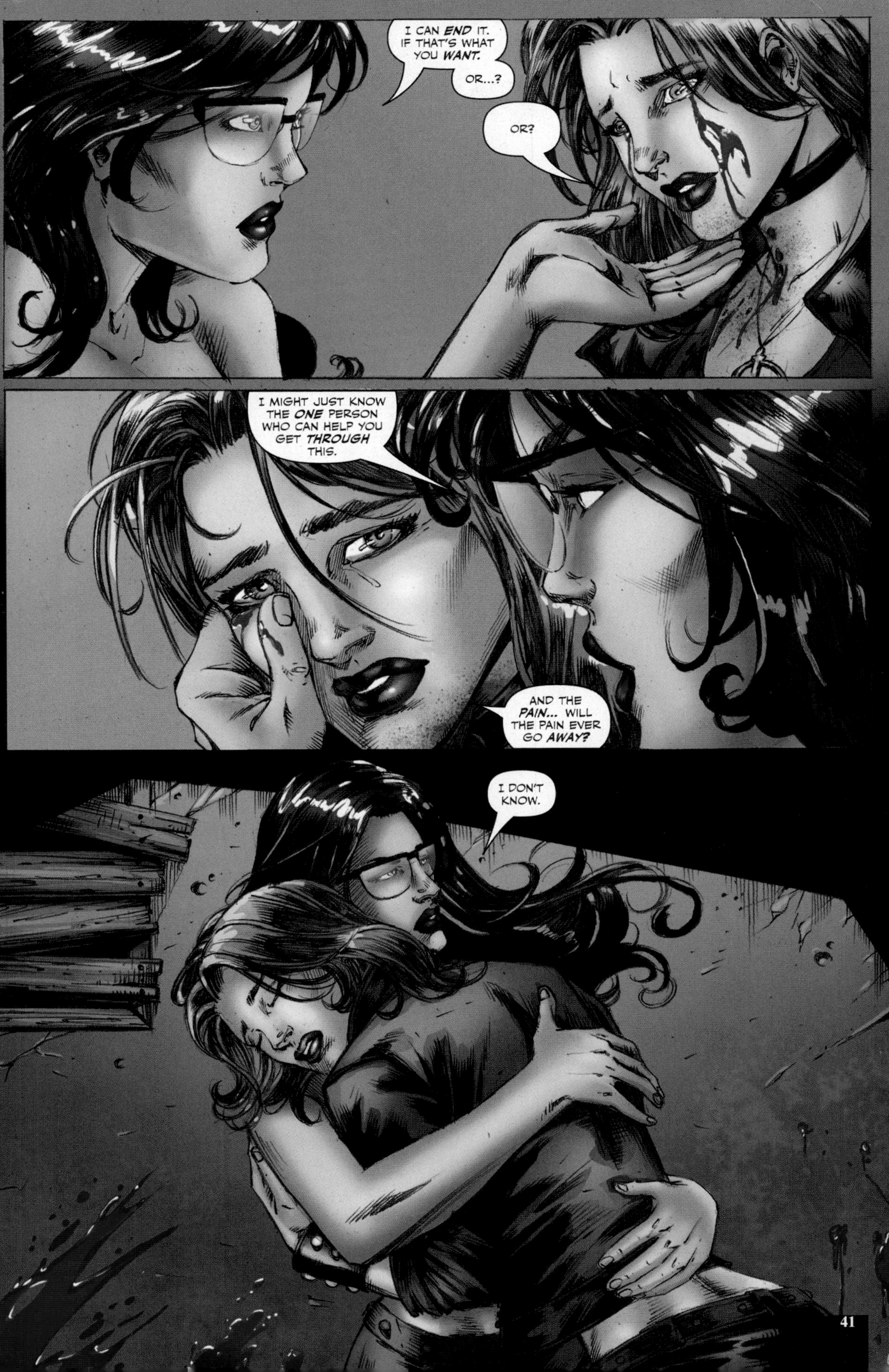
I CAN END IT. IF THAT'S WHAT YOU WANT.
OR...?
OR?
I MIGHT JUST KNOW THE ONE PERSON WHO CAN HELP YOU GET THROUGH THIS.
AND THE PAIN... WILL THE PAIN EVER GO AWAY?
I DON'T KNOW.

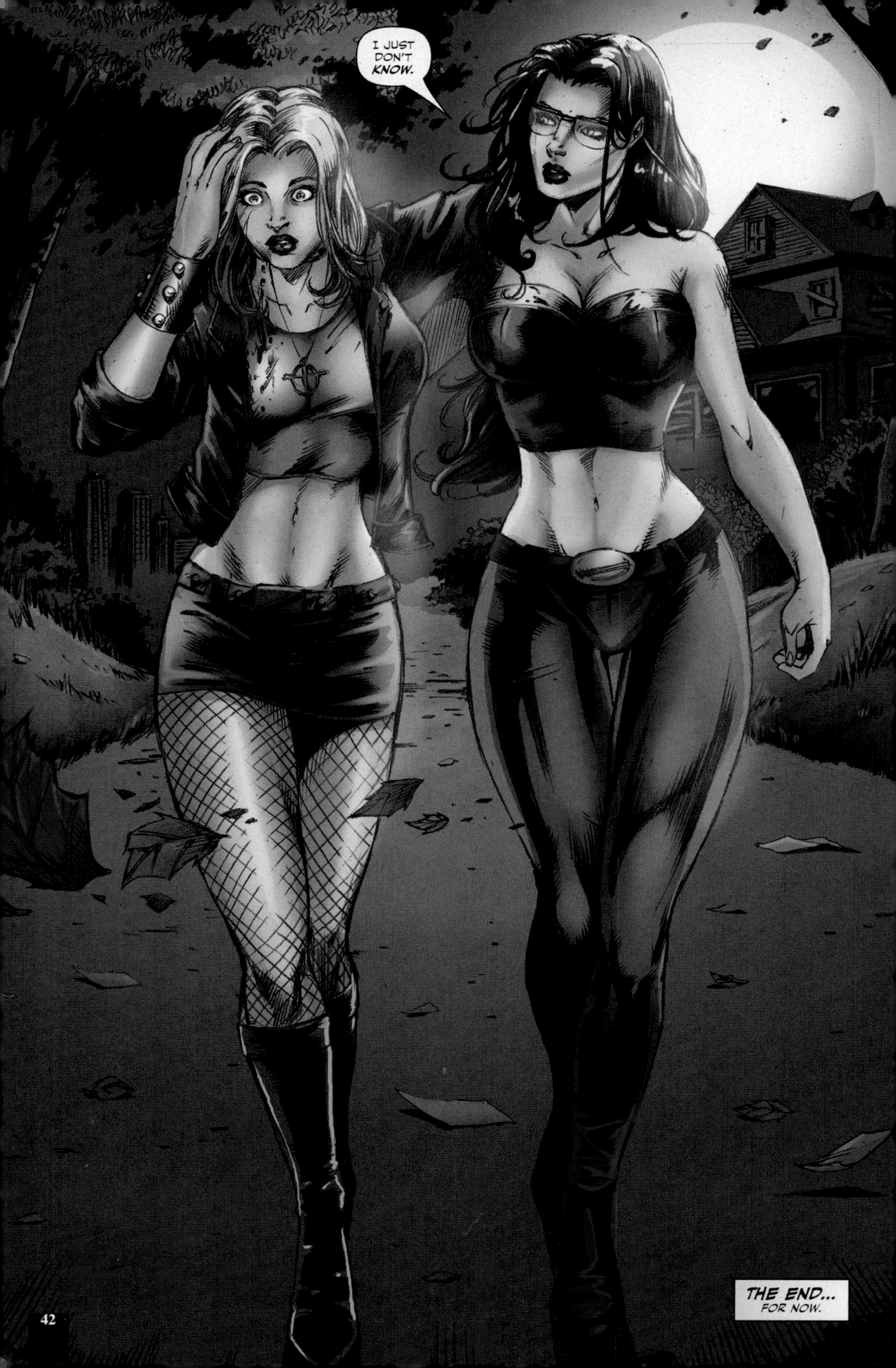
I JUST DON'T KNOW.
THE END... FOR NOW.

Grimm Fairy Tales

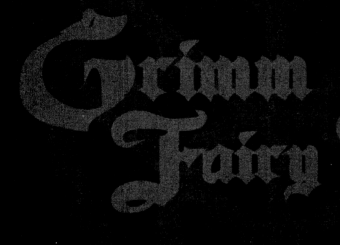

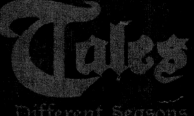

Different Seasons

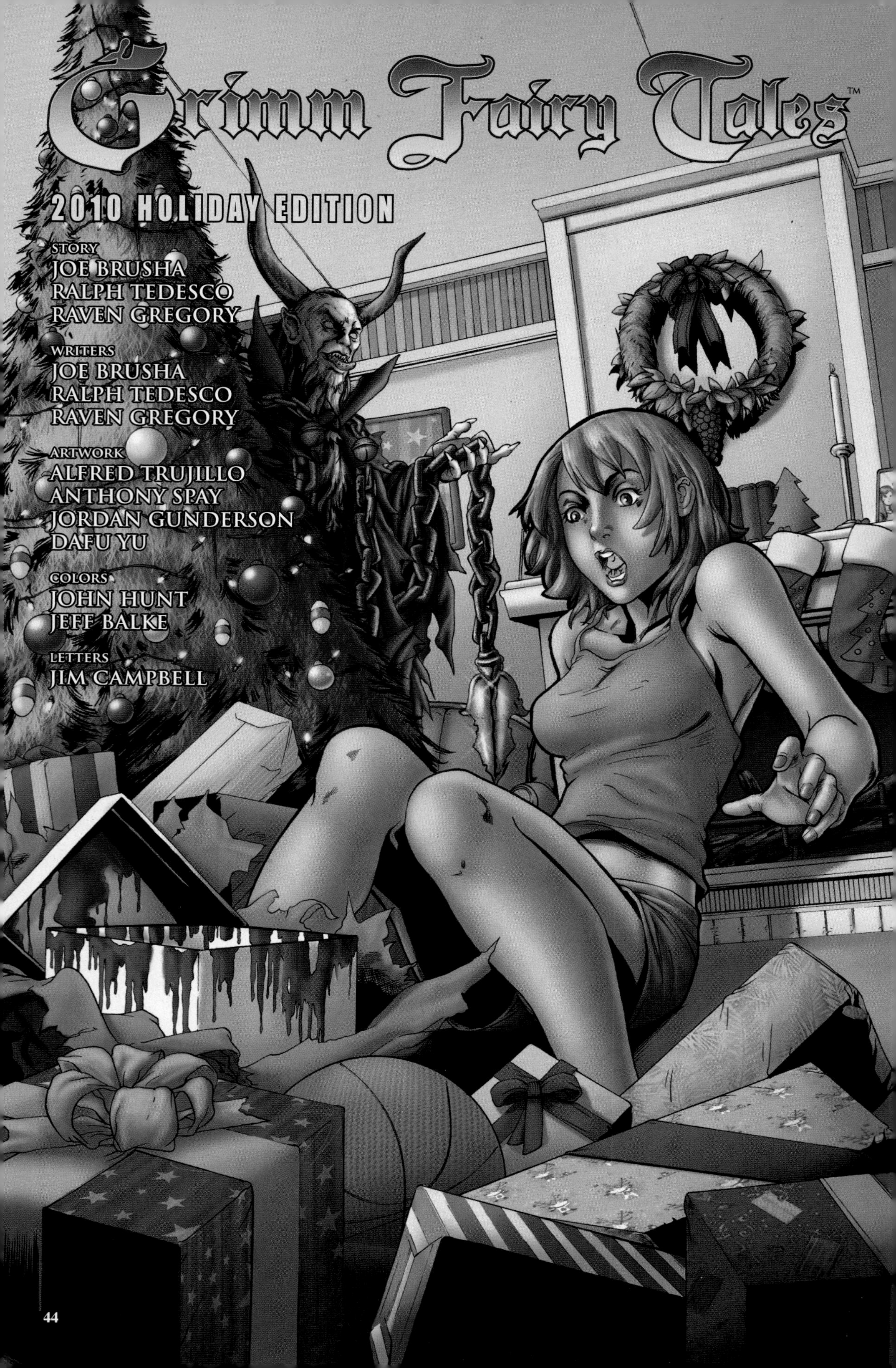
Grimm Fairy Tales™
2010 HOLIDAY EDITION
STORY
JOE BRUSHA
RALPH TEDESCO
RAVEN GREGORY
WRITERS
JOE BRUSHA
RALPH TEDESCO
RAVEN GREGORY
ARTWORK
ALFRED TRUJILLO
ANTHONY SPAY
JORDAN GUNDERSON
DAFU YU
COLORS
JOHN HUNT
JEFF BALKE
LETTERS
JIM CAMPBELL

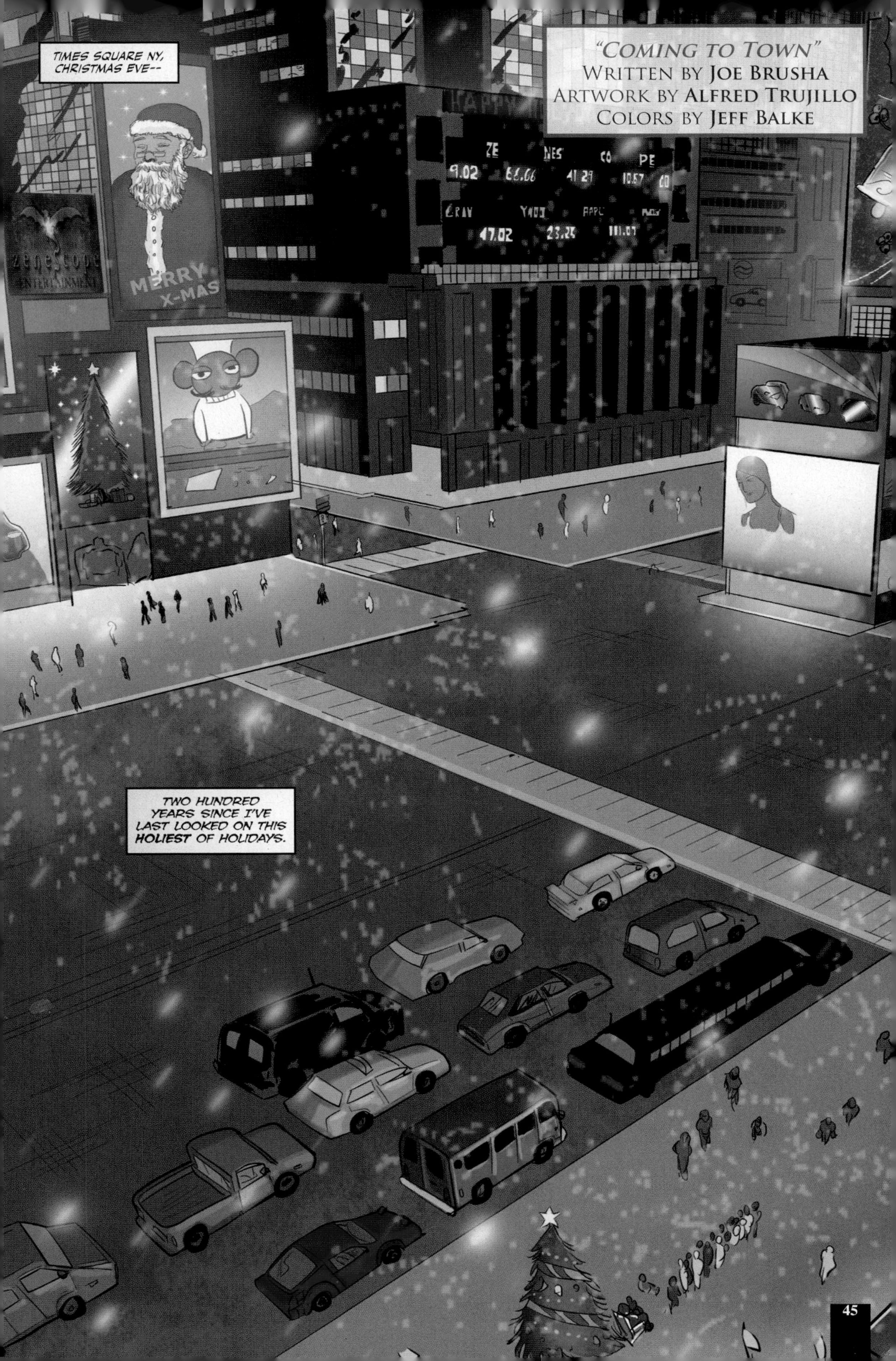
TIMES SQUARE NY, CHRISTMAS EVE--
"COMING TO TOWN"
WRITTEN BY JOE BRUSHA
ARTWORK BY ALFRED TRUJILLO
COLORS BY JEFF BALKE
MERRY X-MAS
TWO HUNDRED YEARS SINCE I'VE LAST LOOKED ON THIS HOLIEST OF HOLIDAYS.

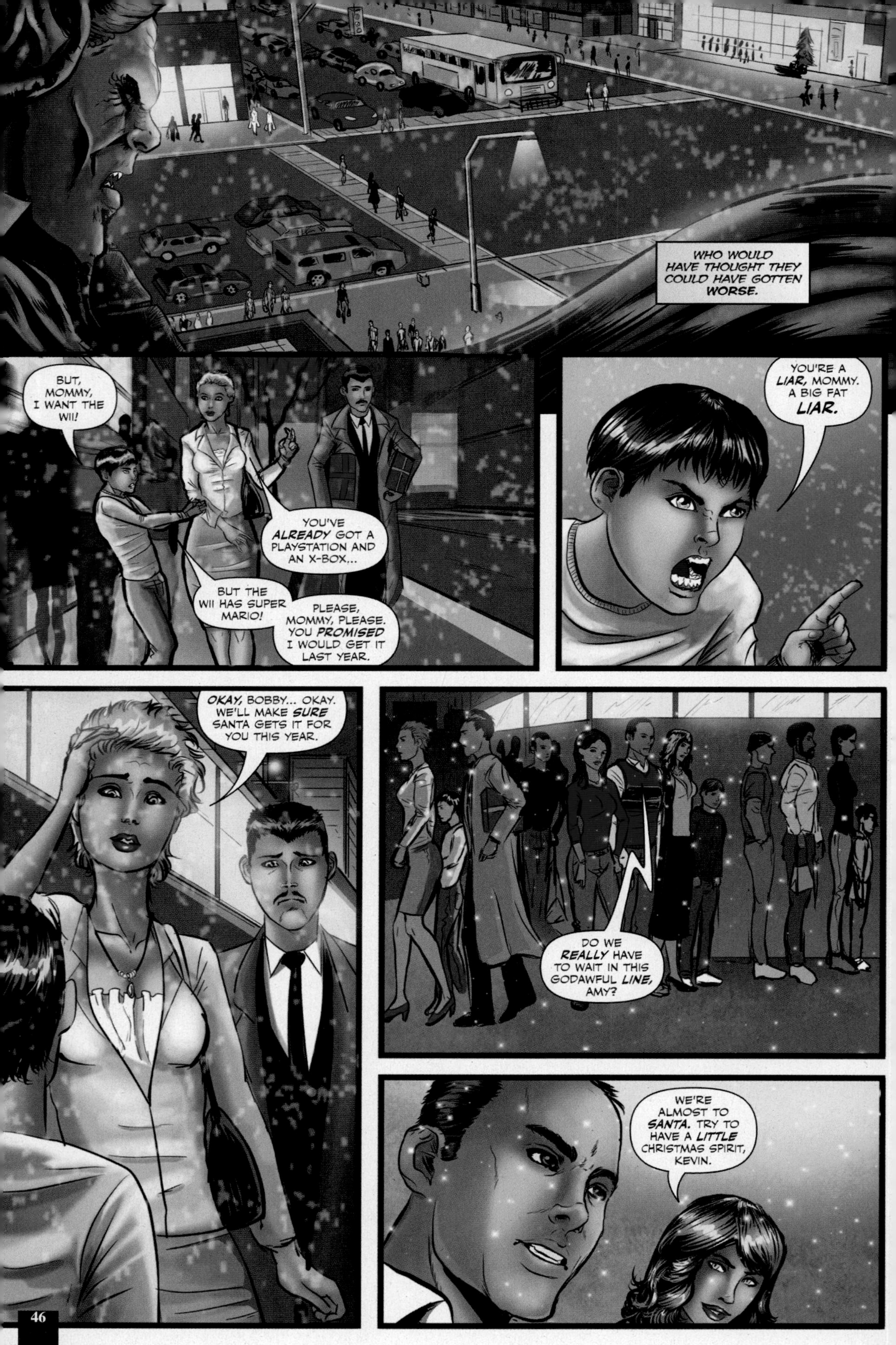
WHO WOULD HAVE THOUGHT THEY COULD HAVE GOTTEN WORSE.
BUT, MOMMY, I WANT THE WII!
YOU'VE ALREADY GOT A PLAYSTATION AND AN X-BOX...
BUT THE WII HAS SUPER MARIO!
PLEASE, MOMMY, PLEASE. YOU PROMISED I WOULD GET IT LAST YEAR.
YOU'RE A LIAR, MOMMY. A BIG FAT LIAR.
OKAY, BOBBY... OKAY. WE'LL MAKE SURE SANTA GETS IT FOR YOU THIS YEAR.
DO WE REALLY HAVE TO WAIT IN THIS GODAWFUL LINE, AMY?
WE'RE ALMOST TO SANTA. TRY TO HAVE A LITTLE CHRISTMAS SPIRIT, KEVIN.

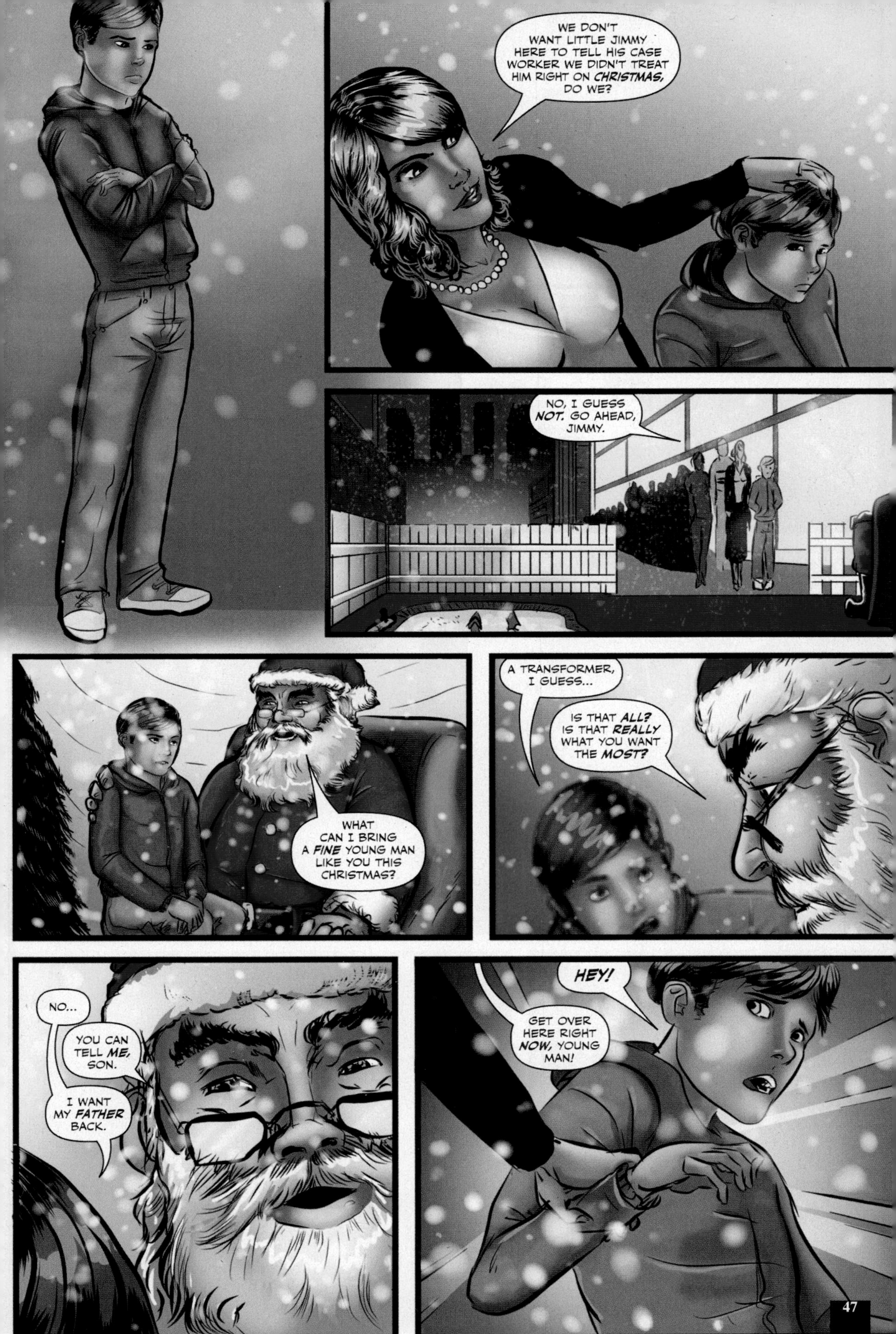
WE DON'T WANT LITTLE JIMMY HERE TO TELL HIS CASE WORKER WE DIDN'T TREAT HIM RIGHT ON *CHRISTMAS,* DO WE?
NO, I GUESS *NOT.* GO AHEAD, JIMMY.
WHAT CAN I BRING A *FINE* YOUNG MAN LIKE YOU THIS CHRISTMAS?
A TRANSFORMER, I GUESS...
IS THAT *ALL?* IS THAT *REALLY* WHAT YOU WANT THE *MOST?*
NO...
YOU CAN TELL *ME,* SON.
I WANT MY *FATHER* BACK.
HEY!
GET OVER HERE RIGHT *NOW,* YOUNG MAN!

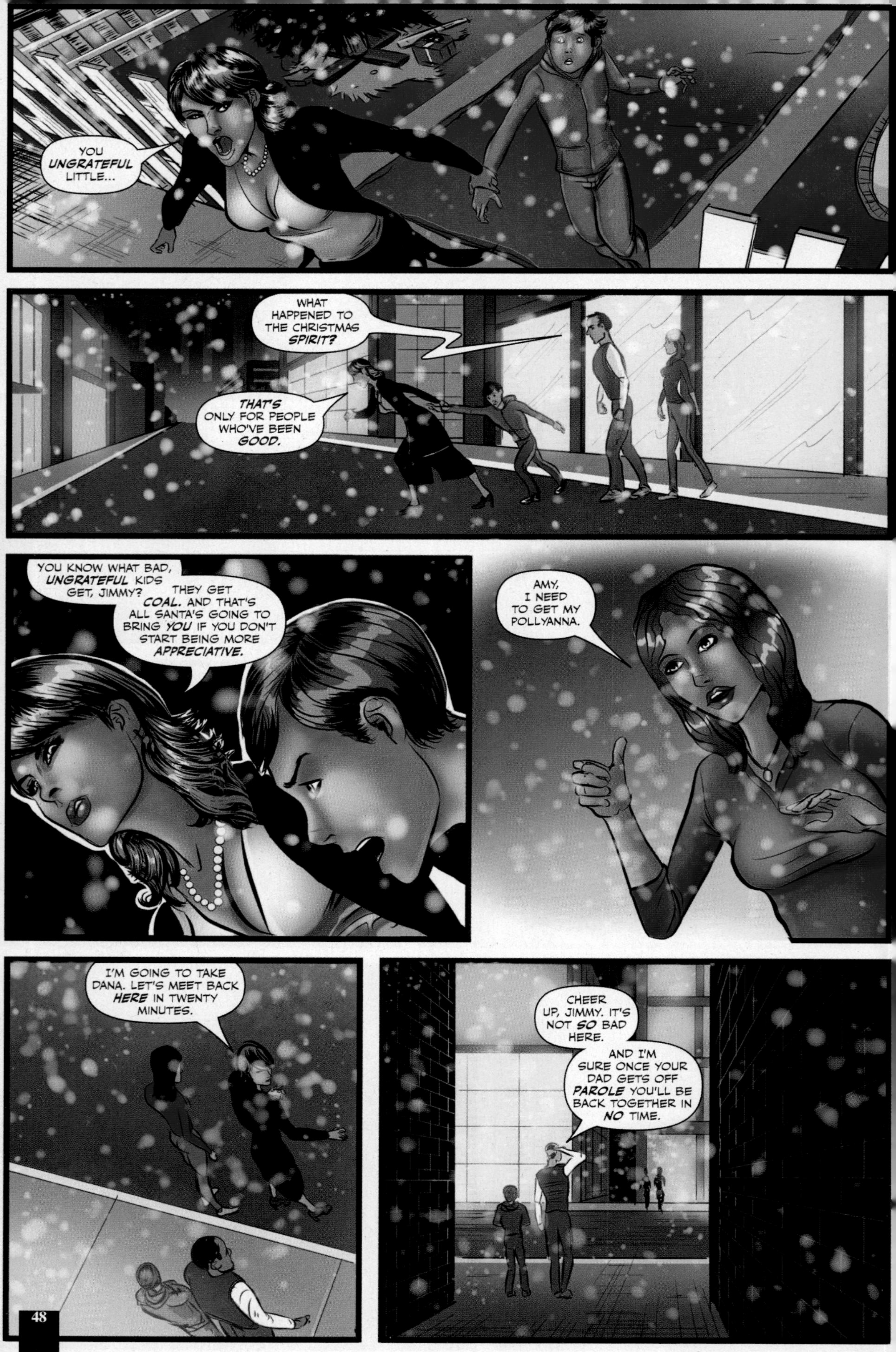
YOU UNGRATEFUL LITTLE...
WHAT HAPPENED TO THE CHRISTMAS SPIRIT?
THAT'S ONLY FOR PEOPLE WHO'VE BEEN GOOD.
YOU KNOW WHAT BAD, UNGRATEFUL KIDS GET, JIMMY?
THEY GET COAL. AND THAT'S ALL SANTA'S GOING TO BRING YOU IF YOU DON'T START BEING MORE APPRECIATIVE.
AMY, I NEED TO GET MY POLLYANNA.
I'M GOING TO TAKE DANA. LET'S MEET BACK HERE IN TWENTY MINUTES.
CHEER UP, JIMMY. IT'S NOT SO BAD HERE.
AND I'M SURE ONCE YOUR DAD GETS OFF PAROLE YOU'LL BE BACK TOGETHER IN NO TIME.

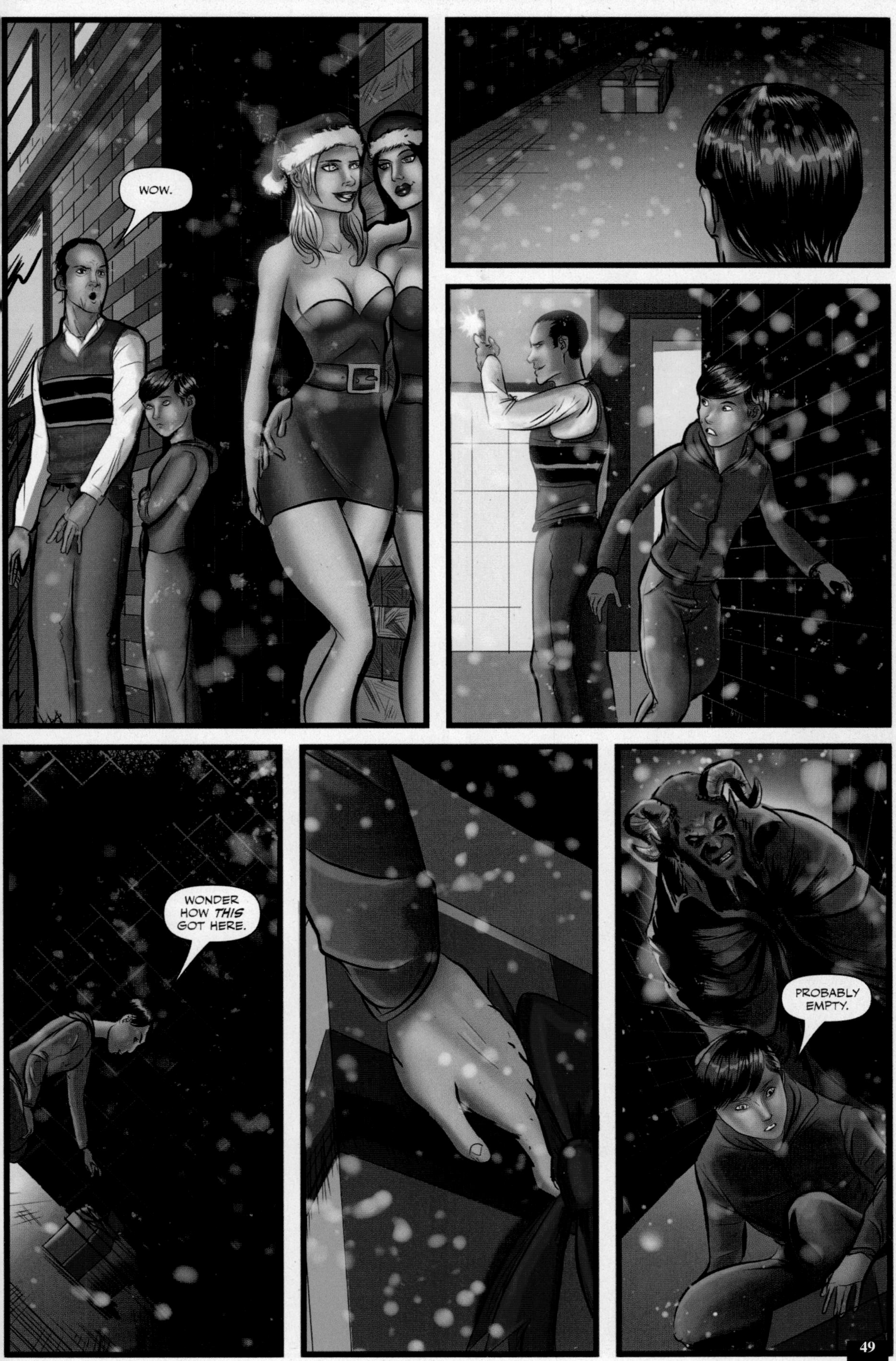
WOW.
WONDER HOW *THIS* GOT HERE.
PROBABLY EMPTY.

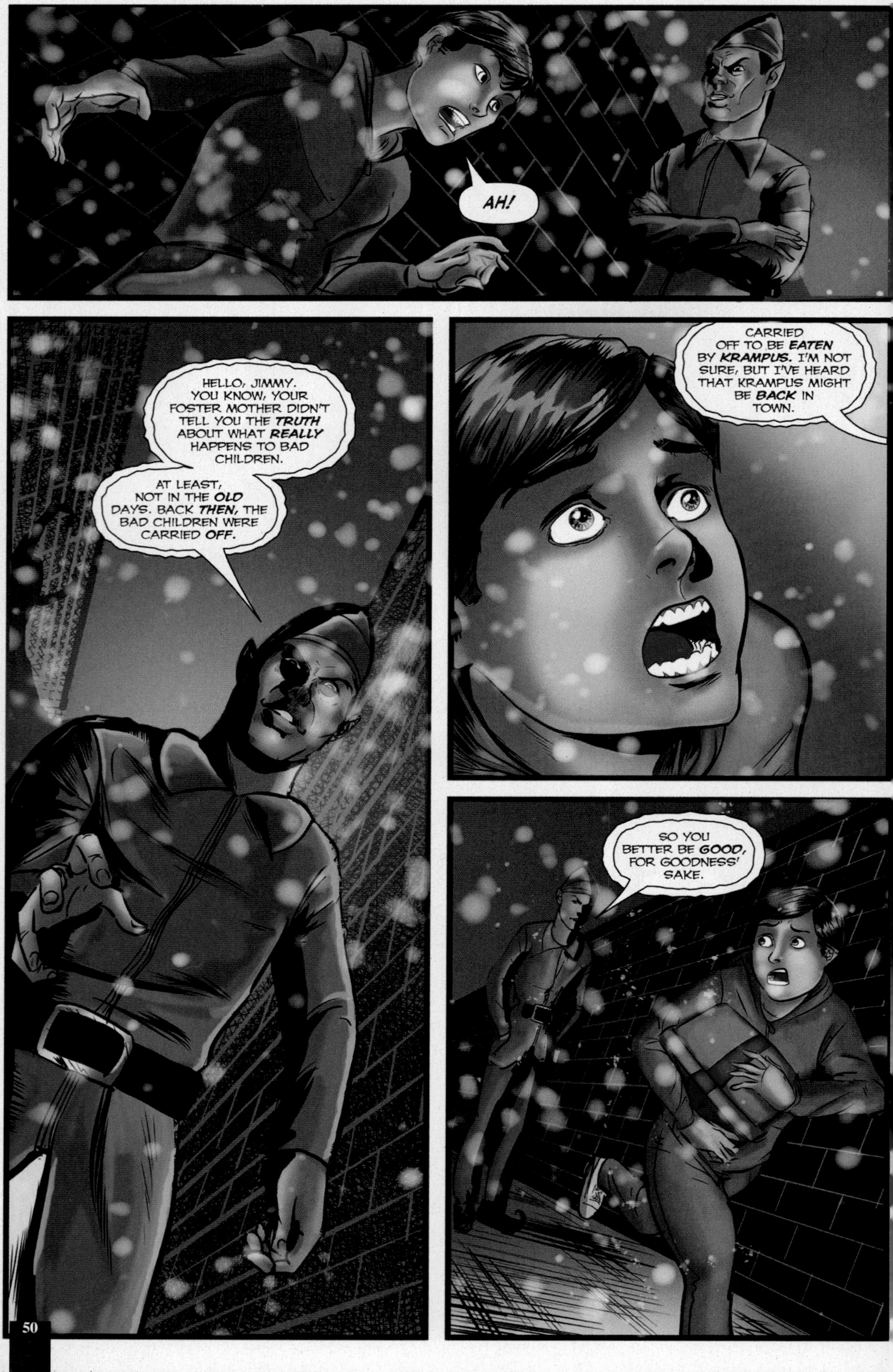
AH!
HELLO, JIMMY. YOU KNOW, YOUR FOSTER MOTHER DIDN'T TELL YOU THE TRUTH ABOUT WHAT REALLY HAPPENS TO BAD CHILDREN.
AT LEAST, NOT IN THE OLD DAYS. BACK THEN, THE BAD CHILDREN WERE CARRIED OFF.
CARRIED OFF TO BE EATEN BY KRAMPUS. I'M NOT SURE, BUT I'VE HEARD THAT KRAMPUS MIGHT BE BACK IN TOWN.
SO YOU BETTER BE GOOD, FOR GOODNESS' SAKE.

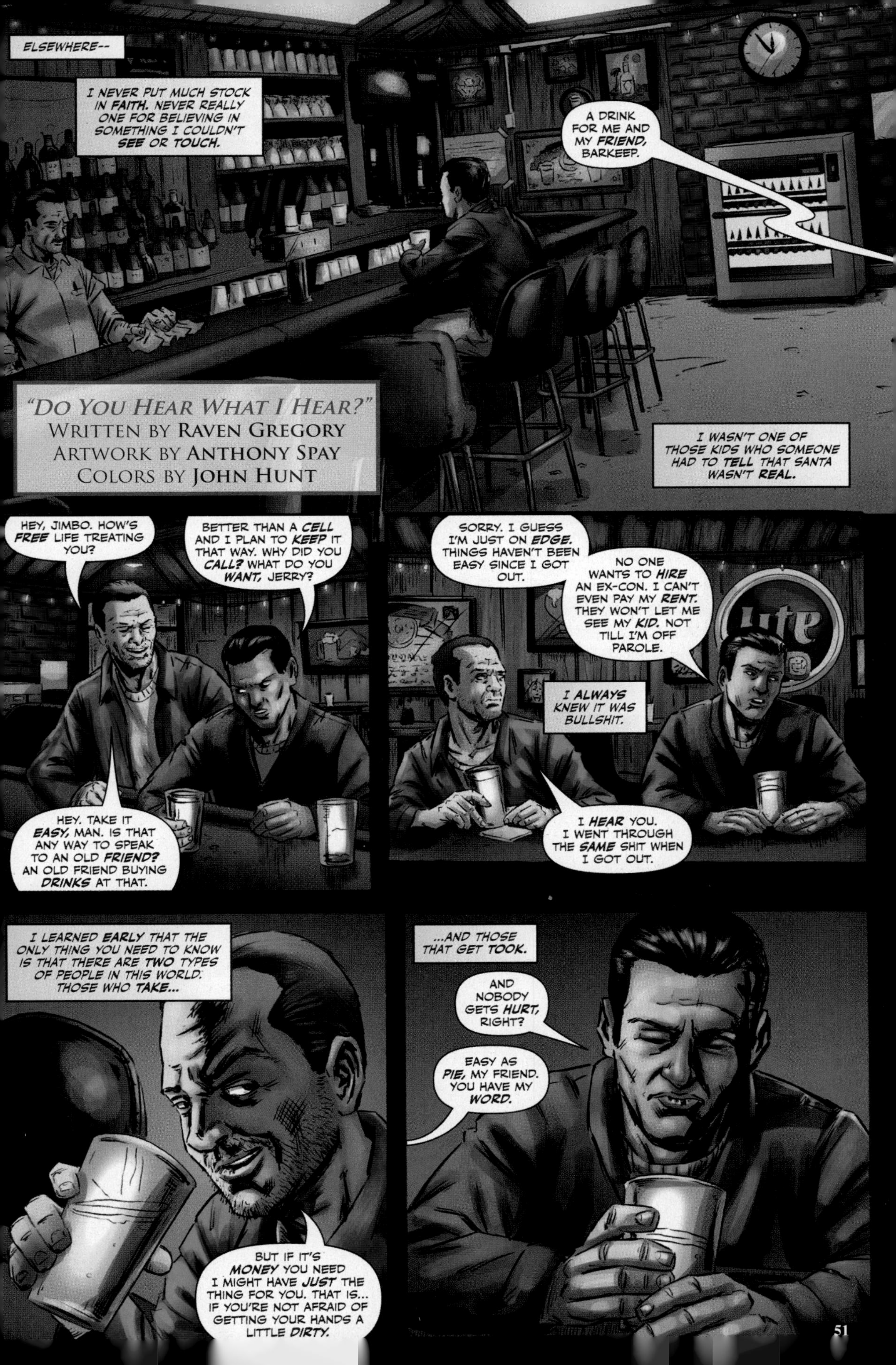
ELSEWHERE--
I NEVER PUT MUCH STOCK IN FAITH. NEVER REALLY ONE FOR BELIEVING IN SOMETHING I COULDN'T SEE OR TOUCH.
A DRINK FOR ME AND MY FRIEND, BARKEEP.
"Do You Hear What I Hear?"
Written by Raven Gregory
Artwork by Anthony Spay
Colors by John Hunt
I WASN'T ONE OF THOSE KIDS WHO SOMEONE HAD TO TELL THAT SANTA WASN'T REAL.
HEY, JIMBO. HOW'S FREE LIFE TREATING YOU?
BETTER THAN A CELL AND I PLAN TO KEEP IT THAT WAY. WHY DID YOU CALL? WHAT DO YOU WANT, JERRY?
HEY. TAKE IT EASY, MAN. IS THAT ANY WAY TO SPEAK TO AN OLD FRIEND? AN OLD FRIEND BUYING DRINKS AT THAT.
SORRY. I GUESS I'M JUST ON EDGE. THINGS HAVEN'T BEEN EASY SINCE I GOT OUT.
NO ONE WANTS TO HIRE AN EX-CON. I CAN'T EVEN PAY MY RENT. THEY WON'T LET ME SEE MY KID. NOT TILL I'M OFF PAROLE.
I ALWAYS KNEW IT WAS BULLSHIT.
I HEAR YOU. I WENT THROUGH THE SAME SHIT WHEN I GOT OUT.
I LEARNED EARLY THAT THE ONLY THING YOU NEED TO KNOW IS THAT THERE ARE TWO TYPES OF PEOPLE IN THIS WORLD. THOSE WHO TAKE...
BUT IF IT'S MONEY YOU NEED I MIGHT HAVE JUST THE THING FOR YOU. THAT IS... IF YOU'RE NOT AFRAID OF GETTING YOUR HANDS A LITTLE DIRTY.
...AND THOSE THAT GET TOOK.
AND NOBODY GETS HURT, RIGHT?
EASY AS PIE, MY FRIEND. YOU HAVE MY WORD.

I BET RIGHT ABOUT NOW YOU'RE WONDERING *HOW* A GUY LIKE *ME* ENDED UP. THE WHOLE NOT BELIEVING IN FAIRY TALES AND WHAT NOT.

IS SOMEONE OUT THERE?

TZZAKK

MERRY *CHRISTMAS*, LITTLE SOY PIGGY.

I'M NOT GONNA *BORE* YOU WITH AN *ABUSIVE* CHILDHOOD OR HOW I WAS RUINED BY SOME *DISILLUSIONMENT* OVER A RELATIONSHIP.

IN FACT, IF ANYTHING, IT REALLY WAS JUST GOOD OLD-FASHIONED *COMMON SENSE* THAT DID IT.

IF YOU DO SOMETHING BAD, UNLESS YOU GET CAUGHT, *NOTHING* HAPPENS. THERE'S NO *CONSEQUENCE*. NO REPERCUSSIONS BY SOME OTHERWORLDLY BEING. THERE'S *NOTHING*.

THERE'S HERE. THERE'S *NOW*.

GET THE @#$% OVER *HERE* AND HELP ME OUT, JIMBO.

NO WAY. THIS *ISN'T* WHAT I SIGNED UP FOR. I AIN'T GETTING LOCKED UP AGAIN OVER *THIS* BULLSHIT. I NEED THE *CASH*, MAN, BUT NOT LIKE *THIS*.

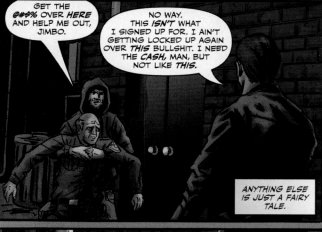

ANYTHING ELSE IS JUST A FAIRY TALE.

HEY, WAIT, COME *ON*. I NEED YOUR *HELP* HERE.

YOU SAID NO ONE WOULD GET *HURT*. I'M *OUTTA* HERE. YOU'RE ON YOUR *OWN*.

AND THE *ONLY* PERSON YOU HAVE TO LIVE WITH... IS YOURSELF.

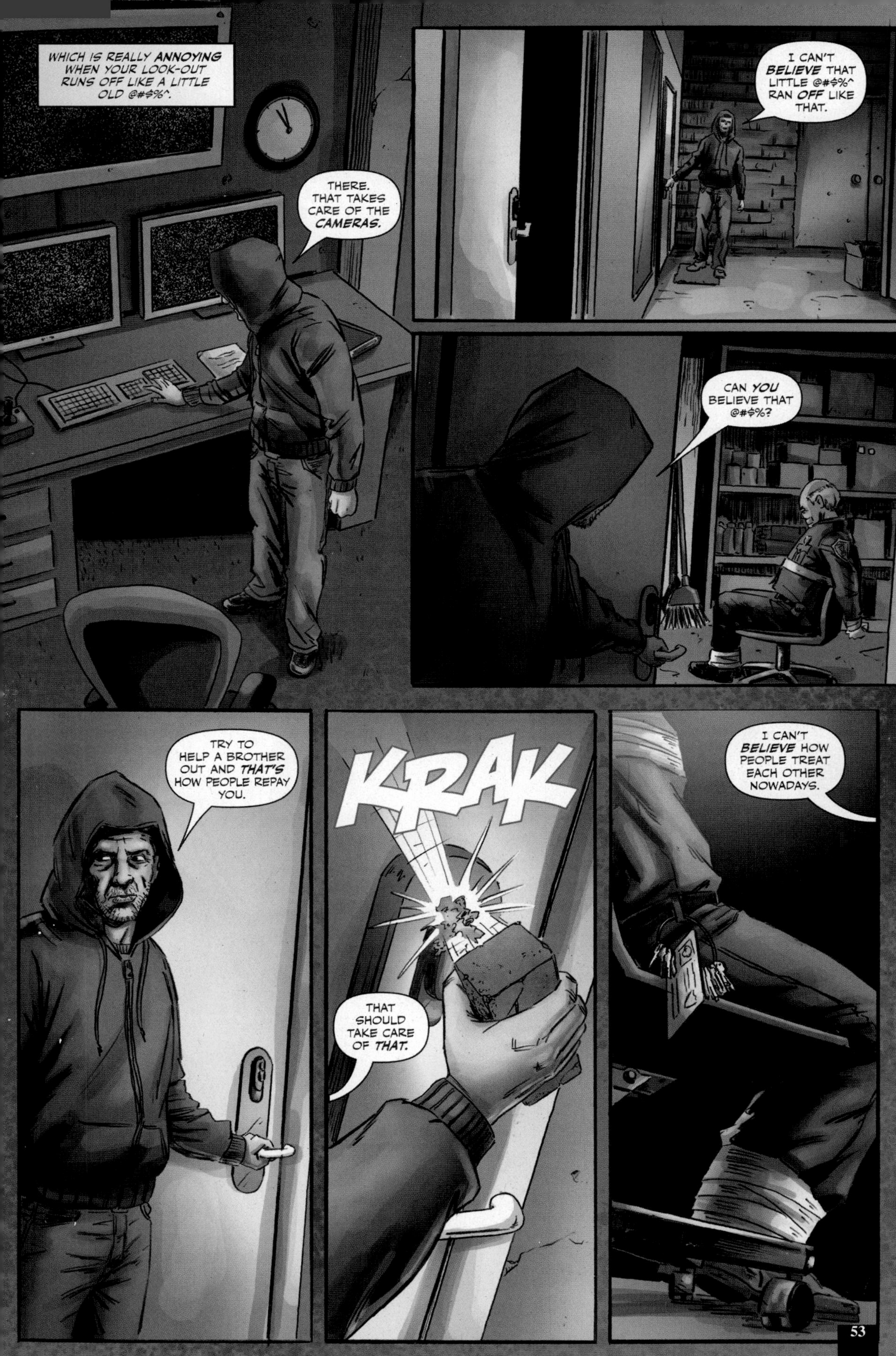
WHICH IS REALLY ANNOYING WHEN YOUR LOOK-OUT RUNS OFF LIKE A LITTLE OLD @#$%^.
THERE. THAT TAKES CARE OF THE CAMERAS.
I CAN'T BELIEVE THAT LITTLE @#$%^ RAN OFF LIKE THAT.
CAN YOU BELIEVE THAT @#$%?
TRY TO HELP A BROTHER OUT AND THAT'S HOW PEOPLE REPAY YOU.
KRAK
THAT SHOULD TAKE CARE OF THAT.
I CAN'T BELIEVE HOW PEOPLE TREAT EACH OTHER NOWADAYS.

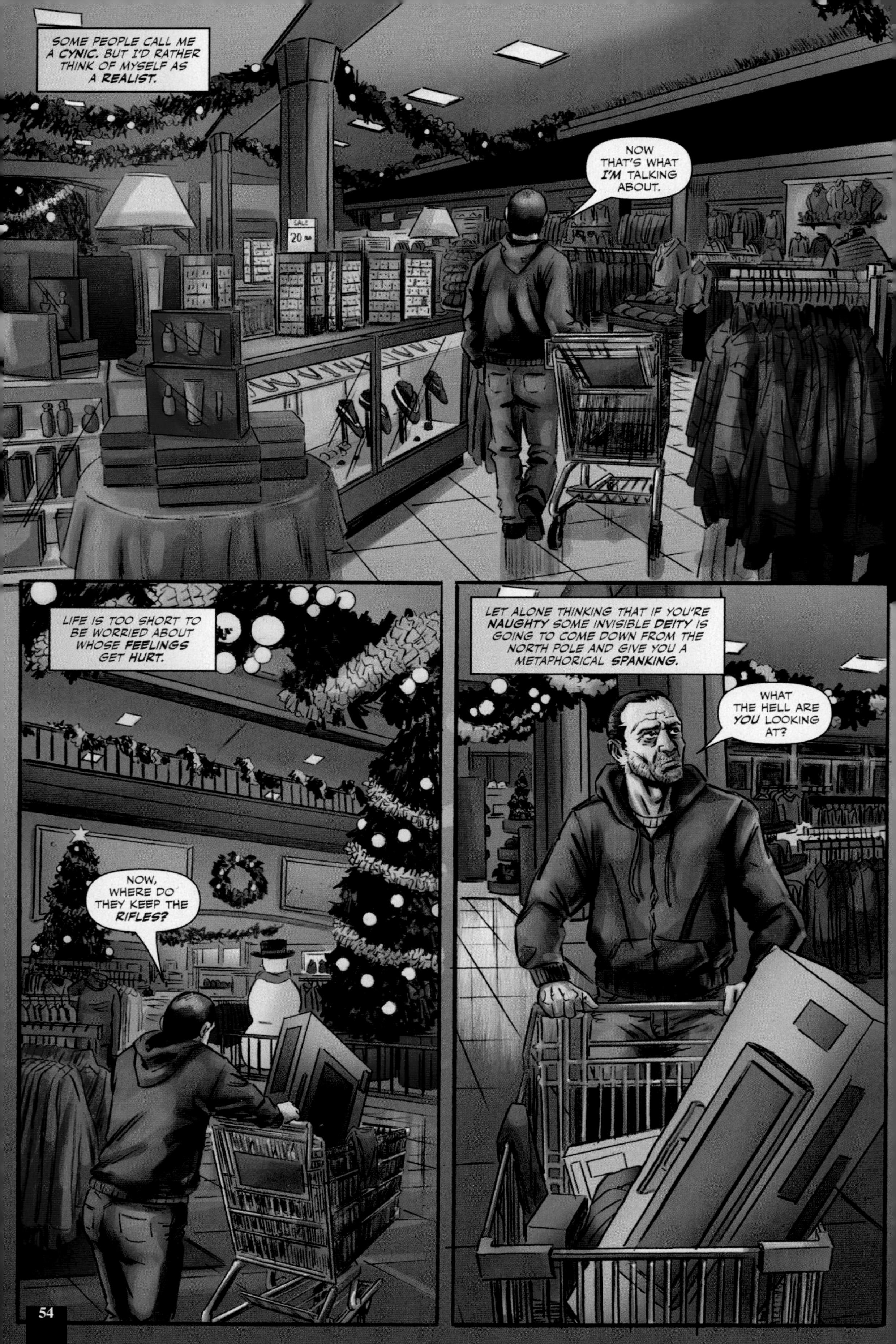
SOME PEOPLE CALL ME A CYNIC. BUT I'D RATHER THINK OF MYSELF AS A REALIST.
NOW THAT'S WHAT I'M TALKING ABOUT.
SALE 20
LIFE IS TOO SHORT TO BE WORRIED ABOUT WHOSE FEELINGS GET HURT.
NOW, WHERE DO THEY KEEP THE RIFLES?
LET ALONE THINKING THAT IF YOU'RE NAUGHTY SOME INVISIBLE DEITY IS GOING TO COME DOWN FROM THE NORTH POLE AND GIVE YOU A METAPHORICAL SPANKING.
WHAT THE HELL ARE YOU LOOKING AT?

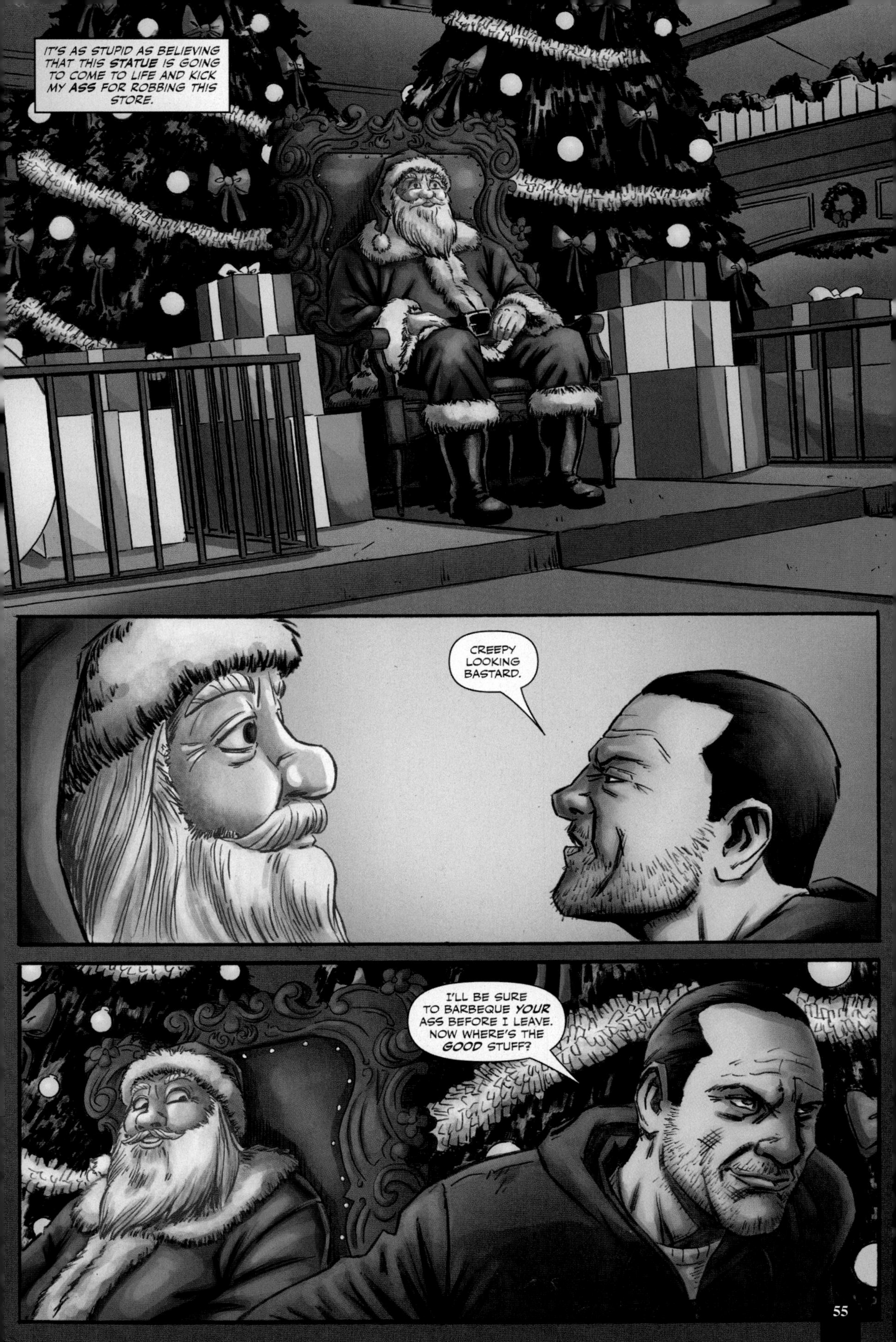
IT'S AS STUPID AS BELIEVING THAT THIS STATUE IS GOING TO COME TO LIFE AND KICK MY ASS FOR ROBBING THIS STORE.
CREEPY LOOKING BASTARD.
I'LL BE SURE TO BARBEQUE YOUR ASS BEFORE I LEAVE. NOW WHERE'S THE GOOD STUFF?

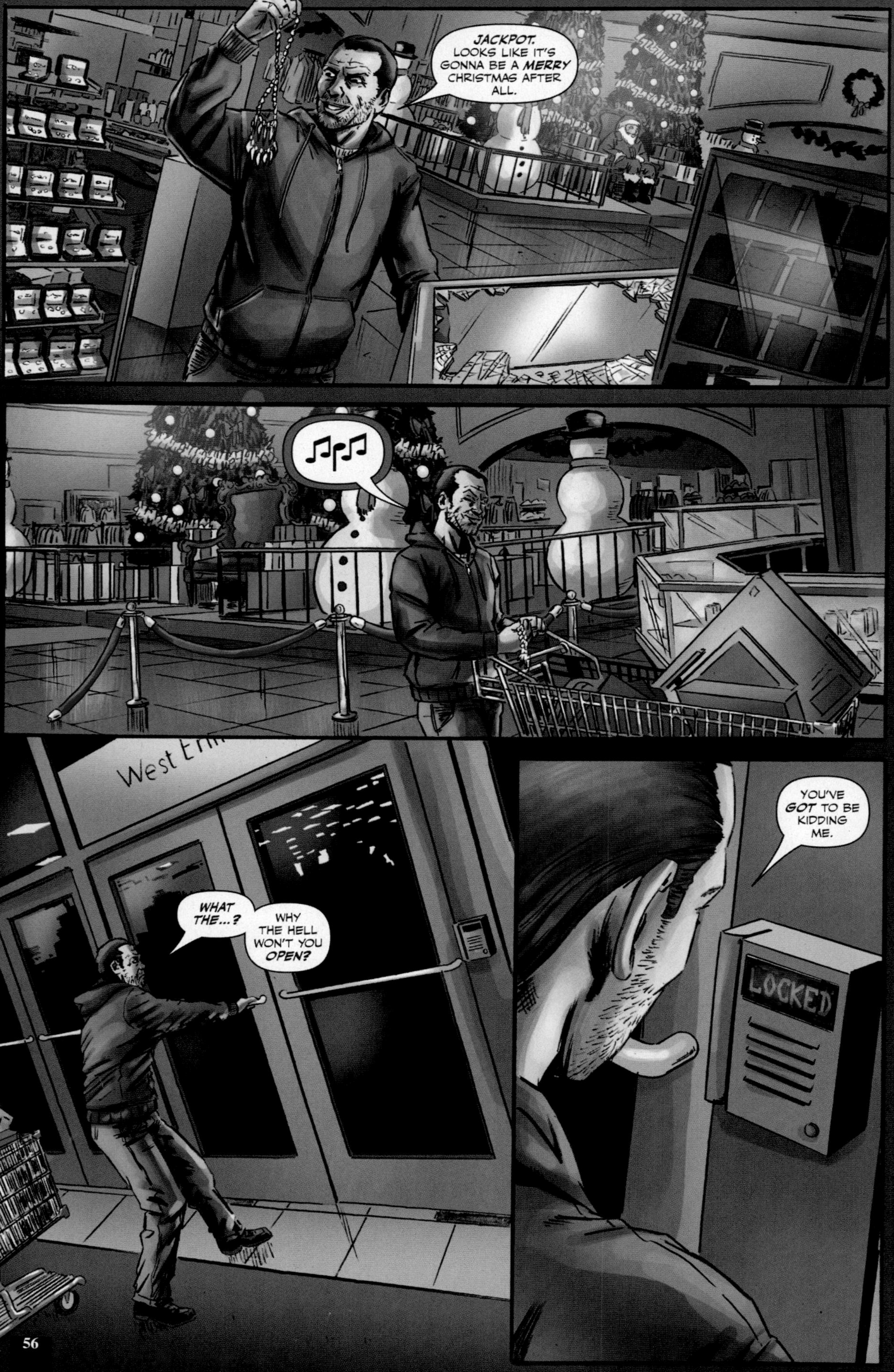
JACKPOT. LOOKS LIKE IT'S GONNA BE A MERRY CHRISTMAS AFTER ALL.
WHAT THE...?
WHY THE HELL WON'T YOU OPEN?
YOU'VE GOT TO BE KIDDING ME.
LOCKED

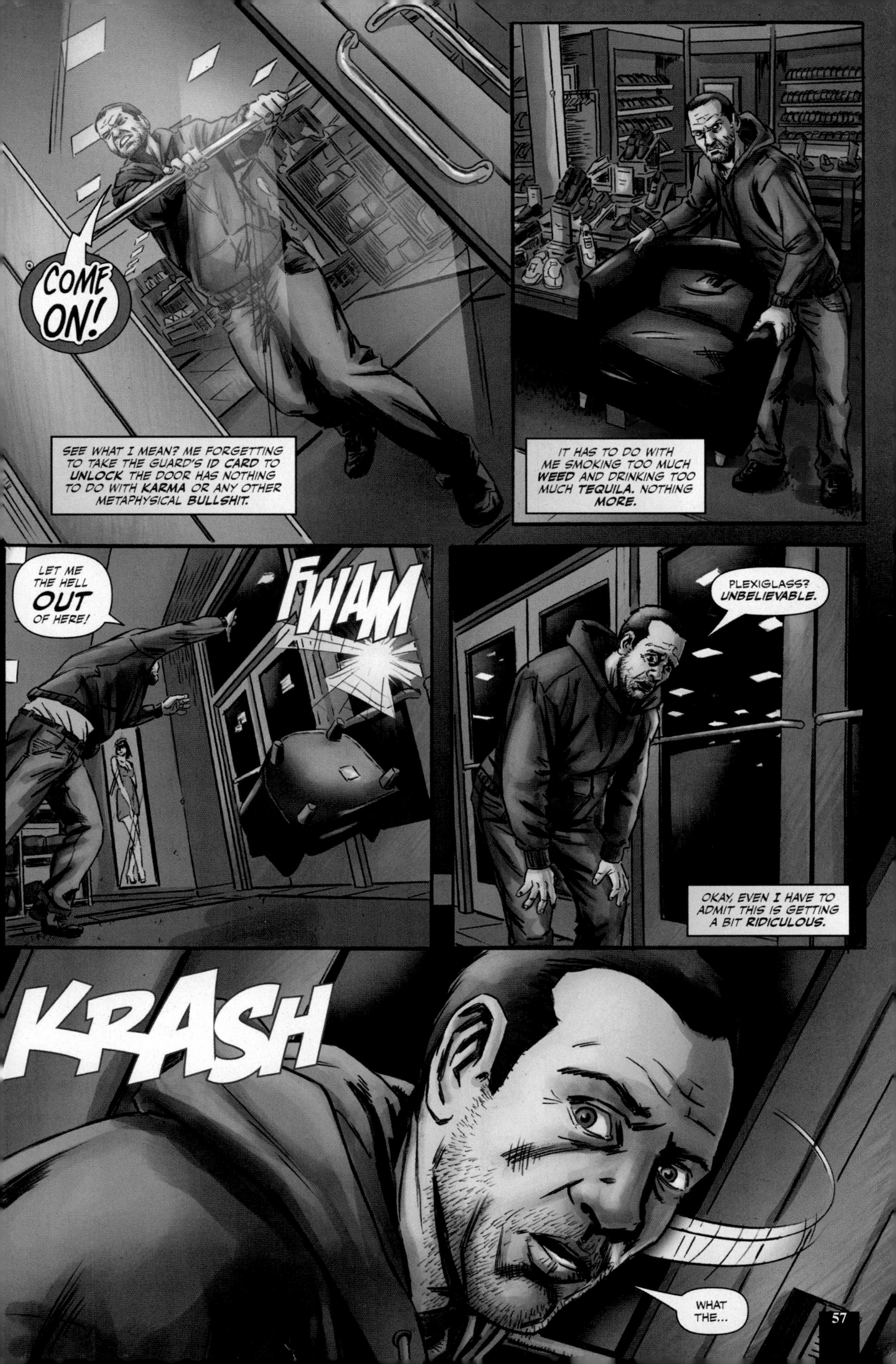
COME ON!
SEE WHAT I MEAN? ME FORGETTING TO TAKE THE GUARD'S ID CARD TO UNLOCK THE DOOR HAS NOTHING TO DO WITH KARMA OR ANY OTHER METAPHYSICAL BULLSHIT.
IT HAS TO DO WITH ME SMOKING TOO MUCH WEED AND DRINKING TOO MUCH TEQUILA. NOTHING MORE.
LET ME THE HELL OUT OF HERE!
FWAM
PLEXIGLASS? UNBELIEVABLE.
OKAY, EVEN I HAVE TO ADMIT THIS IS GETTING A BIT RIDICULOUS.
KRASH
WHAT THE...

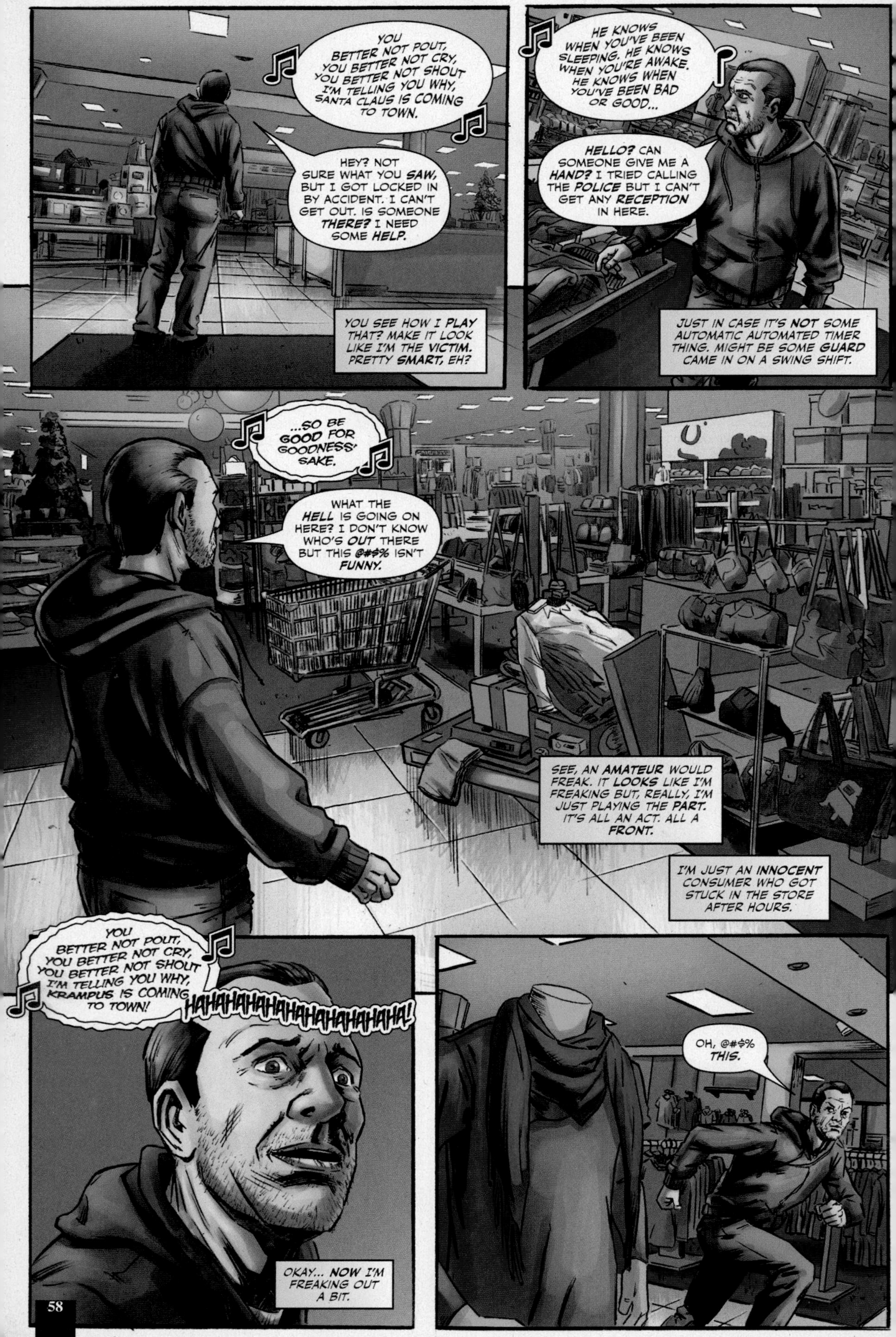
YOU BETTER NOT POUT, YOU BETTER NOT CRY, YOU BETTER NOT SHOUT I'M TELLING YOU WHY, SANTA CLAUS IS COMING TO TOWN.
HEY? NOT SURE WHAT YOU SAW, BUT I GOT LOCKED IN BY ACCIDENT. I CAN'T GET OUT. IS SOMEONE THERE? I NEED SOME HELP.
YOU SEE HOW I PLAY THAT? MAKE IT LOOK LIKE I'M THE VICTIM. PRETTY SMART, EH?
HE KNOWS WHEN YOU'VE BEEN SLEEPING. HE KNOWS WHEN YOU'RE AWAKE. HE KNOWS WHEN YOU'VE BEEN BAD OR GOOD...
HELLO? CAN SOMEONE GIVE ME A HAND? I TRIED CALLING THE POLICE BUT I CAN'T GET ANY RECEPTION IN HERE.
JUST IN CASE IT'S NOT SOME AUTOMATIC AUTOMATED TIMER THING. MIGHT BE SOME GUARD CAME IN ON A SWING SHIFT.
...SO BE GOOD FOR GOODNESS' SAKE.
WHAT THE HELL IS GOING ON HERE? I DON'T KNOW WHO'S OUT THERE BUT THIS @#$% ISN'T FUNNY.
SEE, AN AMATEUR WOULD FREAK. IT LOOKS LIKE I'M FREAKING BUT, REALLY, I'M JUST PLAYING THE PART. IT'S ALL AN ACT. ALL A FRONT.
I'M JUST AN INNOCENT CONSUMER WHO GOT STUCK IN THE STORE AFTER HOURS.
YOU BETTER NOT POUT, YOU BETTER NOT CRY, YOU BETTER NOT SHOUT I'M TELLING YOU WHY, KRAMPUS IS COMING TO TOWN!
HAHAHAHAHAHAHAHAHAHAHAHA!
OKAY... NOW I'M FREAKING OUT A BIT.
OH, @#$% THIS.

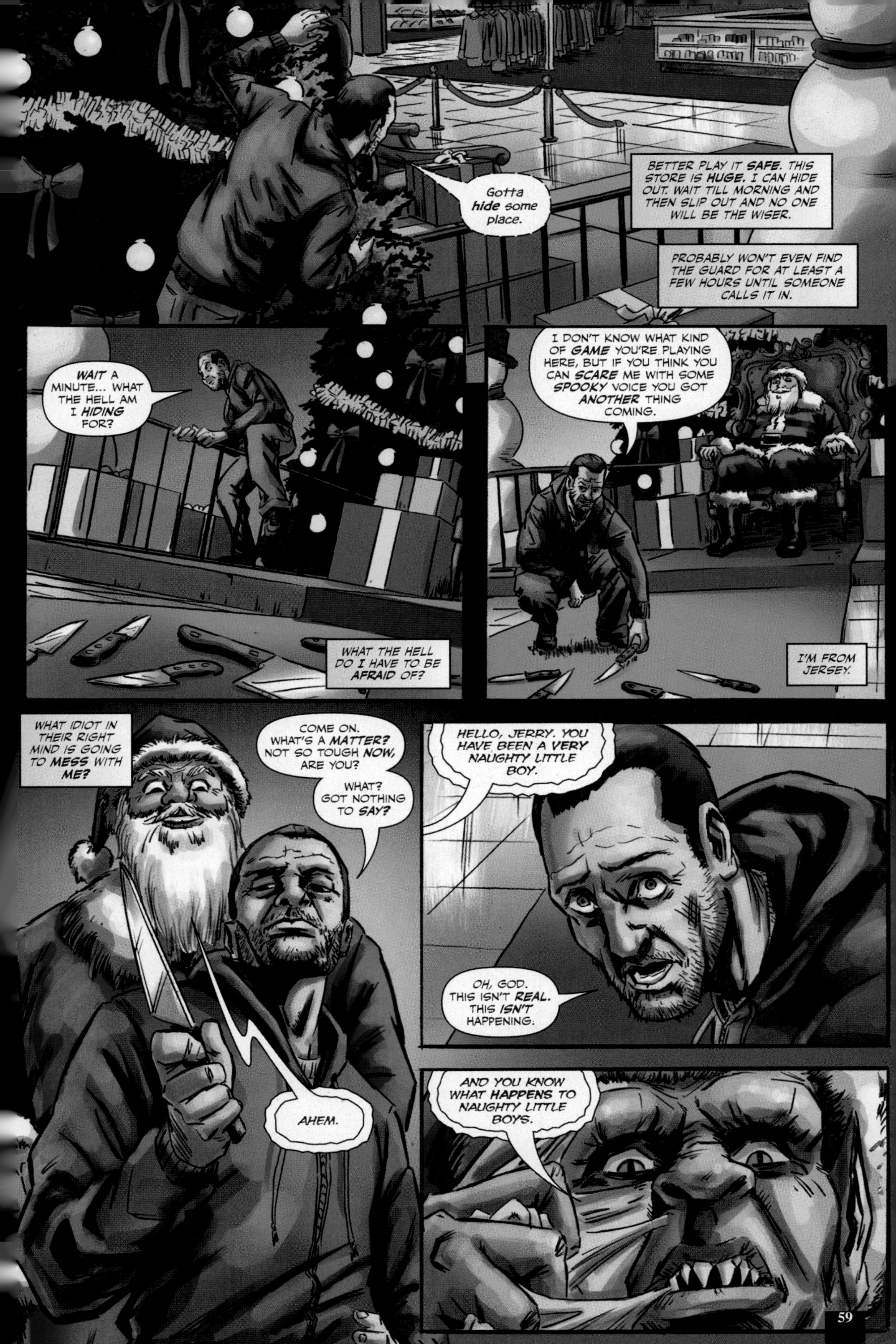
Gotta hide some place.
BETTER PLAY IT SAFE. THIS STORE IS HUGE. I CAN HIDE OUT. WAIT TILL MORNING AND THEN SLIP OUT AND NO ONE WILL BE THE WISER.
PROBABLY WON'T EVEN FIND THE GUARD FOR AT LEAST A FEW HOURS UNTIL SOMEONE CALLS IT IN.
WAIT A MINUTE... WHAT THE HELL AM I HIDING FOR?
WHAT THE HELL DO I HAVE TO BE AFRAID OF?
I DON'T KNOW WHAT KIND OF GAME YOU'RE PLAYING HERE, BUT IF YOU THINK YOU CAN SCARE ME WITH SOME SPOOKY VOICE YOU GOT ANOTHER THING COMING.
I'M FROM JERSEY.
WHAT IDIOT IN THEIR RIGHT MIND IS GOING TO MESS WITH ME?
COME ON. WHAT'S A MATTER? NOT SO TOUGH NOW, ARE YOU?
WHAT? GOT NOTHING TO SAY?
AHEM.
HELLO, JERRY. YOU HAVE BEEN A VERY NAUGHTY LITTLE BOY.
OH, GOD. THIS ISN'T REAL. THIS ISN'T HAPPENING.
AND YOU KNOW WHAT HAPPENS TO NAUGHTY LITTLE BOYS.

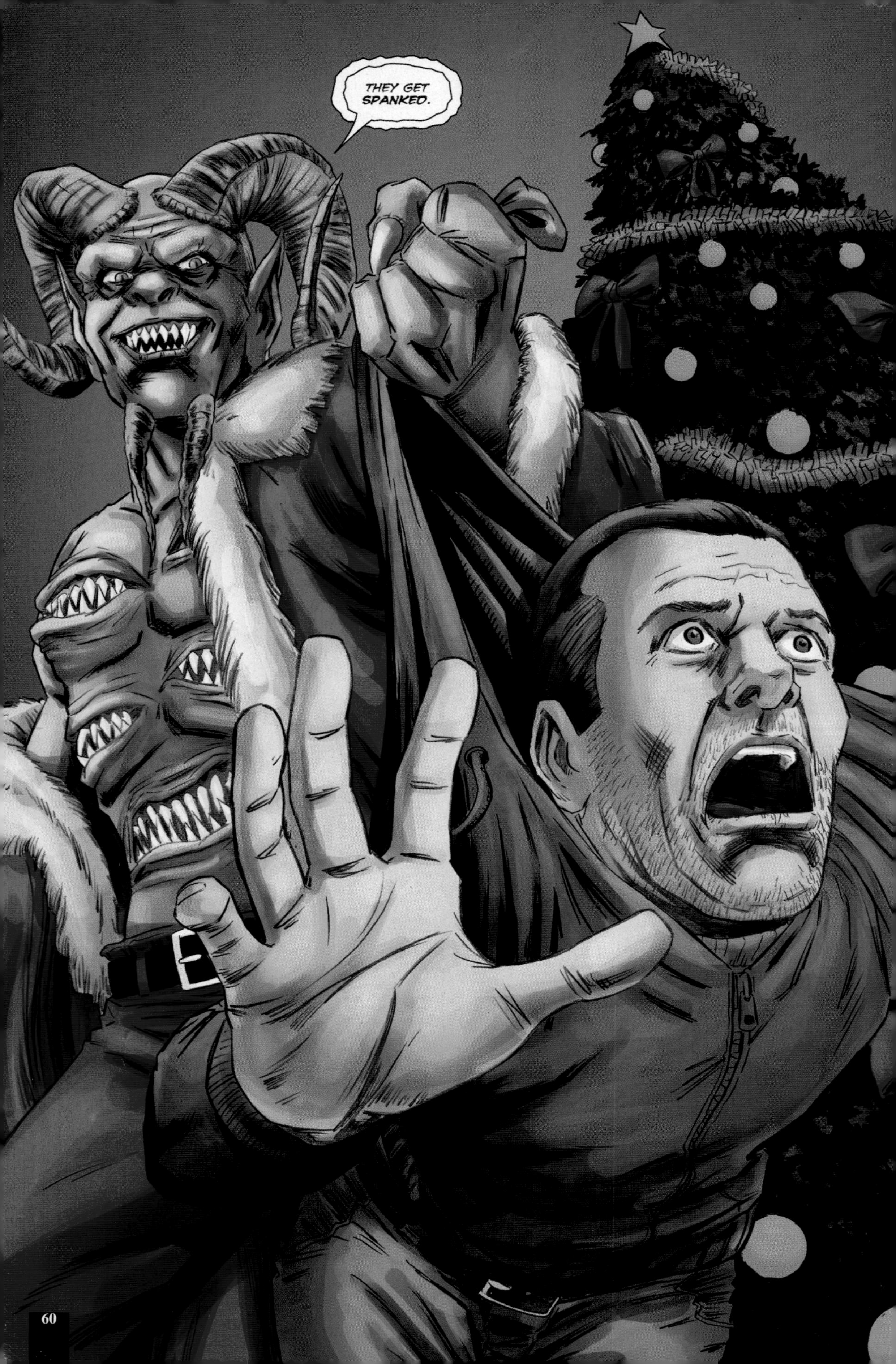
THEY GET SPANKED.

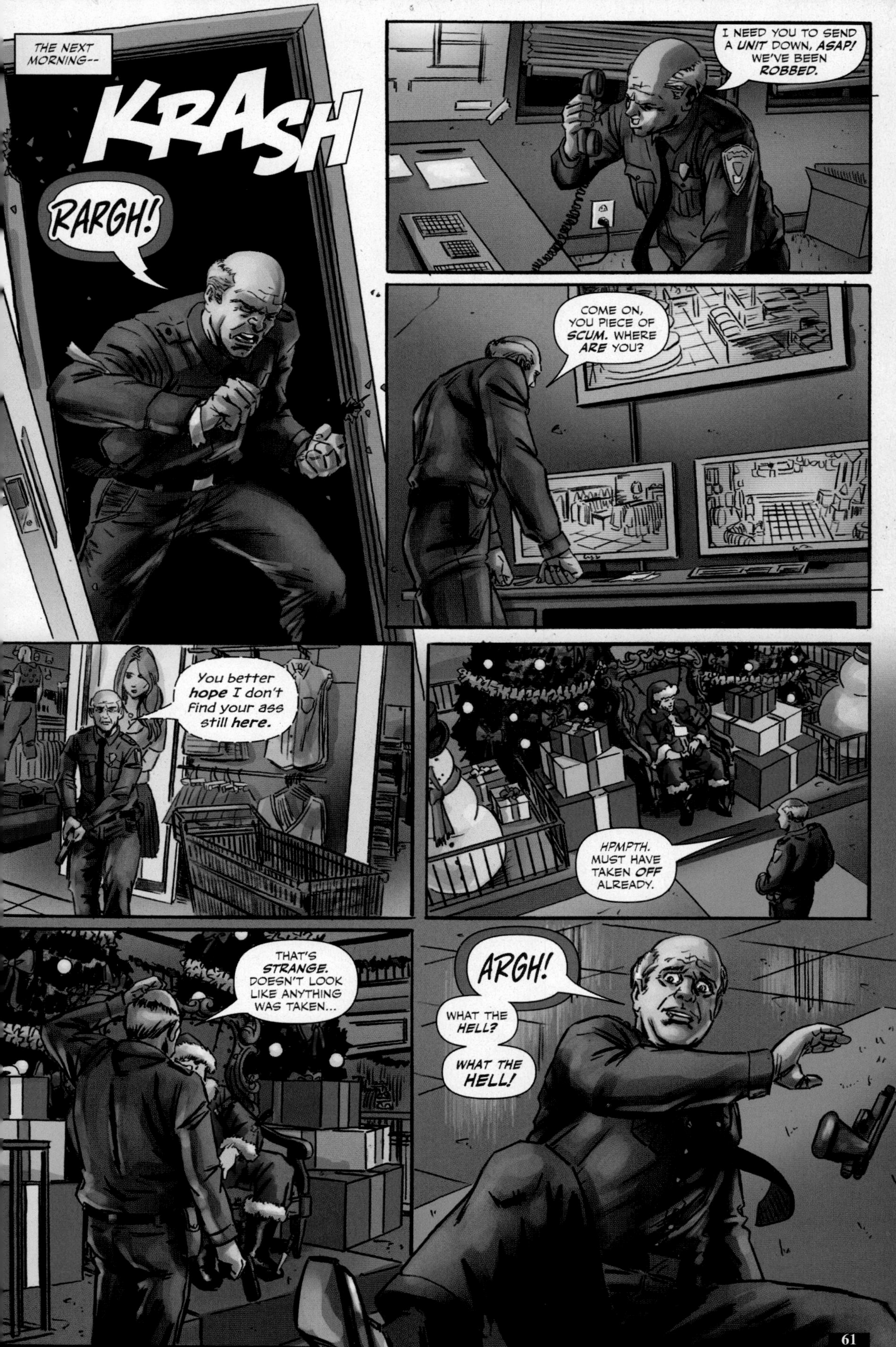
THE NEXT MORNING--
KRASH
RARGH!
I NEED YOU TO SEND A UNIT DOWN, ASAP! WE'VE BEEN ROBBED.
COME ON, YOU PIECE OF SCUM. WHERE ARE YOU?
You better hope I don't find your ass still here.
HPMPTH. MUST HAVE TAKEN OFF ALREADY.
THAT'S STRANGE. DOESN'T LOOK LIKE ANYTHING WAS TAKEN...
ARGH!
WHAT THE HELL?
WHAT THE HELL!

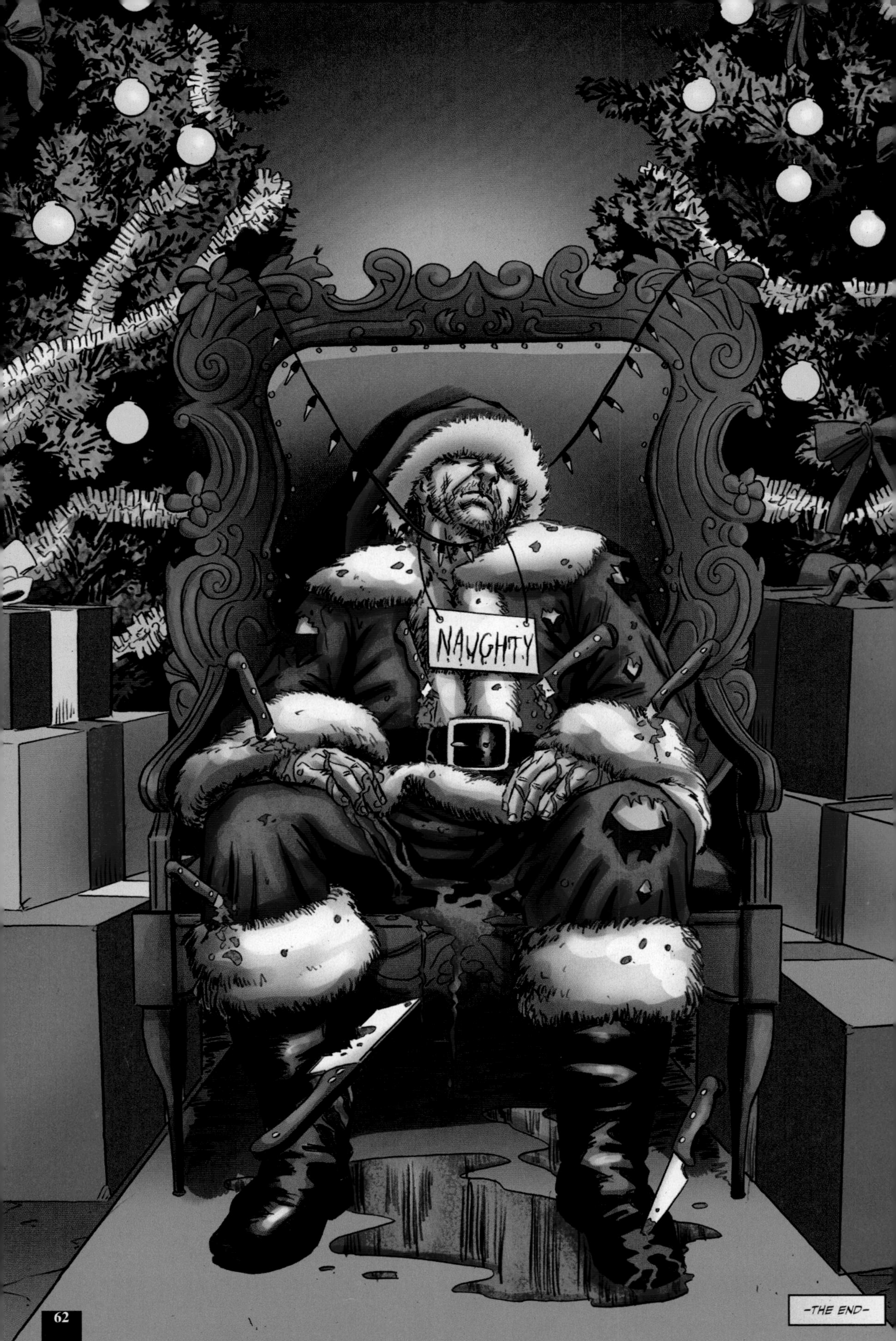
NAUGHTY
-THE END-

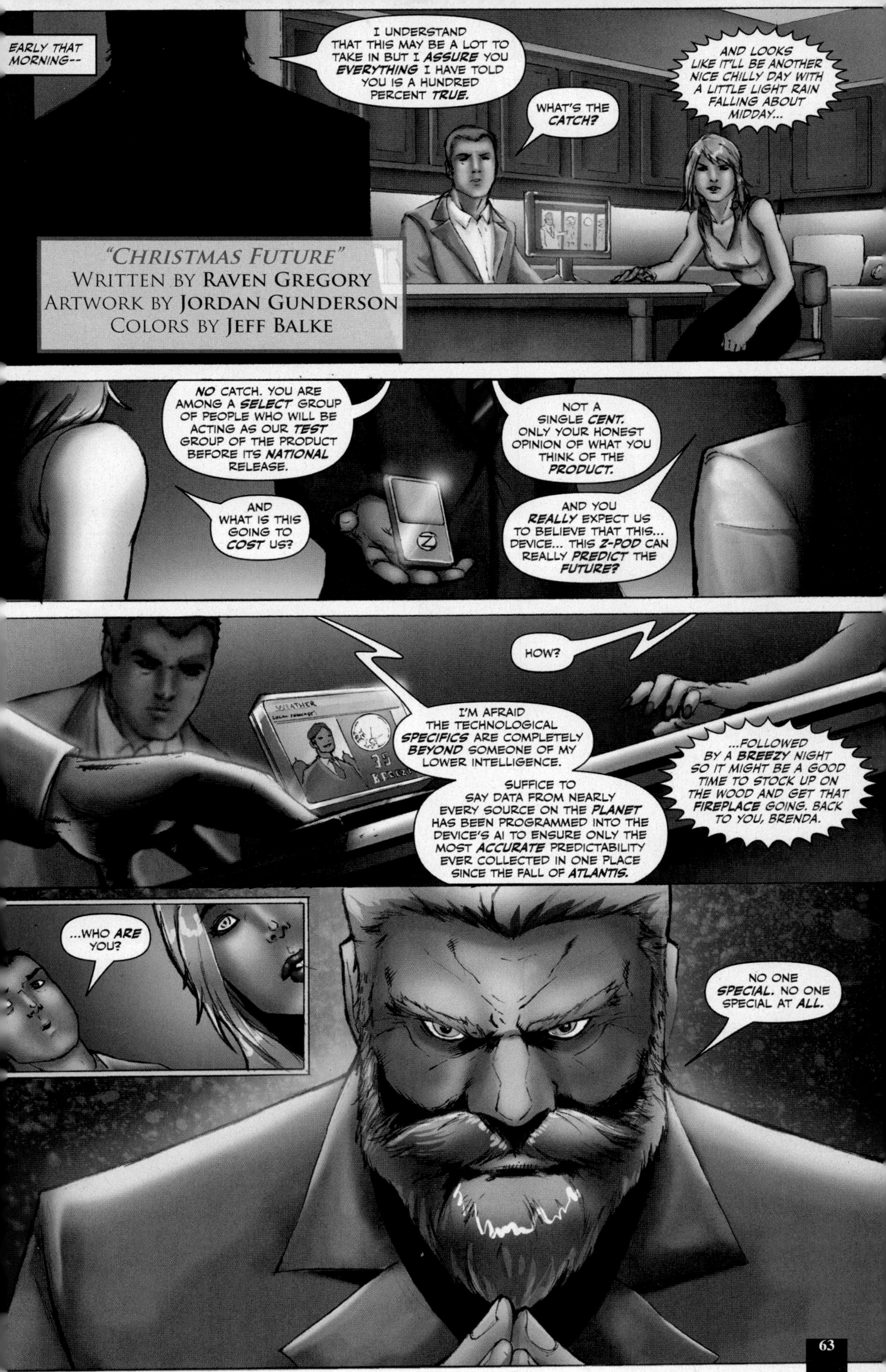

EARLY THAT MORNING--
I UNDERSTAND THAT THIS MAY BE A LOT TO TAKE IN BUT I ASSURE YOU EVERYTHING I HAVE TOLD YOU IS A HUNDRED PERCENT TRUE.
WHAT'S THE CATCH?
AND LOOKS LIKE IT'LL BE ANOTHER NICE CHILLY DAY WITH A LITTLE LIGHT RAIN FALLING ABOUT MIDDAY...
"CHRISTMAS FUTURE"
WRITTEN BY RAVEN GREGORY
ARTWORK BY JORDAN GUNDERSON
COLORS BY JEFF BALKE
NO CATCH. YOU ARE AMONG A SELECT GROUP OF PEOPLE WHO WILL BE ACTING AS OUR TEST GROUP OF THE PRODUCT BEFORE ITS NATIONAL RELEASE.
AND WHAT IS THIS GOING TO COST US?
NOT A SINGLE CENT. ONLY YOUR HONEST OPINION OF WHAT YOU THINK OF THE PRODUCT.
AND YOU REALLY EXPECT US TO BELIEVE THAT THIS... DEVICE... THIS Z-POD CAN REALLY PREDICT THE FUTURE?
HOW?
I'M AFRAID THE TECHNOLOGICAL SPECIFICS ARE COMPLETELY BEYOND SOMEONE OF MY LOWER INTELLIGENCE.
SUFFICE TO SAY DATA FROM NEARLY EVERY SOURCE ON THE PLANET HAS BEEN PROGRAMMED INTO THE DEVICE'S AI TO ENSURE ONLY THE MOST ACCURATE PREDICTABILITY EVER COLLECTED IN ONE PLACE SINCE THE FALL OF ATLANTIS.
...FOLLOWED BY A BREEZY NIGHT SO IT MIGHT BE A GOOD TIME TO STOCK UP ON THE WOOD AND GET THAT FIREPLACE GOING. BACK TO YOU, BRENDA.
...WHO ARE YOU?
NO ONE SPECIAL. NO ONE SPECIAL AT ALL.

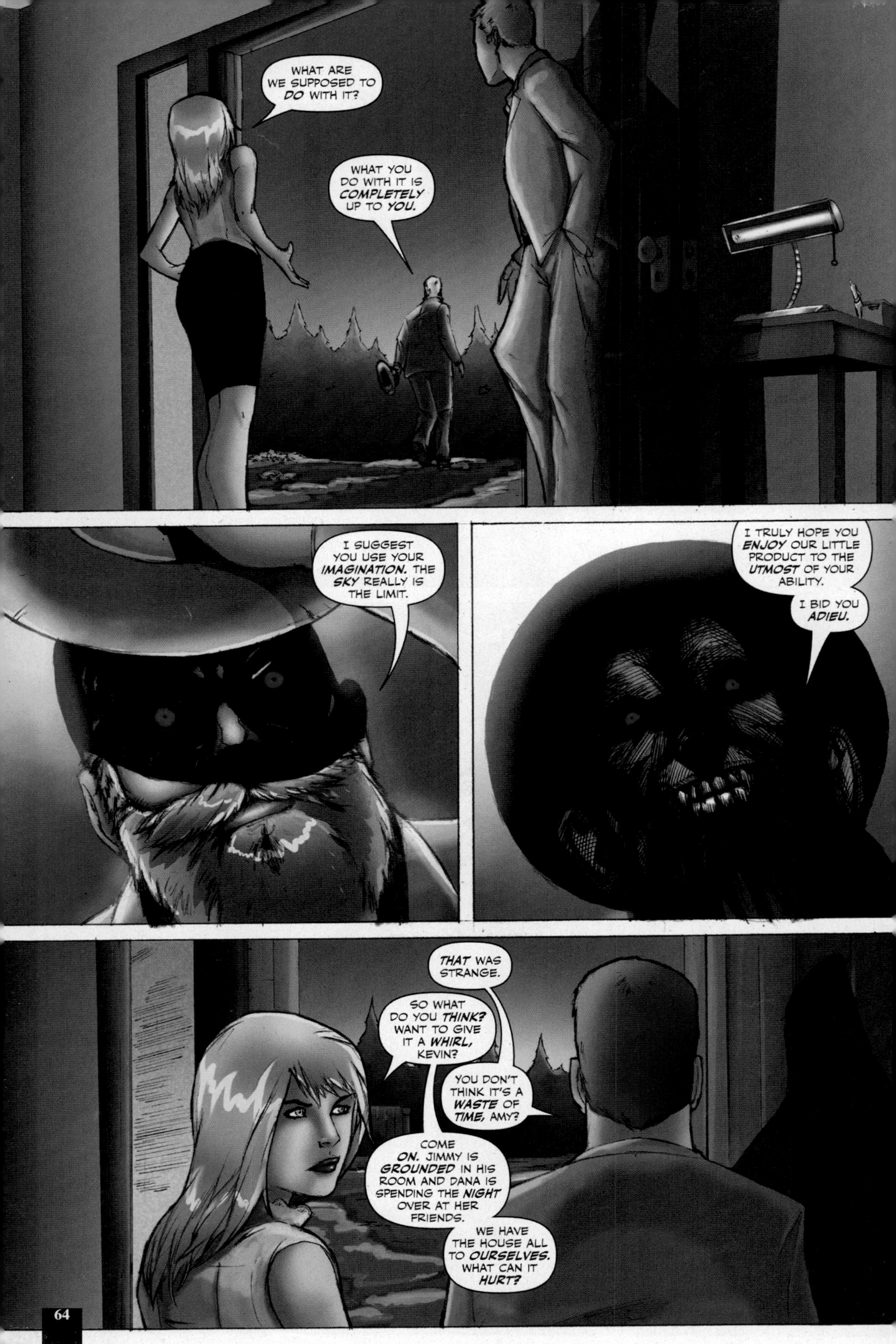
WHAT ARE WE SUPPOSED TO DO WITH IT?
WHAT YOU DO WITH IT IS COMPLETELY UP TO YOU.
I SUGGEST YOU USE YOUR IMAGINATION. THE SKY REALLY IS THE LIMIT.
I TRULY HOPE YOU ENJOY OUR LITTLE PRODUCT TO THE UTMOST OF YOUR ABILITY.
I BID YOU ADIEU.
THAT WAS STRANGE.
SO WHAT DO YOU THINK? WANT TO GIVE IT A WHIRL, KEVIN?
YOU DON'T THINK IT'S A WASTE OF TIME, AMY?
COME ON. JIMMY IS GROUNDED IN HIS ROOM AND DANA IS SPENDING THE NIGHT OVER AT HER FRIENDS.
WE HAVE THE HOUSE ALL TO OURSELVES. WHAT CAN IT HURT?

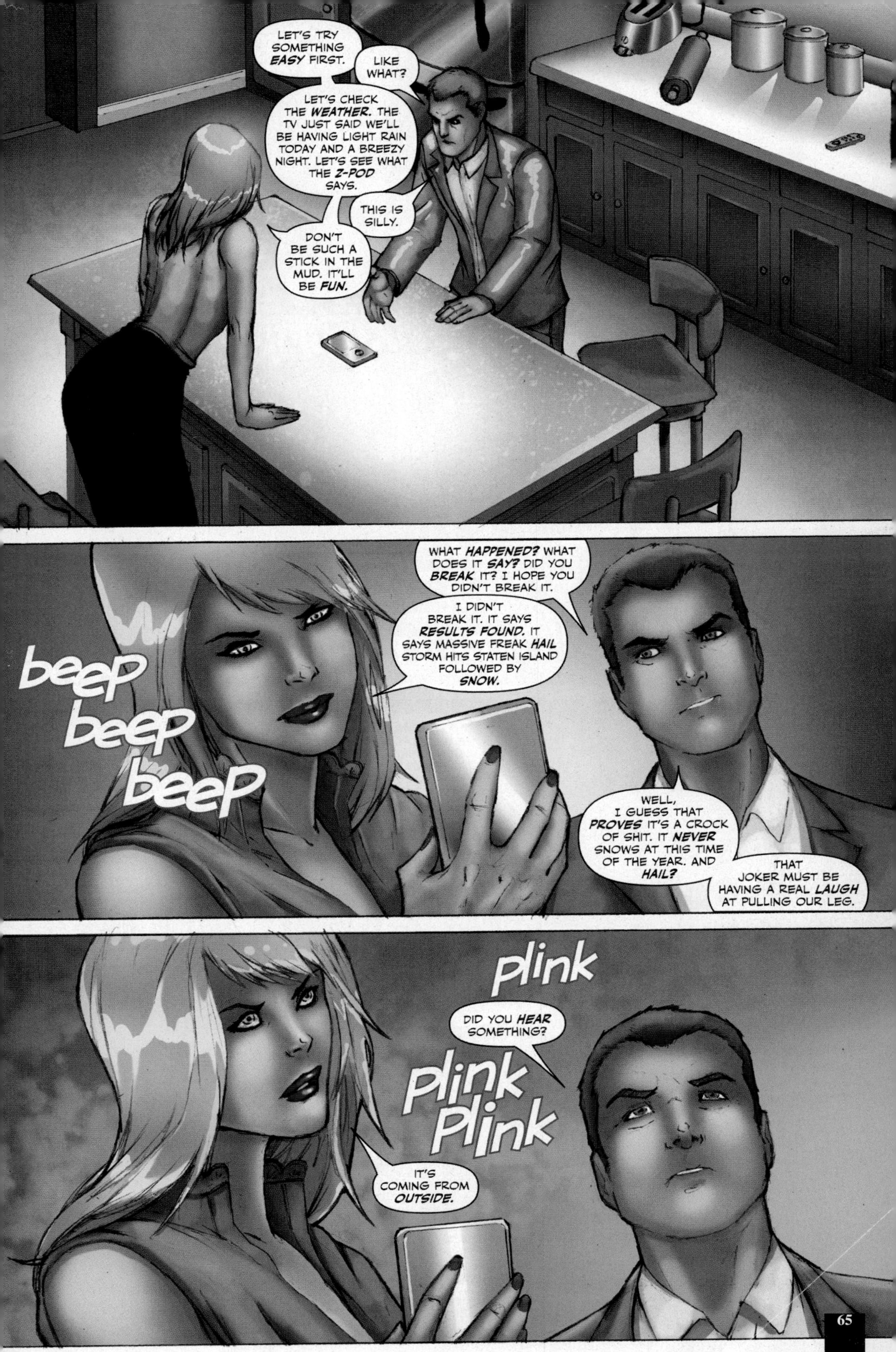
LET'S TRY SOMETHING EASY FIRST.
LIKE WHAT?
LET'S CHECK THE WEATHER. THE TV JUST SAID WE'LL BE HAVING LIGHT RAIN TODAY AND A BREEZY NIGHT. LET'S SEE WHAT THE Z-POD SAYS.
THIS IS SILLY.
DON'T BE SUCH A STICK IN THE MUD. IT'LL BE FUN.
beep beep beep
WHAT HAPPENED? WHAT DOES IT SAY? DID YOU BREAK IT? I HOPE YOU DIDN'T BREAK IT.
I DIDN'T BREAK IT. IT SAYS RESULTS FOUND. IT SAYS MASSIVE FREAK HAIL STORM HITS STATEN ISLAND FOLLOWED BY SNOW.
WELL, I GUESS THAT PROVES IT'S A CROCK OF SHIT. IT NEVER SNOWS AT THIS TIME OF THE YEAR. AND HAIL?
THAT JOKER MUST BE HAVING A REAL LAUGH AT PULLING OUR LEG.
plink
DID YOU HEAR SOMETHING?
plink plink
IT'S COMING FROM OUTSIDE.

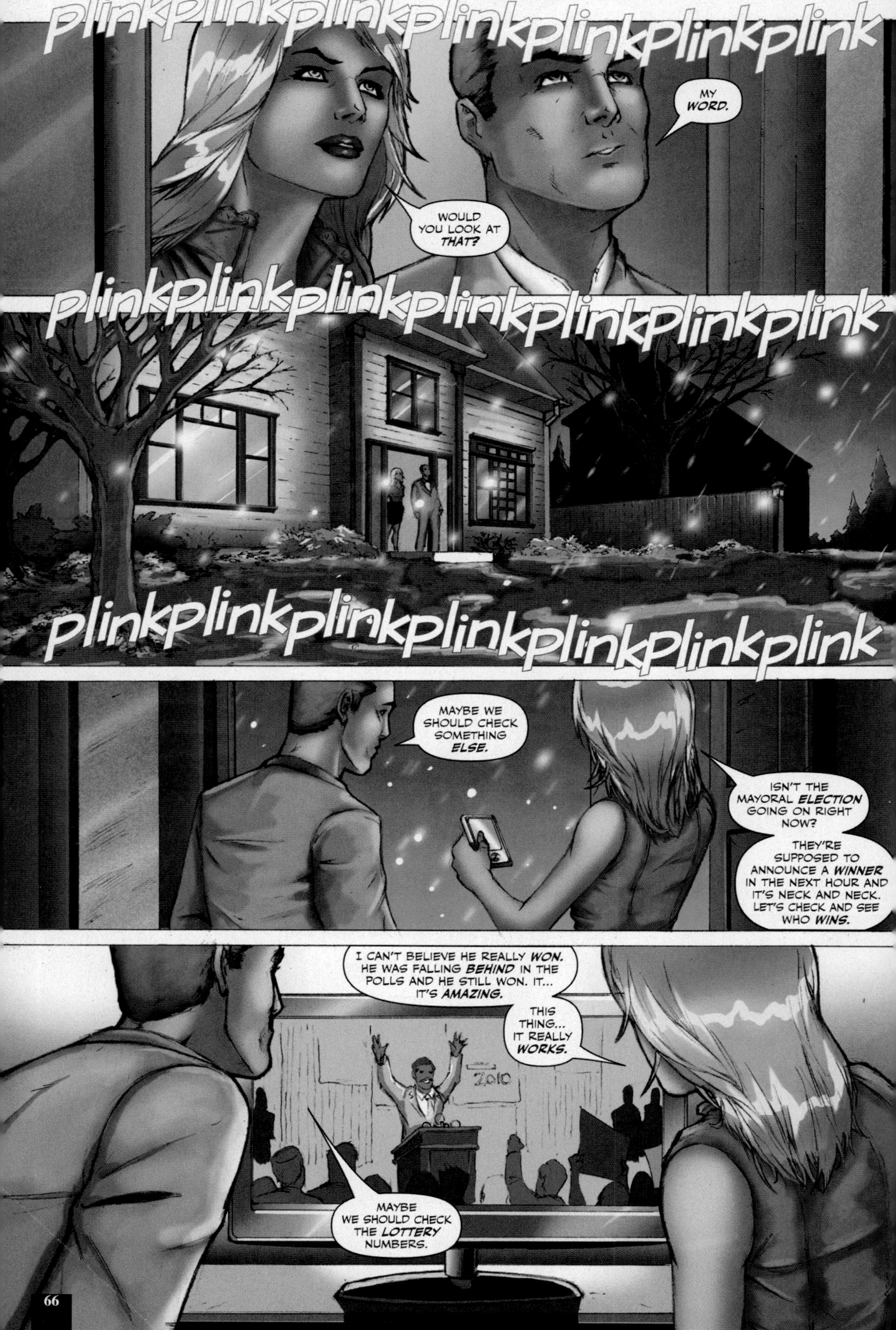
plinkplinkplinkplinkplinkplinkplink
MY WORD.
WOULD YOU LOOK AT THAT?
plinkplinkplinkplinkplinkplinkplink
plinkplinkplinkplinkplinkplinkplink
MAYBE WE SHOULD CHECK SOMETHING ELSE.
ISN'T THE MAYORAL ELECTION GOING ON RIGHT NOW?
THEY'RE SUPPOSED TO ANNOUNCE A WINNER IN THE NEXT HOUR AND IT'S NECK AND NECK. LET'S CHECK AND SEE WHO WINS.
I CAN'T BELIEVE HE REALLY WON. HE WAS FALLING BEHIND IN THE POLLS AND HE STILL WON. IT... IT'S AMAZING.
THIS THING... IT REALLY WORKS.
2010
MAYBE WE SHOULD CHECK THE LOTTERY NUMBERS.

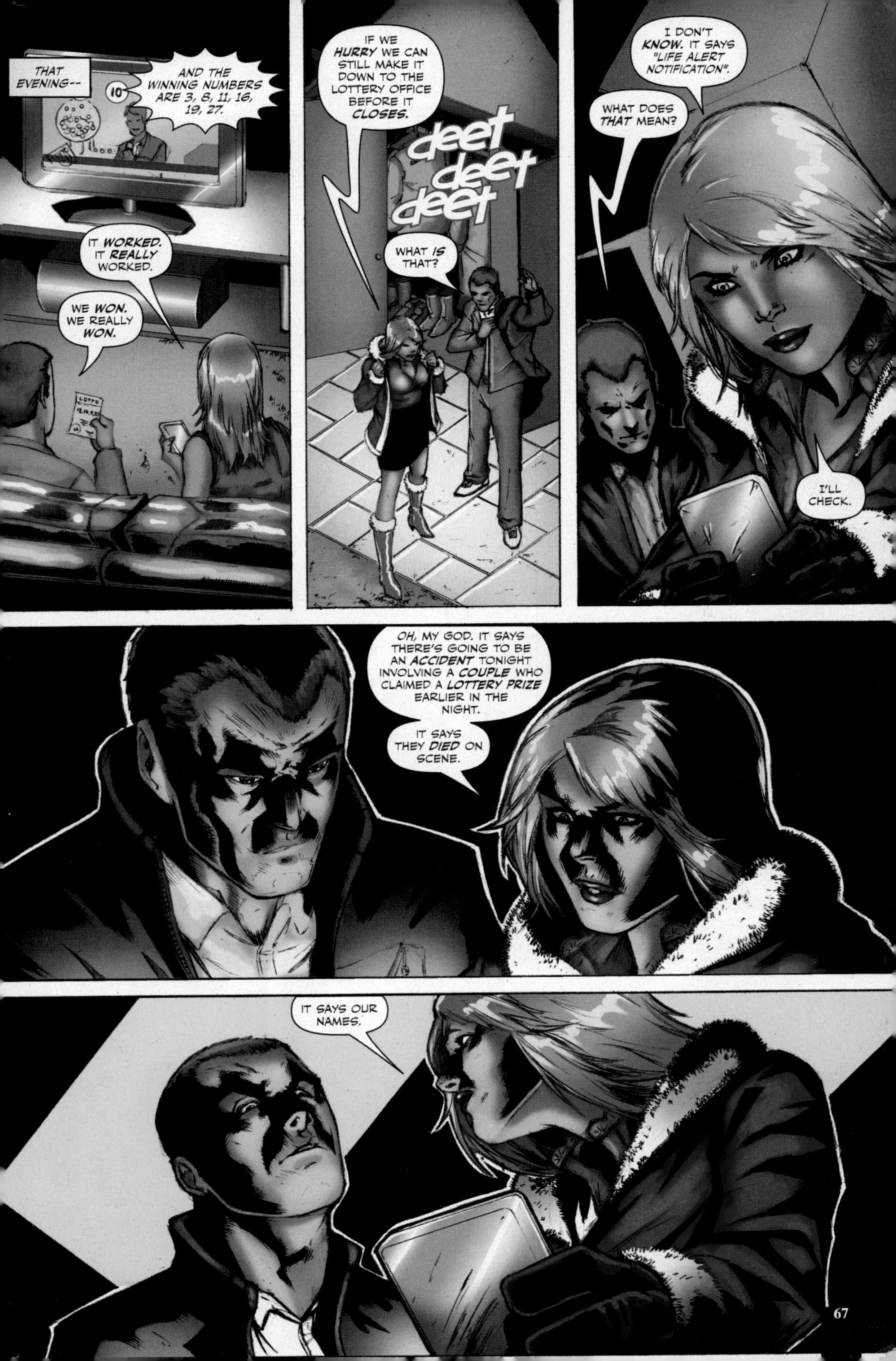
THAT EVENING--
AND THE WINNING NUMBERS ARE 3, 8, 11, 16, 19, 27.
10
IT WORKED. IT REALLY WORKED.
WE WON. WE REALLY WON.
IF WE HURRY WE CAN STILL MAKE IT DOWN TO THE LOTTERY OFFICE BEFORE IT CLOSES.
deet deet deet
WHAT IS THAT?
I DON'T KNOW. IT SAYS "LIFE ALERT NOTIFICATION".
WHAT DOES THAT MEAN?
I'LL CHECK.
OH, MY GOD. IT SAYS THERE'S GOING TO BE AN ACCIDENT TONIGHT INVOLVING A COUPLE WHO CLAIMED A LOTTERY PRIZE EARLIER IN THE NIGHT.
IT SAYS THEY DIED ON SCENE.
IT SAYS OUR NAMES.

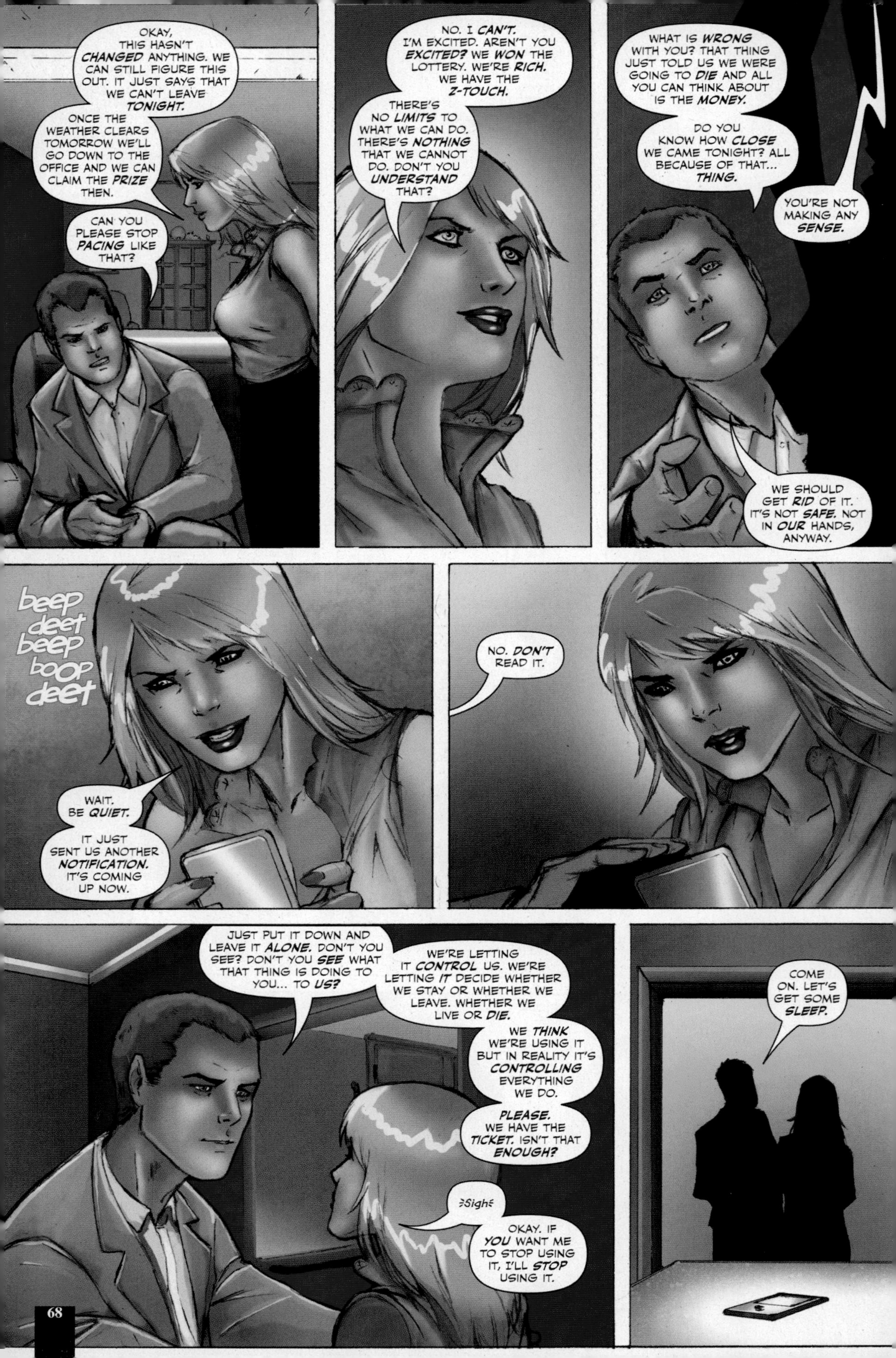
OKAY, THIS HASN'T CHANGED ANYTHING. WE CAN STILL FIGURE THIS OUT. IT JUST SAYS THAT WE CAN'T LEAVE TONIGHT.
ONCE THE WEATHER CLEARS TOMORROW WE'LL GO DOWN TO THE OFFICE AND WE CAN CLAIM THE PRIZE THEN.
CAN YOU PLEASE STOP PACING LIKE THAT?
NO. I CAN'T. I'M EXCITED. AREN'T YOU EXCITED? WE WON THE LOTTERY. WE'RE RICH. WE HAVE THE Z-TOUCH.
THERE'S NO LIMITS TO WHAT WE CAN DO. THERE'S NOTHING THAT WE CANNOT DO. DON'T YOU UNDERSTAND THAT?
WHAT IS WRONG WITH YOU? THAT THING JUST TOLD US WE WERE GOING TO DIE AND ALL YOU CAN THINK ABOUT IS THE MONEY.
DO YOU KNOW HOW CLOSE WE CAME TONIGHT? ALL BECAUSE OF THAT... THING.
YOU'RE NOT MAKING ANY SENSE.
WE SHOULD GET RID OF IT. IT'S NOT SAFE. NOT IN OUR HANDS, ANYWAY.
beep deet beep boop deet
WAIT. BE QUIET.
IT JUST SENT US ANOTHER NOTIFICATION. IT'S COMING UP NOW.
NO. DON'T READ IT.
JUST PUT IT DOWN AND LEAVE IT ALONE. DON'T YOU SEE? DON'T YOU SEE WHAT THAT THING IS DOING TO YOU... TO US?
WE'RE LETTING IT CONTROL US. WE'RE LETTING IT DECIDE WHETHER WE STAY OR WHETHER WE LEAVE. WHETHER WE LIVE OR DIE.
WE THINK WE'RE USING IT BUT IN REALITY IT'S CONTROLLING EVERYTHING WE DO.
PLEASE. WE HAVE THE TICKET. ISN'T THAT ENOUGH?
Sigh
OKAY. IF YOU WANT ME TO STOP USING IT, I'LL STOP USING IT.
COME ON. LET'S GET SOME SLEEP.

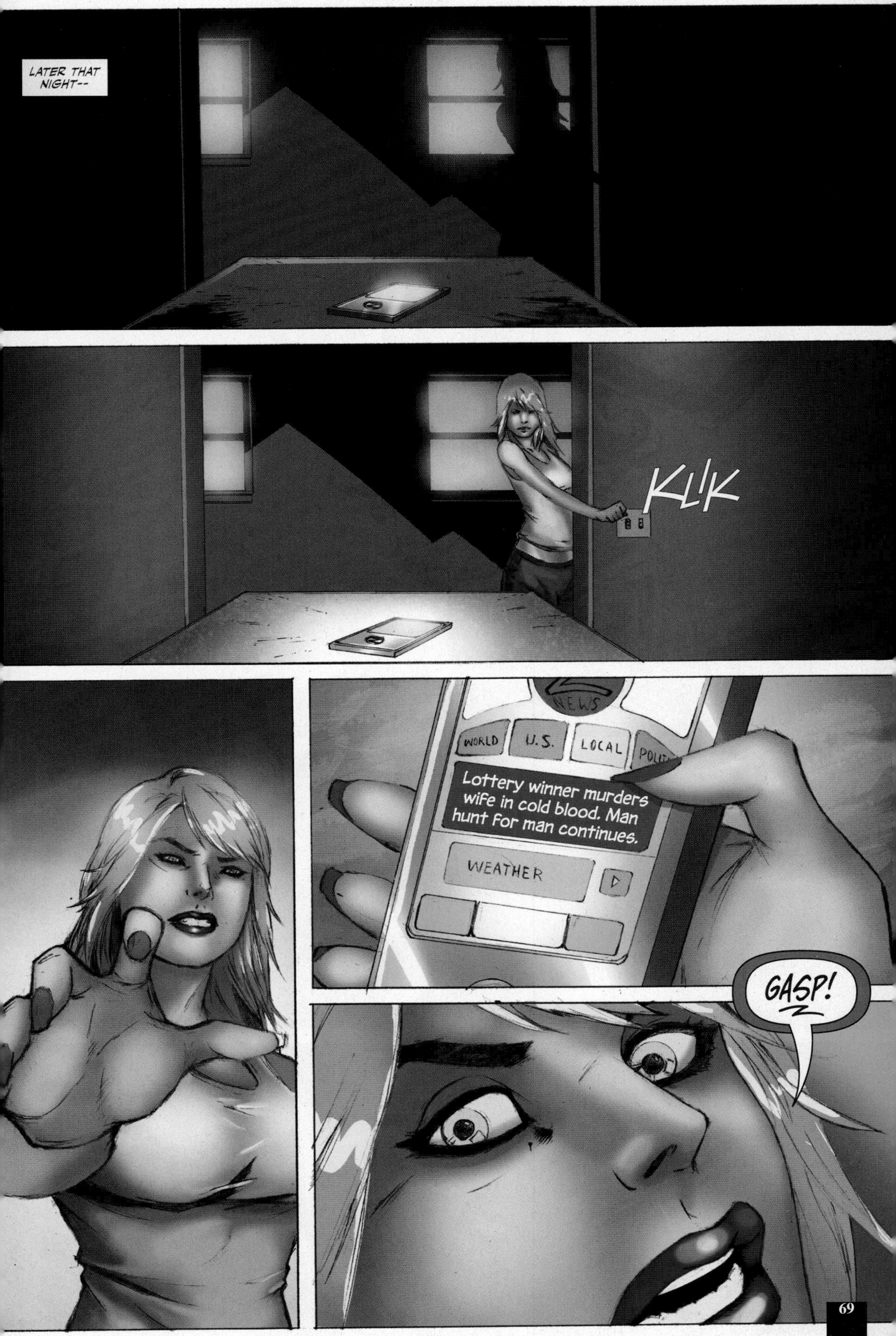
LATER THAT NIGHT--
KLIK
NEWS
WORLD
U.S.
LOCAL
Lottery winner murders wife in cold blood. Man hunt for man continues.
WEATHER
GASP!

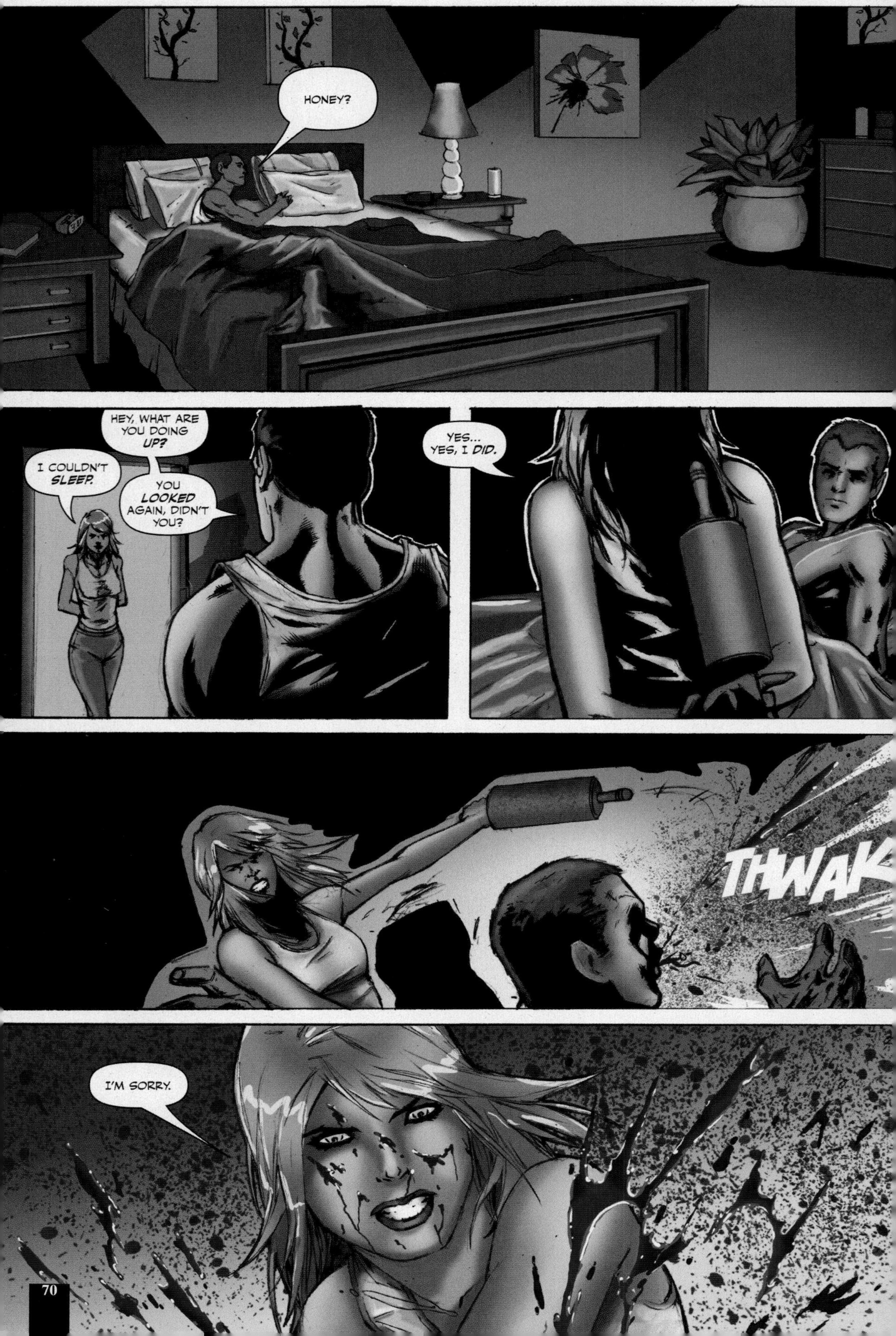
HONEY?
HEY, WHAT ARE YOU DOING UP?
I COULDN'T SLEEP.
YOU LOOKED AGAIN, DIDN'T YOU?
YES... YES, I DID.
THWAK
I'M SORRY.

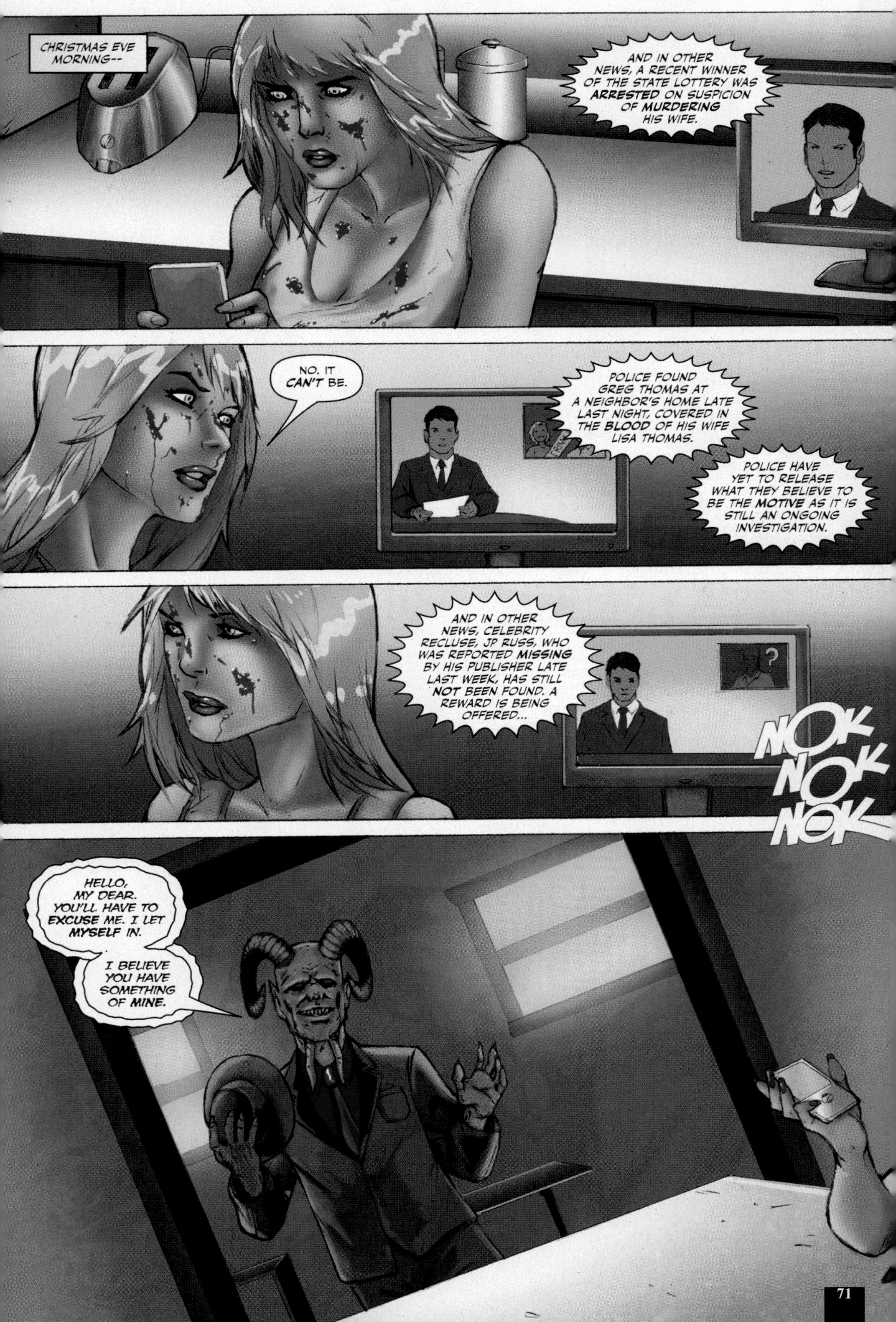
CHRISTMAS EVE MORNING--
AND IN OTHER NEWS, A RECENT WINNER OF THE STATE LOTTERY WAS ARRESTED ON SUSPICION OF MURDERING HIS WIFE.
NO. IT CAN'T BE.
POLICE FOUND GREG THOMAS AT A NEIGHBOR'S HOME LATE LAST NIGHT, COVERED IN THE BLOOD OF HIS WIFE LISA THOMAS.
POLICE HAVE YET TO RELEASE WHAT THEY BELIEVE TO BE THE MOTIVE AS IT IS STILL AN ONGOING INVESTIGATION.
AND IN OTHER NEWS, CELEBRITY RECLUSE, JP RUSS, WHO WAS REPORTED MISSING BY HIS PUBLISHER LATE LAST WEEK, HAS STILL NOT BEEN FOUND. A REWARD IS BEING OFFERED...
?
NOK NOK NOK
HELLO, MY DEAR. YOU'LL HAVE TO EXCUSE ME. I LET MYSELF IN.
I BELIEVE YOU HAVE SOMETHING OF MINE.

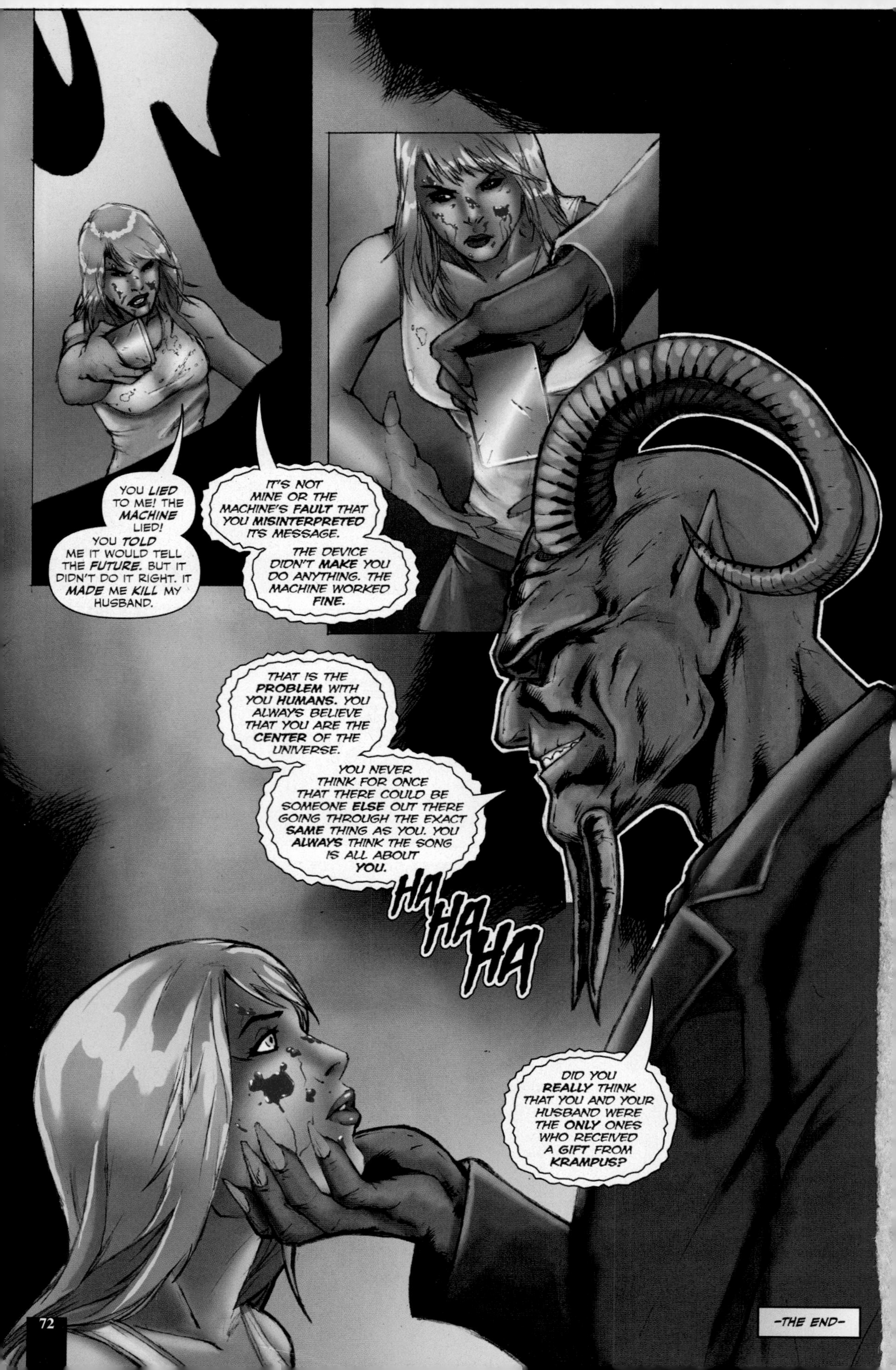
YOU LIED TO ME! THE MACHINE LIED! YOU TOLD ME IT WOULD TELL THE FUTURE. BUT IT DIDN'T DO IT RIGHT. IT MADE ME KILL MY HUSBAND.
IT'S NOT MINE OR THE MACHINE'S FAULT THAT YOU MISINTERPRETED ITS MESSAGE.
THE DEVICE DIDN'T MAKE YOU DO ANYTHING. THE MACHINE WORKED FINE.
THAT IS THE PROBLEM WITH YOU HUMANS. YOU ALWAYS BELIEVE THAT YOU ARE THE CENTER OF THE UNIVERSE.
YOU NEVER THINK FOR ONCE THAT THERE COULD BE SOMEONE ELSE OUT THERE GOING THROUGH THE EXACT SAME THING AS YOU. YOU ALWAYS THINK THE SONG IS ALL ABOUT YOU.
HA HA HA
DID YOU REALLY THINK THAT YOU AND YOUR HUSBAND WERE THE ONLY ONES WHO RECEIVED A GIFT FROM KRAMPUS?
-THE END-

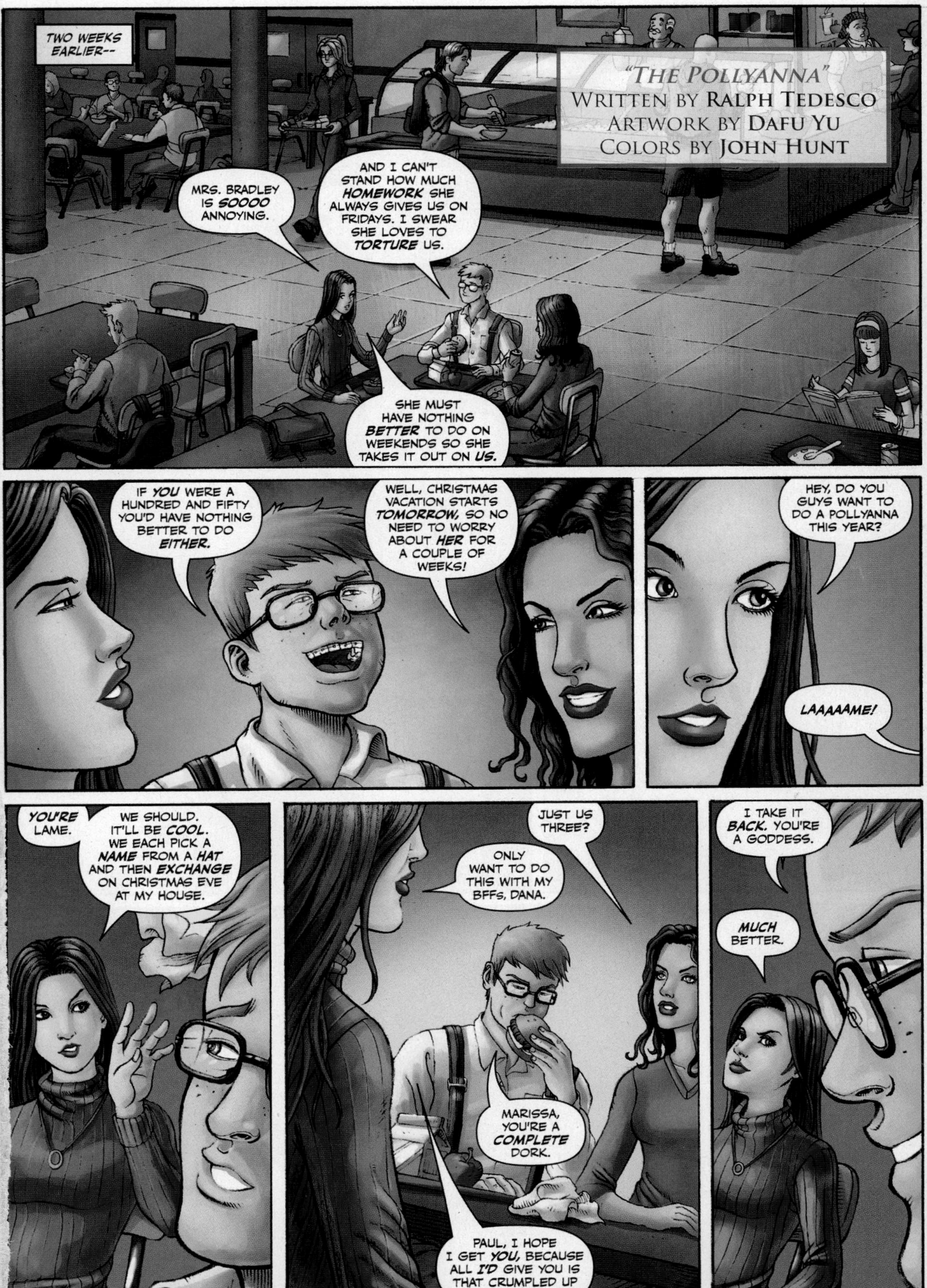
TWO WEEKS EARLIER--
"THE POLLYANNA"
WRITTEN BY RALPH TEDESCO
ARTWORK BY DAFU YU
COLORS BY JOHN HUNT
MRS. BRADLEY IS SOOOO ANNOYING.
AND I CAN'T STAND HOW MUCH HOMEWORK SHE ALWAYS GIVES US ON FRIDAYS. I SWEAR SHE LOVES TO TORTURE US.
SHE MUST HAVE NOTHING BETTER TO DO ON WEEKENDS SO SHE TAKES IT OUT ON US.
IF YOU WERE A HUNDRED AND FIFTY YOU'D HAVE NOTHING BETTER TO DO EITHER.
WELL, CHRISTMAS VACATION STARTS TOMORROW, SO NO NEED TO WORRY ABOUT HER FOR A COUPLE OF WEEKS!
HEY, DO YOU GUYS WANT TO DO A POLLYANNA THIS YEAR?
LAAAAAME!
YOU'RE LAME.
WE SHOULD. IT'LL BE COOL. WE EACH PICK A NAME FROM A HAT AND THEN EXCHANGE ON CHRISTMAS EVE AT MY HOUSE.
JUST US THREE?
ONLY WANT TO DO THIS WITH MY BFFs, DANA.
MARISSA, YOU'RE A COMPLETE DORK.
PAUL, I HOPE I GET YOU, BECAUSE ALL I'D GIVE YOU IS THAT CRUMPLED UP NAPKIN.
I TAKE IT BACK. YOU'RE A GODDESS.
MUCH BETTER.

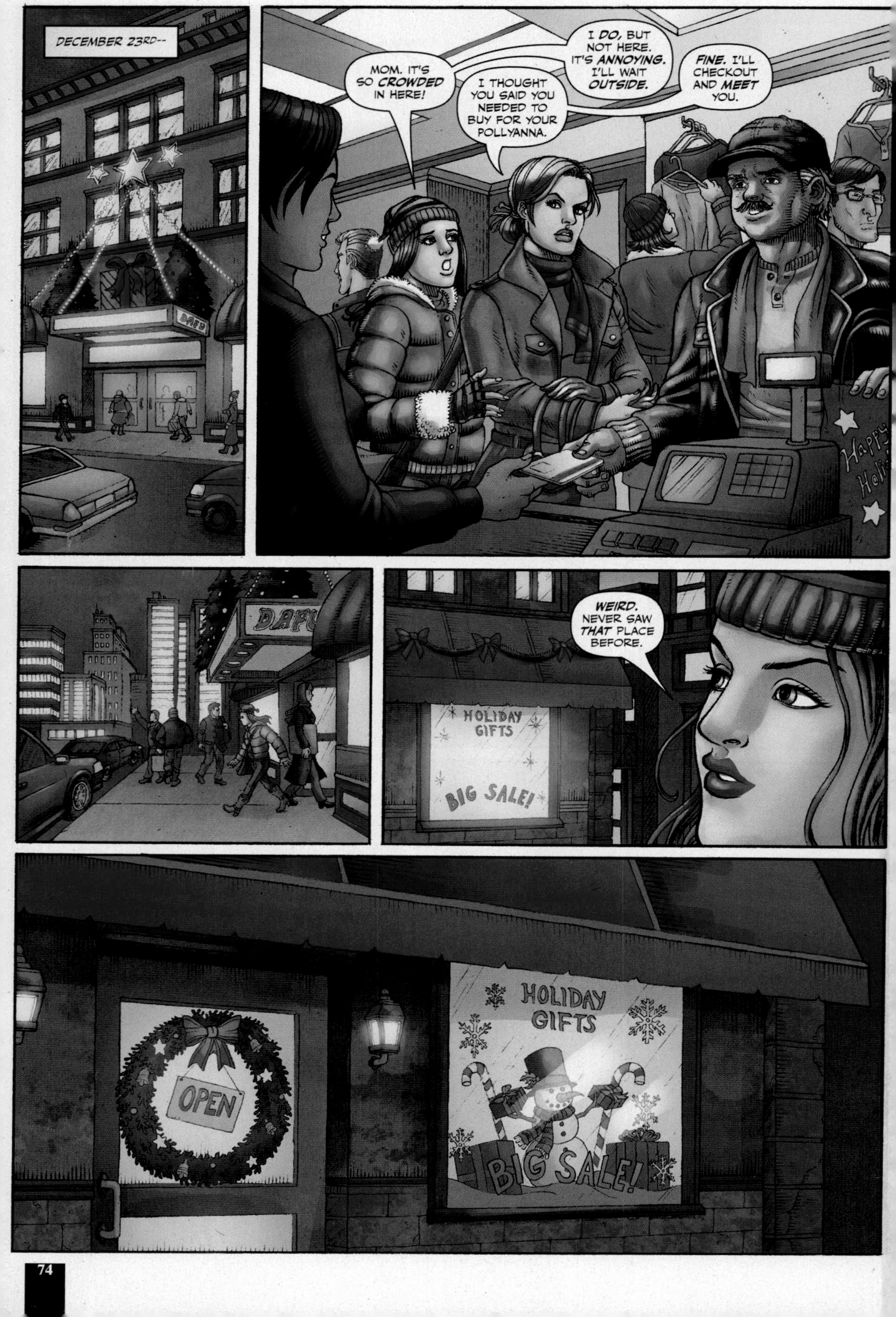
DECEMBER 23RD--
MOM. IT'S SO CROWDED IN HERE!
I THOUGHT YOU SAID YOU NEEDED TO BUY FOR YOUR POLLYANNA.
I DO, BUT NOT HERE. IT'S ANNOYING. I'LL WAIT OUTSIDE.
FINE. I'LL CHECKOUT AND MEET YOU.
WEIRD. NEVER SAW THAT PLACE BEFORE.
HOLIDAY GIFTS
BIG SALE!
HOLIDAY GIFTS
OPEN
BIG SALE!

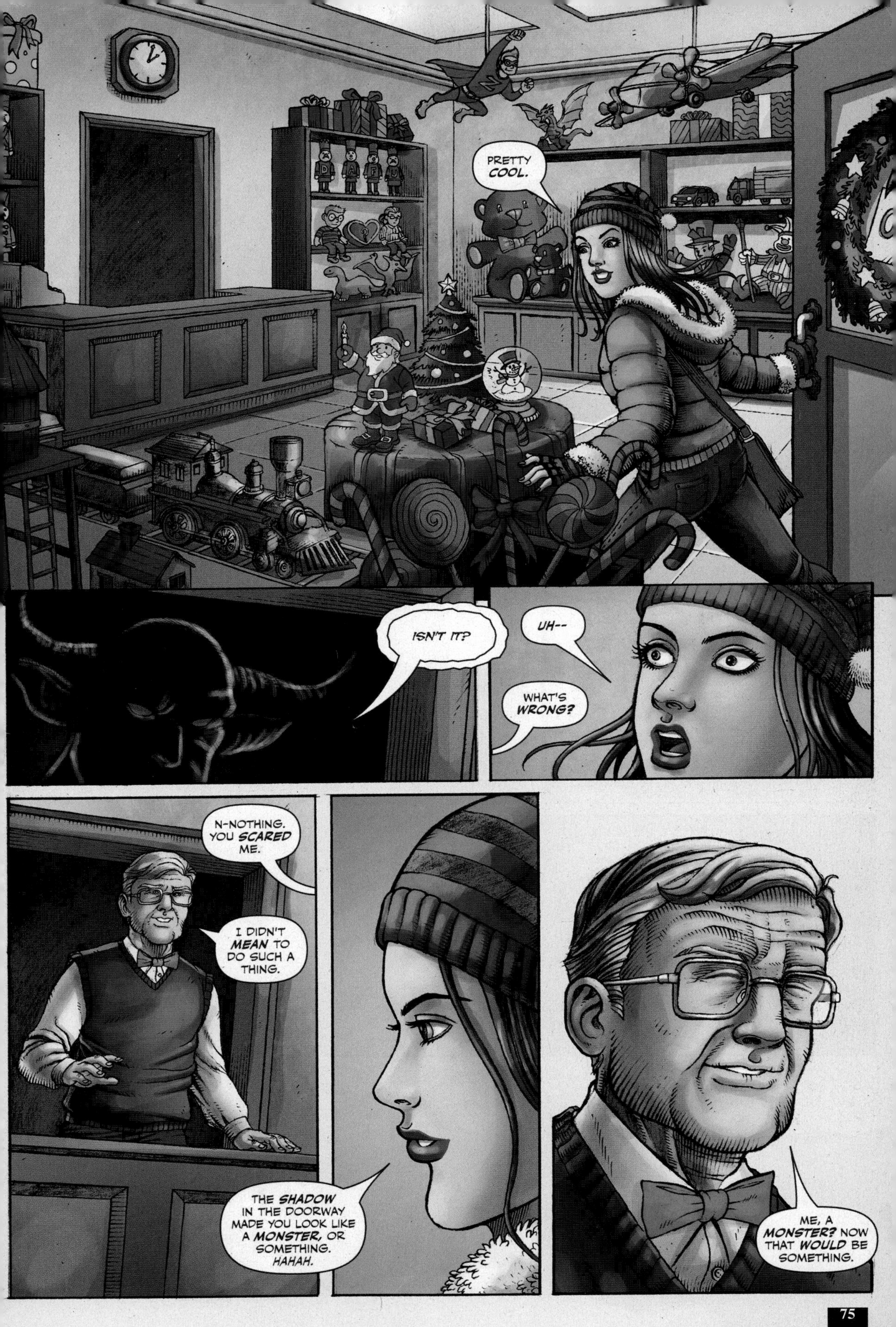

PRETTY COOL.
ISN'T IT?
UH--
WHAT'S WRONG?
N-NOTHING. YOU SCARED ME.
I DIDN'T MEAN TO DO SUCH A THING.
THE SHADOW IN THE DOORWAY MADE YOU LOOK LIKE A MONSTER, OR SOMETHING. HAHAH.
ME, A MONSTER? NOW THAT WOULD BE SOMETHING.

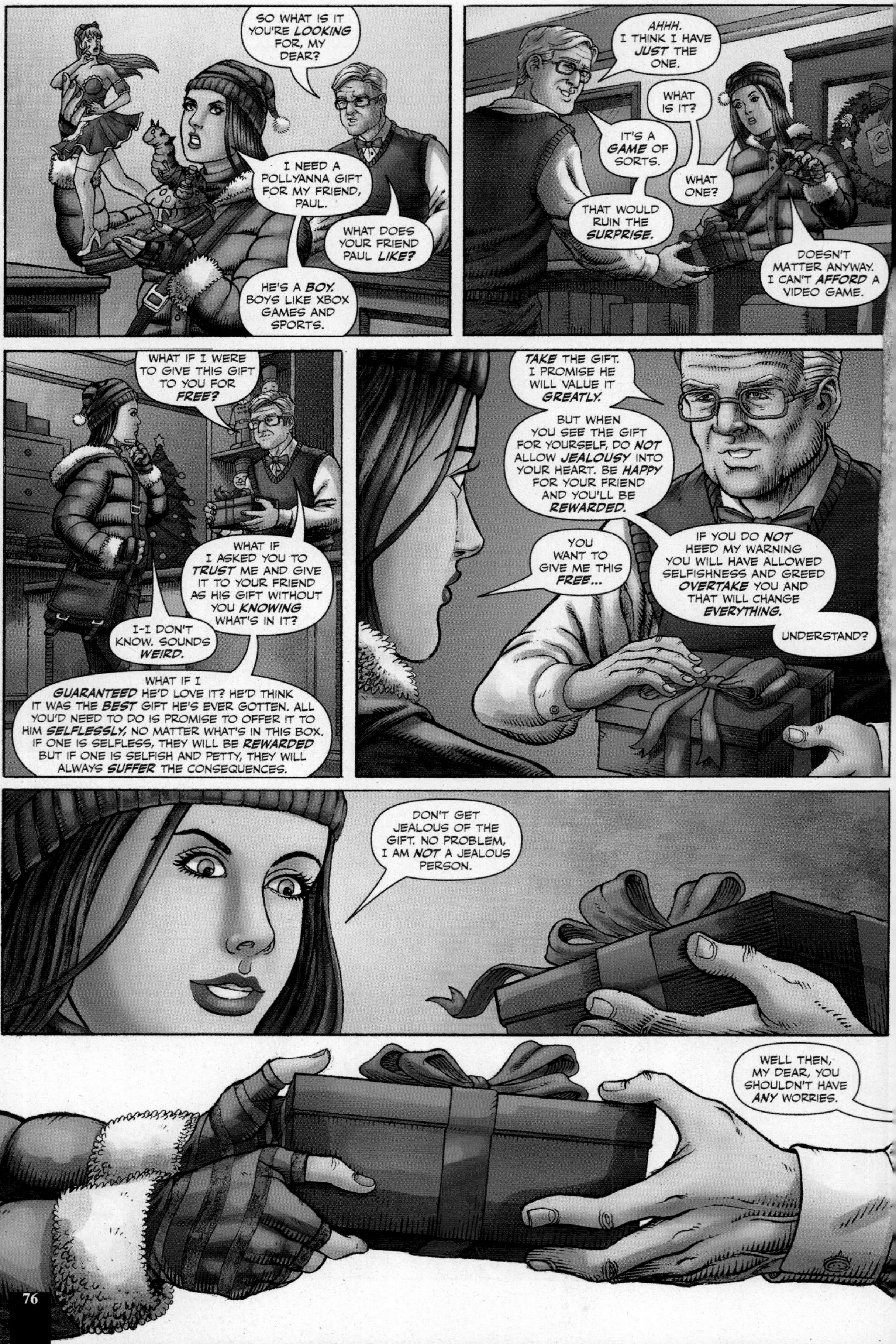
SO WHAT IS IT YOU'RE LOOKING FOR, MY DEAR?
I NEED A POLLYANNA GIFT FOR MY FRIEND, PAUL.
WHAT DOES YOUR FRIEND PAUL LIKE?
HE'S A BOY. BOYS LIKE XBOX GAMES AND SPORTS.
AHHH. I THINK I HAVE JUST THE ONE.
WHAT IS IT?
IT'S A GAME OF SORTS.
WHAT ONE?
THAT WOULD RUIN THE SURPRISE.
DOESN'T MATTER ANYWAY. I CAN'T AFFORD A VIDEO GAME.
WHAT IF I WERE TO GIVE THIS GIFT TO YOU FOR FREE?
WHAT IF I ASKED YOU TO TRUST ME AND GIVE IT TO YOUR FRIEND AS HIS GIFT WITHOUT YOU KNOWING WHAT'S IN IT?
I-I DON'T KNOW. SOUNDS WEIRD.
WHAT IF I GUARANTEED HE'D LOVE IT? HE'D THINK IT WAS THE BEST GIFT HE'S EVER GOTTEN. ALL YOU'D NEED TO DO IS PROMISE TO OFFER IT TO HIM SELFLESSLY, NO MATTER WHAT'S IN THIS BOX. IF ONE IS SELFLESS, THEY WILL BE REWARDED BUT IF ONE IS SELFISH AND PETTY, THEY WILL ALWAYS SUFFER THE CONSEQUENCES.
TAKE THE GIFT. I PROMISE HE WILL VALUE IT GREATLY.
BUT WHEN YOU SEE THE GIFT FOR YOURSELF, DO NOT ALLOW JEALOUSY INTO YOUR HEART. BE HAPPY FOR YOUR FRIEND AND YOU'LL BE REWARDED.
YOU WANT TO GIVE ME THIS FREE...
IF YOU DO NOT HEED MY WARNING YOU WILL HAVE ALLOWED SELFISHNESS AND GREED OVERTAKE YOU AND THAT WILL CHANGE EVERYTHING.
UNDERSTAND?
DON'T GET JEALOUS OF THE GIFT. NO PROBLEM, I AM NOT A JEALOUS PERSON.
WELL THEN, MY DEAR, YOU SHOULDN'T HAVE ANY WORRIES.

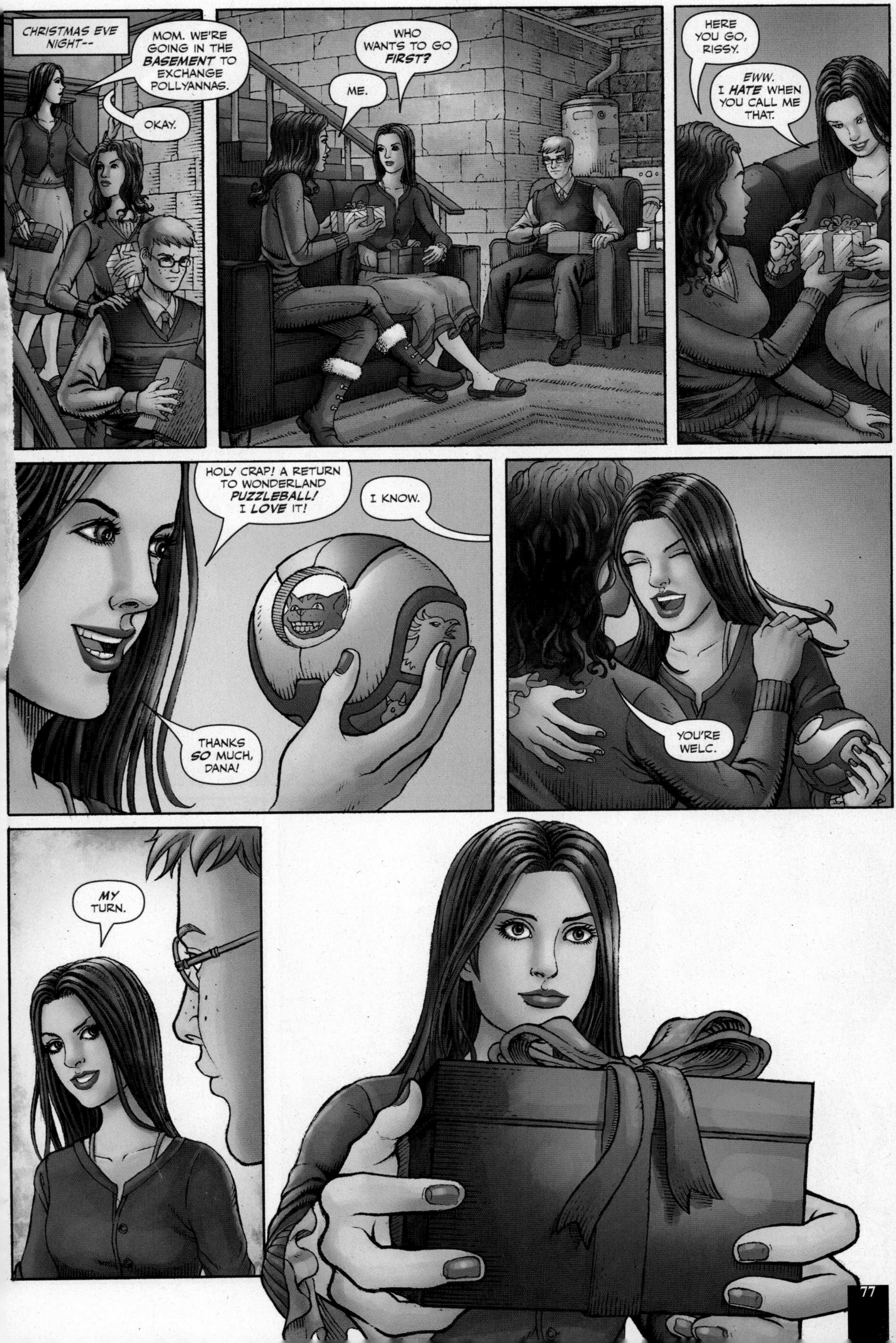
CHRISTMAS EVE NIGHT--
MOM. WE'RE GOING IN THE BASEMENT TO EXCHANGE POLLYANNAS.
OKAY.
WHO WANTS TO GO FIRST?
ME.
HERE YOU GO, RISSY.
EWW. I HATE WHEN YOU CALL ME THAT.
HOLY CRAP! A RETURN TO WONDERLAND PUZZLEBALL! I LOVE IT!
I KNOW.
THANKS SO MUCH, DANA!
YOU'RE WELC.
MY TURN.

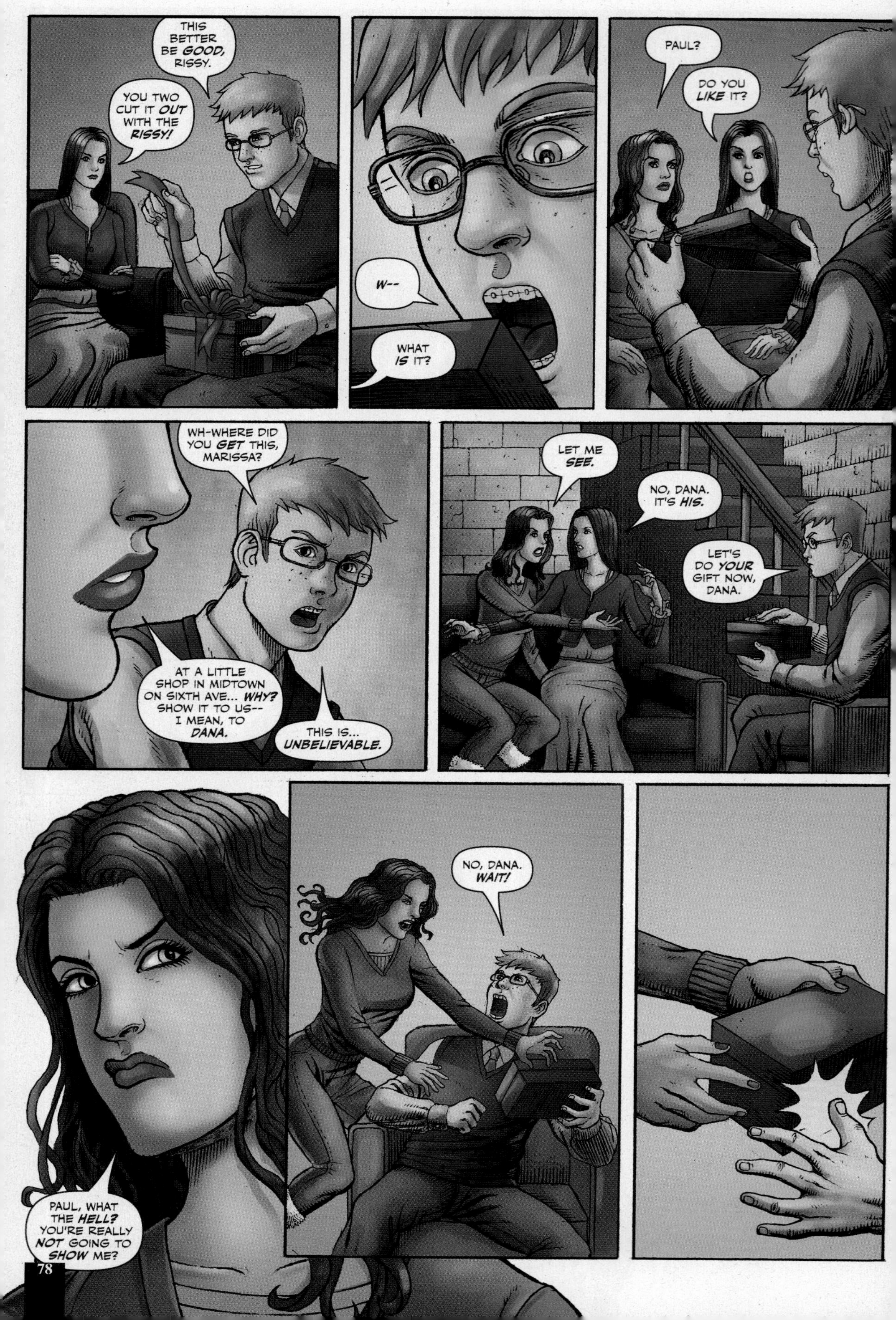
THIS BETTER BE GOOD, RISSY.
YOU TWO CUT IT OUT WITH THE RISSY!
W--
WHAT IS IT?
PAUL?
DO YOU LIKE IT?
WH-WHERE DID YOU GET THIS, MARISSA?
AT A LITTLE SHOP IN MIDTOWN ON SIXTH AVE... WHY? SHOW IT TO US-- I MEAN, TO DANA.
THIS IS... UNBELIEVABLE.
LET ME SEE.
NO, DANA. IT'S HIS.
LET'S DO YOUR GIFT NOW, DANA.
PAUL, WHAT THE HELL? YOU'RE REALLY NOT GOING TO SHOW ME?
NO, DANA. WAIT!

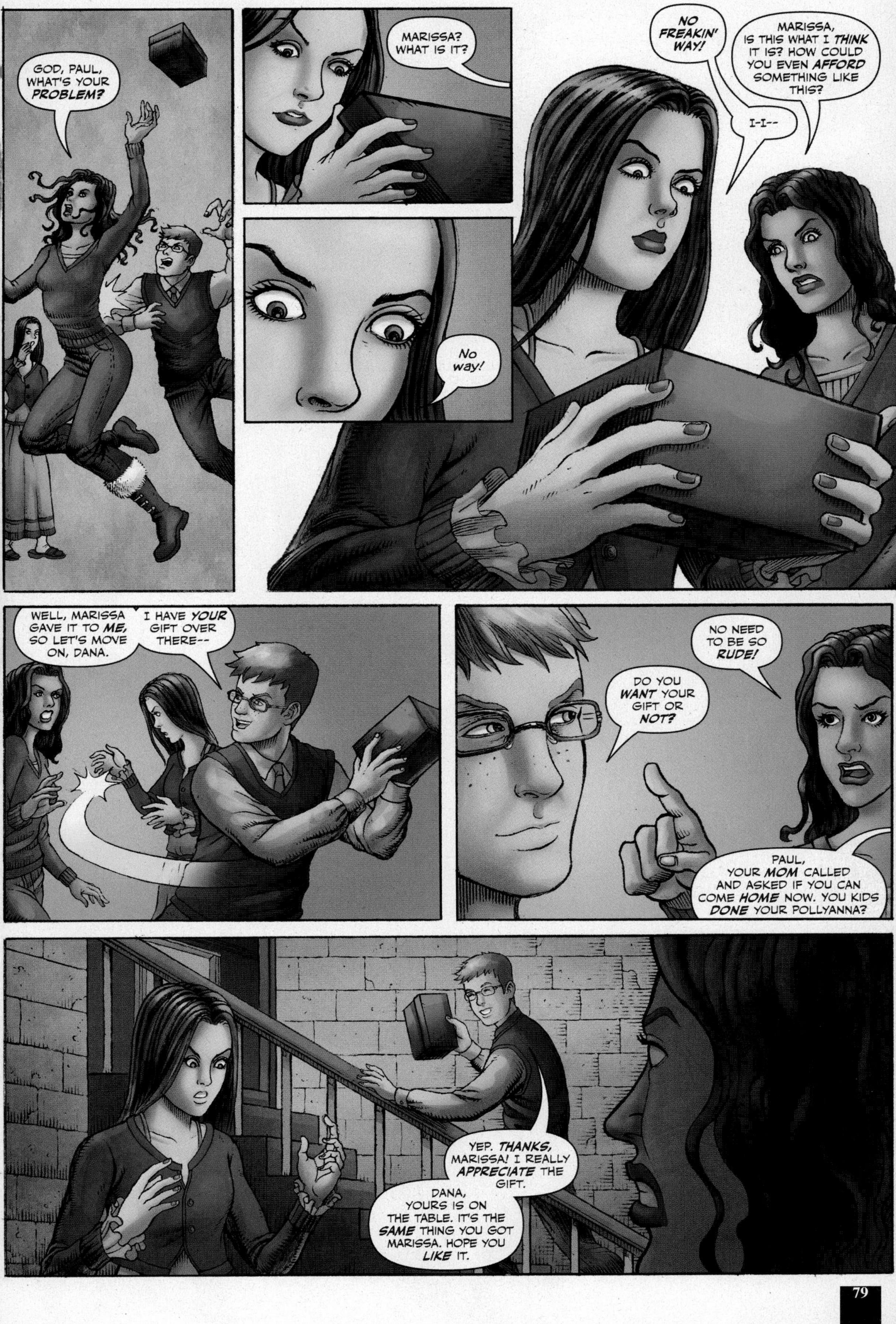
GOD, PAUL, WHAT'S YOUR *PROBLEM?*
MARISSA? WHAT IS IT?
No way!
NO FREAKIN' WAY!
MARISSA, IS THIS WHAT I *THINK* IT IS? HOW COULD YOU EVEN *AFFORD* SOMETHING LIKE THIS?
I-I--
WELL, MARISSA GAVE IT TO *ME,* SO LET'S MOVE ON, DANA.
I HAVE *YOUR* GIFT OVER THERE--
NO NEED TO BE SO *RUDE!*
DO YOU *WANT* YOUR GIFT OR *NOT?*
PAUL, YOUR *MOM* CALLED AND ASKED IF YOU CAN COME *HOME* NOW. YOU KIDS *DONE* YOUR POLLYANNA?
YEP. *THANKS,* MARISSA! I REALLY *APPRECIATE* THE GIFT.
DANA, YOURS IS ON THE TABLE. IT'S THE *SAME* THING YOU GOT MARISSA. HOPE YOU *LIKE* IT.

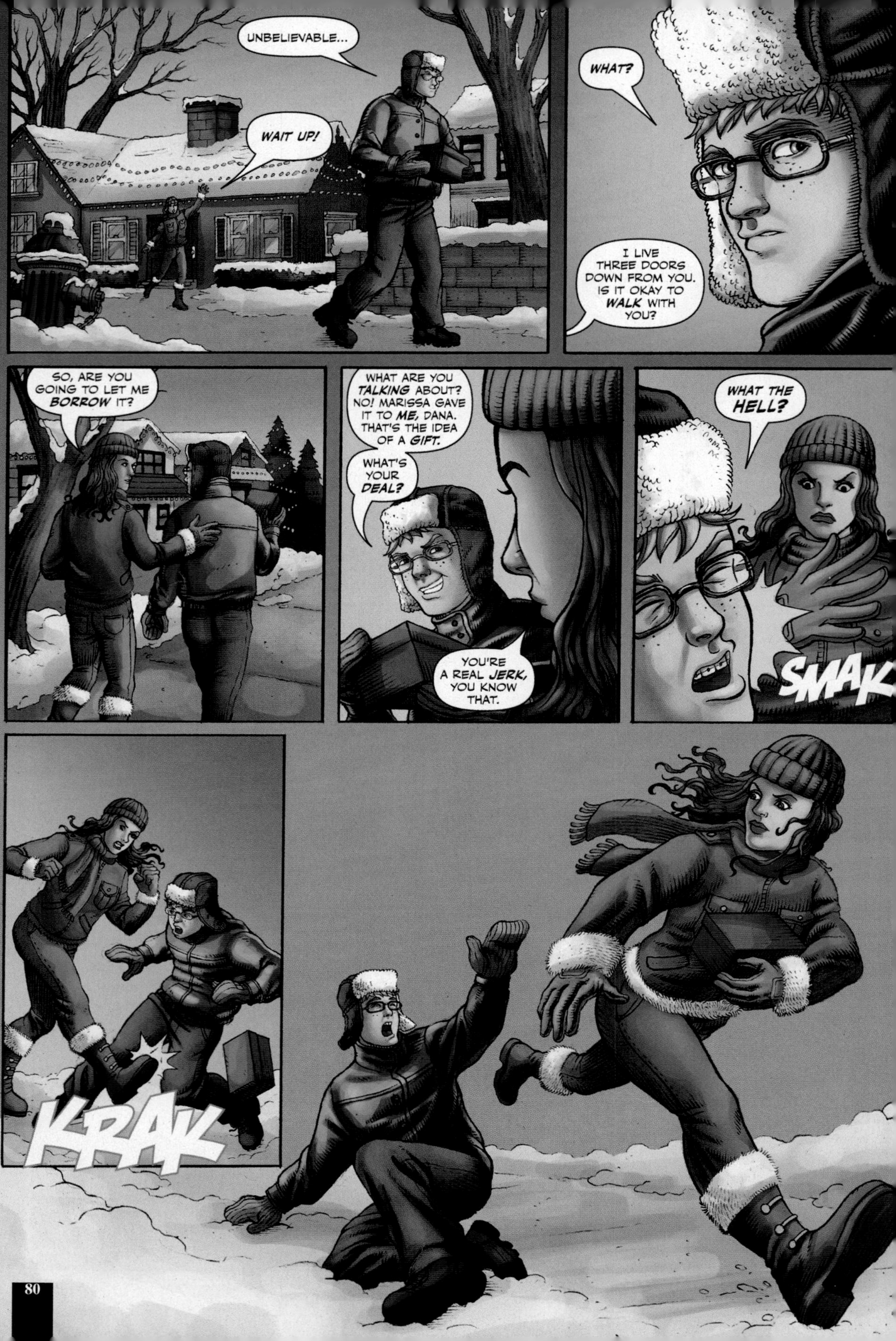
UNBELIEVABLE...
WAIT UP!
WHAT?
I LIVE THREE DOORS DOWN FROM YOU. IS IT OKAY TO WALK WITH YOU?
SO, ARE YOU GOING TO LET ME BORROW IT?
WHAT ARE YOU TALKING ABOUT? NO! MARISSA GAVE IT TO ME, DANA. THAT'S THE IDEA OF A GIFT.
WHAT'S YOUR DEAL?
YOU'RE A REAL JERK, YOU KNOW THAT.
WHAT THE HELL?
SMAK
KRAK

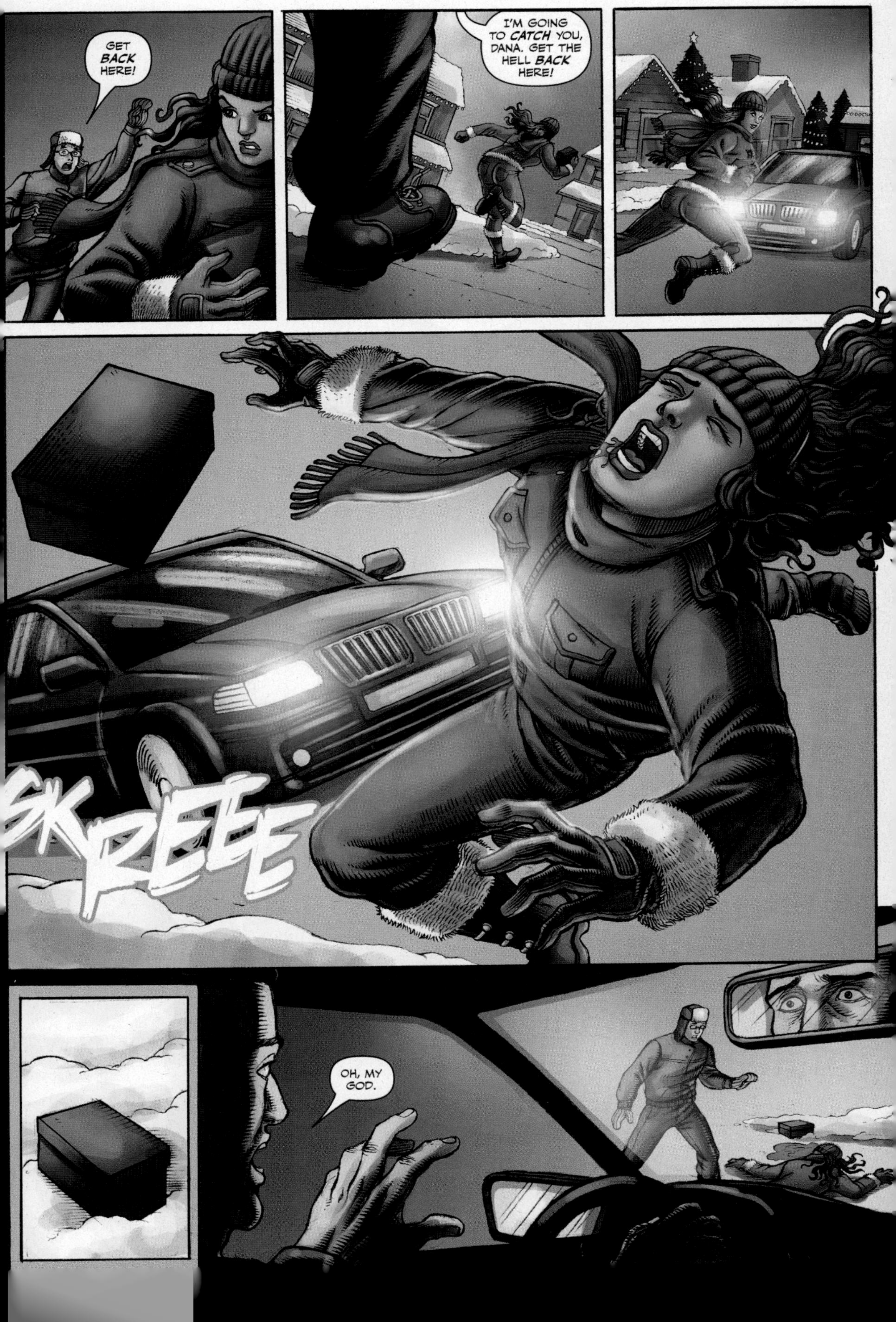
GET BACK HERE!
I'M GOING TO CATCH YOU, DANA. GET THE HELL BACK HERE!
SKREEE
OH, MY GOD.

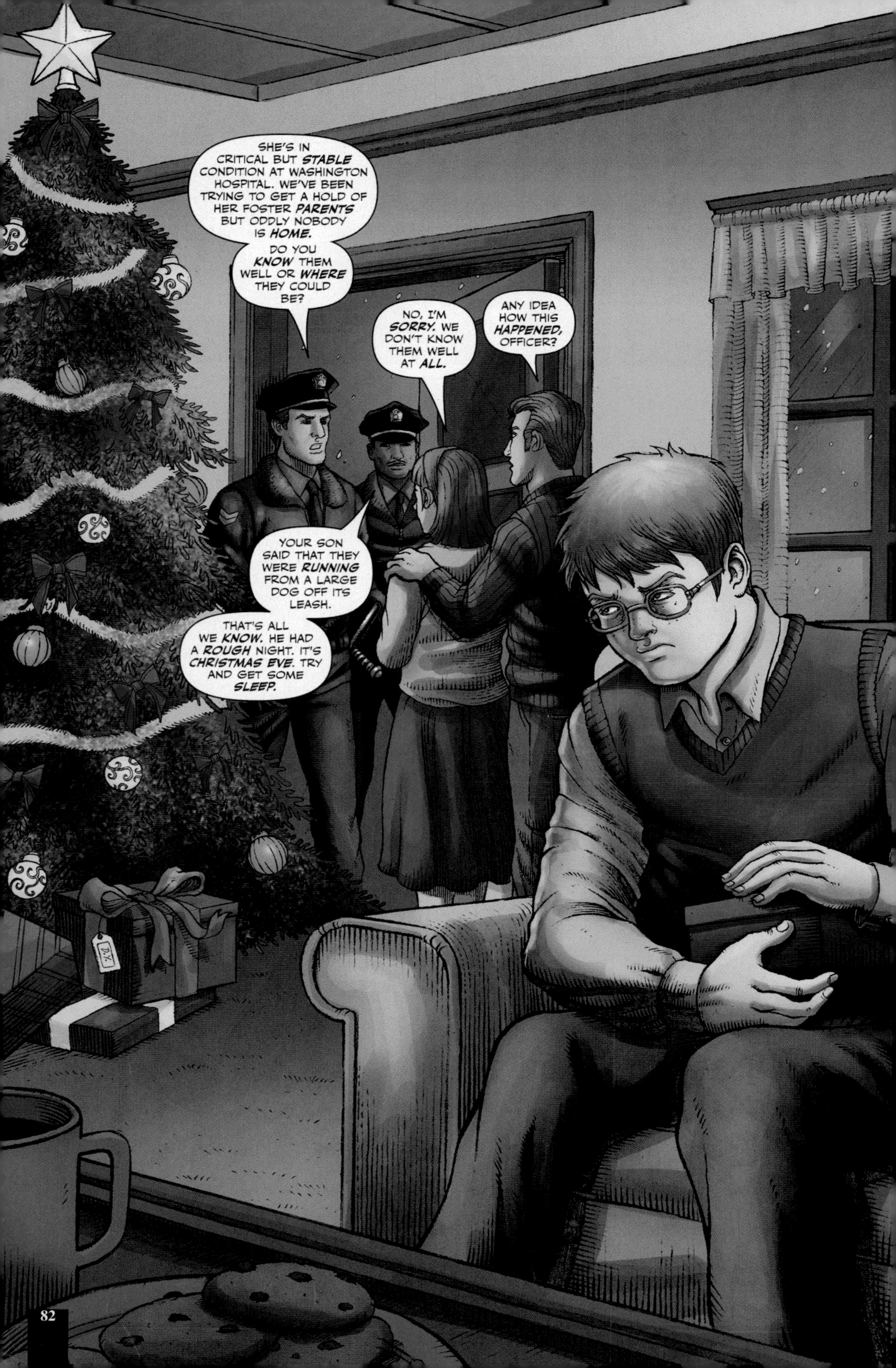
SHE'S IN CRITICAL BUT STABLE CONDITION AT WASHINGTON HOSPITAL. WE'VE BEEN TRYING TO GET A HOLD OF HER FOSTER PARENTS BUT ODDLY NOBODY IS HOME.
DO YOU KNOW THEM WELL OR WHERE THEY COULD BE?
NO, I'M SORRY. WE DON'T KNOW THEM WELL AT ALL.
ANY IDEA HOW THIS HAPPENED, OFFICER?
YOUR SON SAID THAT THEY WERE RUNNING FROM A LARGE DOG OFF ITS LEASH.
THAT'S ALL WE KNOW. HE HAD A ROUGH NIGHT. IT'S CHRISTMAS EVE. TRY AND GET SOME SLEEP.

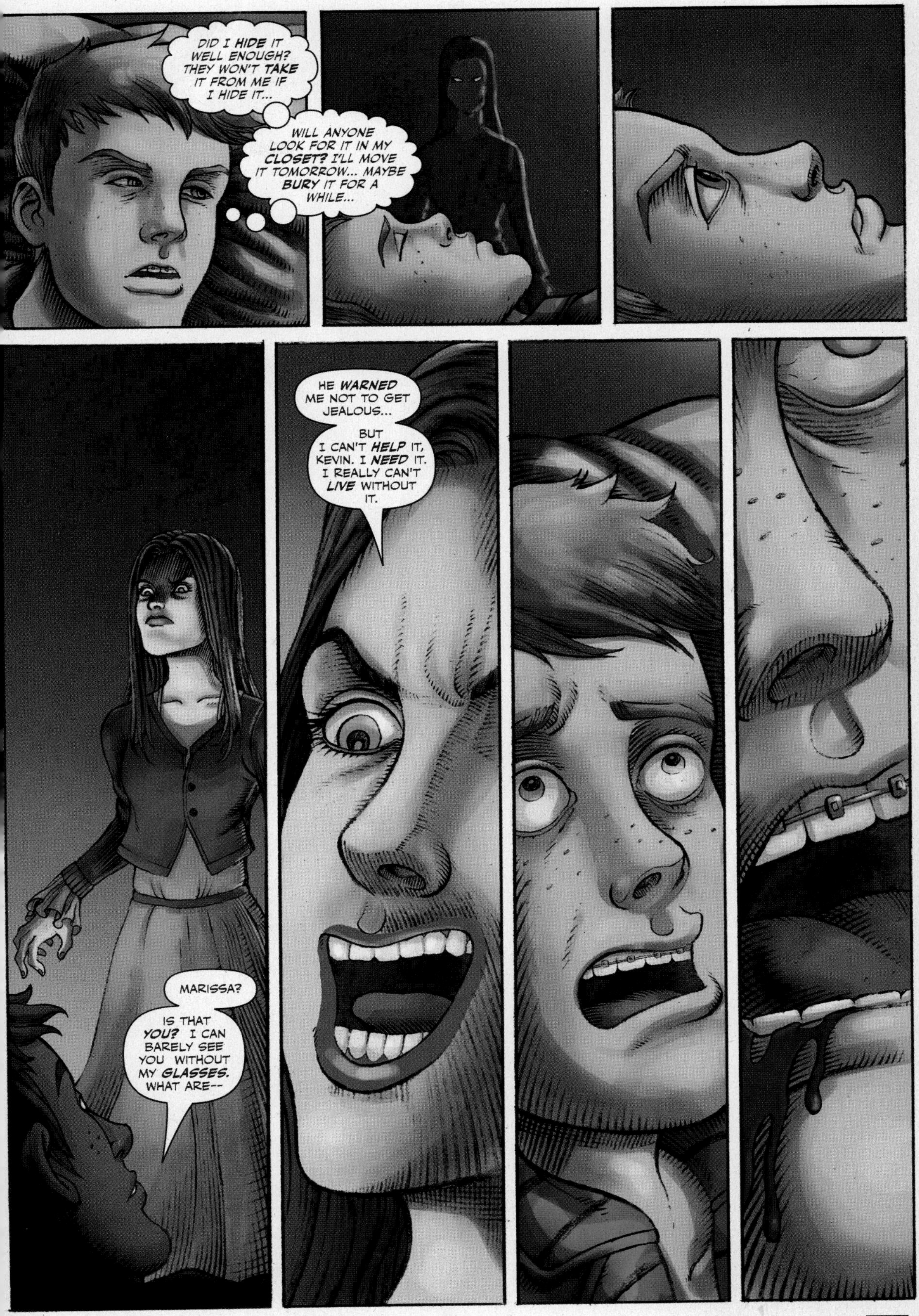
DID I HIDE IT WELL ENOUGH? THEY WON'T TAKE IT FROM ME IF I HIDE IT...
WILL ANYONE LOOK FOR IT IN MY CLOSET? I'LL MOVE IT TOMORROW... MAYBE BURY IT FOR A WHILE...
MARISSA?
IS THAT YOU? I CAN BARELY SEE YOU WITHOUT MY GLASSES. WHAT ARE--
HE WARNED ME NOT TO GET JEALOUS...
BUT I CAN'T HELP IT, KEVIN. I NEED IT. I REALLY CAN'T LIVE WITHOUT IT.

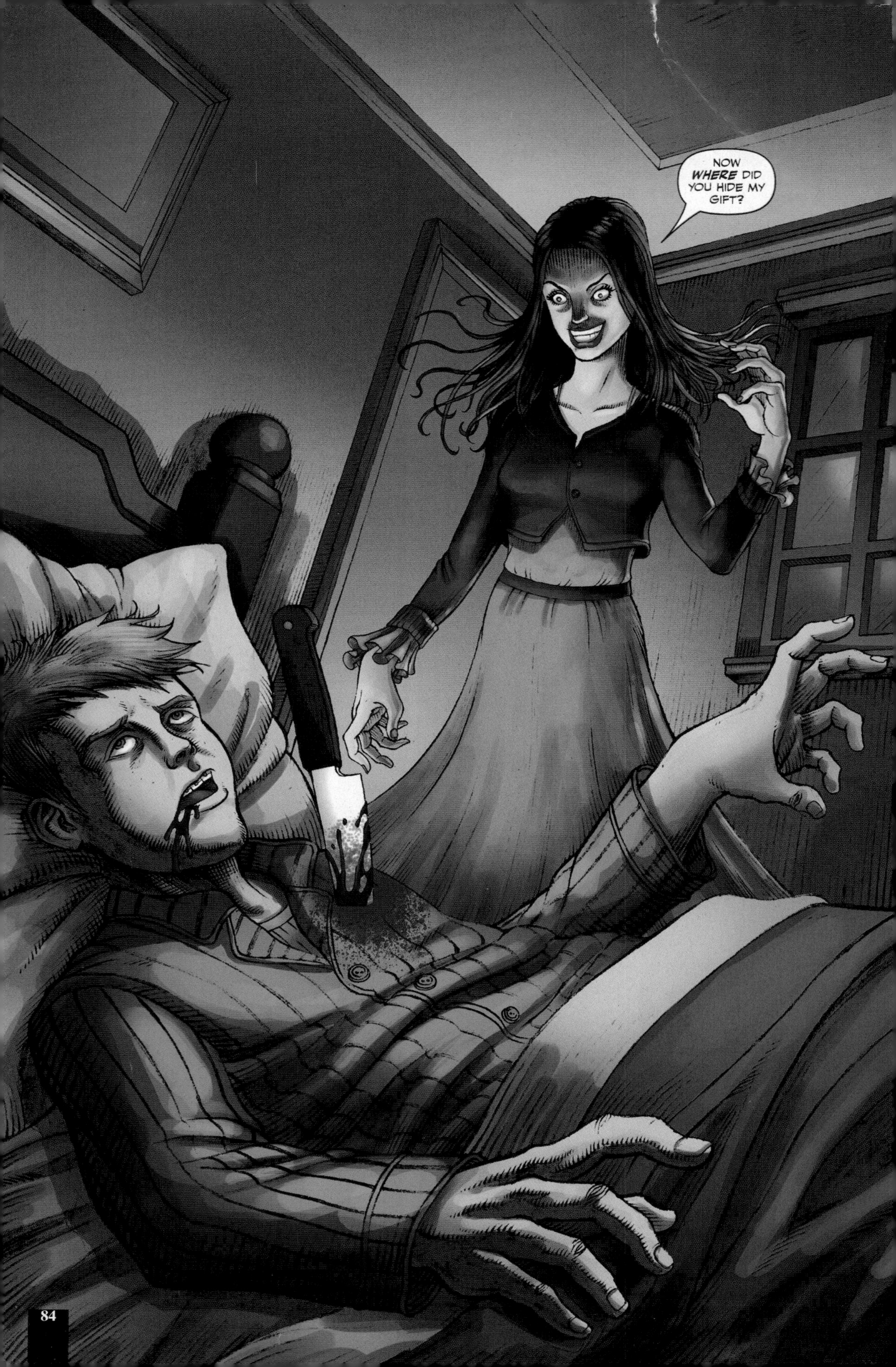
NOW WHERE DID YOU HIDE MY GIFT?

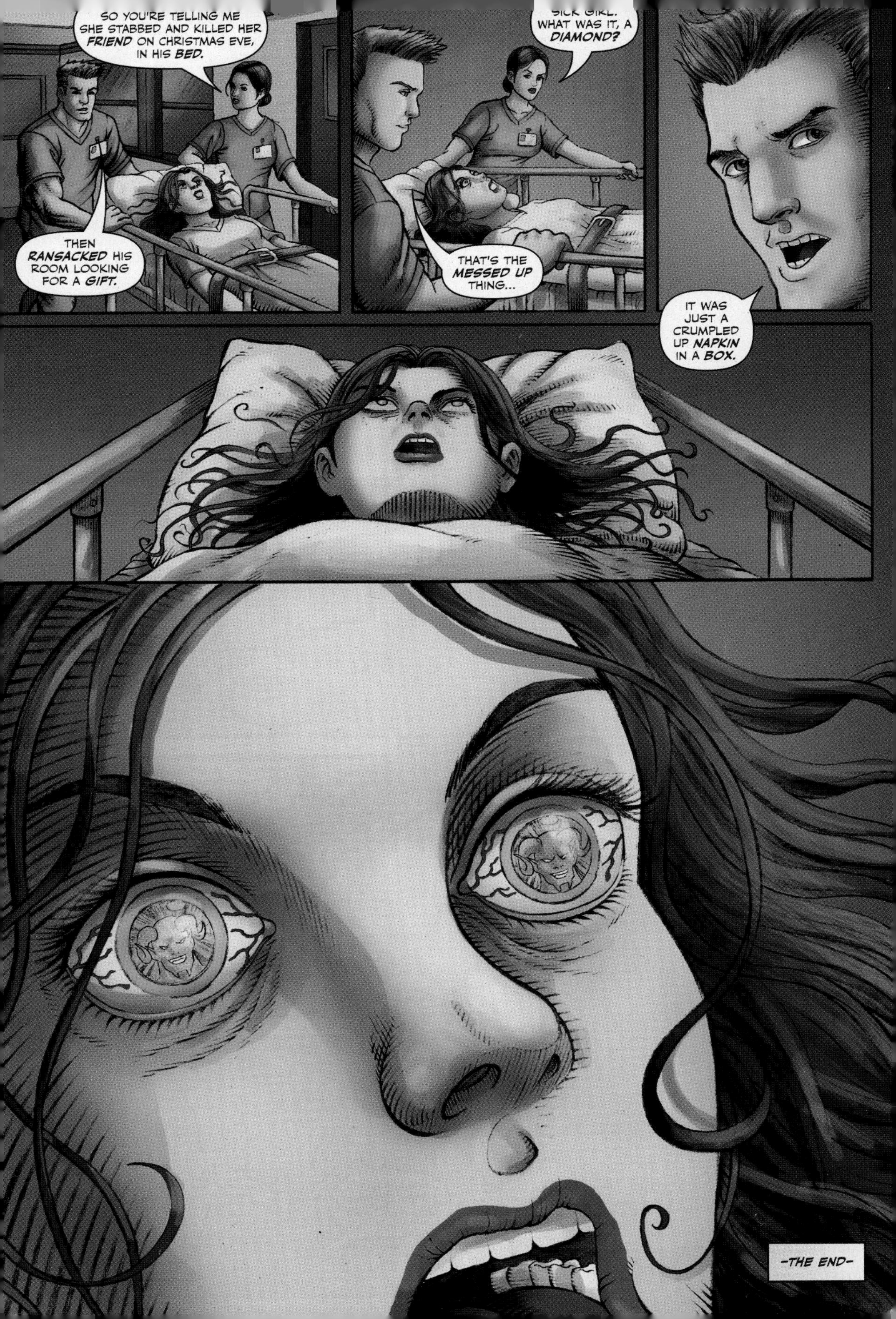

SO YOU'RE TELLING ME SHE STABBED AND KILLED HER FRIEND ON CHRISTMAS EVE, IN HIS BED.
THEN RANSACKED HIS ROOM LOOKING FOR A GIFT.
SICK GIRL. WHAT WAS IT, A DIAMOND?
THAT'S THE MESSED UP THING...
IT WAS JUST A CRUMPLED UP NAPKIN IN A BOX.
-THE END-

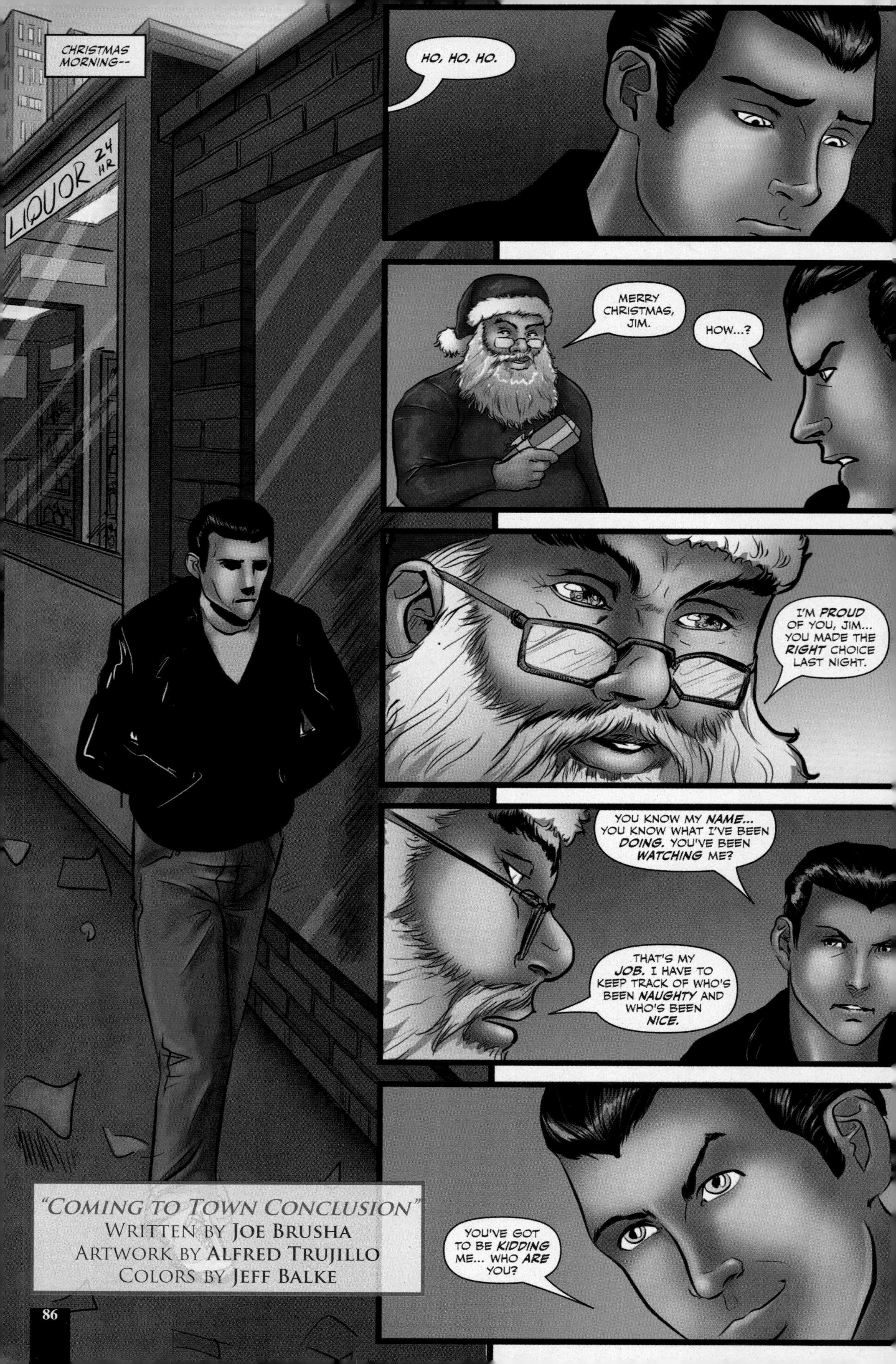
CHRISTMAS MORNING--
LIQUOR 24 HR
HO, HO, HO.
MERRY CHRISTMAS, JIM.
HOW...?
I'M PROUD OF YOU, JIM... YOU MADE THE RIGHT CHOICE LAST NIGHT.
YOU KNOW MY NAME... YOU KNOW WHAT I'VE BEEN DOING. YOU'VE BEEN WATCHING ME?
THAT'S MY JOB. I HAVE TO KEEP TRACK OF WHO'S BEEN NAUGHTY AND WHO'S BEEN NICE.
YOU'VE GOT TO BE KIDDING ME... WHO ARE YOU?
"COMING TO TOWN CONCLUSION"
WRITTEN BY JOE BRUSHA
ARTWORK BY ALFRED TRUJILLO
COLORS BY JEFF BALKE

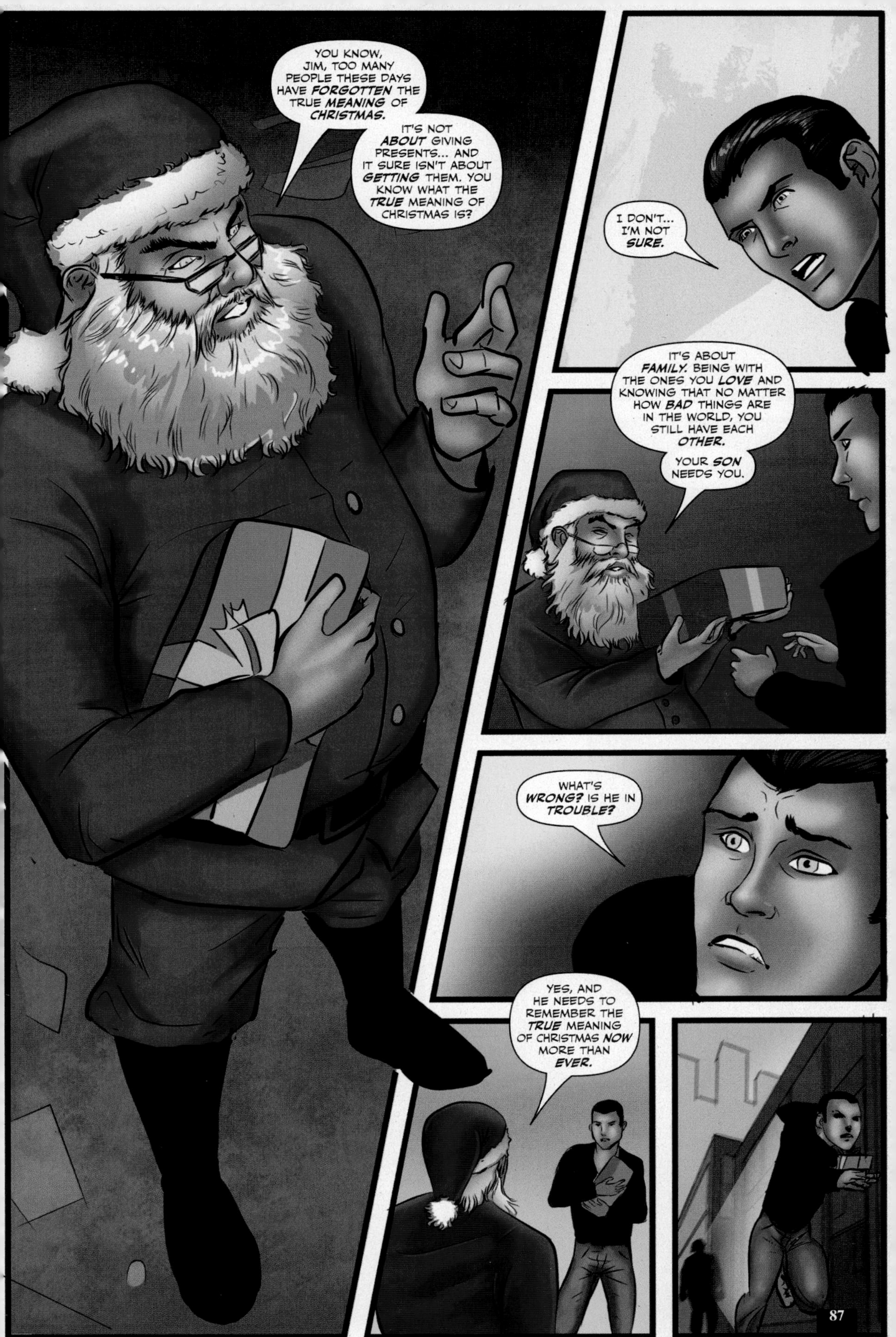
YOU KNOW, JIM, TOO MANY PEOPLE THESE DAYS HAVE FORGOTTEN THE TRUE MEANING OF CHRISTMAS.
IT'S NOT ABOUT GIVING PRESENTS... AND IT SURE ISN'T ABOUT GETTING THEM. YOU KNOW WHAT THE TRUE MEANING OF CHRISTMAS IS?
I DON'T... I'M NOT SURE.
IT'S ABOUT FAMILY. BEING WITH THE ONES YOU LOVE AND KNOWING THAT NO MATTER HOW BAD THINGS ARE IN THE WORLD, YOU STILL HAVE EACH OTHER.
YOUR SON NEEDS YOU.
WHAT'S WRONG? IS HE IN TROUBLE?
YES, AND HE NEEDS TO REMEMBER THE TRUE MEANING OF CHRISTMAS NOW MORE THAN EVER.

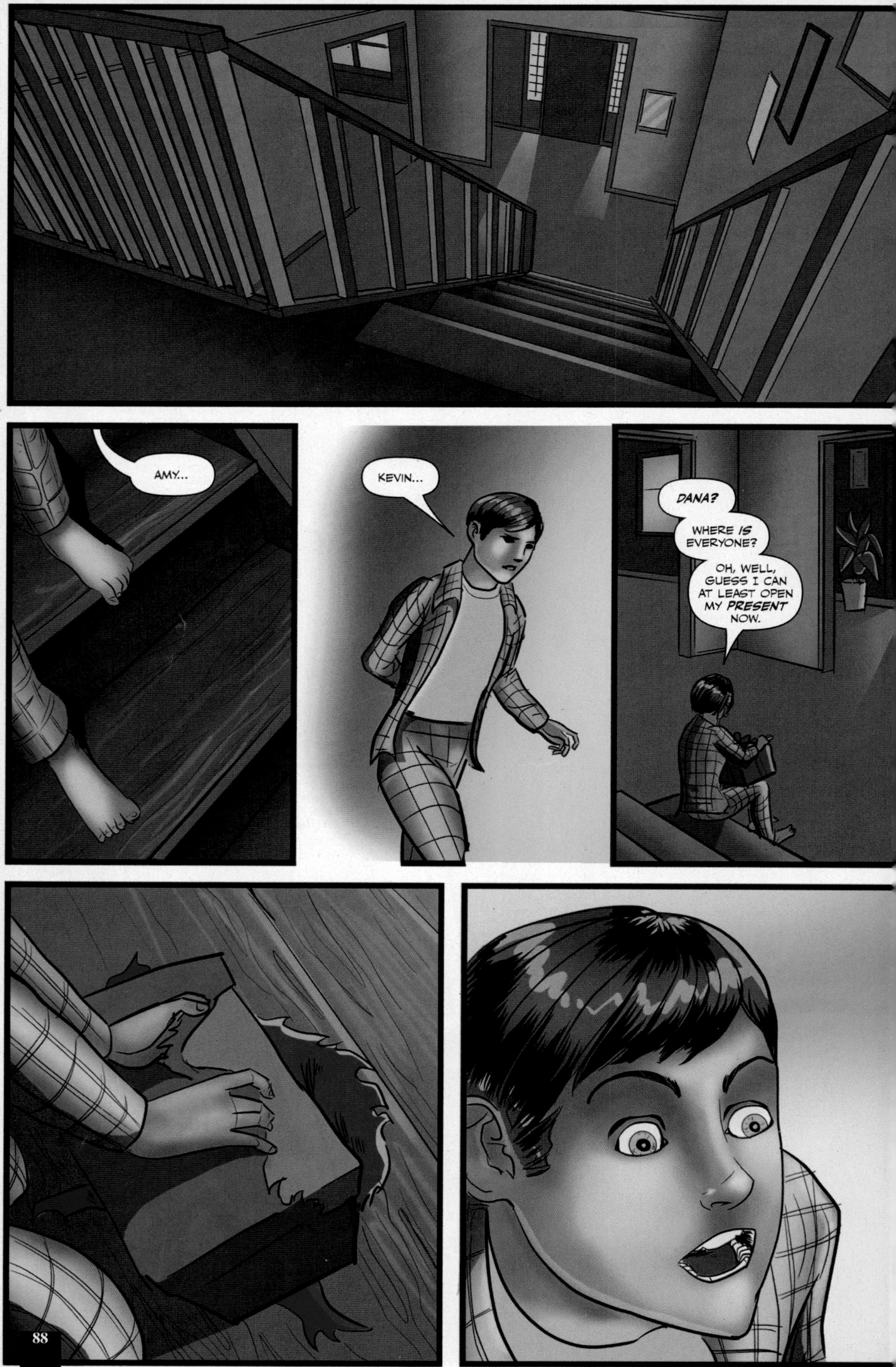
AMY...
KEVIN...
DANA?
WHERE IS EVERYONE?
OH, WELL, GUESS I CAN AT LEAST OPEN MY PRESENT NOW.

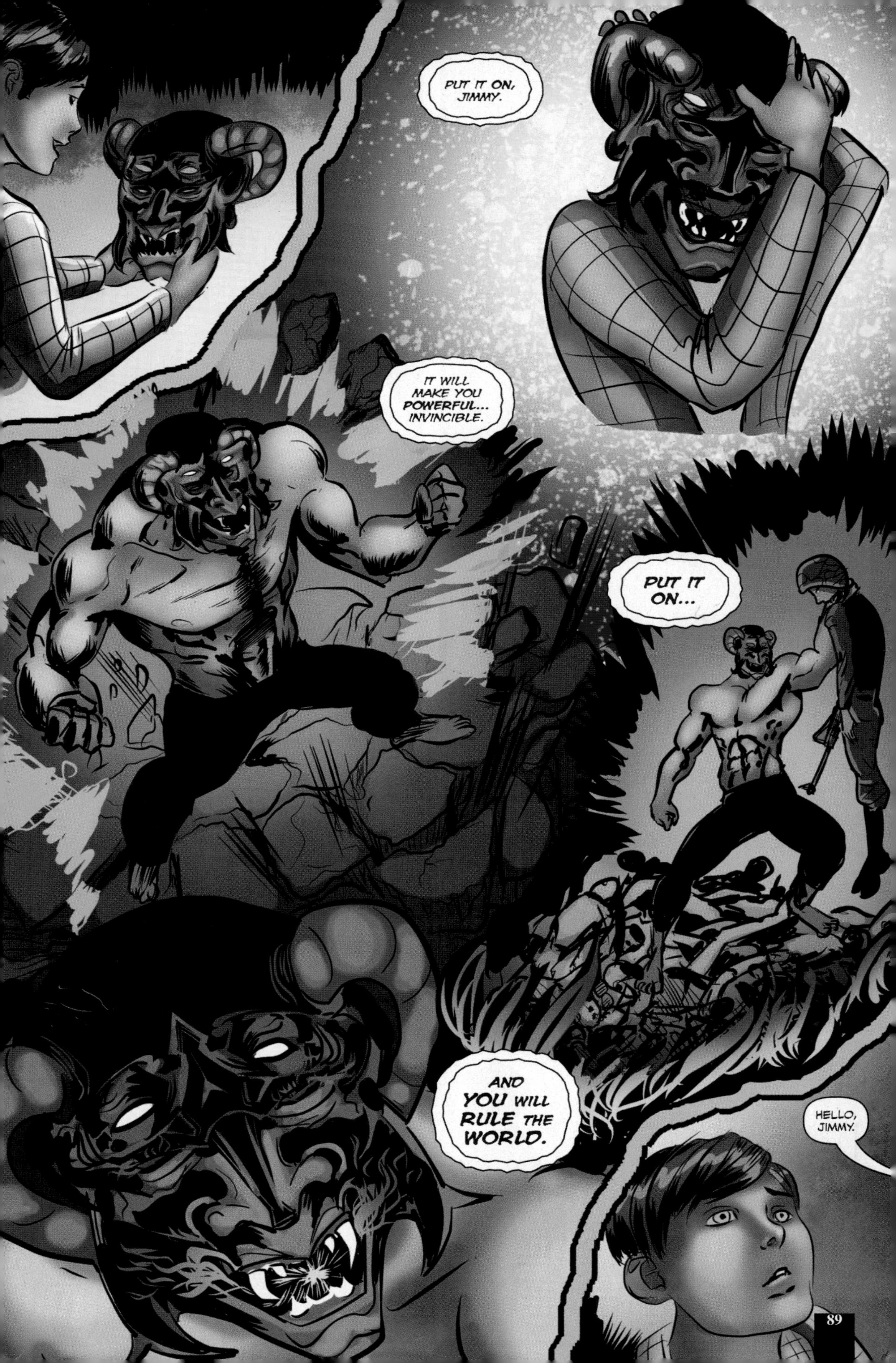
PUT IT ON, JIMMY.
IT WILL MAKE YOU POWERFUL... INVINCIBLE.
PUT IT ON...
AND YOU WILL RULE THE WORLD.
HELLO, JIMMY.

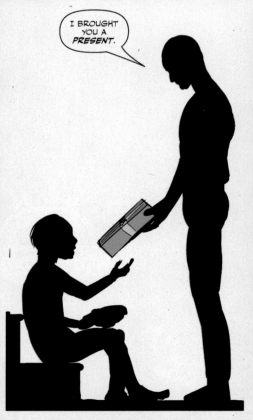

HOW HAVE YOU *BEEN*, BUD?

DAD?

I'VE REALLY *MISSED* YOU.

I'M *SORRY* THAT I HAD TO LEAVE YOU. A FATHER SHOULD *NEVER* LEAVE HIS KIDS...

BUT I'M *BACK* NOW... AND I'M *NEVER* GOING TO LEAVE YOU ALONE *AGAIN*.

BECAUSE I LOVE YOU.

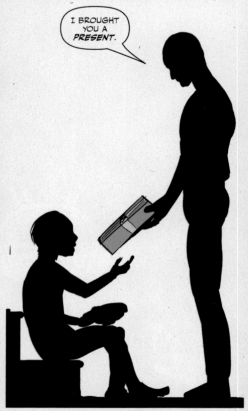

I BROUGHT YOU A *PRESENT*.

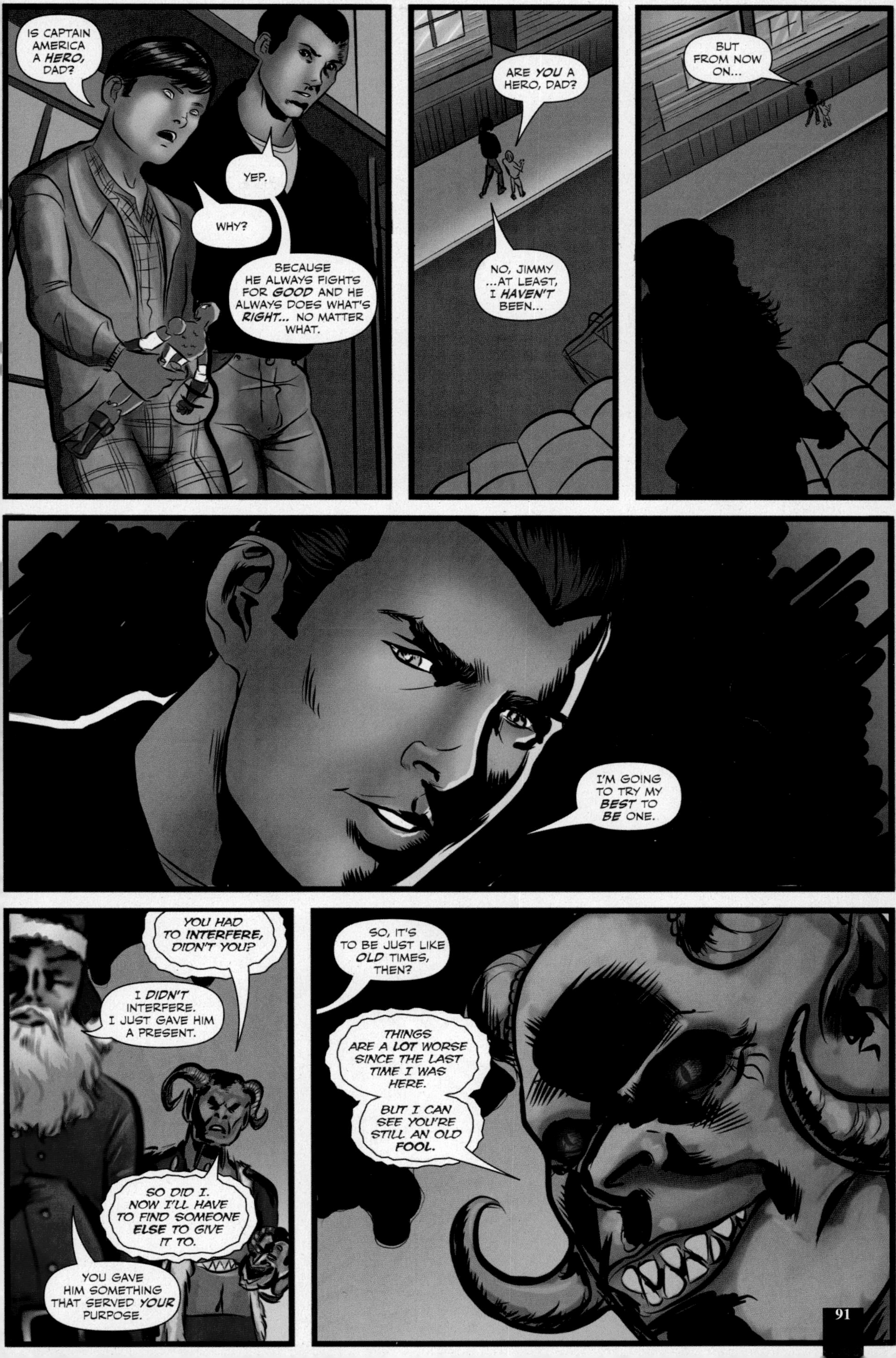
IS CAPTAIN AMERICA A HERO, DAD?
YEP.
WHY?
BECAUSE HE ALWAYS FIGHTS FOR GOOD AND HE ALWAYS DOES WHAT'S RIGHT... NO MATTER WHAT.
ARE YOU A HERO, DAD?
NO, JIMMY ...AT LEAST, I HAVEN'T BEEN...
BUT FROM NOW ON...
I'M GOING TO TRY MY BEST TO BE ONE.
YOU HAD TO INTERFERE, DIDN'T YOU?
I DIDN'T INTERFERE. I JUST GAVE HIM A PRESENT.
SO DID I. NOW I'LL HAVE TO FIND SOMEONE ELSE TO GIVE IT TO.
YOU GAVE HIM SOMETHING THAT SERVED YOUR PURPOSE.
SO, IT'S TO BE JUST LIKE OLD TIMES, THEN?
THINGS ARE A LOT WORSE SINCE THE LAST TIME I WAS HERE.
BUT I CAN SEE YOU'RE STILL AN OLD FOOL.

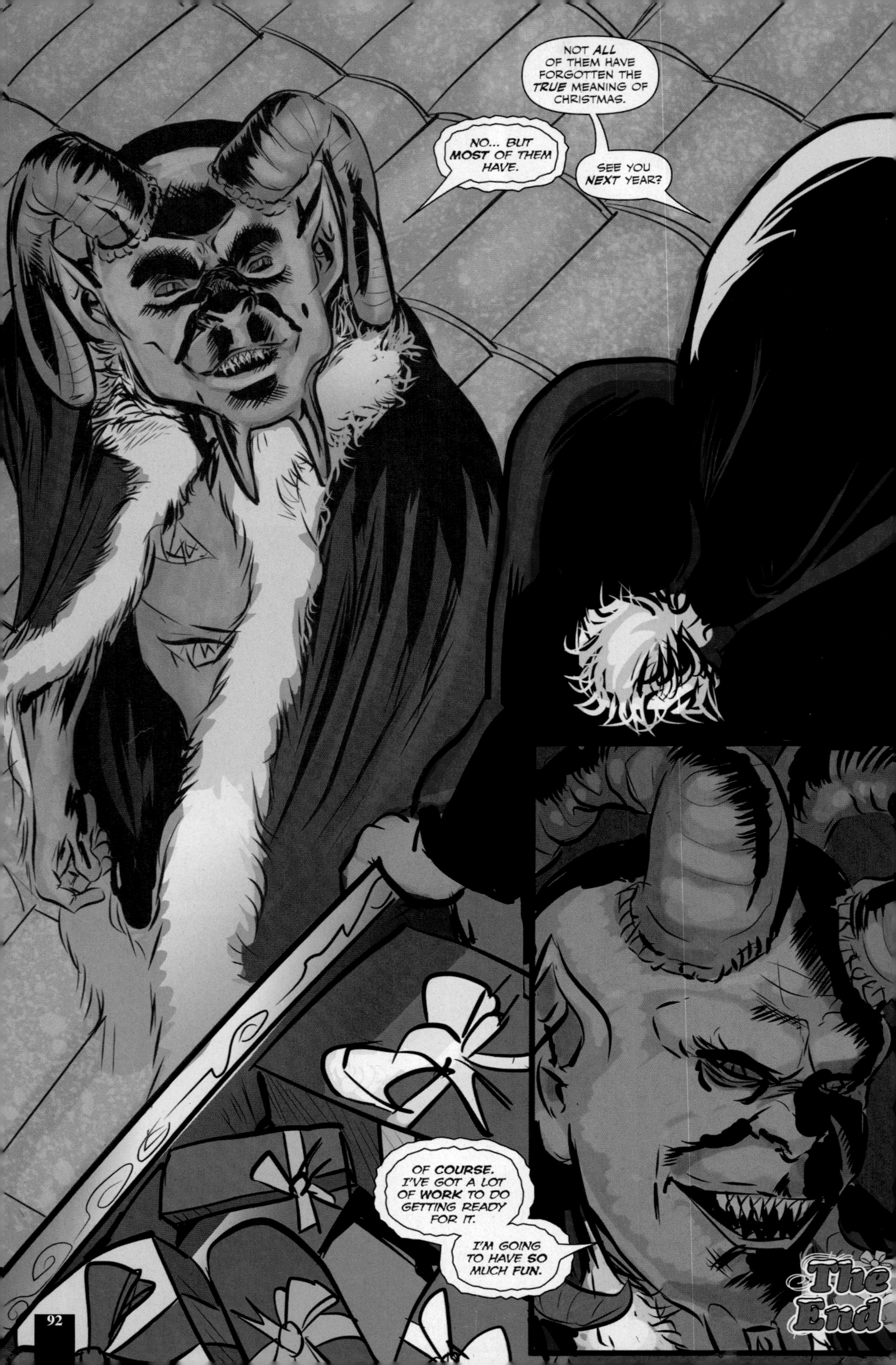
NOT ALL OF THEM HAVE FORGOTTEN THE TRUE MEANING OF CHRISTMAS.
NO... BUT MOST OF THEM HAVE.
SEE YOU NEXT YEAR?
OF COURSE. I'VE GOT A LOT OF WORK TO DO GETTING READY FOR IT.
I'M GOING TO HAVE SO MUCH FUN.
The End

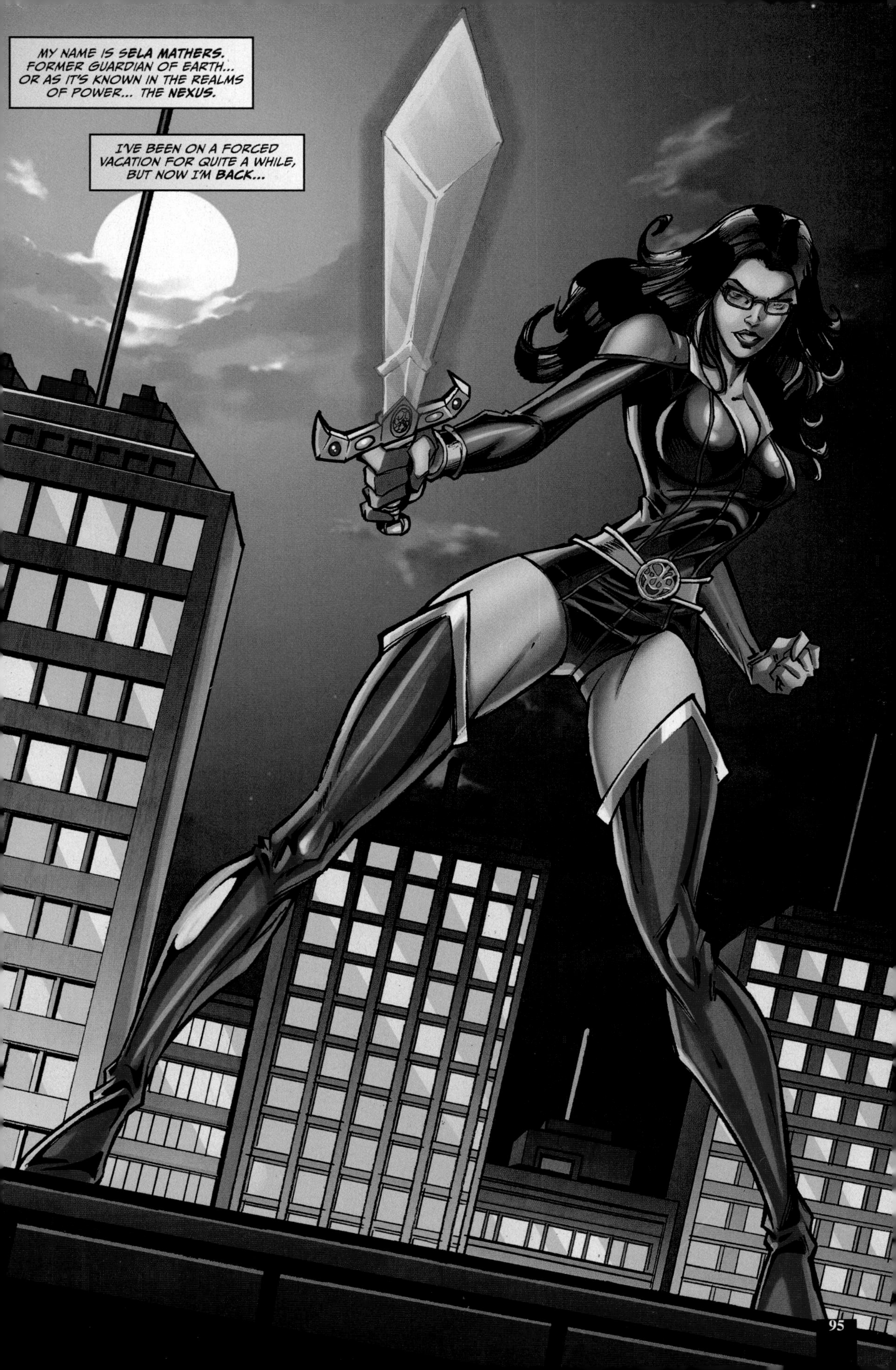
MY NAME IS SELA MATHERS. FORMER GUARDIAN OF EARTH... OR AS IT'S KNOWN IN THE REALMS OF POWER... THE NEXUS.
I'VE BEEN ON A FORCED VACATION FOR QUITE A WHILE, BUT NOW I'M BACK...

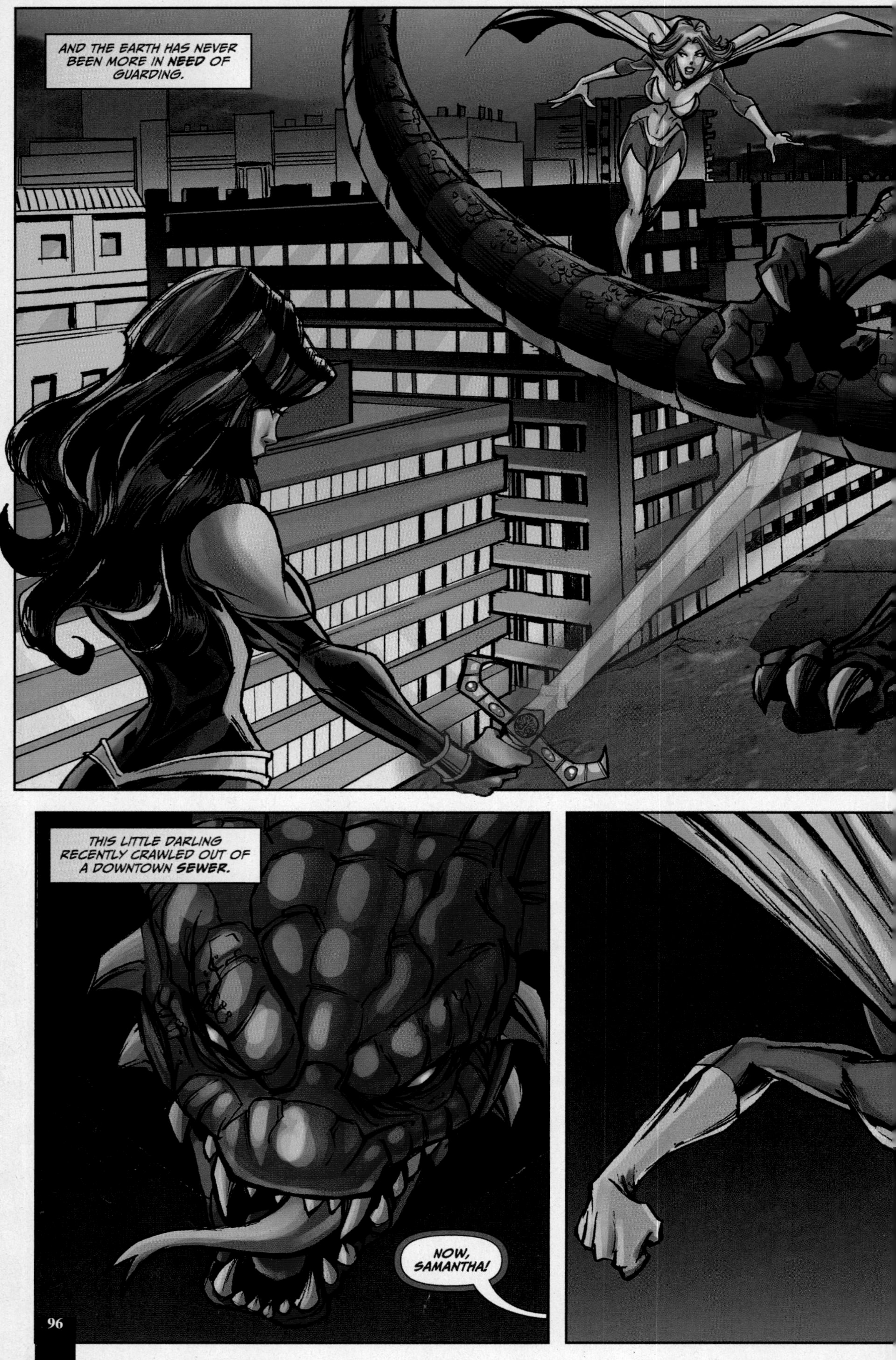
AND THE EARTH HAS NEVER BEEN MORE IN NEED OF GUARDING.
THIS LITTLE DARLING RECENTLY CRAWLED OUT OF A DOWNTOWN SEWER.
NOW, SAMANTHA!

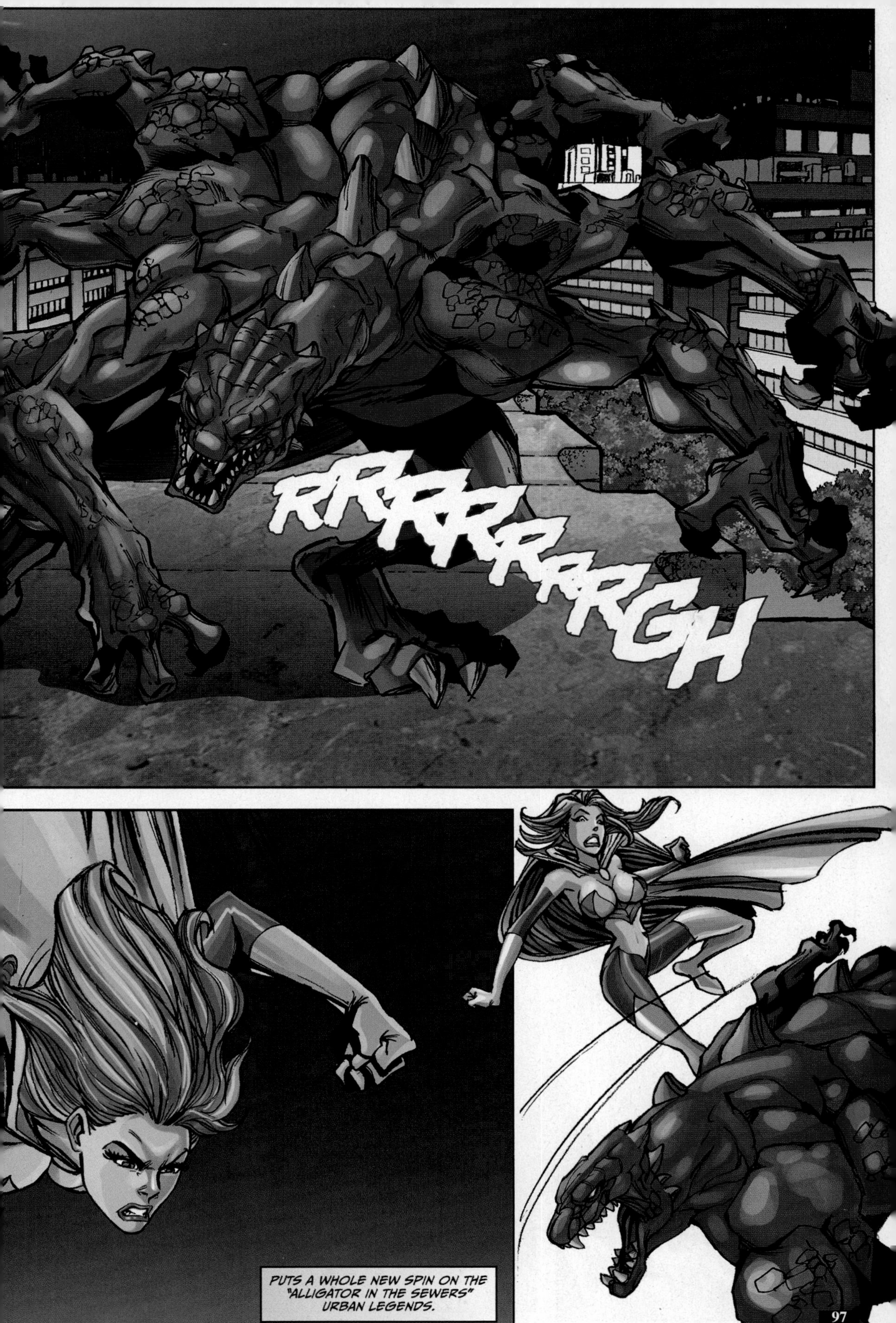
RRRRRRRRRGH
PUTS A WHOLE NEW SPIN ON THE "ALLIGATOR IN THE SEWERS" URBAN LEGENDS.

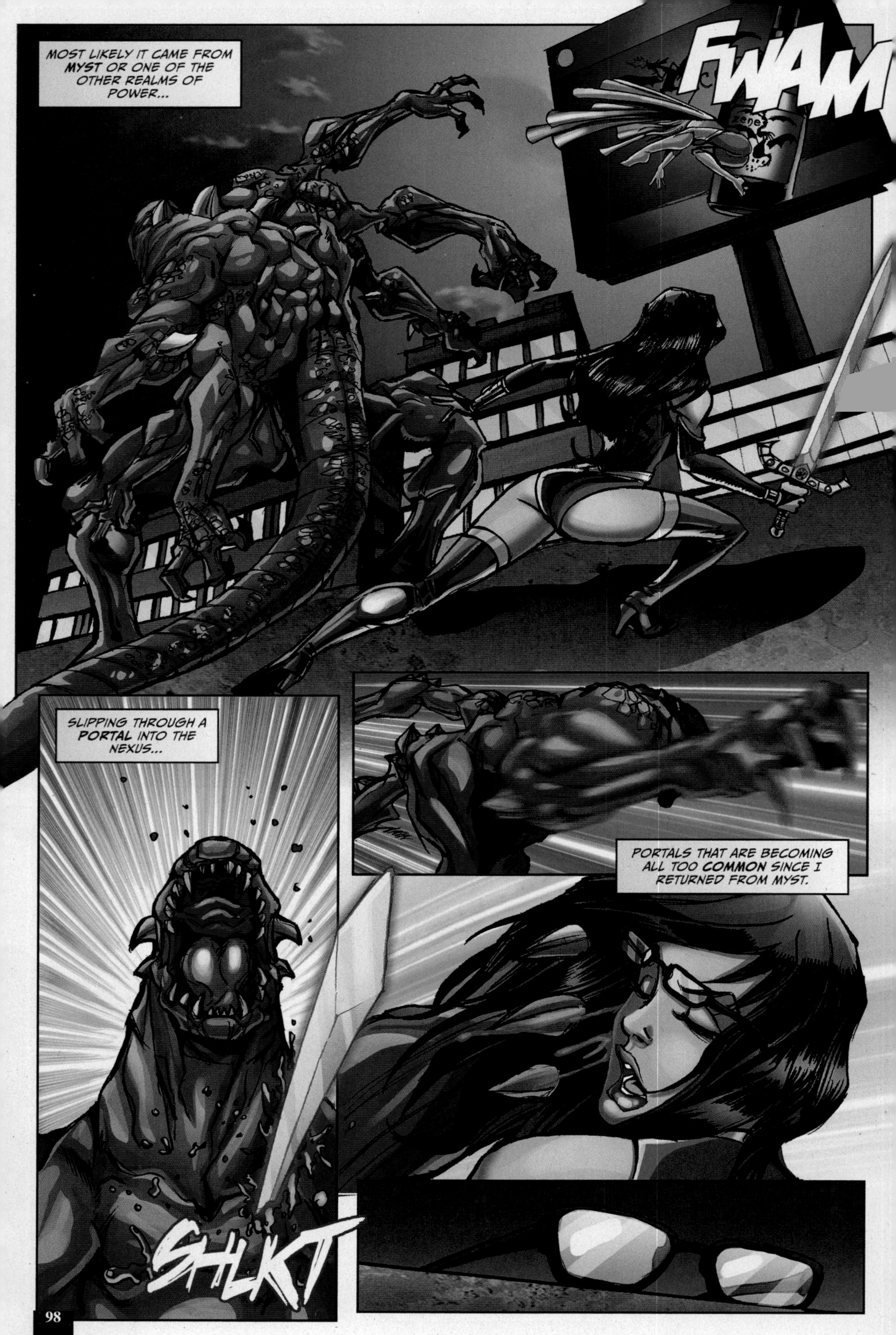
MOST LIKELY IT CAME FROM MYST OR ONE OF THE OTHER REALMS OF POWER...
FWAM
SLIPPING THROUGH A PORTAL INTO THE NEXUS...
PORTALS THAT ARE BECOMING ALL TOO COMMON SINCE I RETURNED FROM MYST.
SHLKT

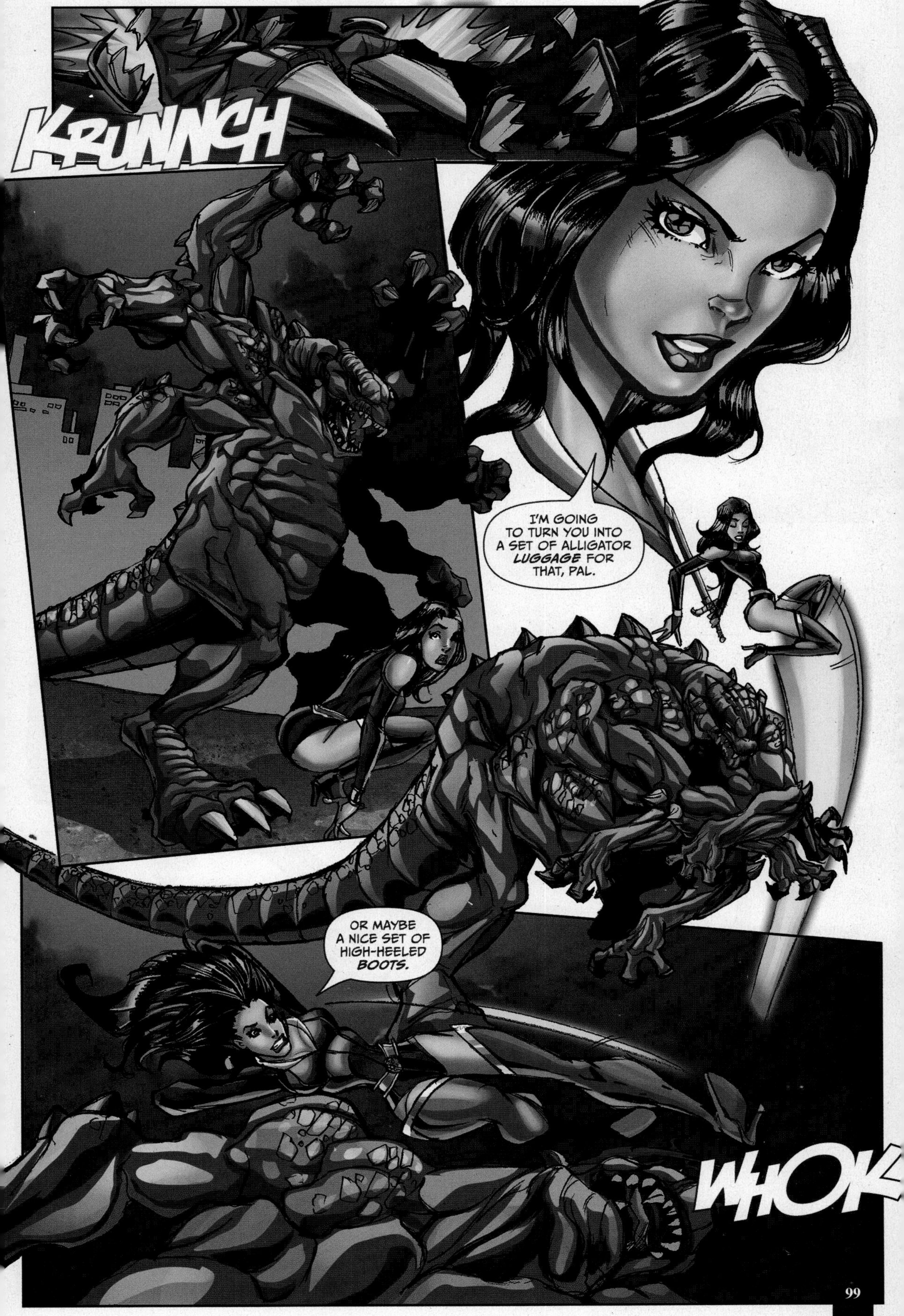
KRUNNCH
I'M GOING TO TURN YOU INTO A SET OF ALLIGATOR LUGGAGE FOR THAT, PAL.
OR MAYBE A NICE SET OF HIGH-HEELED BOOTS.
WHOK

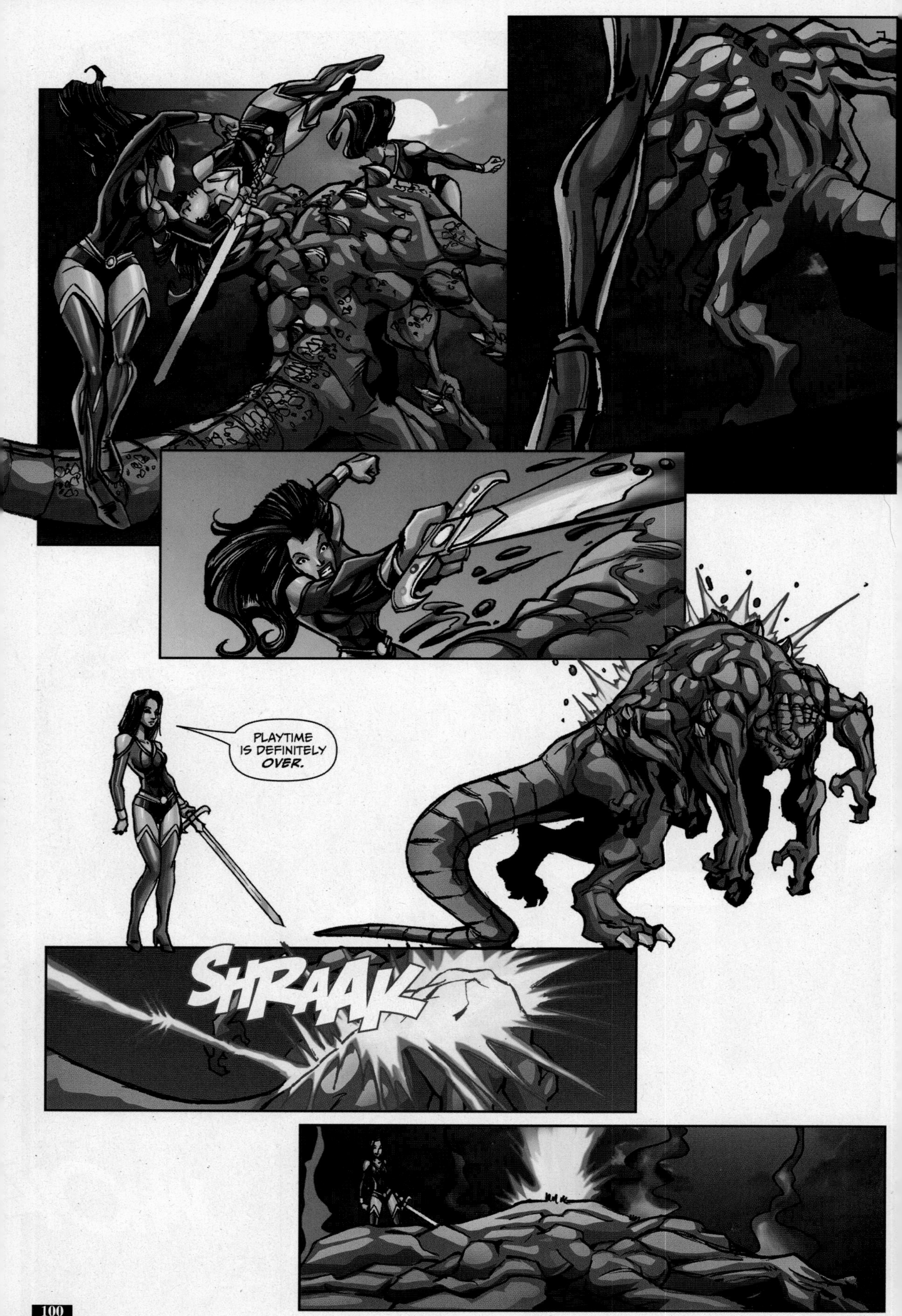
PLAYTIME
IS DEFINITELY
OVER.
SHRAAK

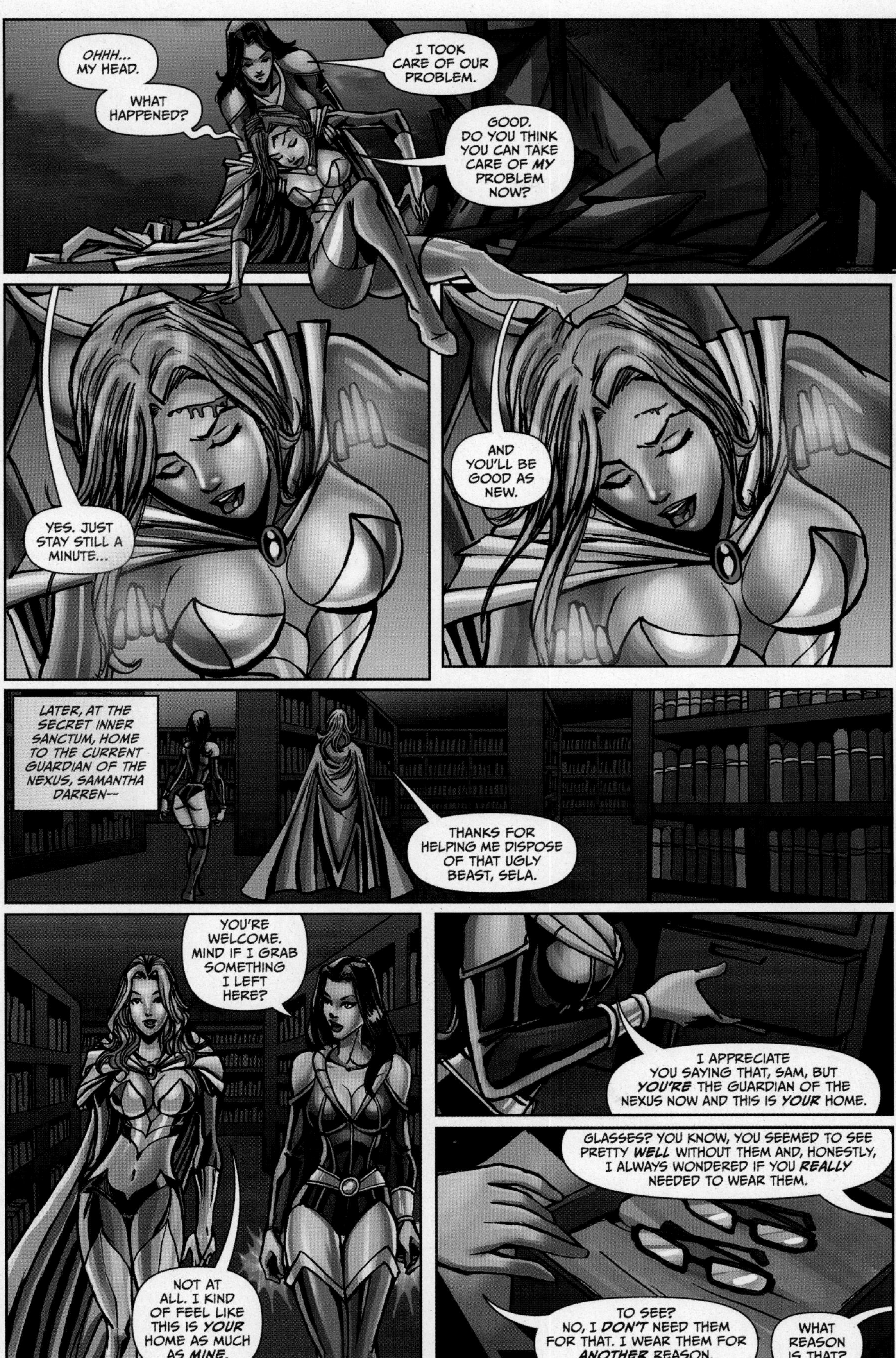
OHHH... MY HEAD.
WHAT HAPPENED?
I TOOK CARE OF OUR PROBLEM.
GOOD. DO YOU THINK YOU CAN TAKE CARE OF MY PROBLEM NOW?
YES. JUST STAY STILL A MINUTE...
AND YOU'LL BE GOOD AS NEW.
LATER, AT THE SECRET INNER SANCTUM, HOME TO THE CURRENT GUARDIAN OF THE NEXUS, SAMANTHA DARREN--
THANKS FOR HELPING ME DISPOSE OF THAT UGLY BEAST, SELA.
YOU'RE WELCOME. MIND IF I GRAB SOMETHING I LEFT HERE?
NOT AT ALL. I KIND OF FEEL LIKE THIS IS YOUR HOME AS MUCH AS MINE.
I APPRECIATE YOU SAYING THAT, SAM, BUT YOU'RE THE GUARDIAN OF THE NEXUS NOW AND THIS IS YOUR HOME.
GLASSES? YOU KNOW, YOU SEEMED TO SEE PRETTY WELL WITHOUT THEM AND, HONESTLY, I ALWAYS WONDERED IF YOU REALLY NEEDED TO WEAR THEM.
TO SEE? NO, I DON'T NEED THEM FOR THAT. I WEAR THEM FOR ANOTHER REASON.
WHAT REASON IS THAT?

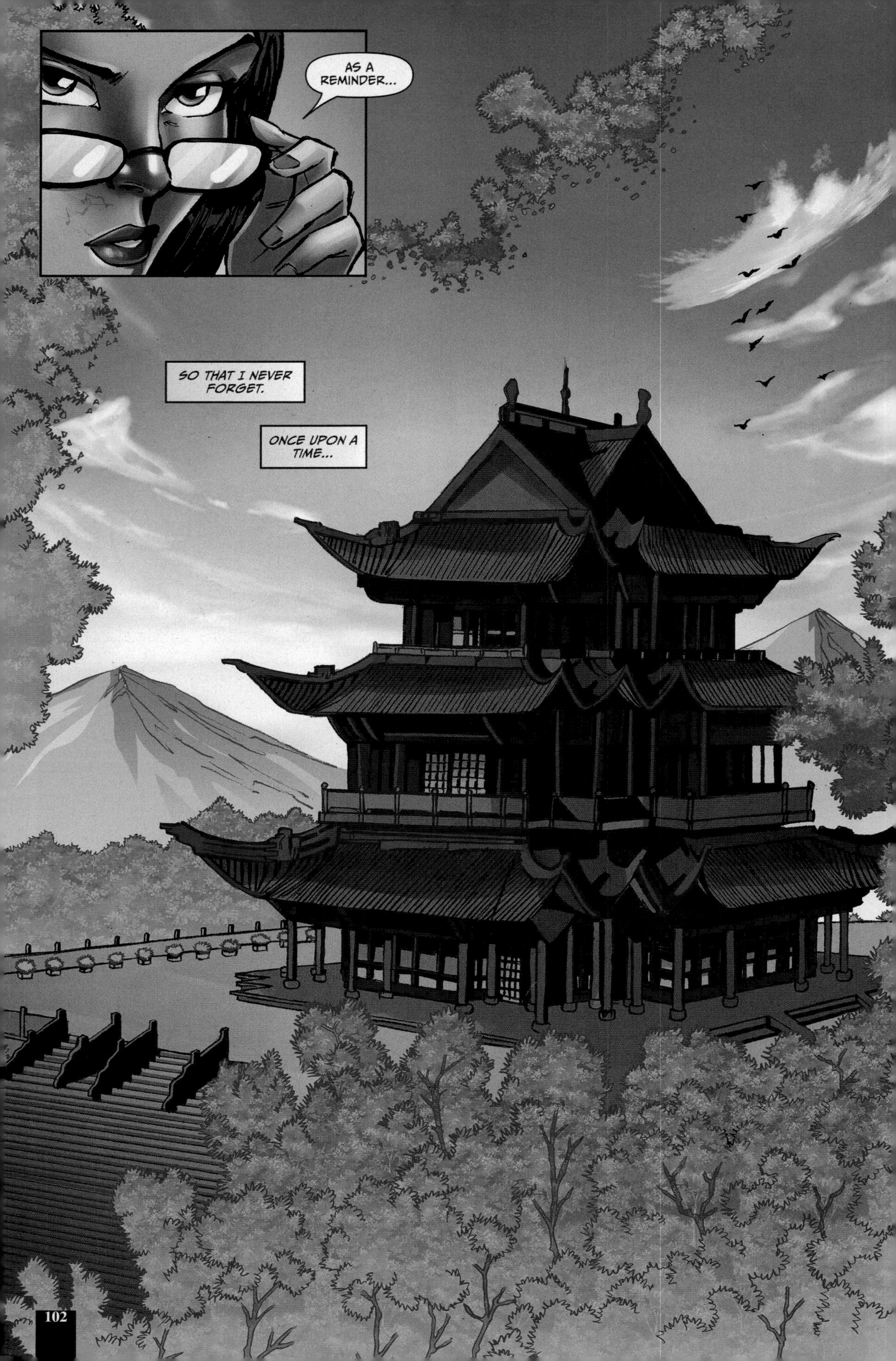
AS A REMINDER...
SO THAT I NEVER FORGET.
ONCE UPON A TIME...

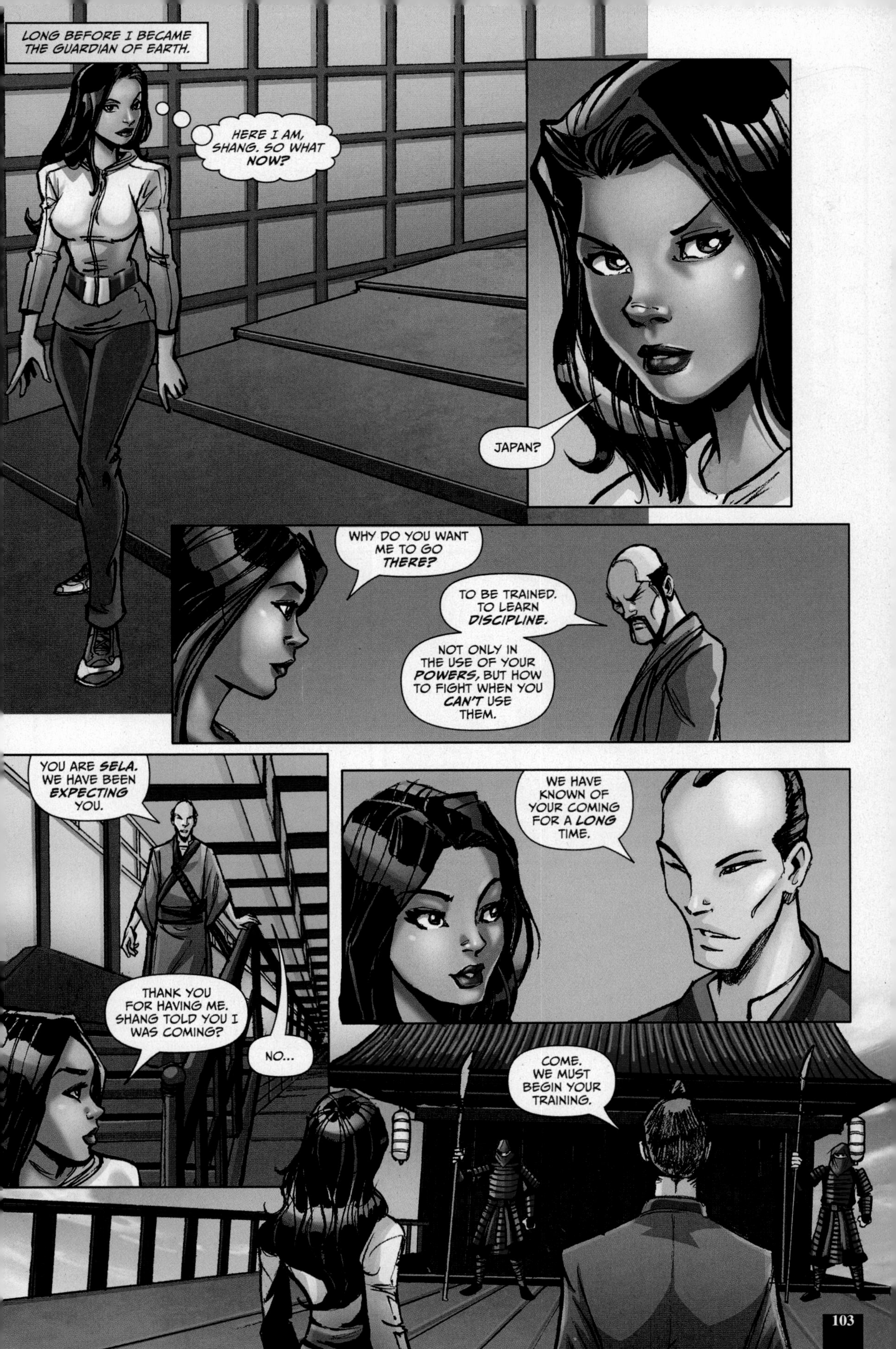

LONG BEFORE I BECAME THE GUARDIAN OF EARTH.
HERE I AM, SHANG. SO WHAT NOW?
JAPAN?
WHY DO YOU WANT ME TO GO THERE?
TO BE TRAINED. TO LEARN DISCIPLINE.
NOT ONLY IN THE USE OF YOUR POWERS, BUT HOW TO FIGHT WHEN YOU CAN'T USE THEM.
YOU ARE SELA. WE HAVE BEEN EXPECTING YOU.
THANK YOU FOR HAVING ME. SHANG TOLD YOU I WAS COMING?
NO...
WE HAVE KNOWN OF YOUR COMING FOR A LONG TIME.
COME. WE MUST BEGIN YOUR TRAINING.

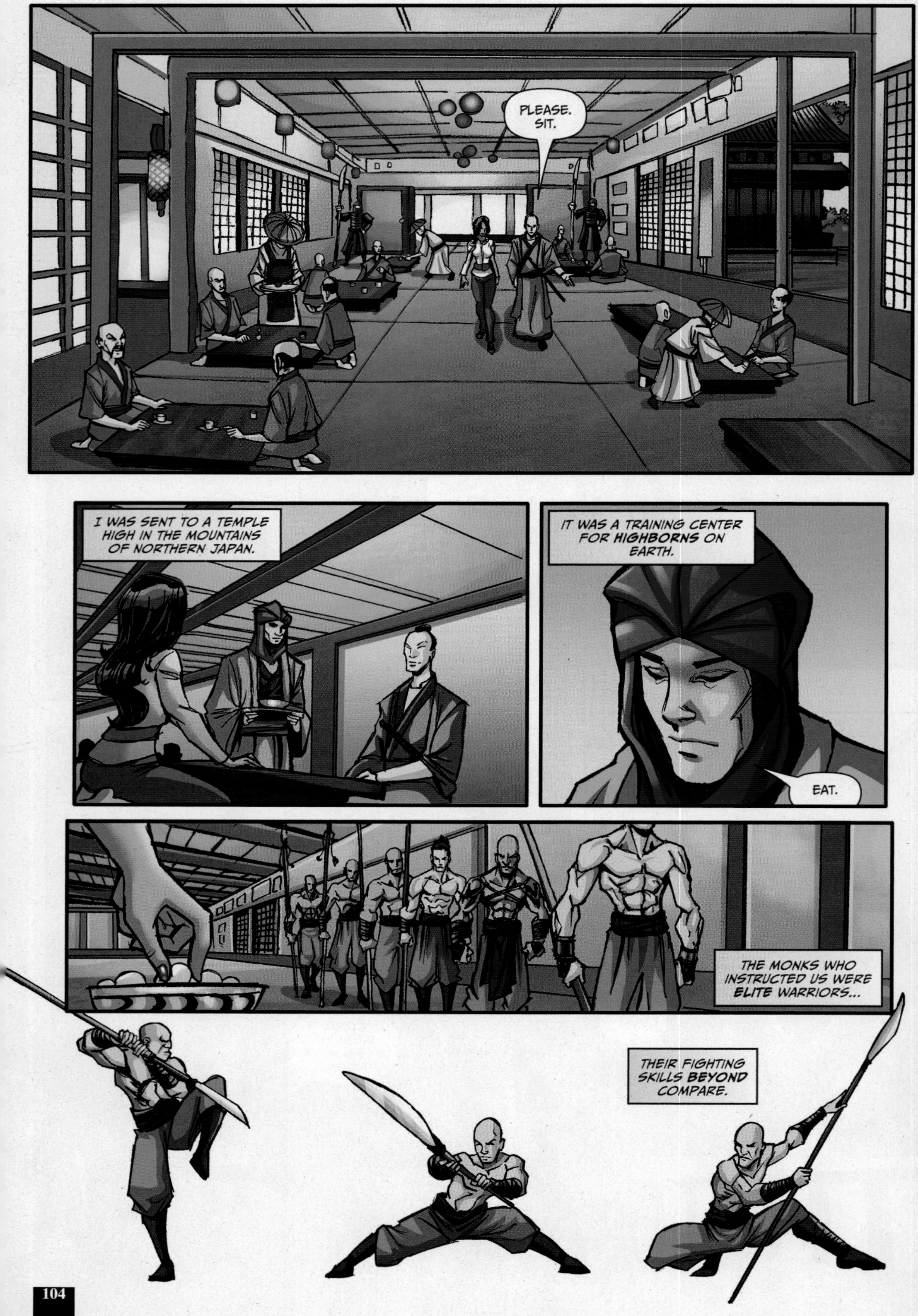
PLEASE. SIT.
I WAS SENT TO A TEMPLE HIGH IN THE MOUNTAINS OF NORTHERN JAPAN.
IT WAS A TRAINING CENTER FOR HIGHBORNS ON EARTH.
EAT.
THE MONKS WHO INSTRUCTED US WERE ELITE WARRIORS...
THEIR FIGHTING SKILLS BEYOND COMPARE.

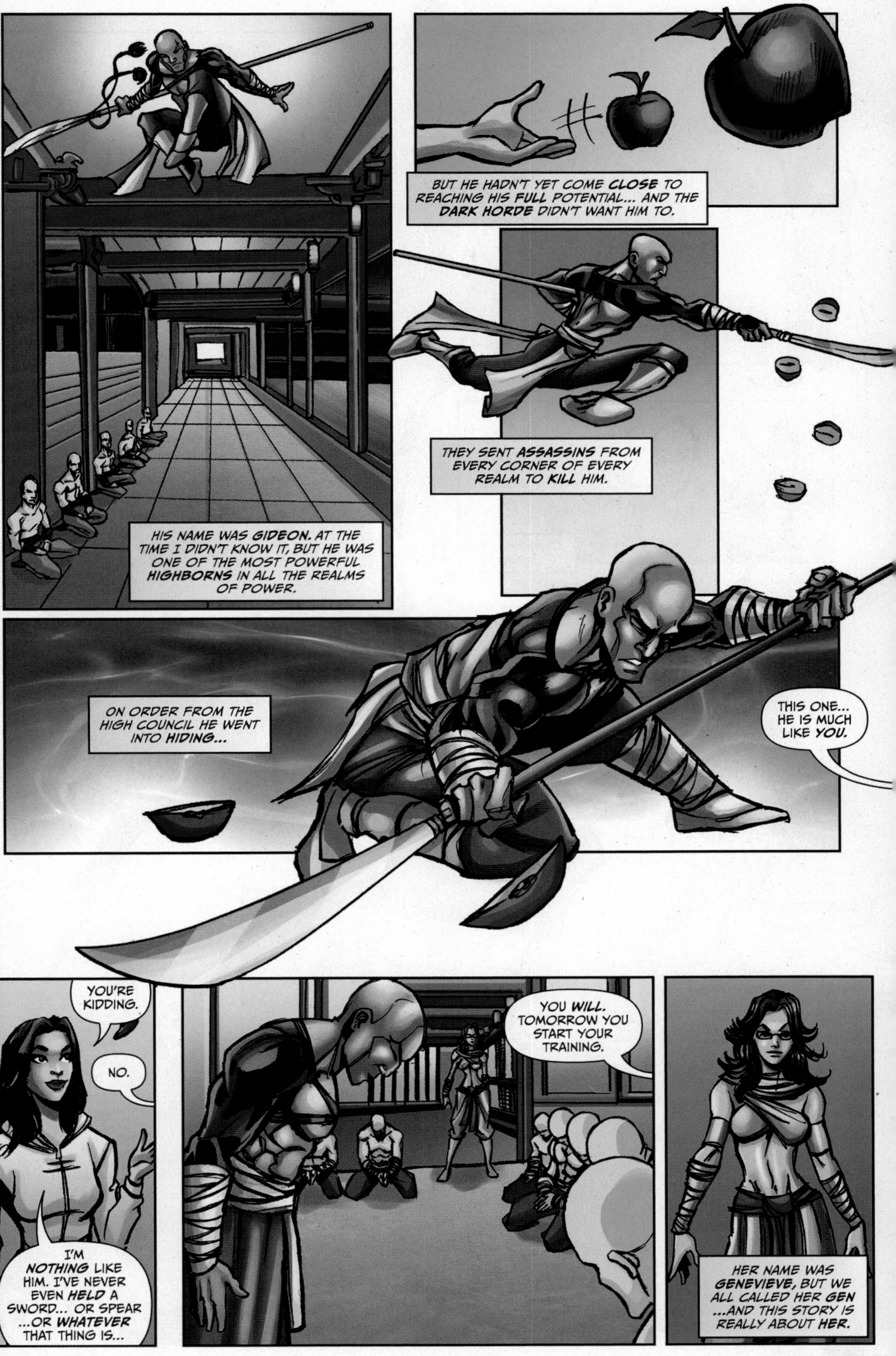
HIS NAME WAS GIDEON. AT THE TIME I DIDN'T KNOW IT, BUT HE WAS ONE OF THE MOST POWERFUL HIGHBORNS IN ALL THE REALMS OF POWER.
BUT HE HADN'T YET COME CLOSE TO REACHING HIS FULL POTENTIAL... AND THE DARK HORDE DIDN'T WANT HIM TO.
THEY SENT ASSASSINS FROM EVERY CORNER OF EVERY REALM TO KILL HIM.
ON ORDER FROM THE HIGH COUNCIL HE WENT INTO HIDING...
THIS ONE... HE IS MUCH LIKE YOU.
YOU'RE KIDDING.
NO.
I'M NOTHING LIKE HIM. I'VE NEVER EVEN HELD A SWORD... OR SPEAR ...OR WHATEVER THAT THING IS...
YOU WILL. TOMORROW YOU START YOUR TRAINING.
HER NAME WAS GENEVIEVE, BUT WE ALL CALLED HER GEN ...AND THIS STORY IS REALLY ABOUT HER.

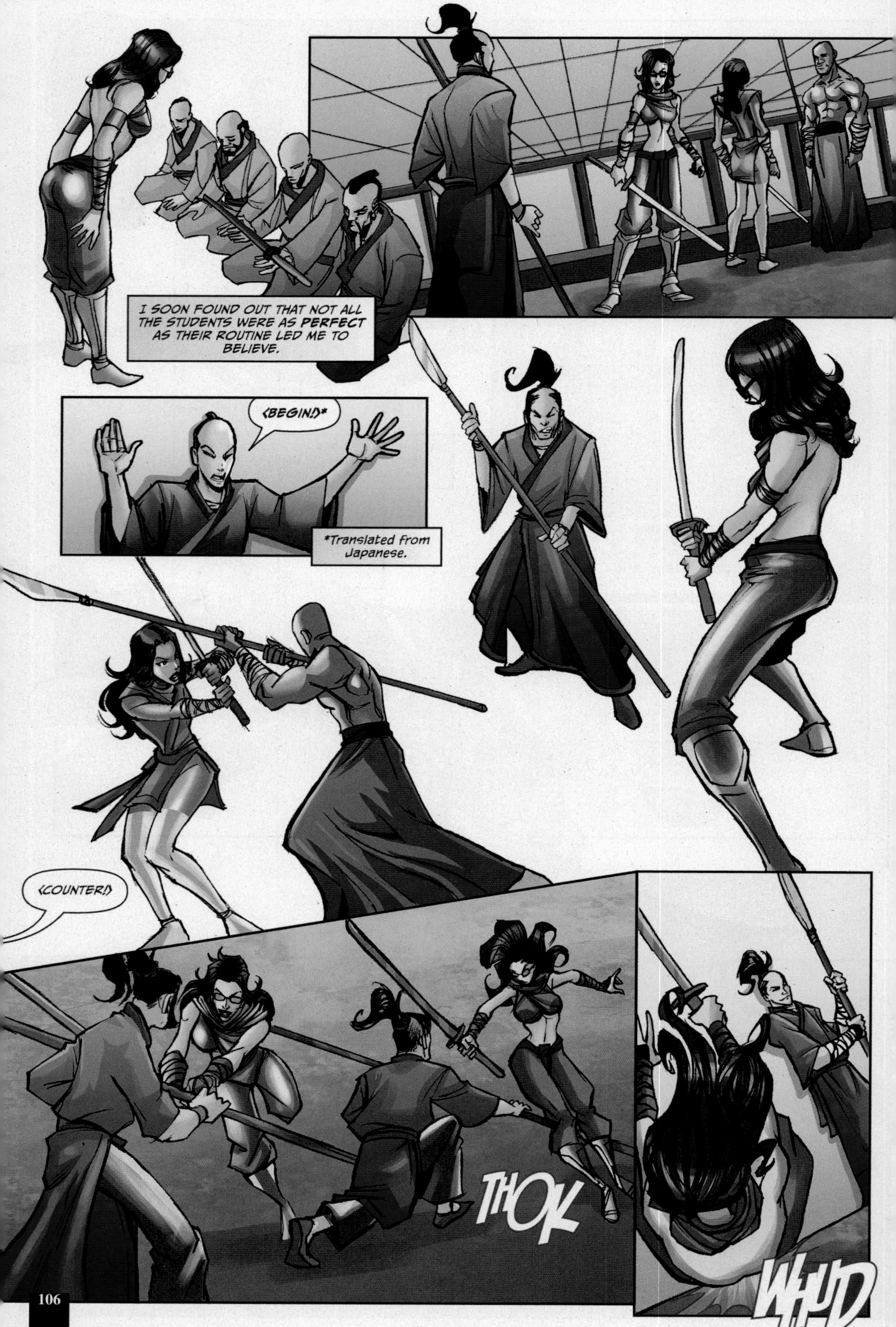
I SOON FOUND OUT THAT NOT ALL THE STUDENTS WERE AS PERFECT AS THEIR ROUTINE LED ME TO BELIEVE.
<BEGIN!>*
*Translated from Japanese.
<COUNTER!>
THOK
WHUD

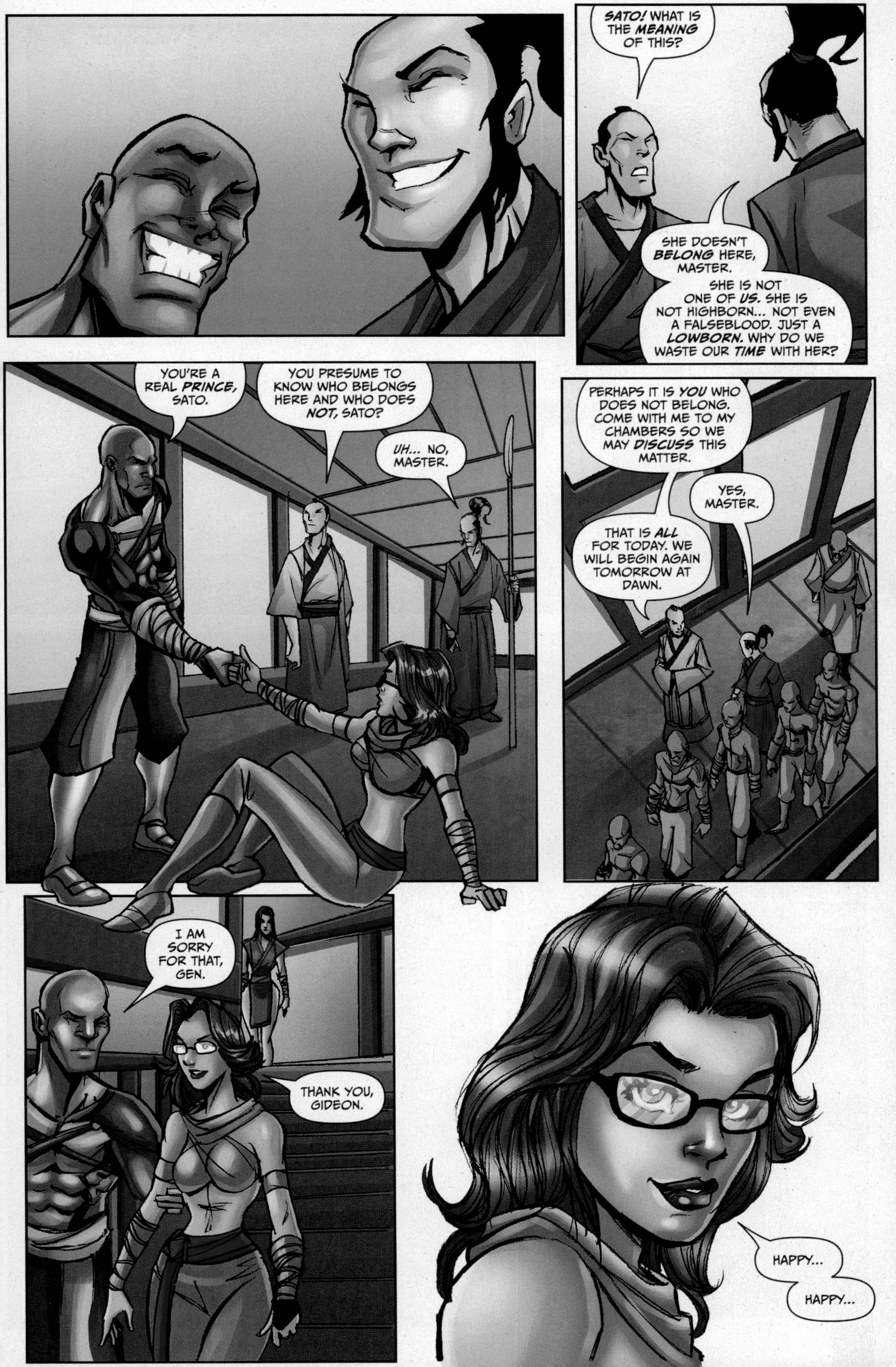
SATO! WHAT IS THE MEANING OF THIS?
SHE DOESN'T BELONG HERE, MASTER.
SHE IS NOT ONE OF US. SHE IS NOT HIGHBORN... NOT EVEN A FALSEBLOOD. JUST A LOWBORN. WHY DO WE WASTE OUR TIME WITH HER?
YOU'RE A REAL PRINCE, SATO.
YOU PRESUME TO KNOW WHO BELONGS HERE AND WHO DOES NOT, SATO?
UH... NO, MASTER.
PERHAPS IT IS YOU WHO DOES NOT BELONG. COME WITH ME TO MY CHAMBERS SO WE MAY DISCUSS THIS MATTER.
YES, MASTER.
THAT IS ALL FOR TODAY. WE WILL BEGIN AGAIN TOMORROW AT DAWN.
I AM SORRY FOR THAT, GEN.
THANK YOU, GIDEON.
HAPPY...
HAPPY...

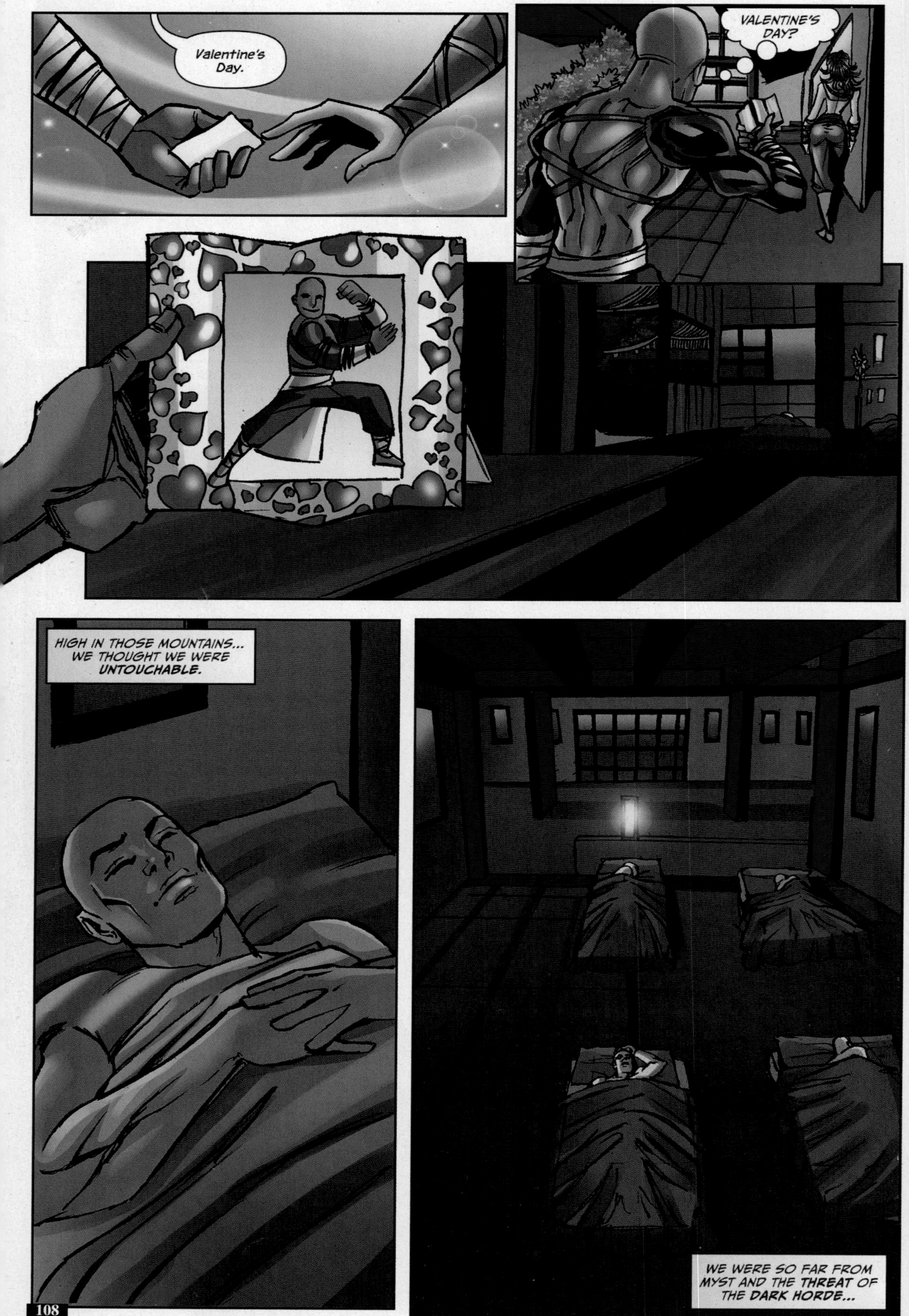

Valentine's Day.
VALENTINE'S DAY?
HIGH IN THOSE MOUNTAINS... WE THOUGHT WE WERE UNTOUCHABLE.
WE WERE SO FAR FROM MYST AND THE THREAT OF THE DARK HORDE...

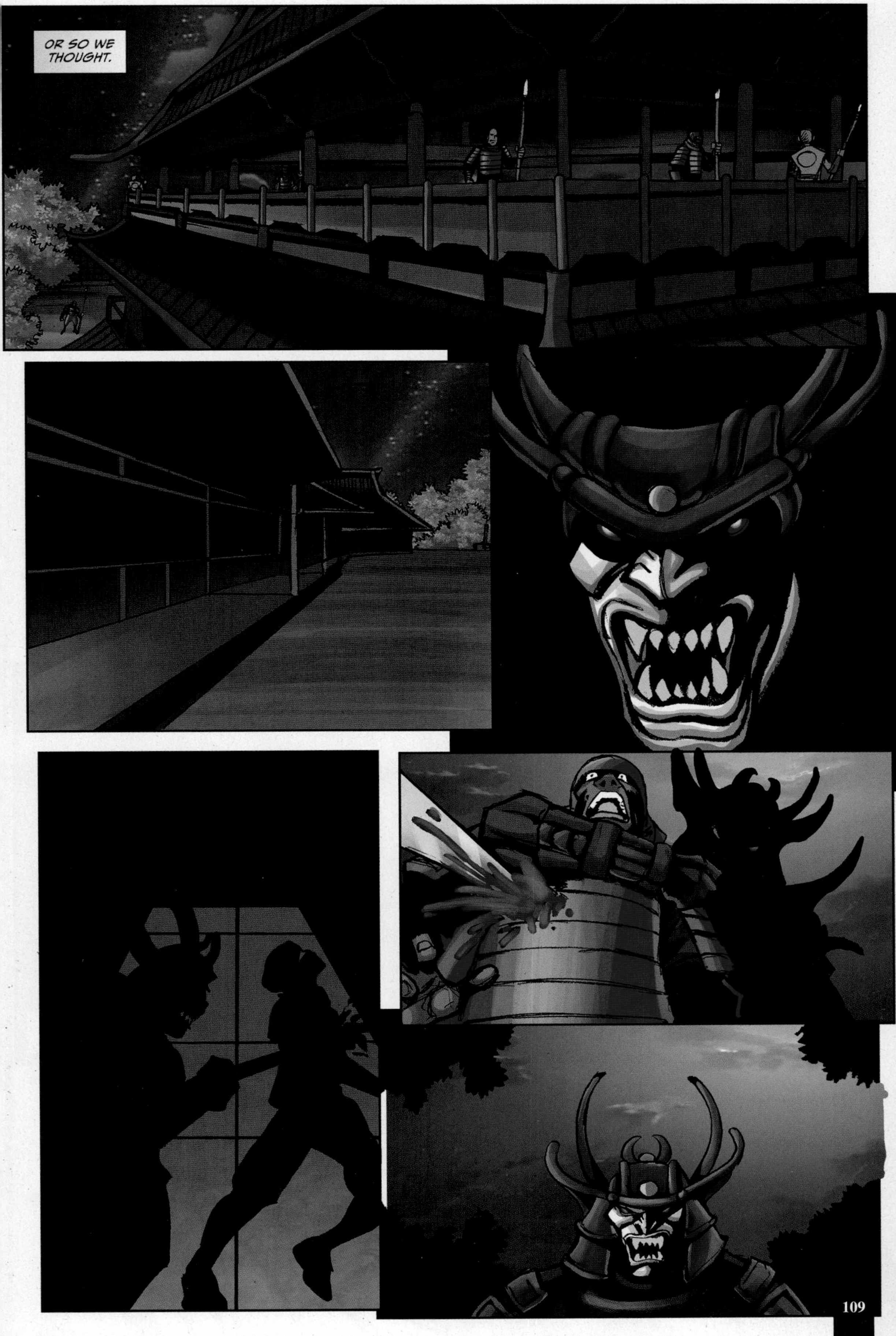
OR SO WE THOUGHT.

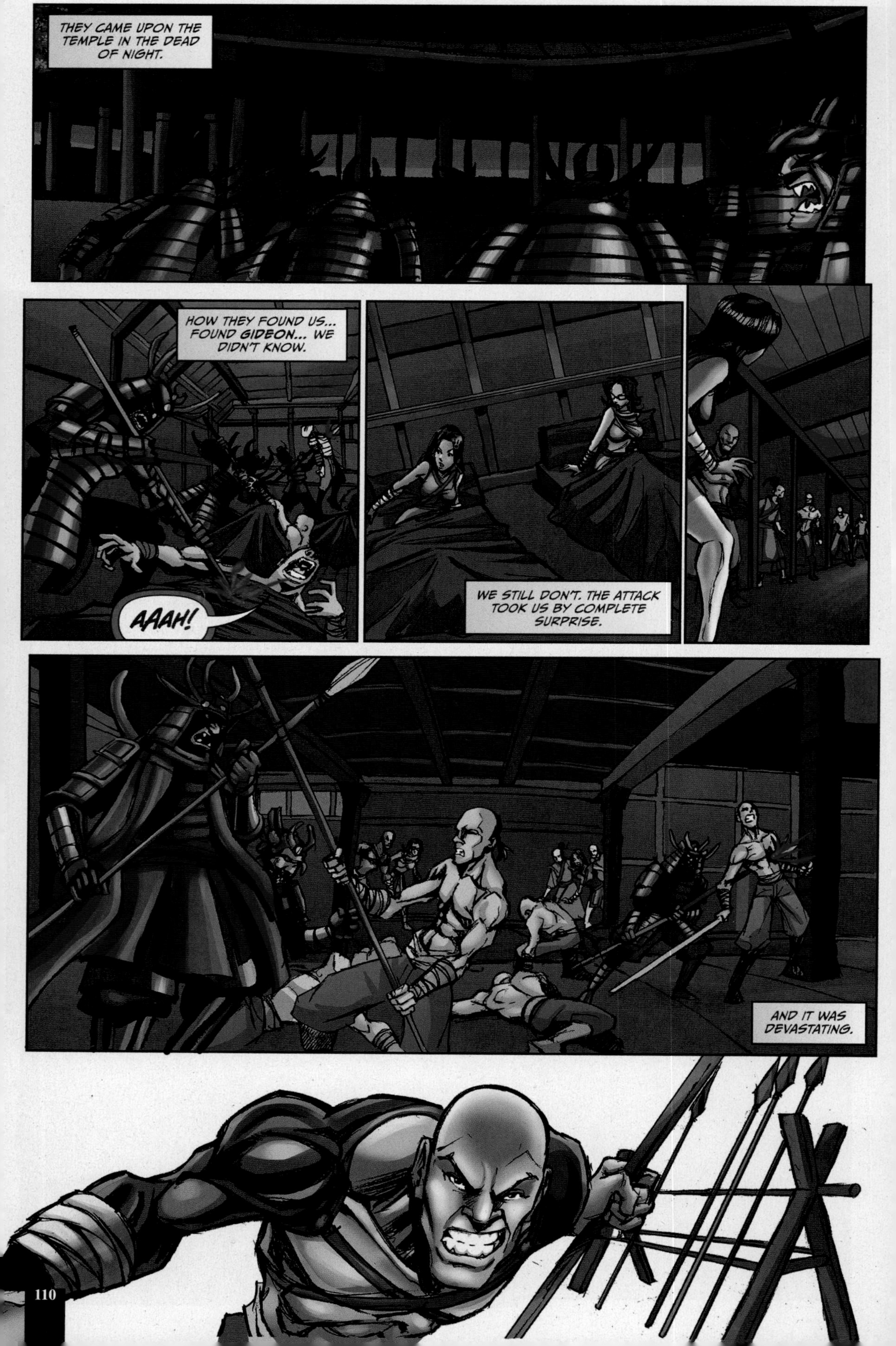
THEY CAME UPON THE TEMPLE IN THE DEAD OF NIGHT.
HOW THEY FOUND US... FOUND GIDEON... WE DIDN'T KNOW.
AAAH!
WE STILL DON'T. THE ATTACK TOOK US BY COMPLETE SURPRISE.
AND IT WAS DEVASTATING.

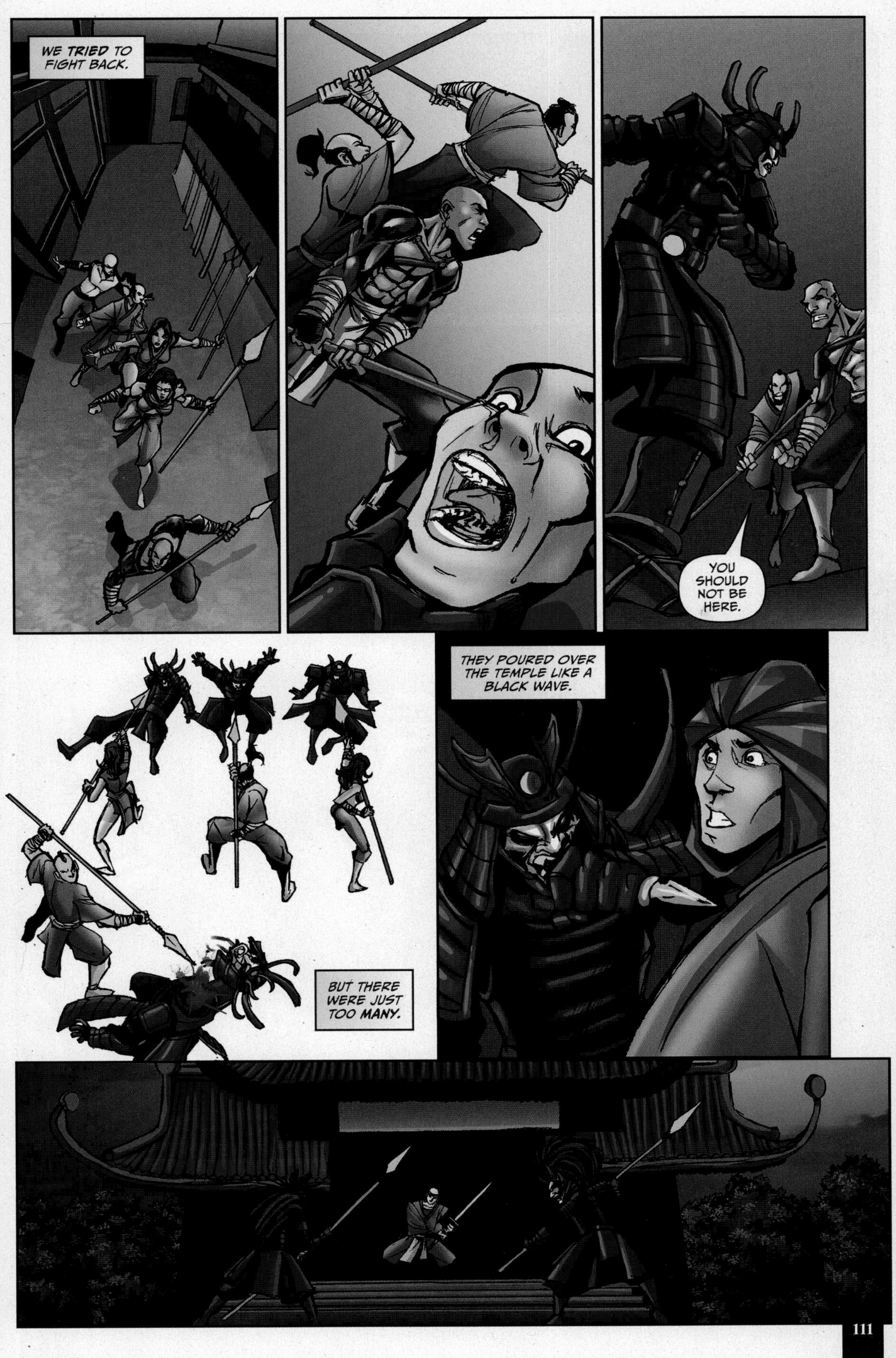
WE TRIED TO FIGHT BACK.
YOU SHOULD NOT BE HERE.
BUT THERE WERE JUST TOO MANY.
THEY POURED OVER THE TEMPLE LIKE A BLACK WAVE.

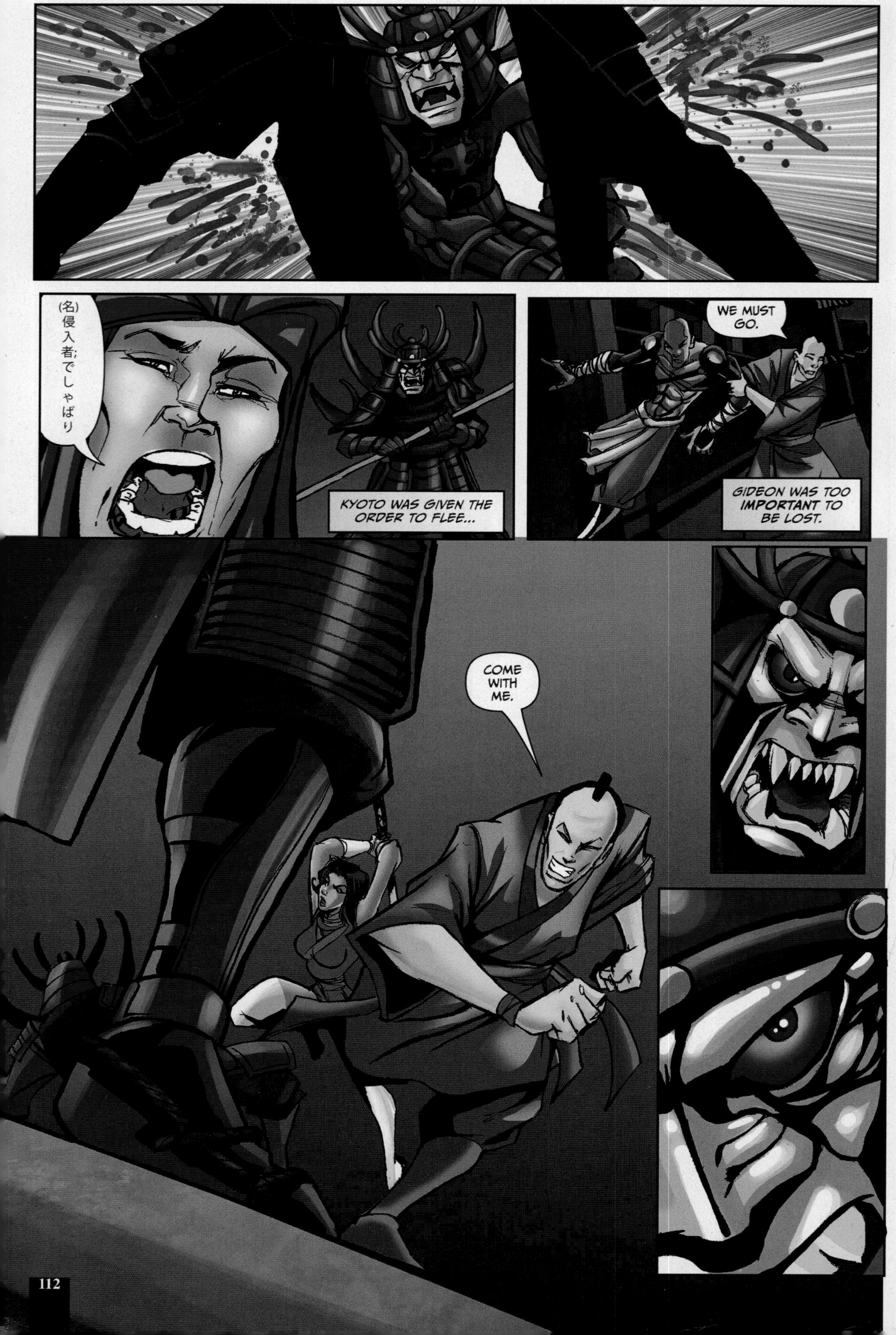
(名)侵入者;でしゃばり
KYOTO WAS GIVEN THE ORDER TO FLEE...
WE MUST GO.
GIDEON WAS TOO IMPORTANT TO BE LOST.
COME WITH ME.

SHZAAK

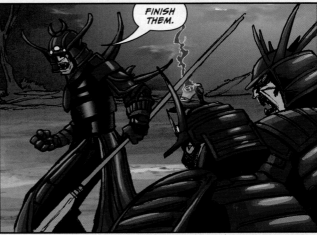

FINISH THEM.

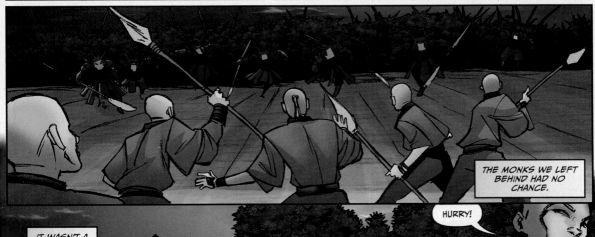

THE MONKS WE LEFT BEHIND HAD NO CHANCE.

IT WASN'T A BATTLE...

HURRY!

113

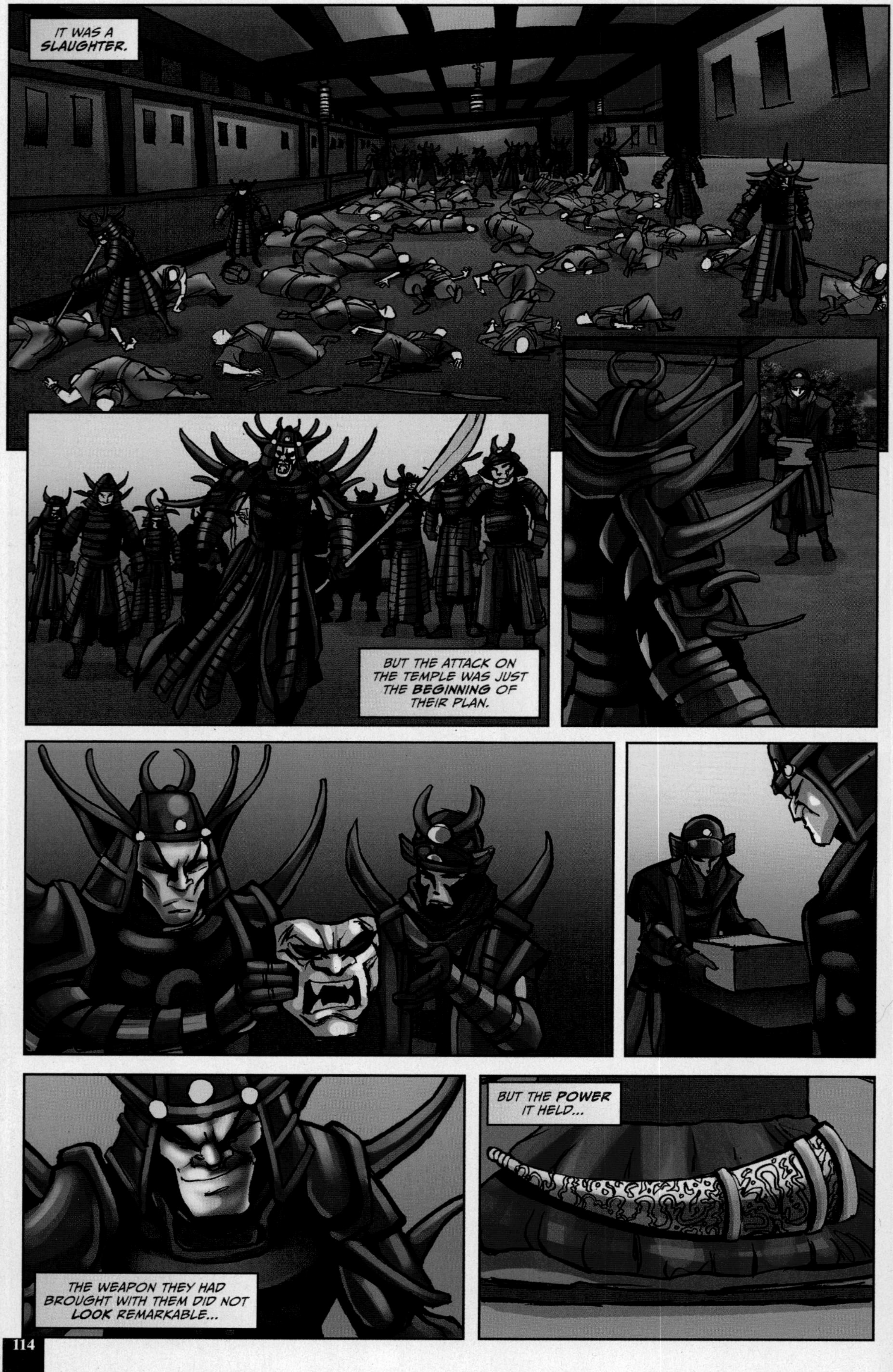
IT WAS A SLAUGHTER.
BUT THE ATTACK ON THE TEMPLE WAS JUST THE BEGINNING OF THEIR PLAN.
THE WEAPON THEY HAD BROUGHT WITH THEM DID NOT LOOK REMARKABLE...
BUT THE POWER IT HELD...

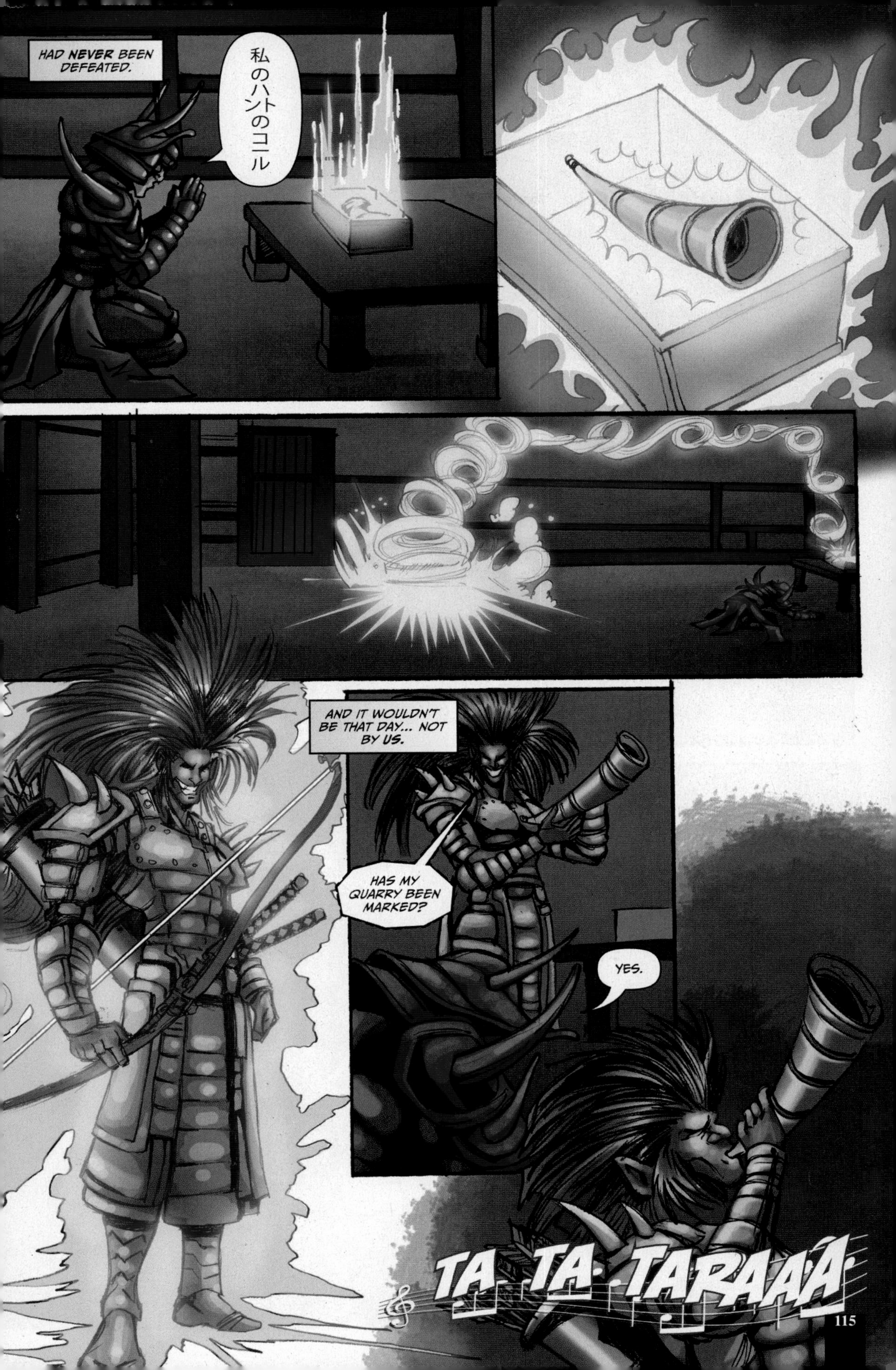
HAD NEVER BEEN DEFEATED.
私のハントのコル
AND IT WOULDN'T BE THAT DAY... NOT BY US.
HAS MY QUARRY BEEN MARKED?
YES.
TA TA TARAAA

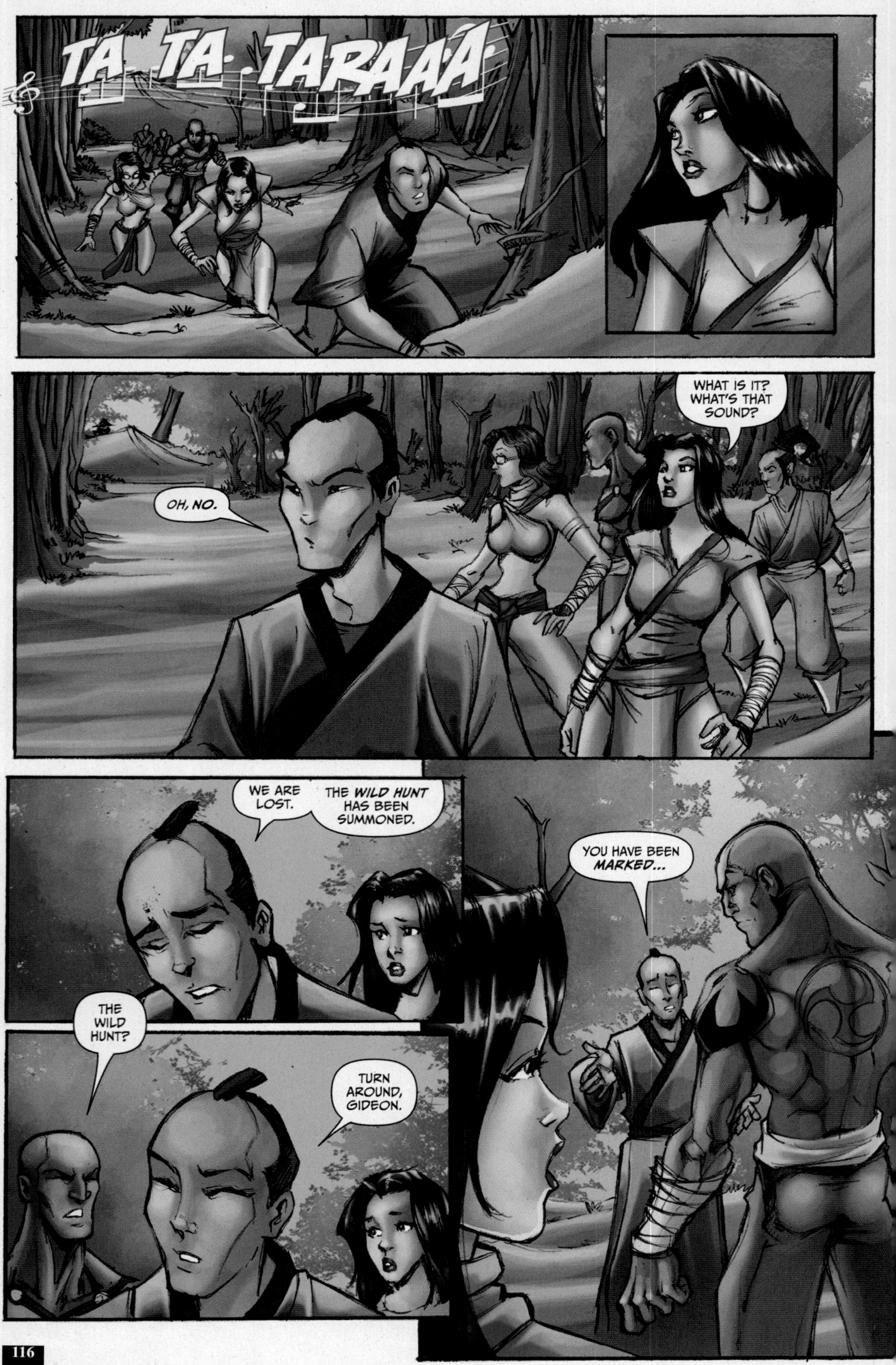
TA TA TARAAA
WHAT IS IT? WHAT'S THAT SOUND?
OH, NO.
WE ARE LOST.
THE WILD HUNT HAS BEEN SUMMONED.
YOU HAVE BEEN MARKED...
THE WILD HUNT?
TURN AROUND, GIDEON.

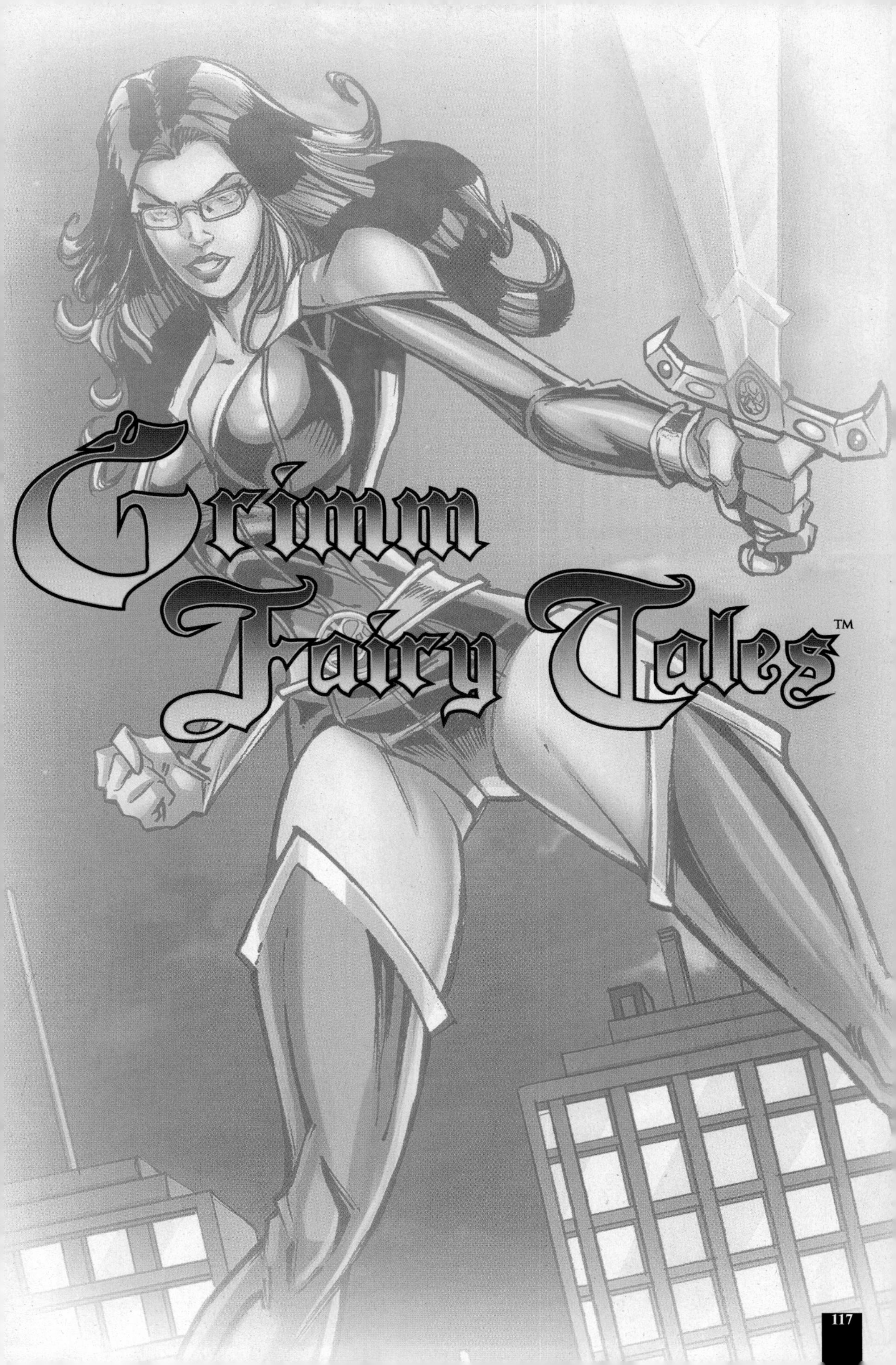
Grimm Fairy Tales™

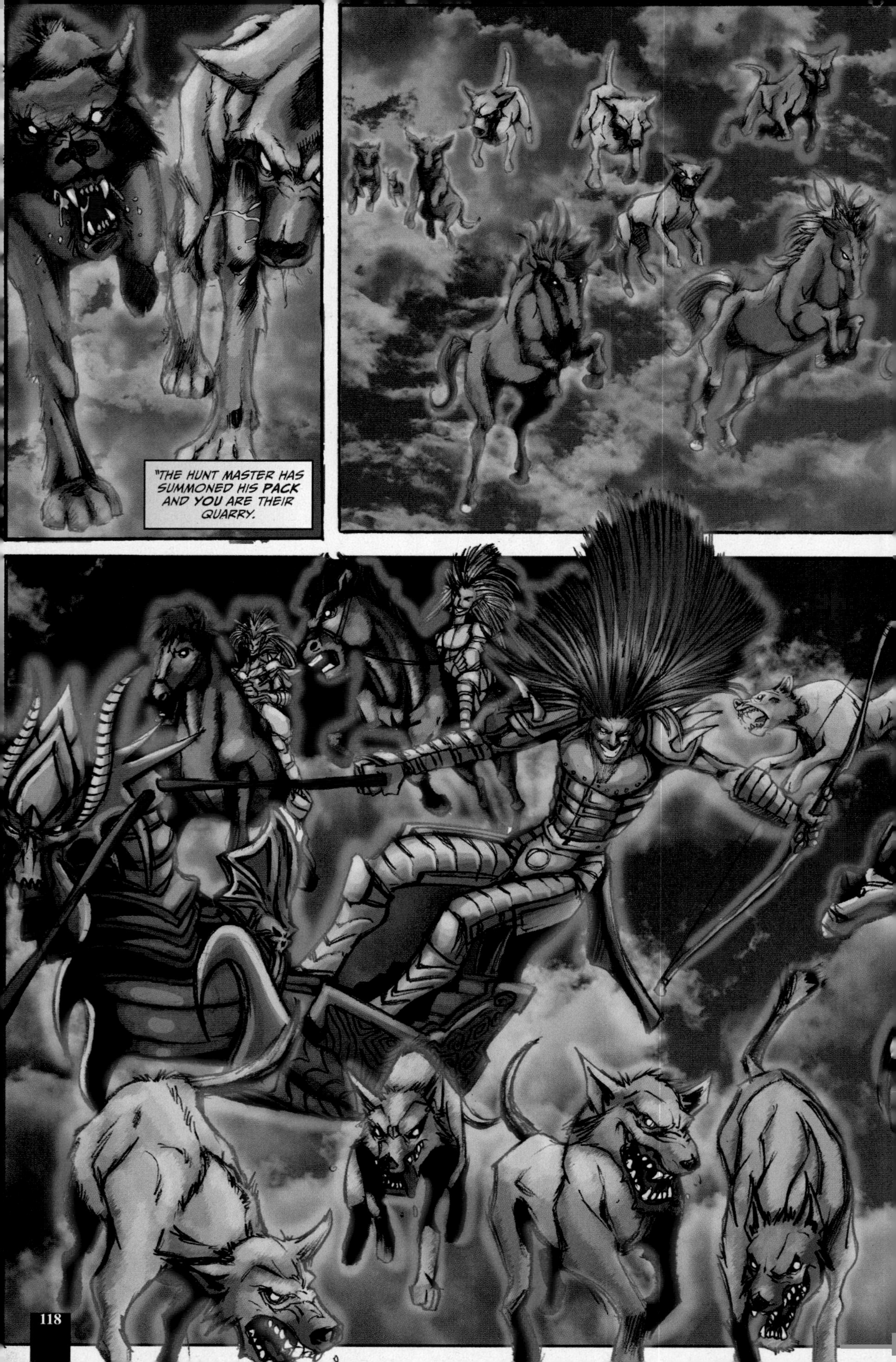
"THE HUNT MASTER HAS SUMMONED HIS PACK AND YOU ARE THEIR QUARRY.

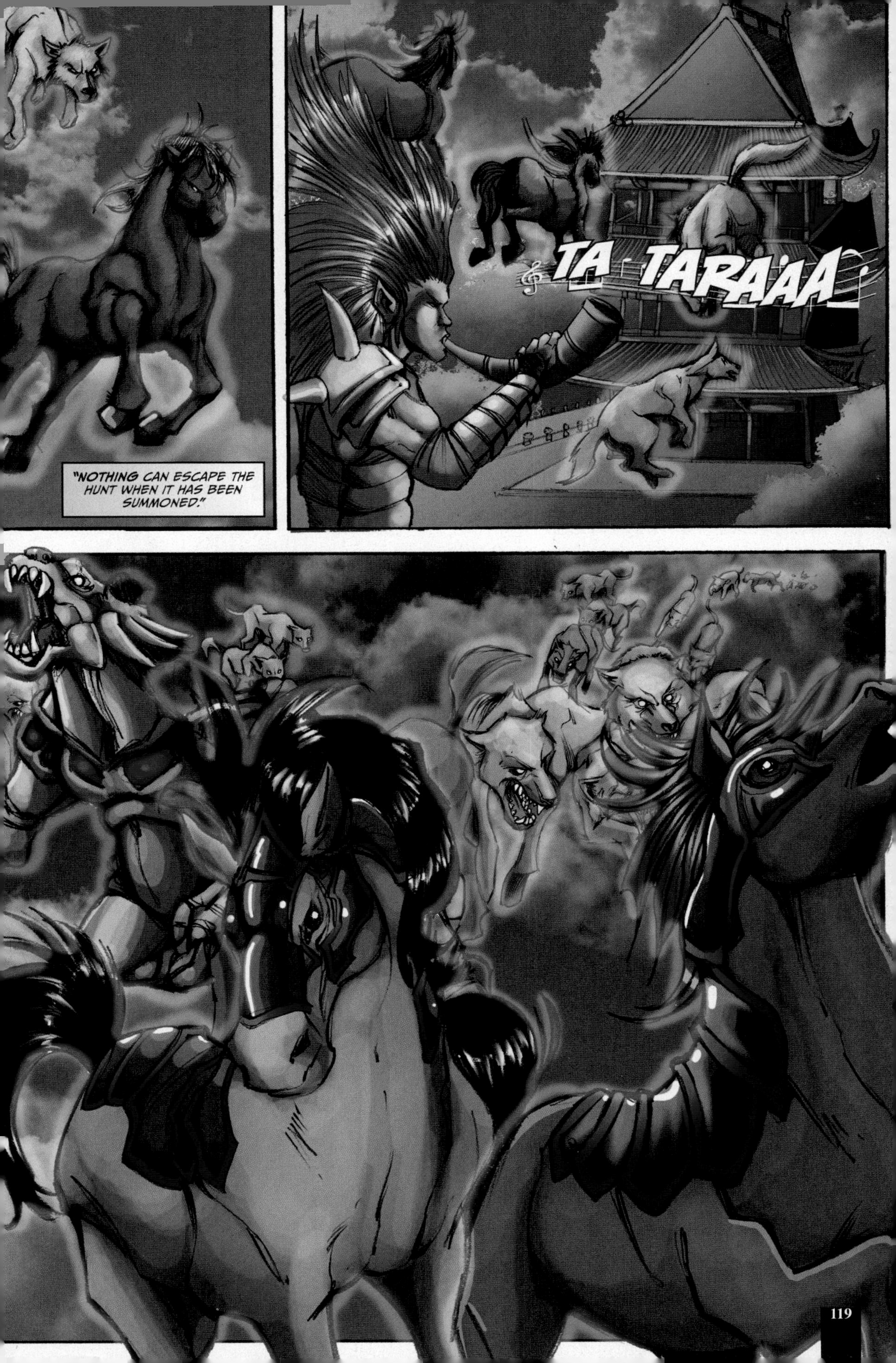
"NOTHING CAN ESCAPE THE HUNT WHEN IT HAS BEEN SUMMONED."
TA TARAAA

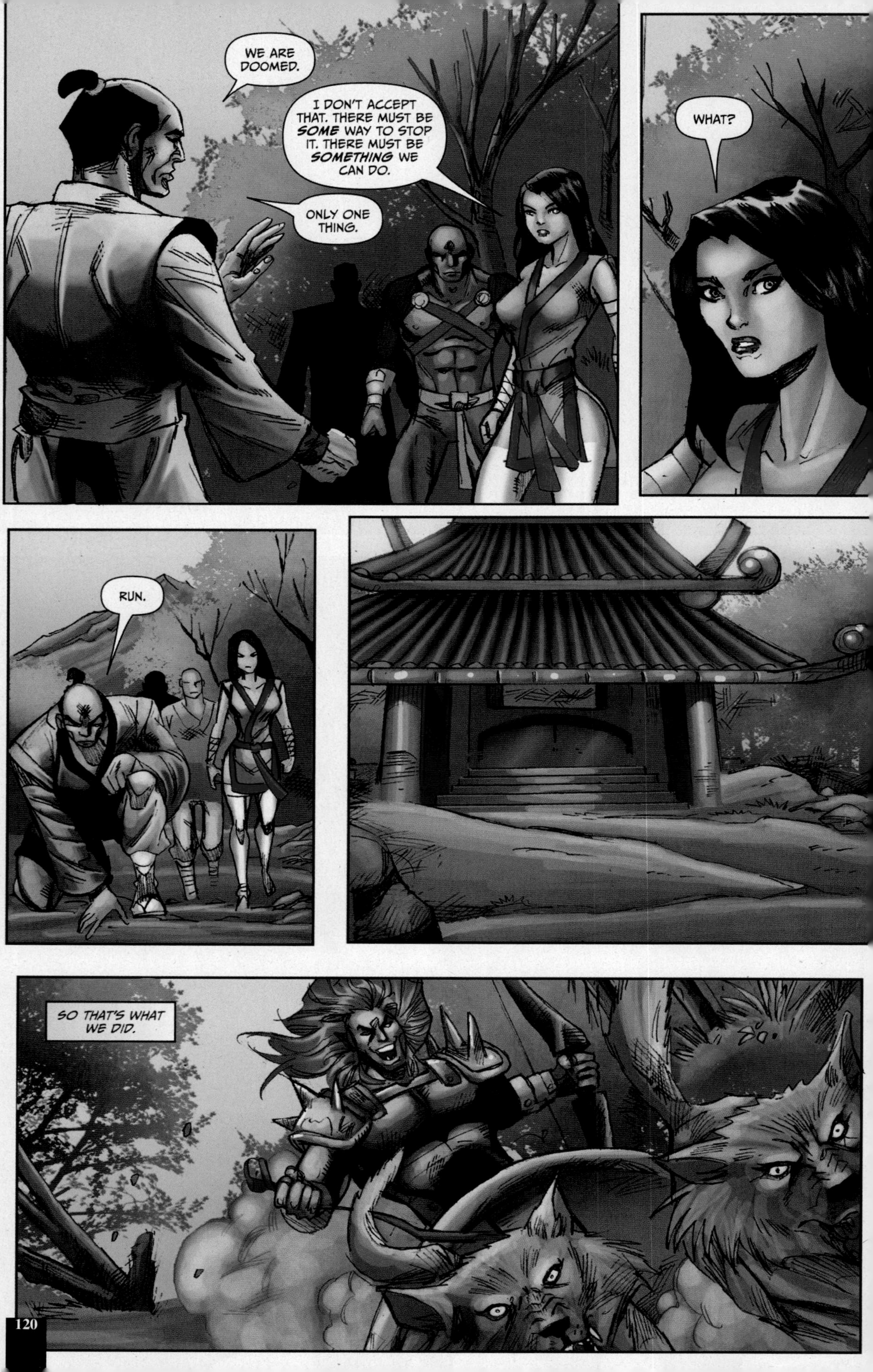
WE ARE DOOMED.
I DON'T ACCEPT THAT. THERE MUST BE SOME WAY TO STOP IT. THERE MUST BE SOMETHING WE CAN DO.
ONLY ONE THING.
WHAT?
RUN.
SO THAT'S WHAT WE DID.

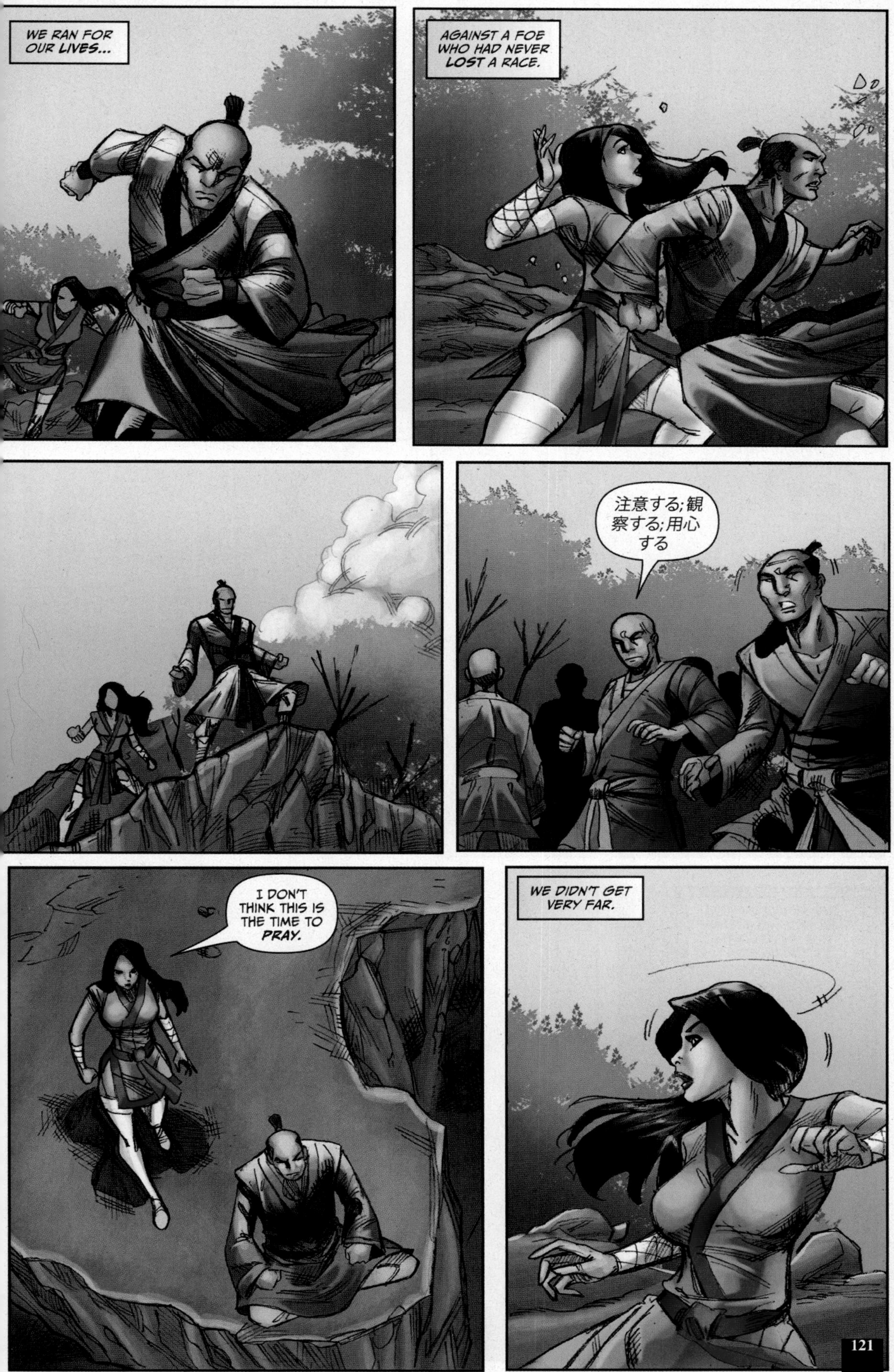
WE RAN FOR OUR LIVES...
AGAINST A FOE WHO HAD NEVER LOST A RACE.
注意する;観察する;用心する
I DON'T THINK THIS IS THE TIME TO PRAY.
WE DIDN'T GET VERY FAR.

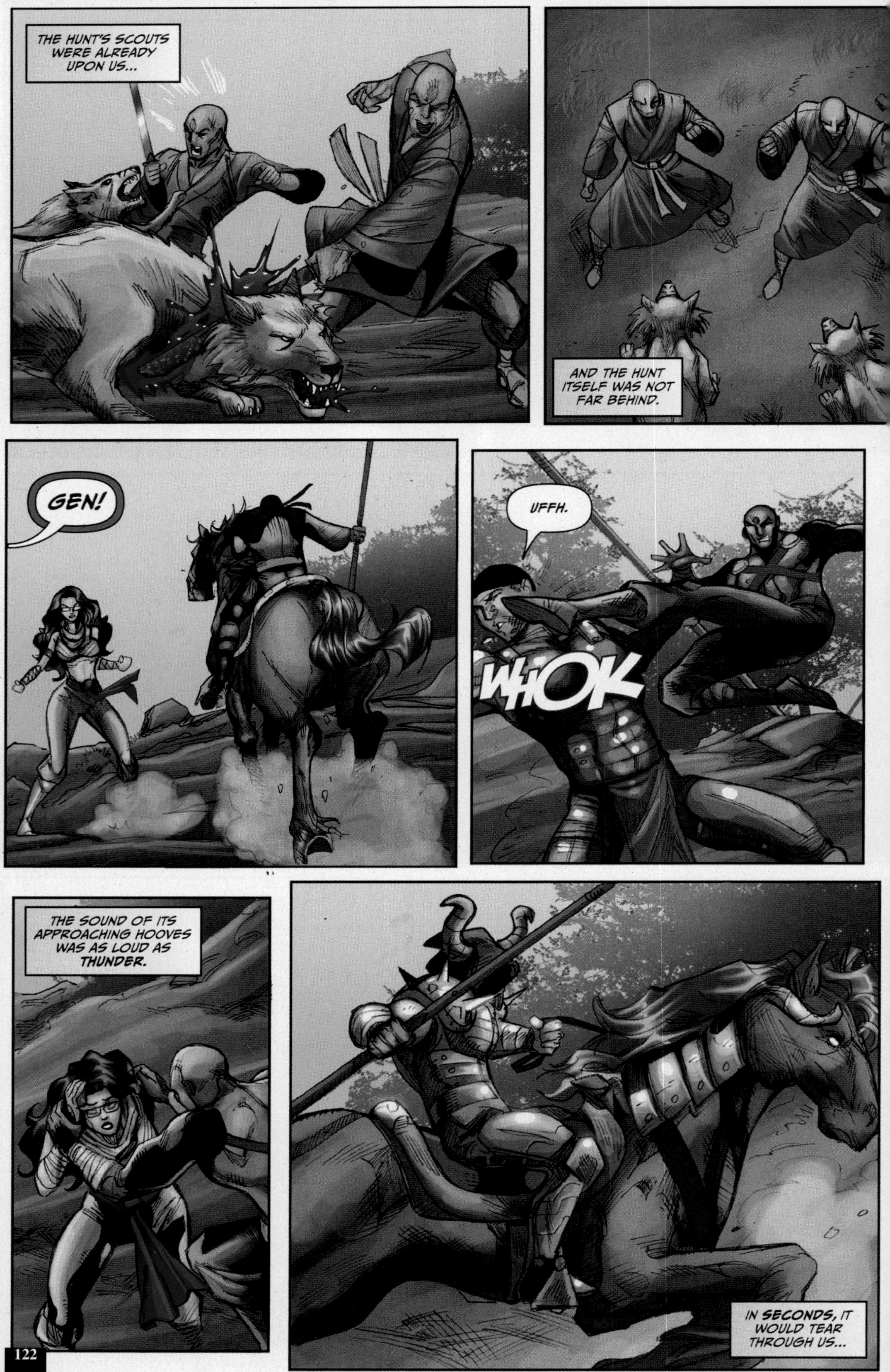
THE HUNT'S SCOUTS WERE ALREADY UPON US...
AND THE HUNT ITSELF WAS NOT FAR BEHIND.
GEN!
UFFH.
WHOK
THE SOUND OF ITS APPROACHING HOOVES WAS AS LOUD AS THUNDER.
IN SECONDS, IT WOULD TEAR THROUGH US...

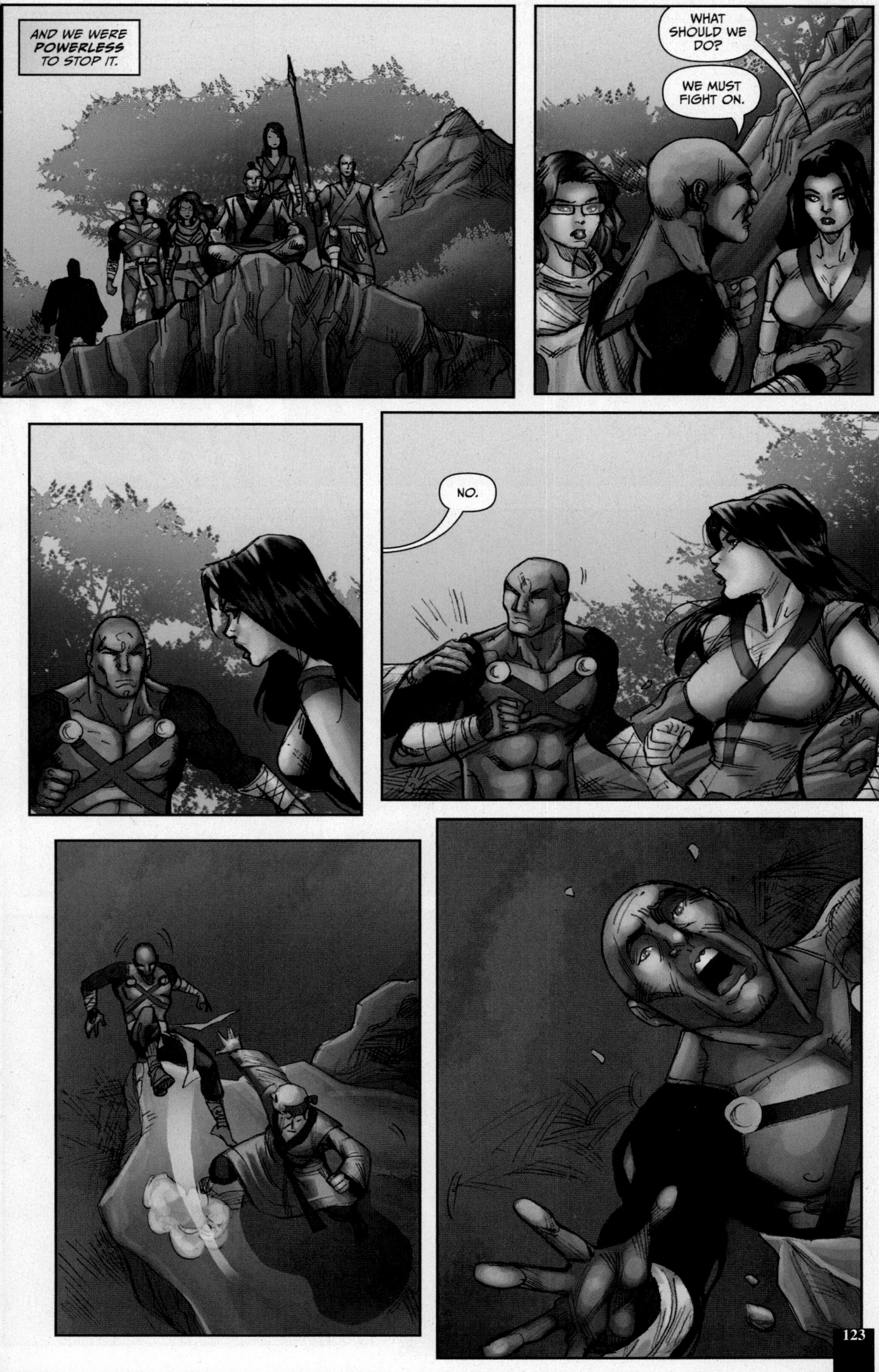
AND WE WERE POWERLESS TO STOP IT.
WHAT SHOULD WE DO?
WE MUST FIGHT ON.
NO.

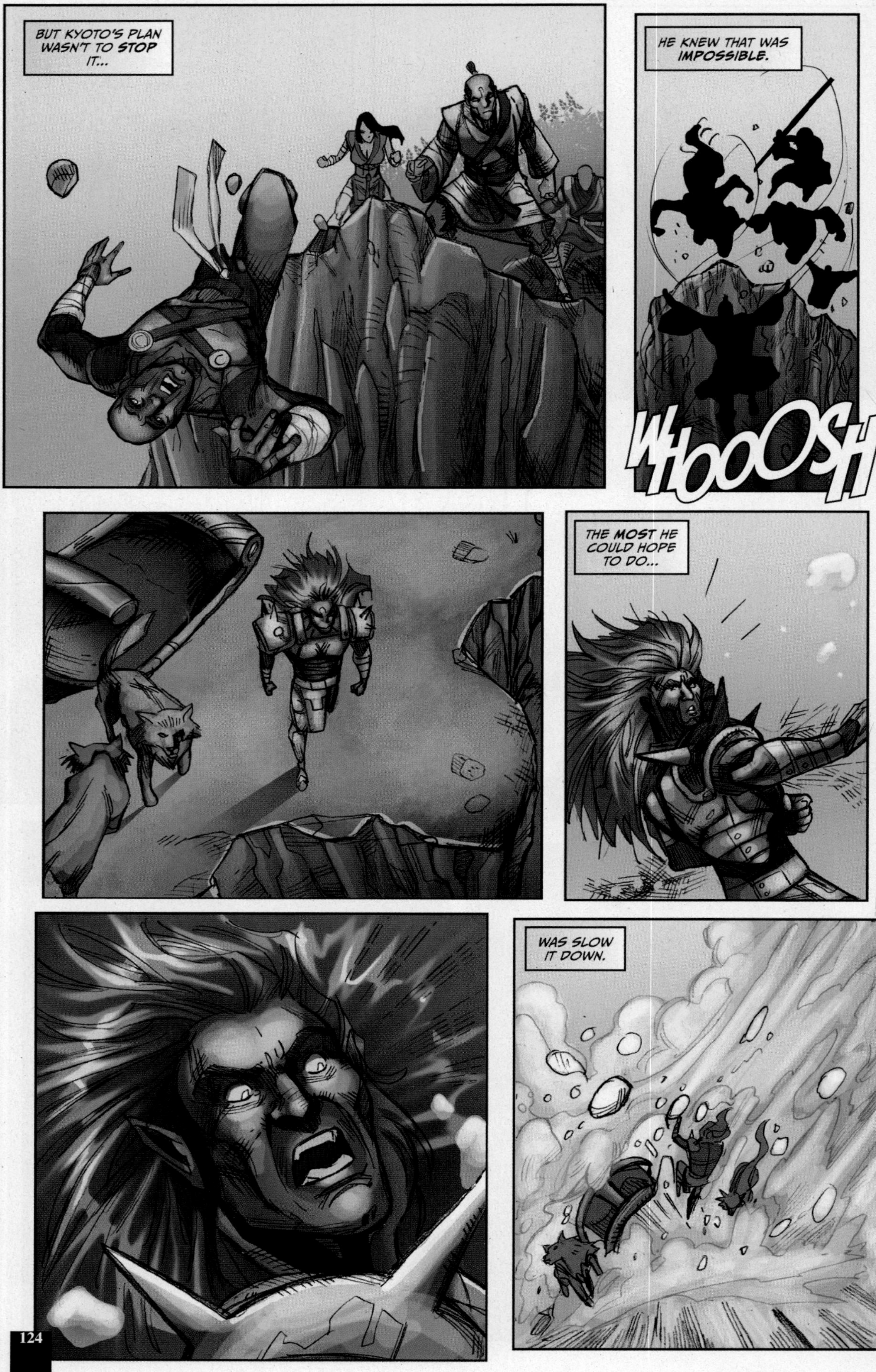

BUT KYOTO'S PLAN WASN'T TO STOP IT...
HE KNEW THAT WAS IMPOSSIBLE.
WHOOOSH
THE MOST HE COULD HOPE TO DO...
WAS SLOW IT DOWN.

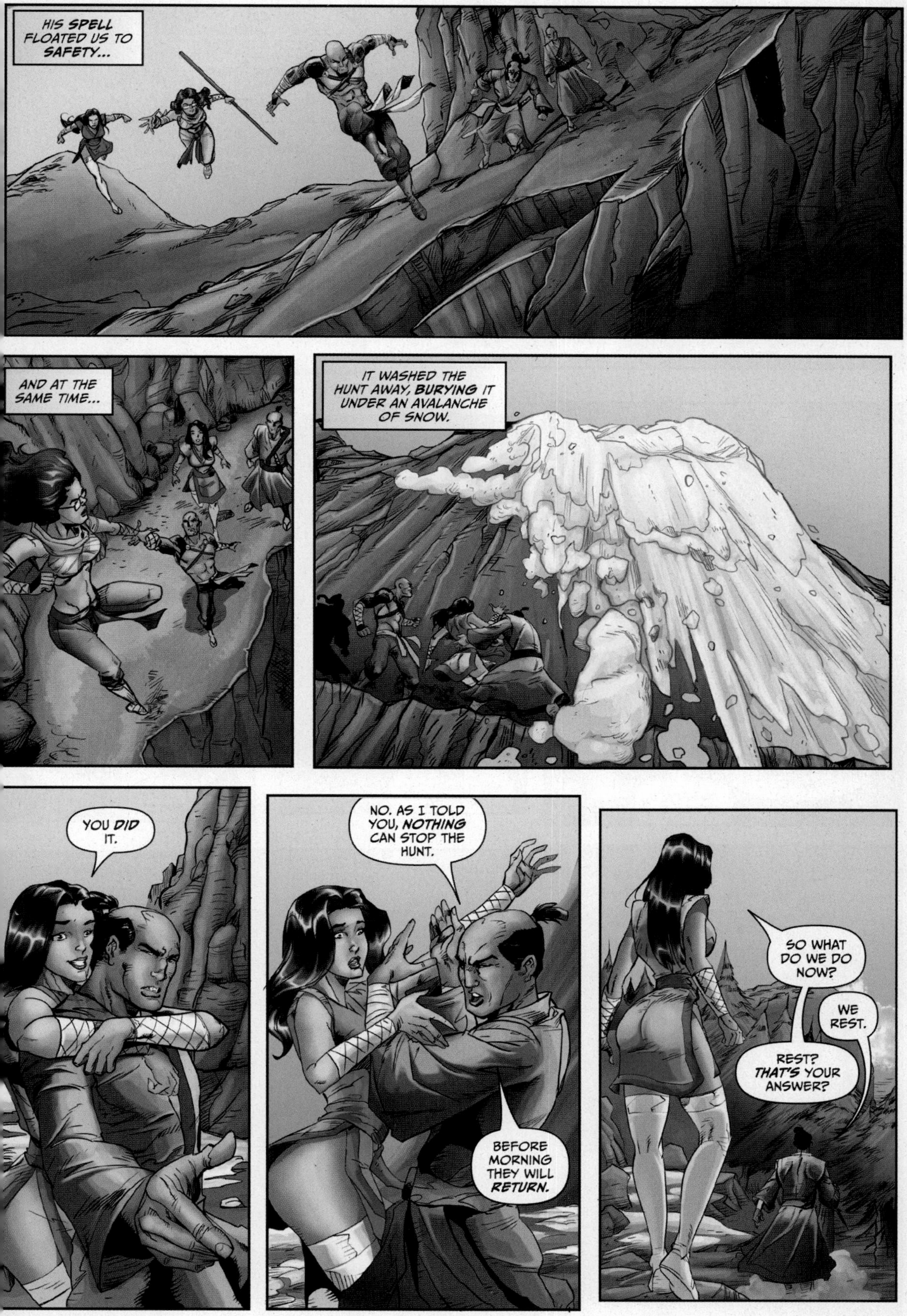

HIS SPELL FLOATED US TO SAFETY...
AND AT THE SAME TIME...
IT WASHED THE HUNT AWAY, BURYING IT UNDER AN AVALANCHE OF SNOW.
YOU DID IT.
NO. AS I TOLD YOU, NOTHING CAN STOP THE HUNT.
BEFORE MORNING THEY WILL RETURN.
SO WHAT DO WE DO NOW?
WE REST.
REST? THAT'S YOUR ANSWER?

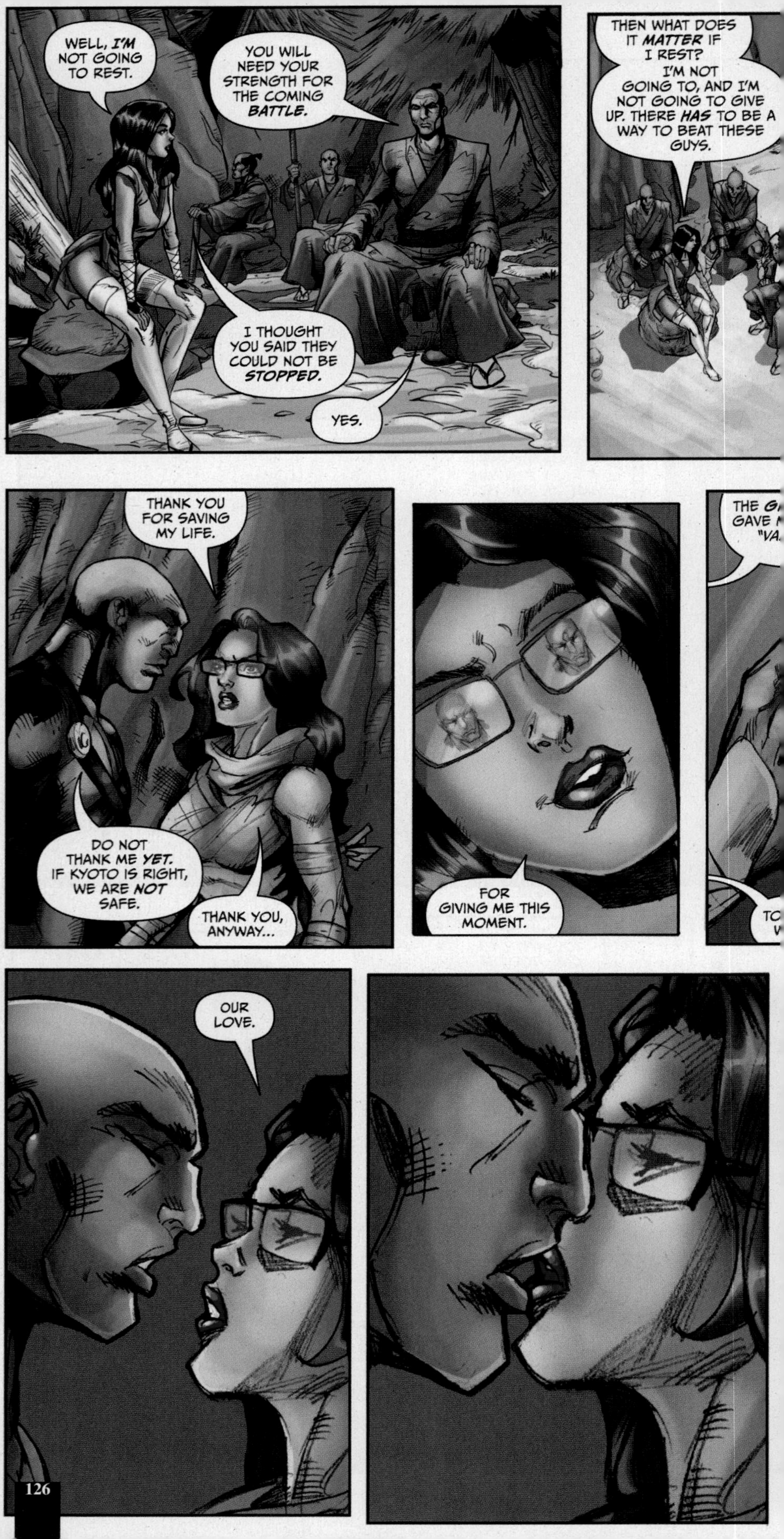
WELL, *I'M* NOT GOING TO REST.
YOU WILL NEED YOUR STRENGTH FOR THE COMING *BATTLE.*
I THOUGHT YOU SAID THEY COULD NOT BE *STOPPED.*
YES.
THEN WHAT DOES IT *MATTER* IF I REST?
I'M NOT GOING TO, AND I'M NOT GOING TO GIVE UP. THERE *HAS* TO BE A WAY TO BEAT THESE GUYS.
THANK YOU FOR SAVING MY LIFE.
DO NOT THANK ME *YET.* IF KYOTO IS RIGHT, WE ARE *NOT* SAFE.
THANK YOU, ANYWAY...
FOR GIVING ME THIS MOMENT.
THE
OUR LOVE.

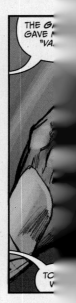

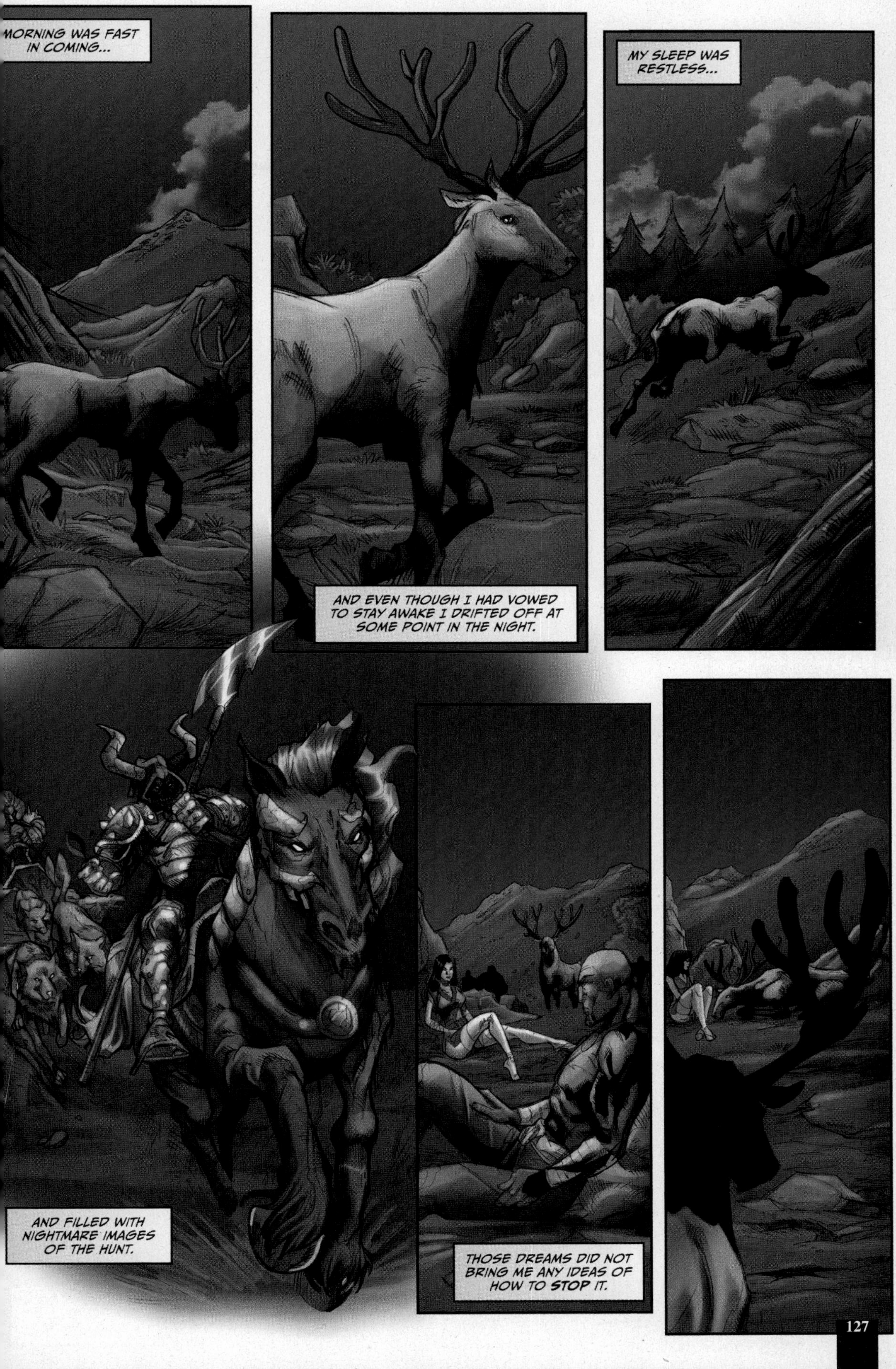
MORNING WAS FAST IN COMING...
AND EVEN THOUGH I HAD VOWED TO STAY AWAKE I DRIFTED OFF AT SOME POINT IN THE NIGHT.
MY SLEEP WAS RESTLESS...
AND FILLED WITH NIGHTMARE IMAGES OF THE HUNT.
THOSE DREAMS DID NOT BRING ME ANY IDEAS OF HOW TO STOP IT.

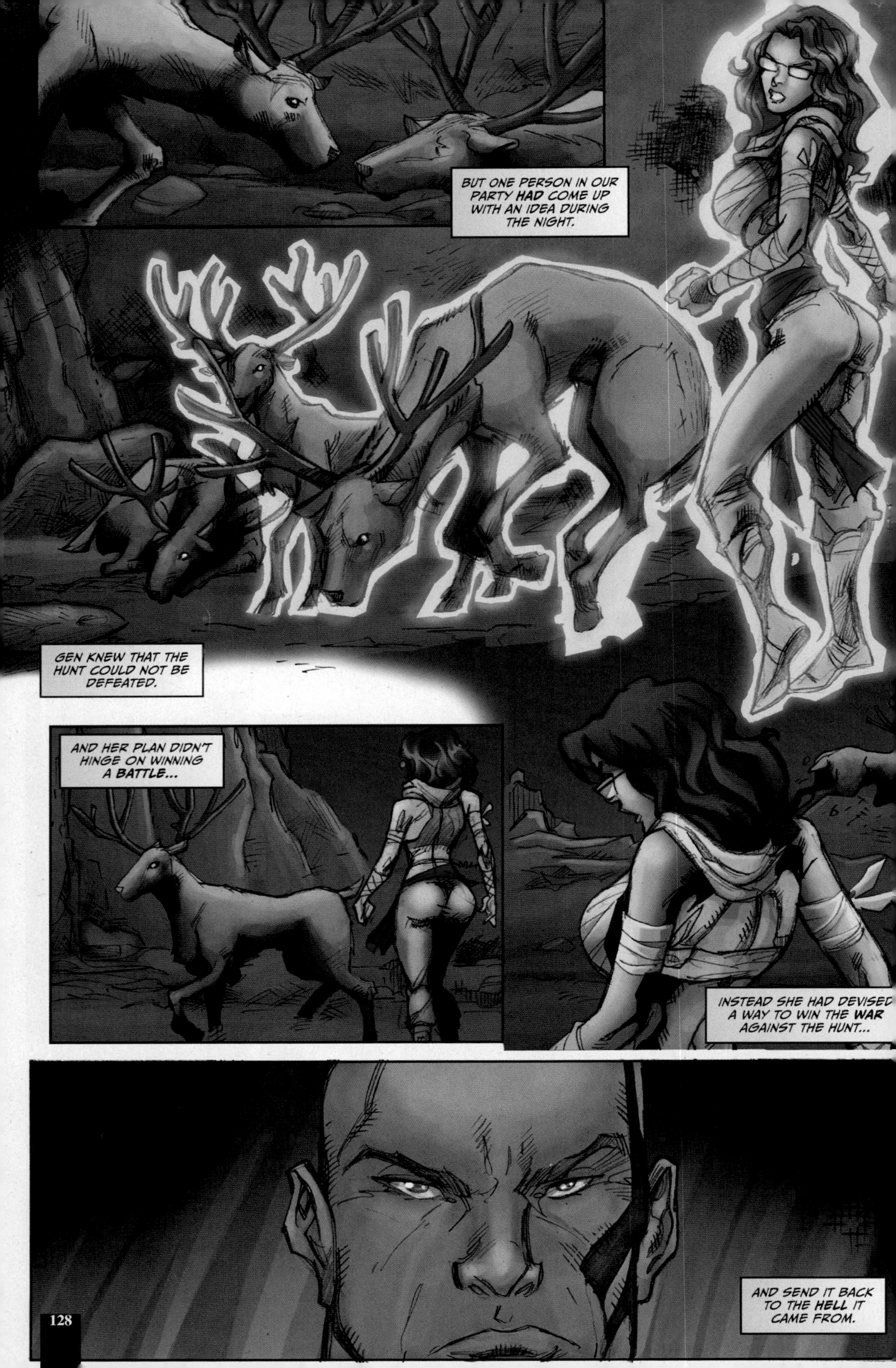
BUT ONE PERSON IN OUR PARTY HAD COME UP WITH AN IDEA DURING THE NIGHT.
GEN KNEW THAT THE HUNT COULD NOT BE DEFEATED.
AND HER PLAN DIDN'T HINGE ON WINNING A BATTLE...
INSTEAD SHE HAD DEVISED A WAY TO WIN THE WAR AGAINST THE HUNT...
AND SEND IT BACK TO THE HELL IT CAME FROM.

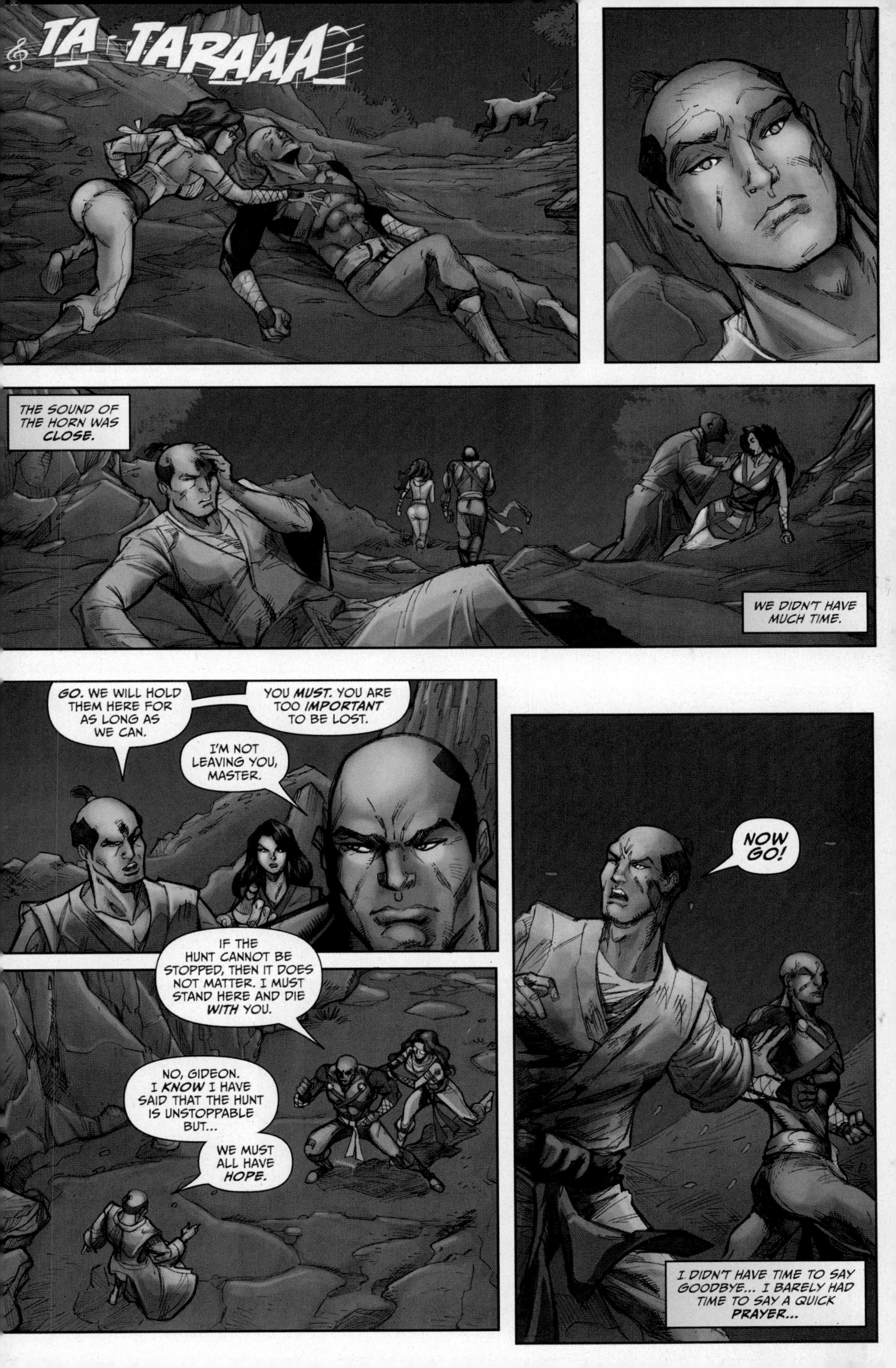
TA-TARAAA
THE SOUND OF THE HORN WAS CLOSE.
WE DIDN'T HAVE MUCH TIME.
GO. WE WILL HOLD THEM HERE FOR AS LONG AS WE CAN.
YOU MUST. YOU ARE TOO IMPORTANT TO BE LOST.
I'M NOT LEAVING YOU, MASTER.
IF THE HUNT CANNOT BE STOPPED, THEN IT DOES NOT MATTER. I MUST STAND HERE AND DIE WITH YOU.
NO, GIDEON. I KNOW I HAVE SAID THAT THE HUNT IS UNSTOPPABLE BUT...
WE MUST ALL HAVE HOPE.
NOW GO!
I DIDN'T HAVE TIME TO SAY GOODBYE... I BARELY HAD TIME TO SAY A QUICK PRAYER...

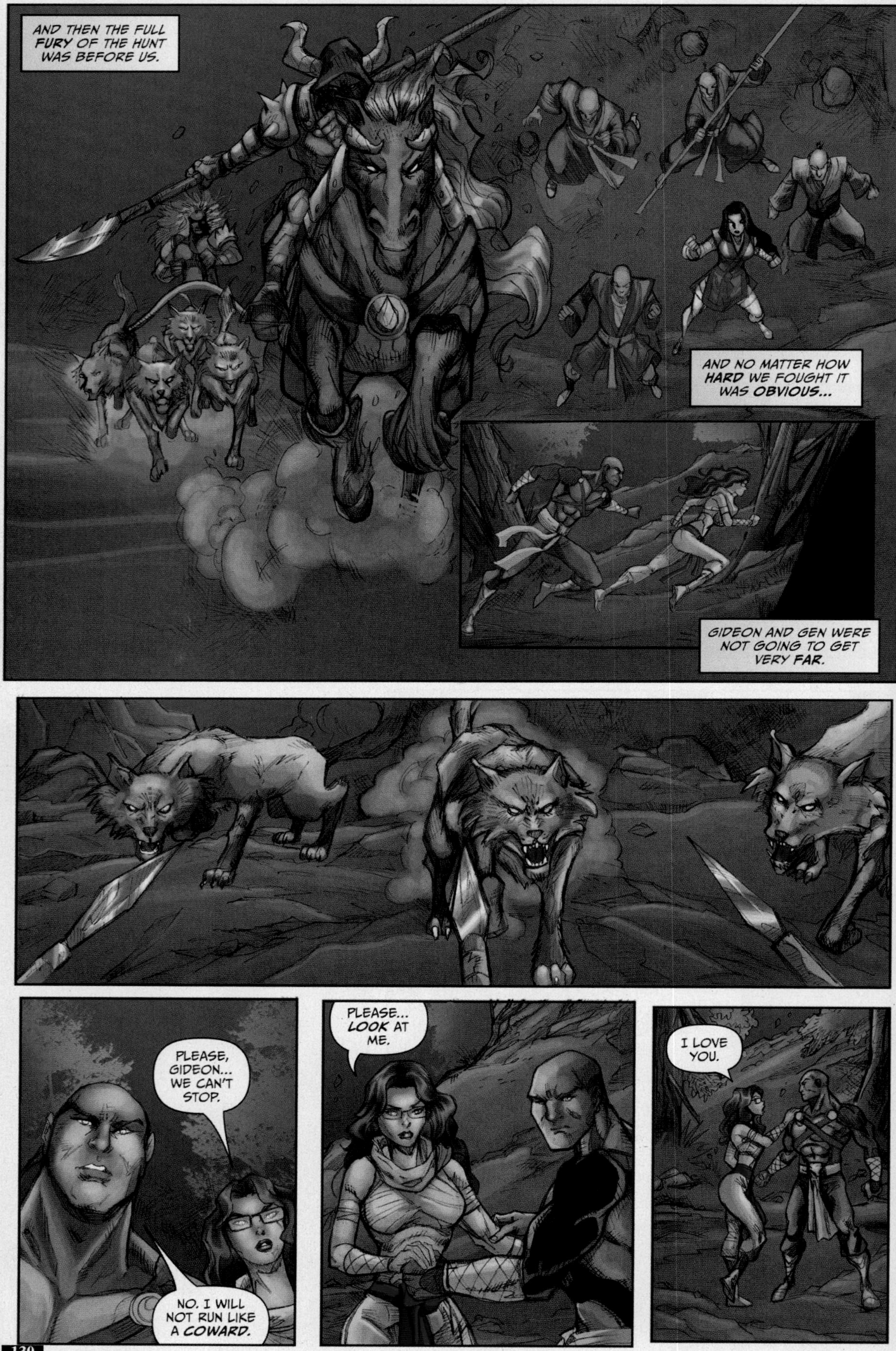
AND THEN THE FULL FURY OF THE HUNT WAS BEFORE US.
AND NO MATTER HOW HARD WE FOUGHT IT WAS OBVIOUS...
GIDEON AND GEN WERE NOT GOING TO GET VERY FAR.
PLEASE, GIDEON... WE CAN'T STOP.
NO. I WILL NOT RUN LIKE A COWARD.
PLEASE... LOOK AT ME.
I LOVE YOU.

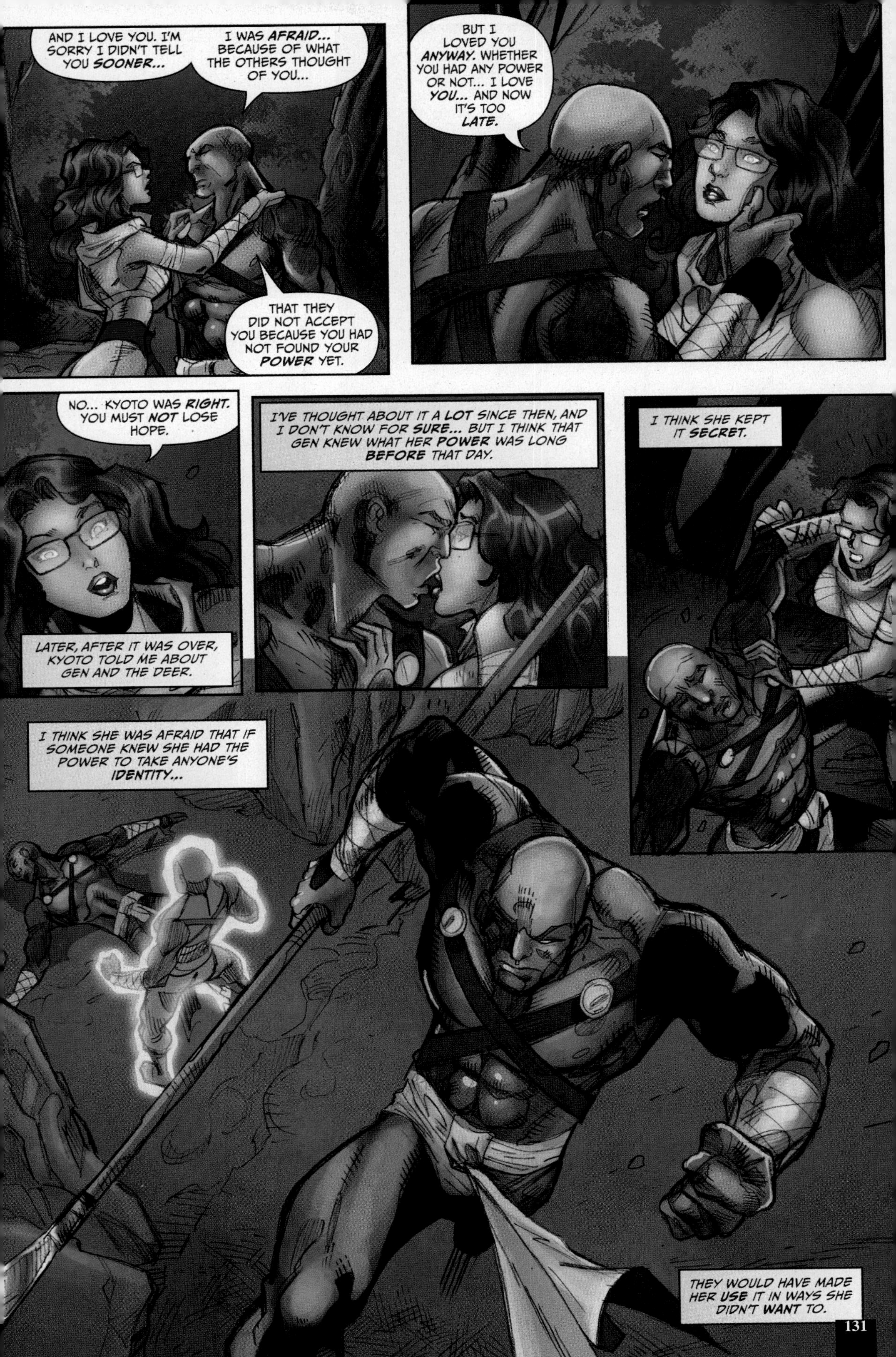
AND I LOVE YOU. I'M SORRY I DIDN'T TELL YOU SOONER...
I WAS AFRAID... BECAUSE OF WHAT THE OTHERS THOUGHT OF YOU...
THAT THEY DID NOT ACCEPT YOU BECAUSE YOU HAD NOT FOUND YOUR POWER YET.
BUT I LOVED YOU ANYWAY. WHETHER YOU HAD ANY POWER OR NOT... I LOVE YOU... AND NOW IT'S TOO LATE.
NO... KYOTO WAS RIGHT. YOU MUST NOT LOSE HOPE.
LATER, AFTER IT WAS OVER, KYOTO TOLD ME ABOUT GEN AND THE DEER.
I'VE THOUGHT ABOUT IT A LOT SINCE THEN, AND I DON'T KNOW FOR SURE... BUT I THINK THAT GEN KNEW WHAT HER POWER WAS LONG BEFORE THAT DAY.
I THINK SHE KEPT IT SECRET.
I THINK SHE WAS AFRAID THAT IF SOMEONE KNEW SHE HAD THE POWER TO TAKE ANYONE'S IDENTITY...
THEY WOULD HAVE MADE HER USE IT IN WAYS SHE DIDN'T WANT TO.

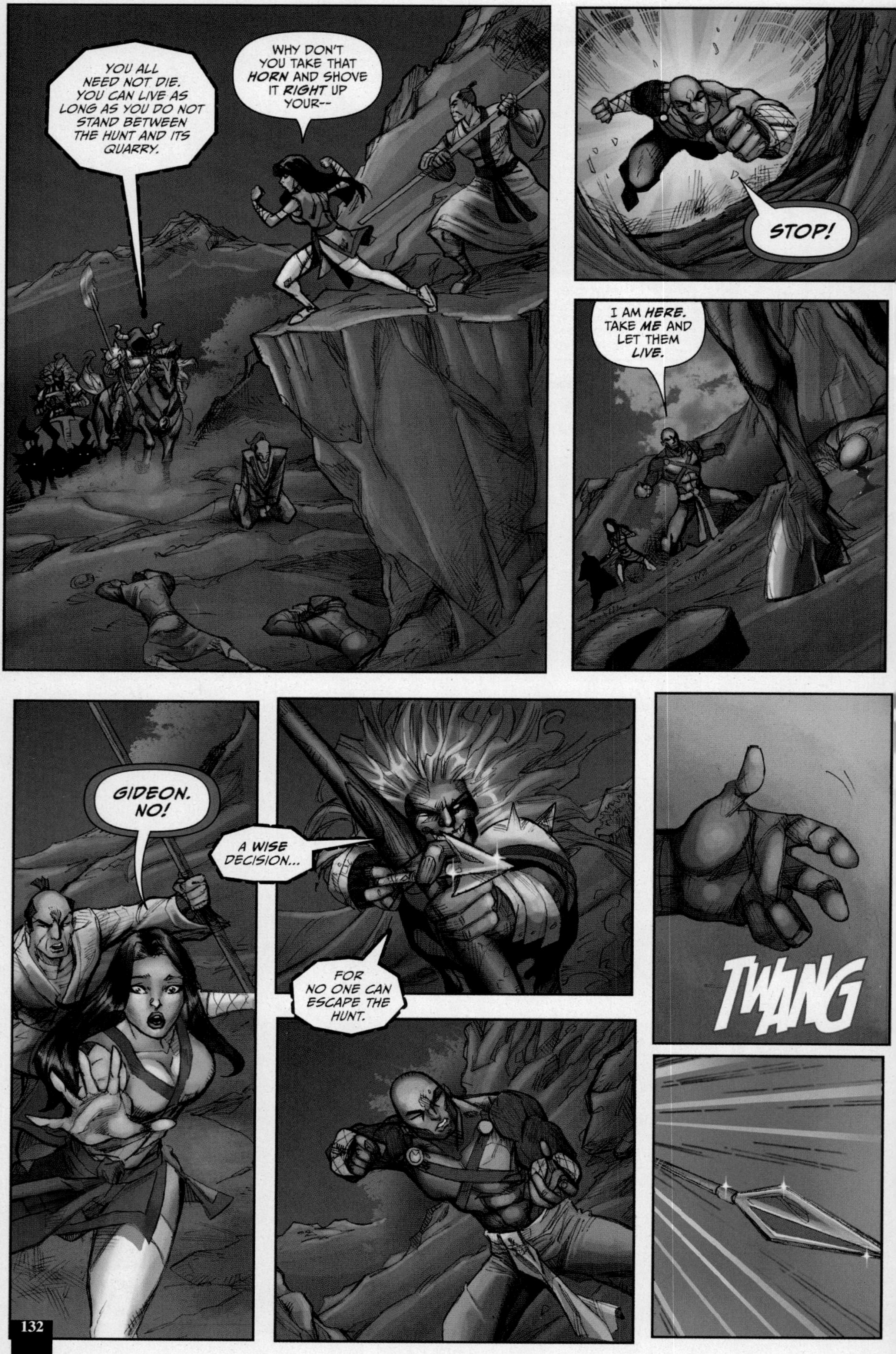
YOU ALL NEED NOT DIE. YOU CAN LIVE AS LONG AS YOU DO NOT STAND BETWEEN THE HUNT AND ITS QUARRY.
WHY DON'T YOU TAKE THAT HORN AND SHOVE IT RIGHT UP YOUR--
STOP!
I AM HERE. TAKE ME AND LET THEM LIVE.
GIDEON. NO!
A WISE DECISION...
FOR NO ONE CAN ESCAPE THE HUNT.
TWANG

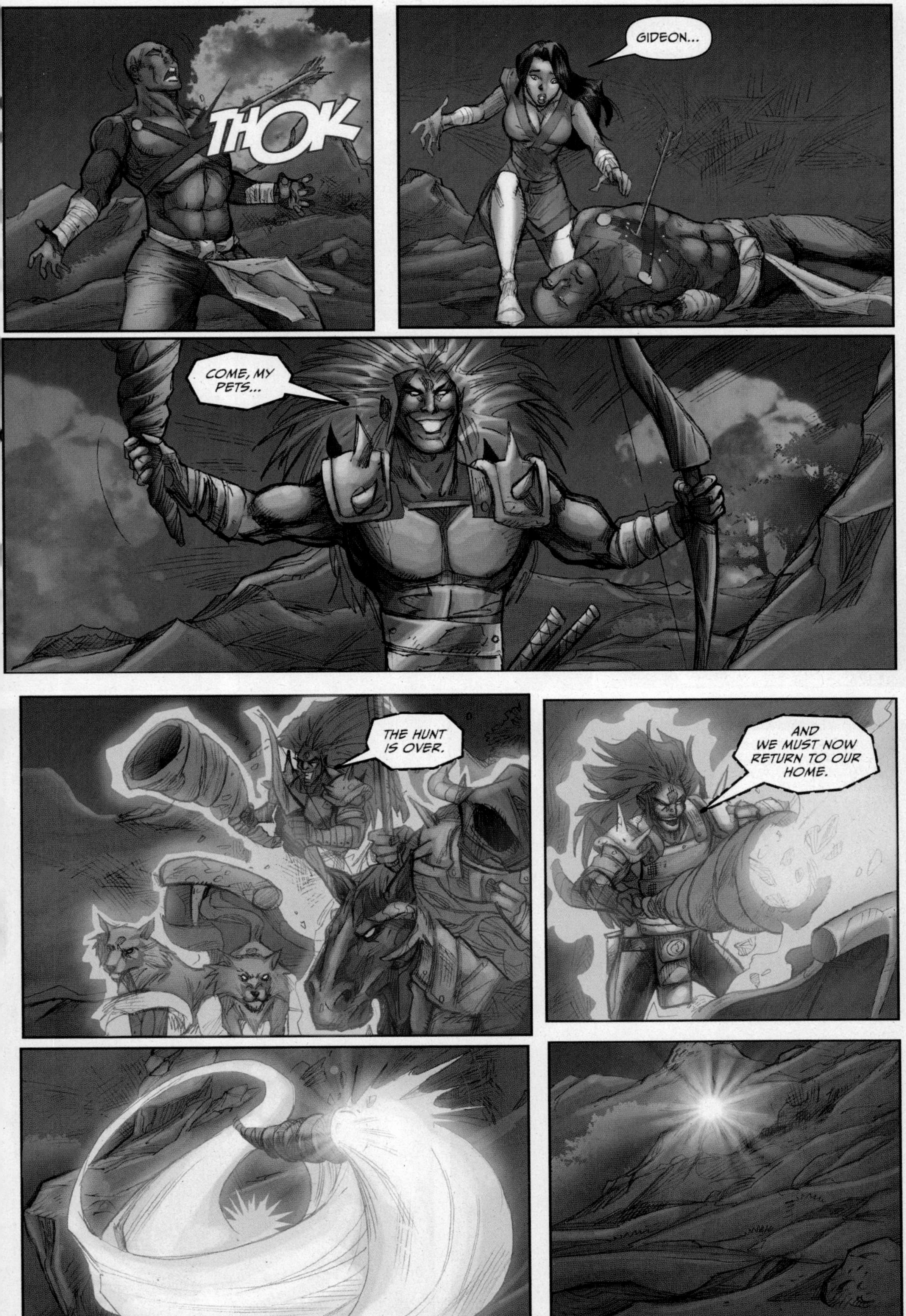
THOK
GIDEON...
COME, MY PETS...
THE HUNT IS OVER.
AND WE MUST NOW RETURN TO OUR HOME.

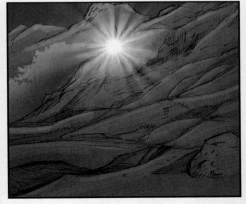

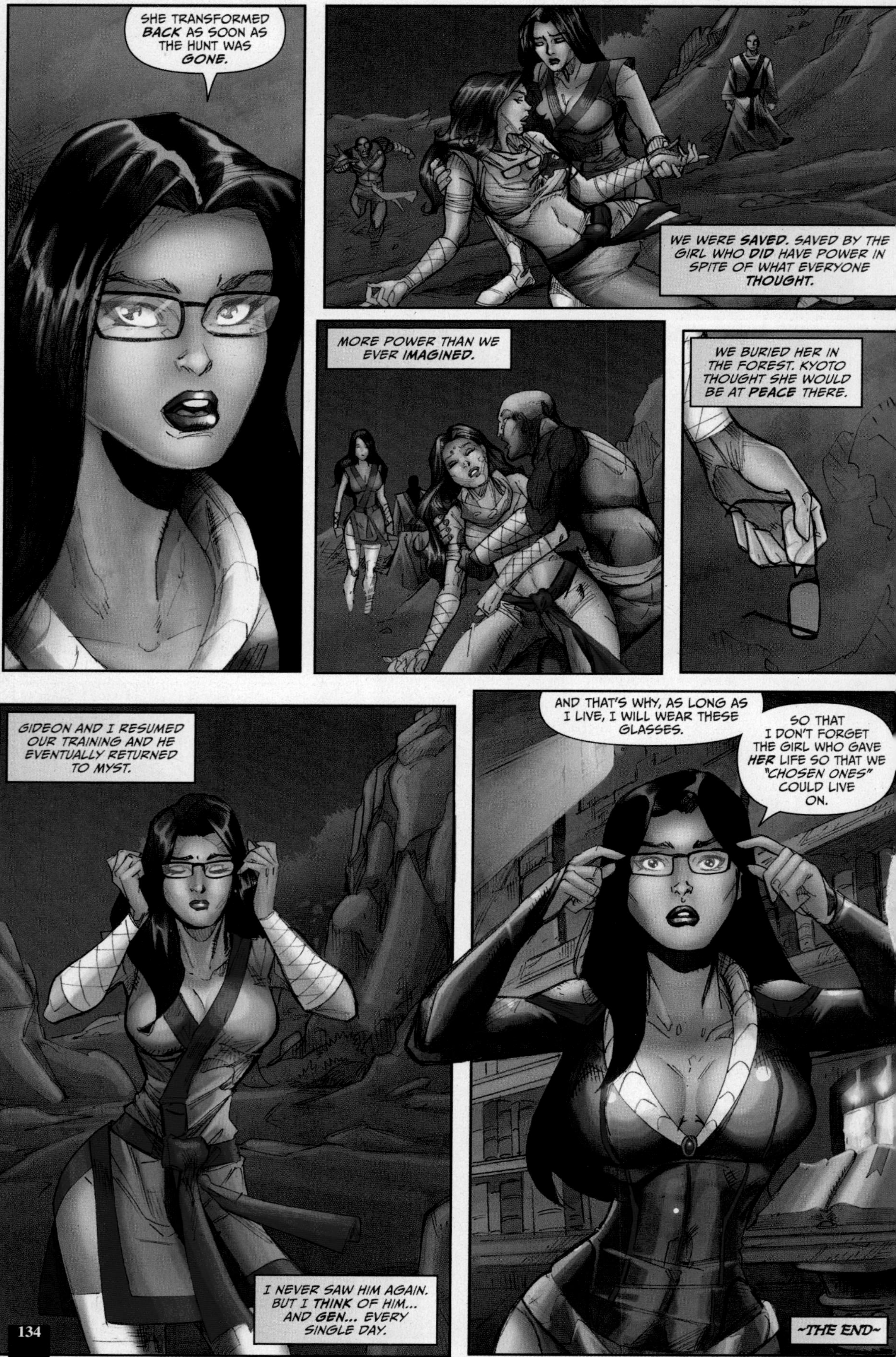
SHE TRANSFORMED BACK AS SOON AS THE HUNT WAS GONE.
WE WERE SAVED. SAVED BY THE GIRL WHO DID HAVE POWER IN SPITE OF WHAT EVERYONE THOUGHT.
MORE POWER THAN WE EVER IMAGINED.
WE BURIED HER IN THE FOREST. KYOTO THOUGHT SHE WOULD BE AT PEACE THERE.
GIDEON AND I RESUMED OUR TRAINING AND HE EVENTUALLY RETURNED TO MYST.
I NEVER SAW HIM AGAIN. BUT I THINK OF HIM... AND GEN... EVERY SINGLE DAY.
AND THAT'S WHY, AS LONG AS I LIVE, I WILL WEAR THESE GLASSES.
SO THAT I DON'T FORGET THE GIRL WHO GAVE HER LIFE SO THAT WE "CHOSEN ONES" COULD LIVE ON.
~THE END~

Grimm Fairy Tales

Different Seasons

Grimm Fairy Tales™

ST. PATRICK'S DAY SPECIAL 2013

STORY
JOE BRUSHA
RAVEN GREGORY
RALPH TEDESCO
PAT SHAND

WRITER
PAT SHAND

ARTWORK
MARCELLO COSTA
LUIS CZERNAWSKI
FERRAN SELLARES
FRANCESCO GASTON

COLORS
PASCAL NINO
JOSE EXPO
LEONARDO PACIAROTTI

LETTERS
JIM CAMPBELL

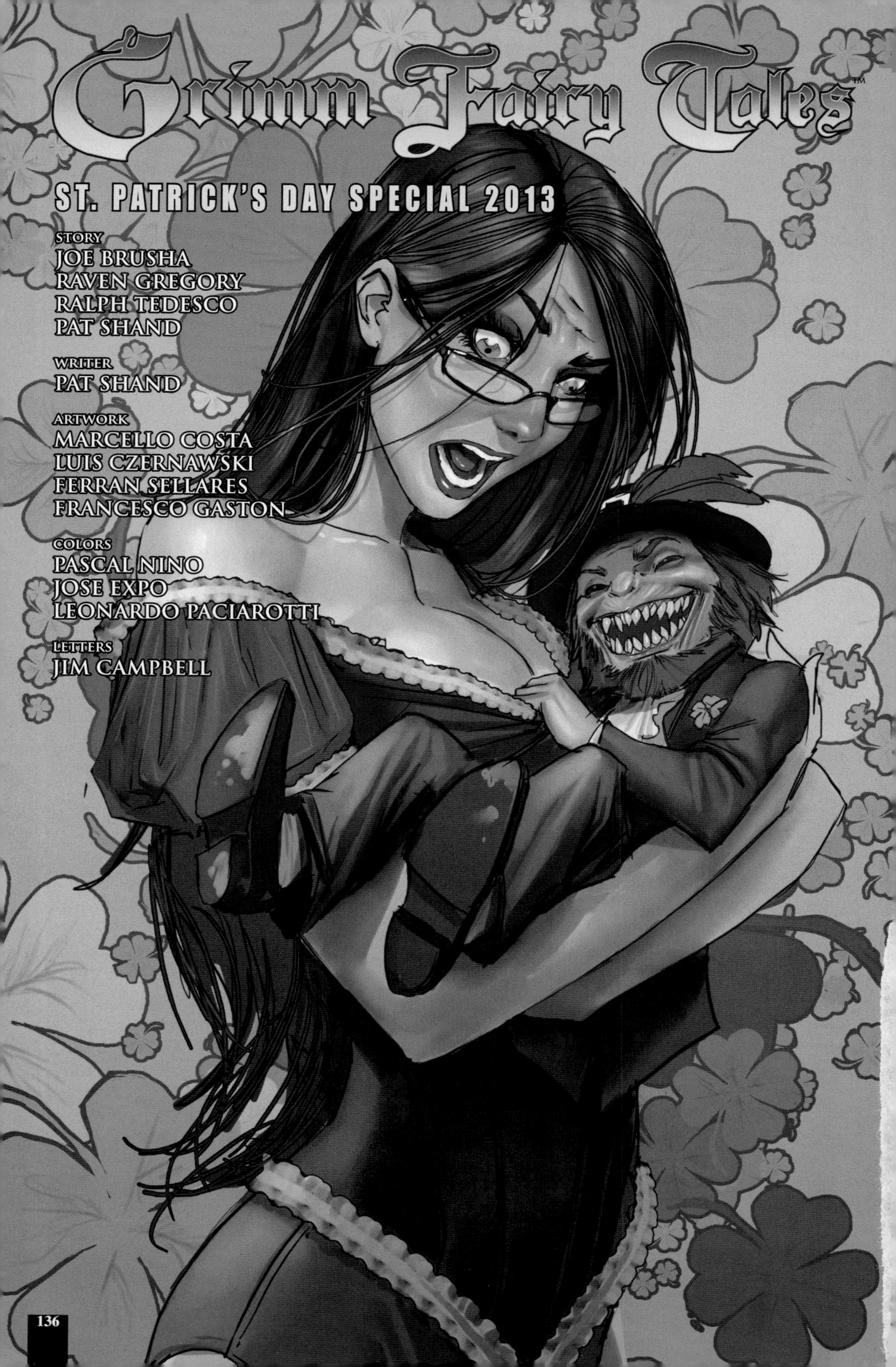

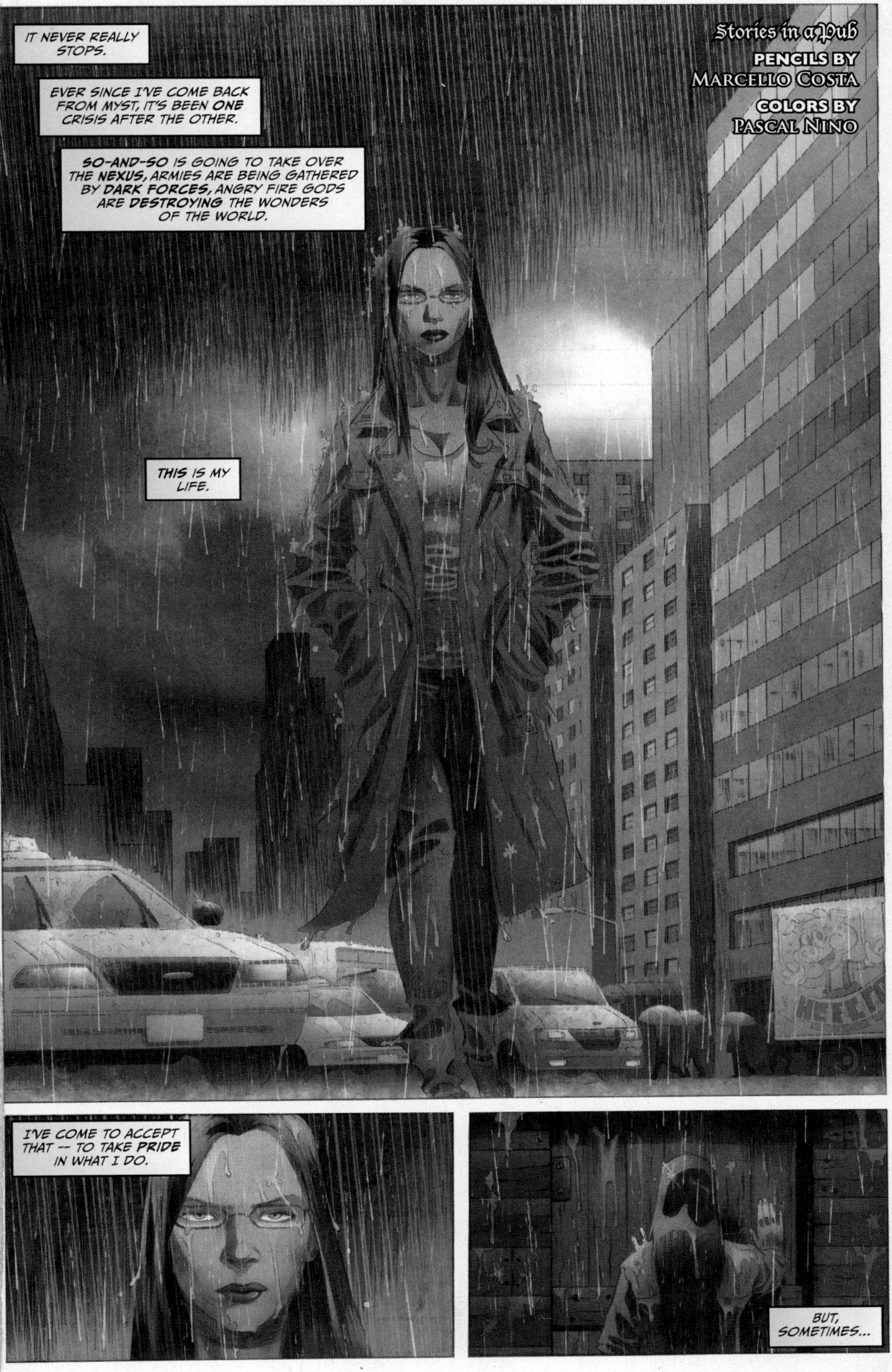
Stories in a Pub
PENCILS BY
MARCELLO COSTA
COLORS BY
PASCAL NINO
IT NEVER REALLY STOPS.
EVER SINCE I'VE COME BACK FROM MYST, IT'S BEEN ONE CRISIS AFTER THE OTHER.
SO-AND-SO IS GOING TO TAKE OVER THE NEXUS, ARMIES ARE BEING GATHERED BY DARK FORCES, ANGRY FIRE GODS ARE DESTROYING THE WONDERS OF THE WORLD.
THIS IS MY LIFE.
I'VE COME TO ACCEPT THAT -- TO TAKE PRIDE IN WHAT I DO.
BUT, SOMETIMES...

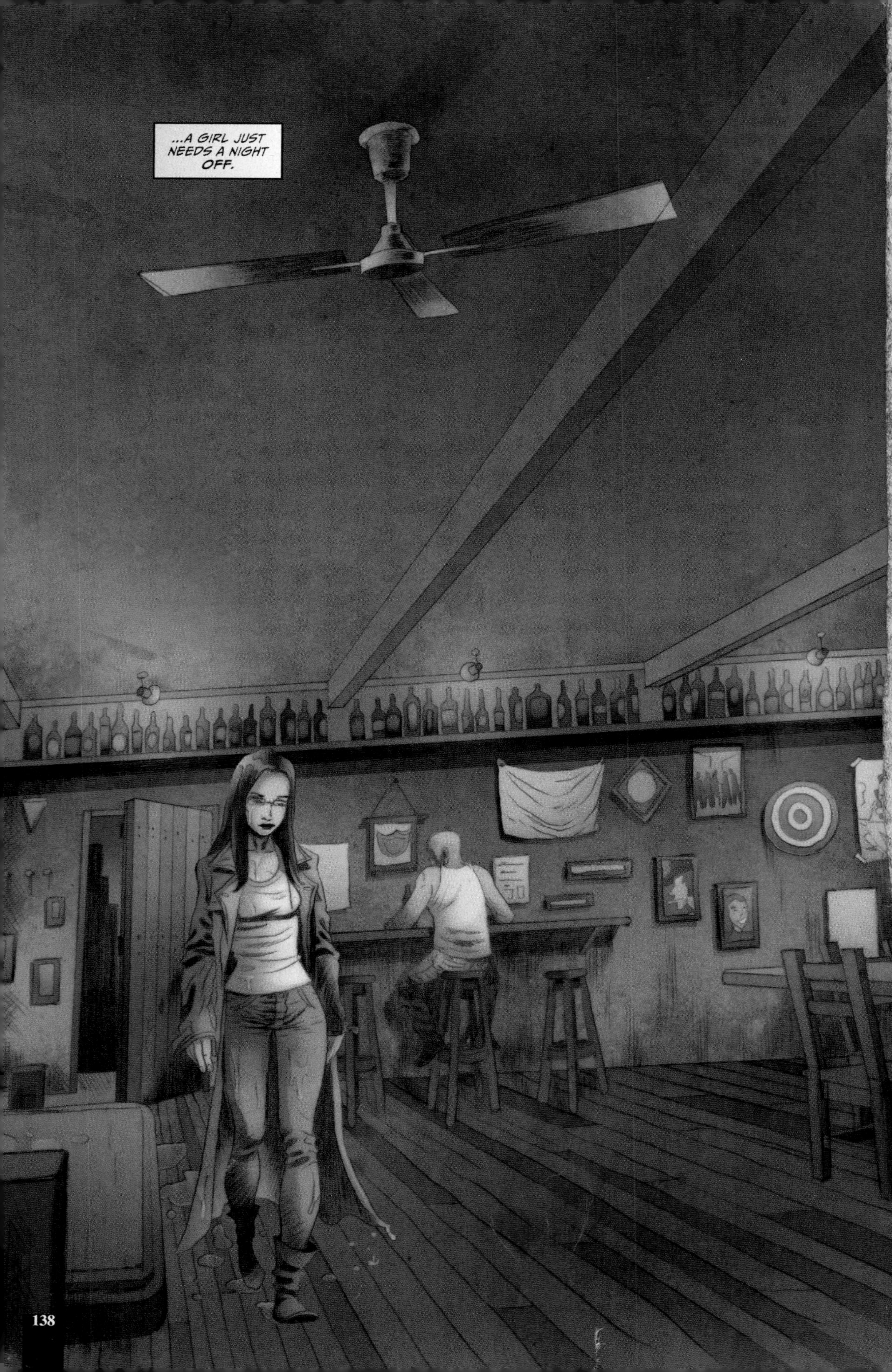
...A GIRL JUST NEEDS A NIGHT OFF.

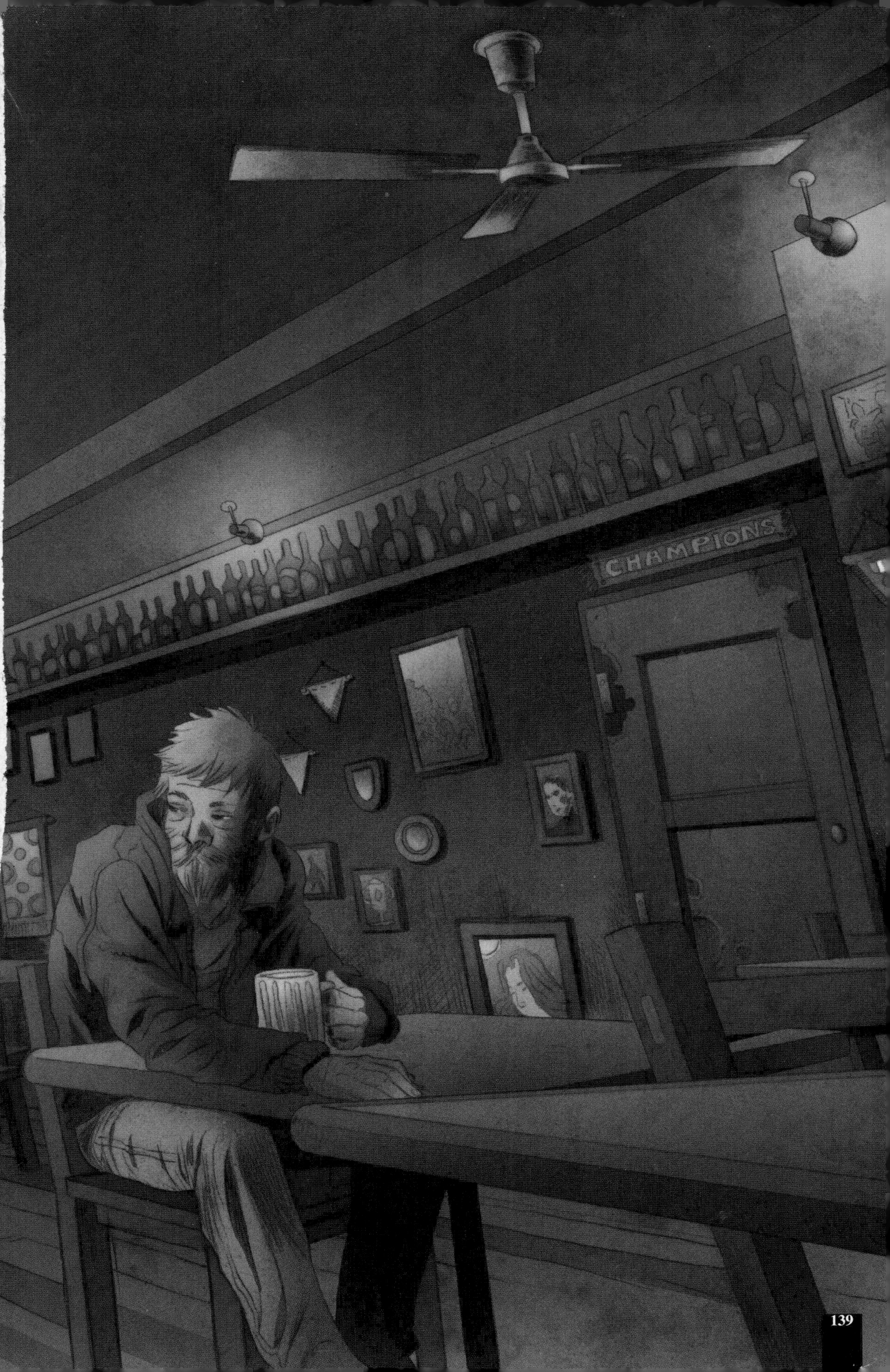
CHAMPIONS

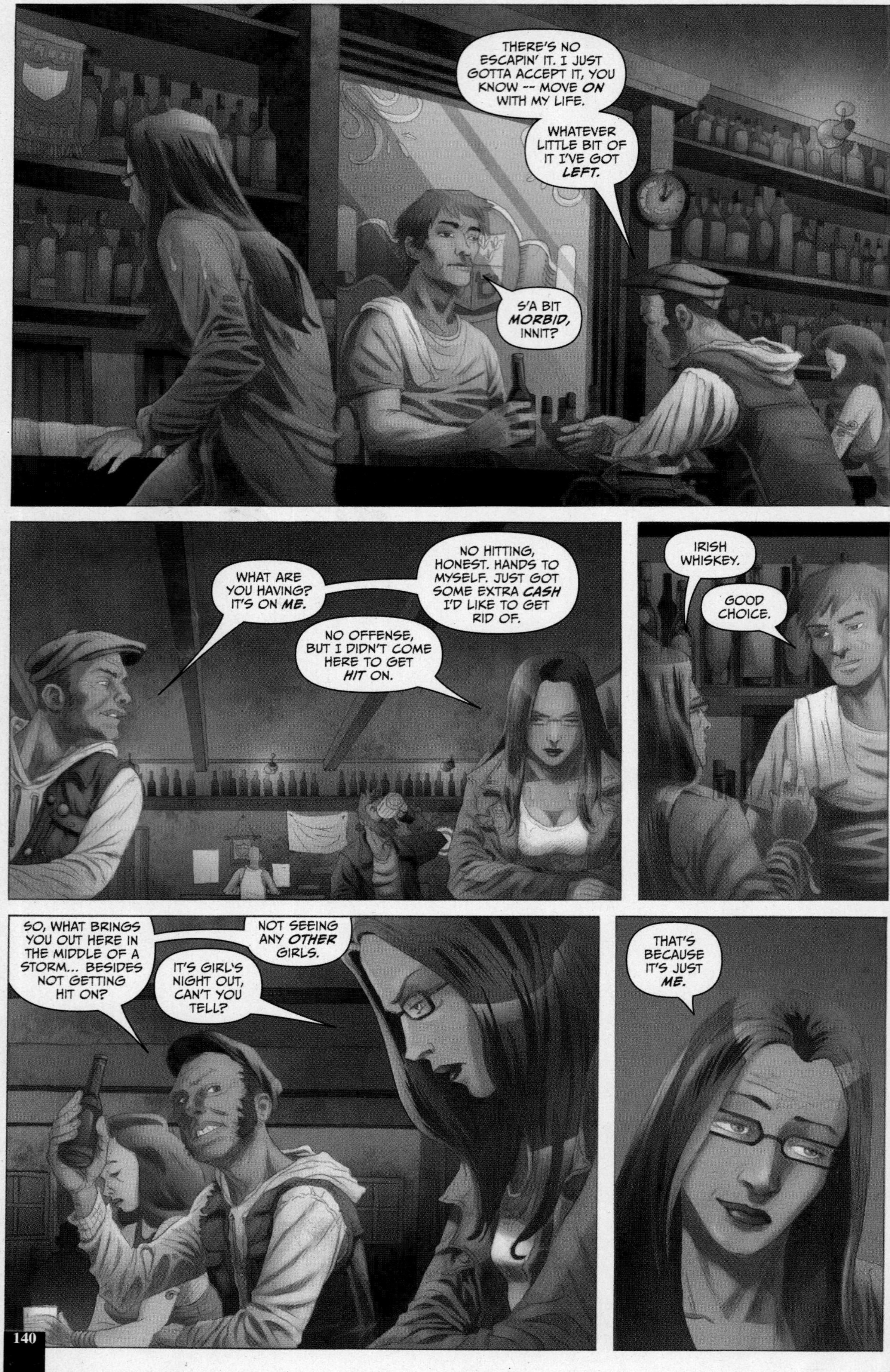
THERE'S NO ESCAPIN' IT. I JUST GOTTA ACCEPT IT, YOU KNOW -- MOVE ON WITH MY LIFE.
WHATEVER LITTLE BIT OF IT I'VE GOT LEFT.
S'A BIT MORBID, INNIT?
WHAT ARE YOU HAVING? IT'S ON ME.
NO HITTING, HONEST. HANDS TO MYSELF. JUST GOT SOME EXTRA CASH I'D LIKE TO GET RID OF.
NO OFFENSE, BUT I DIDN'T COME HERE TO GET HIT ON.
IRISH WHISKEY.
GOOD CHOICE.
SO, WHAT BRINGS YOU OUT HERE IN THE MIDDLE OF A STORM... BESIDES NOT GETTING HIT ON?
IT'S GIRL'S NIGHT OUT, CAN'T YOU TELL?
NOT SEEING ANY OTHER GIRLS.
THAT'S BECAUSE IT'S JUST ME.

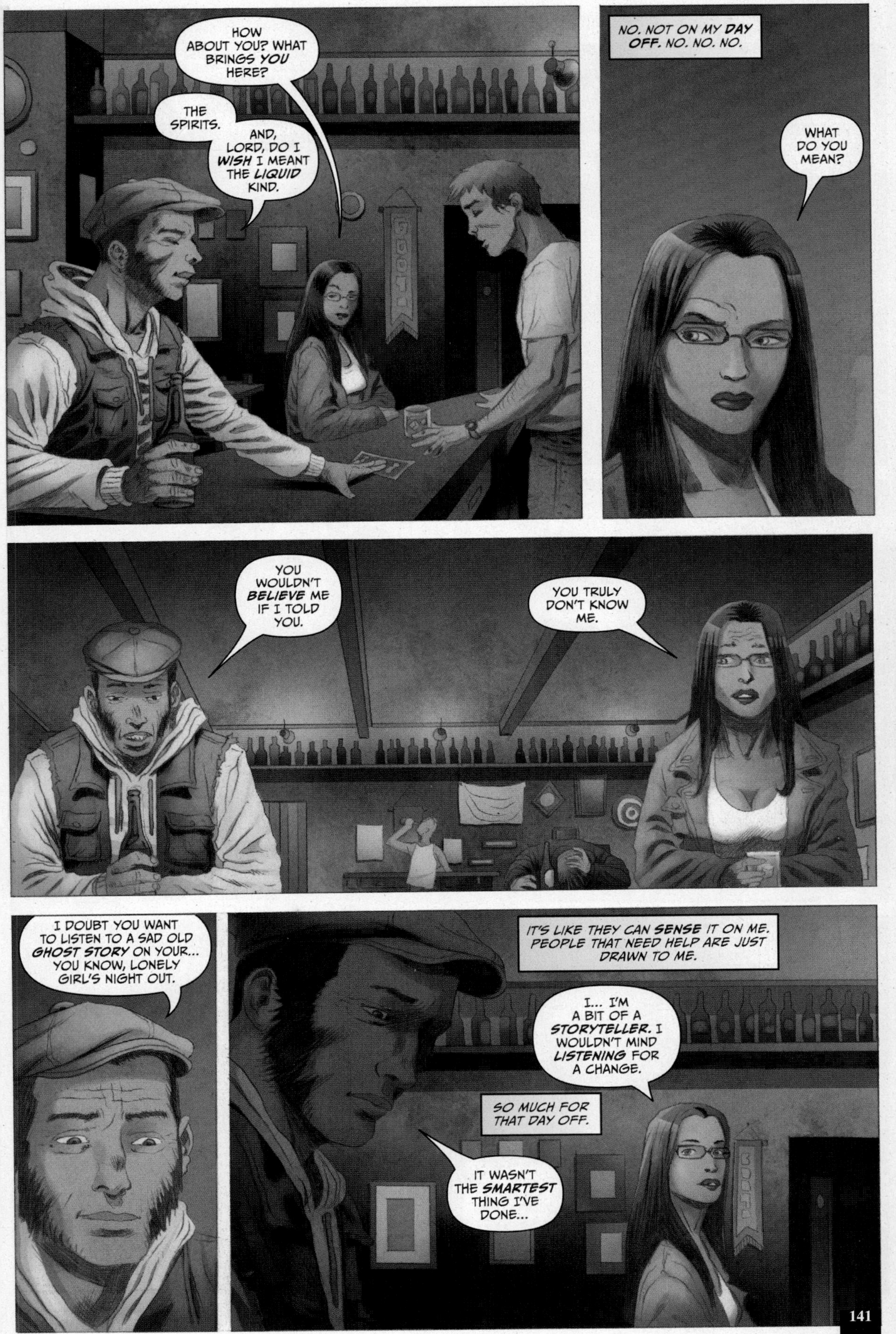
HOW ABOUT YOU? WHAT BRINGS YOU HERE?
THE SPIRITS.
AND, LORD, DO I WISH I MEANT THE LIQUID KIND.
NO. NOT ON MY DAY OFF. NO. NO. NO.
WHAT DO YOU MEAN?
YOU WOULDN'T BELIEVE ME IF I TOLD YOU.
YOU TRULY DON'T KNOW ME.
I DOUBT YOU WANT TO LISTEN TO A SAD OLD GHOST STORY ON YOUR... YOU KNOW, LONELY GIRL'S NIGHT OUT.
IT'S LIKE THEY CAN SENSE IT ON ME. PEOPLE THAT NEED HELP ARE JUST DRAWN TO ME.
I... I'M A BIT OF A STORYTELLER. I WOULDN'T MIND LISTENING FOR A CHANGE.
SO MUCH FOR THAT DAY OFF.
IT WASN'T THE SMARTEST THING I'VE DONE...

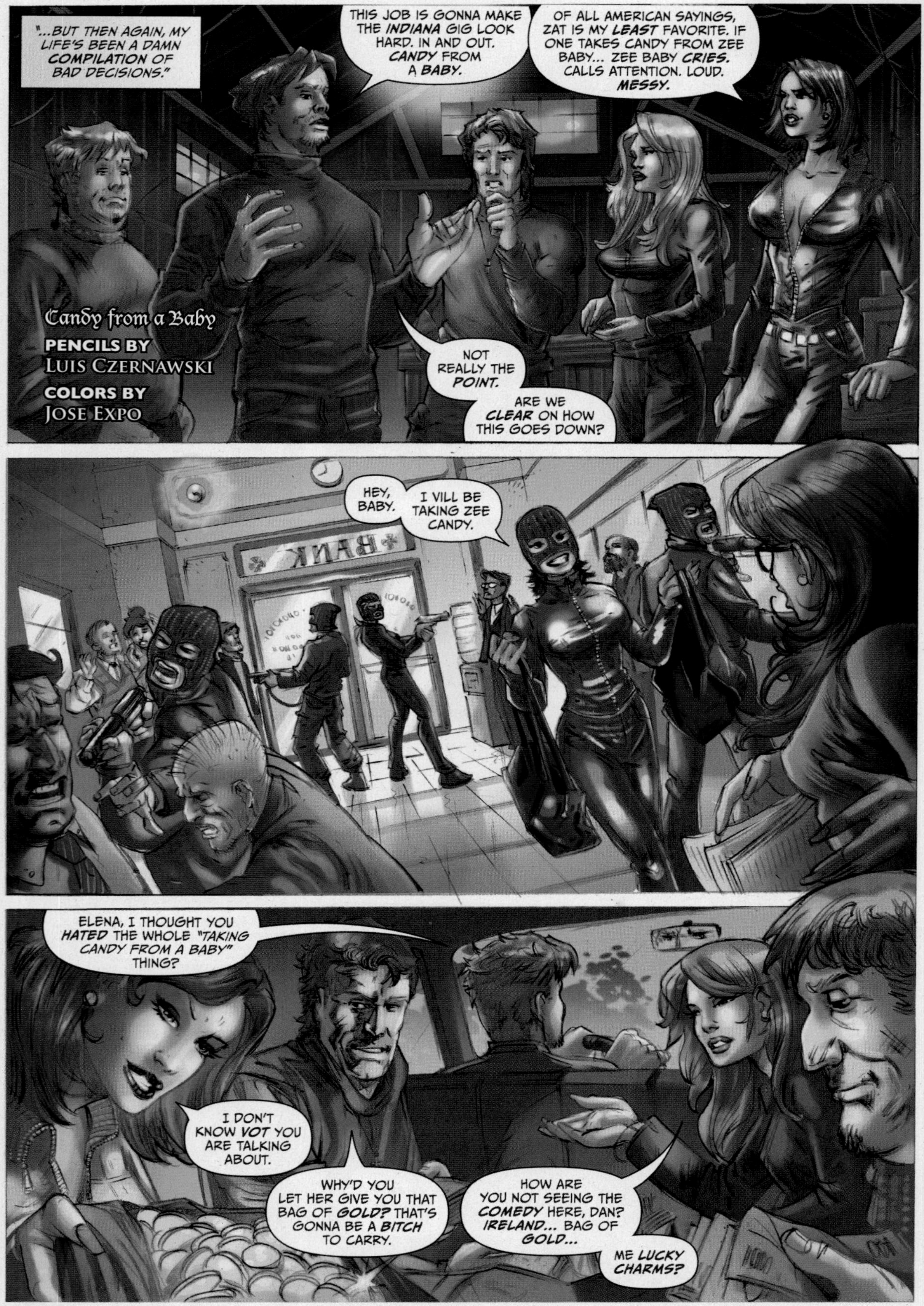
"...BUT THEN AGAIN, MY LIFE'S BEEN A DAMN COMPILATION OF BAD DECISIONS."
THIS JOB IS GONNA MAKE THE INDIANA GIG LOOK HARD. IN AND OUT. CANDY FROM A BABY.
OF ALL AMERICAN SAYINGS, ZAT IS MY LEAST FAVORITE. IF ONE TAKES CANDY FROM ZEE BABY... ZEE BABY CRIES. CALLS ATTENTION. LOUD. MESSY.
Candy from a Baby
PENCILS BY
LUIS CZERNAWSKI
COLORS BY
JOSE EXPO
NOT REALLY THE POINT.
ARE WE CLEAR ON HOW THIS GOES DOWN?
HEY, BABY.
I VILL BE TAKING ZEE CANDY.
BANK
ELENA, I THOUGHT YOU HATED THE WHOLE "TAKING CANDY FROM A BABY" THING?
I DON'T KNOW VOT YOU ARE TALKING ABOUT.
WHY'D YOU LET HER GIVE YOU THAT BAG OF GOLD? THAT'S GONNA BE A BITCH TO CARRY.
HOW ARE YOU NOT SEEING THE COMEDY HERE, DAN? IRELAND... BAG OF GOLD...
ME LUCKY CHARMS?

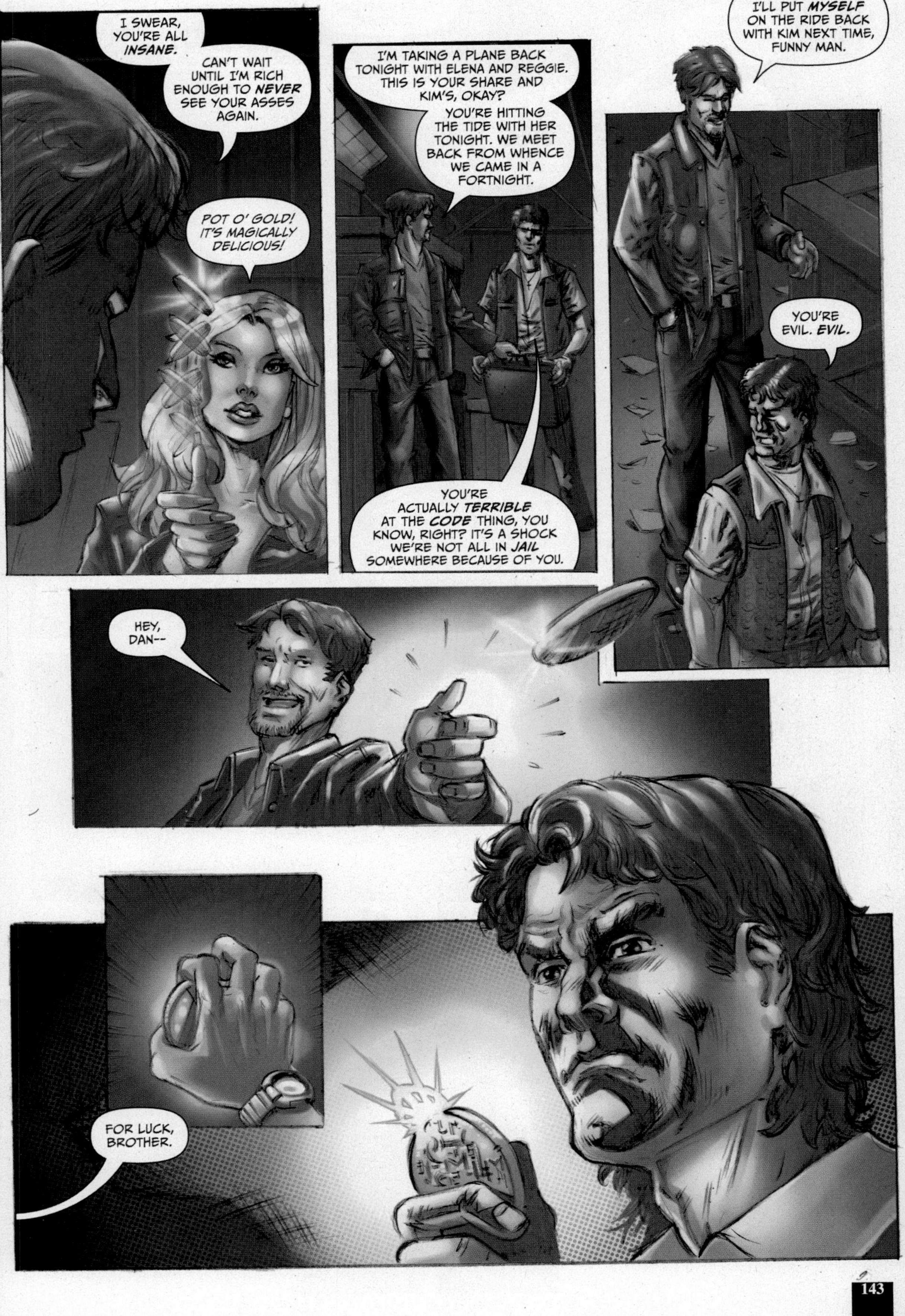
I SWEAR, YOU'RE ALL INSANE.
CAN'T WAIT UNTIL I'M RICH ENOUGH TO NEVER SEE YOUR ASSES AGAIN.
POT O' GOLD! IT'S MAGICALLY DELICIOUS!
I'M TAKING A PLANE BACK TONIGHT WITH ELENA AND REGGIE. THIS IS YOUR SHARE AND KIM'S, OKAY?
YOU'RE HITTING THE TIDE WITH HER TONIGHT. WE MEET BACK FROM WHENCE WE CAME IN A FORTNIGHT.
YOU'RE ACTUALLY TERRIBLE AT THE CODE THING, YOU KNOW, RIGHT? IT'S A SHOCK WE'RE NOT ALL IN JAIL SOMEWHERE BECAUSE OF YOU.
MAYBE I'LL PUT MYSELF ON THE RIDE BACK WITH KIM NEXT TIME, FUNNY MAN.
YOU'RE EVIL. EVIL.
HEY, DAN--
FOR LUCK, BROTHER.

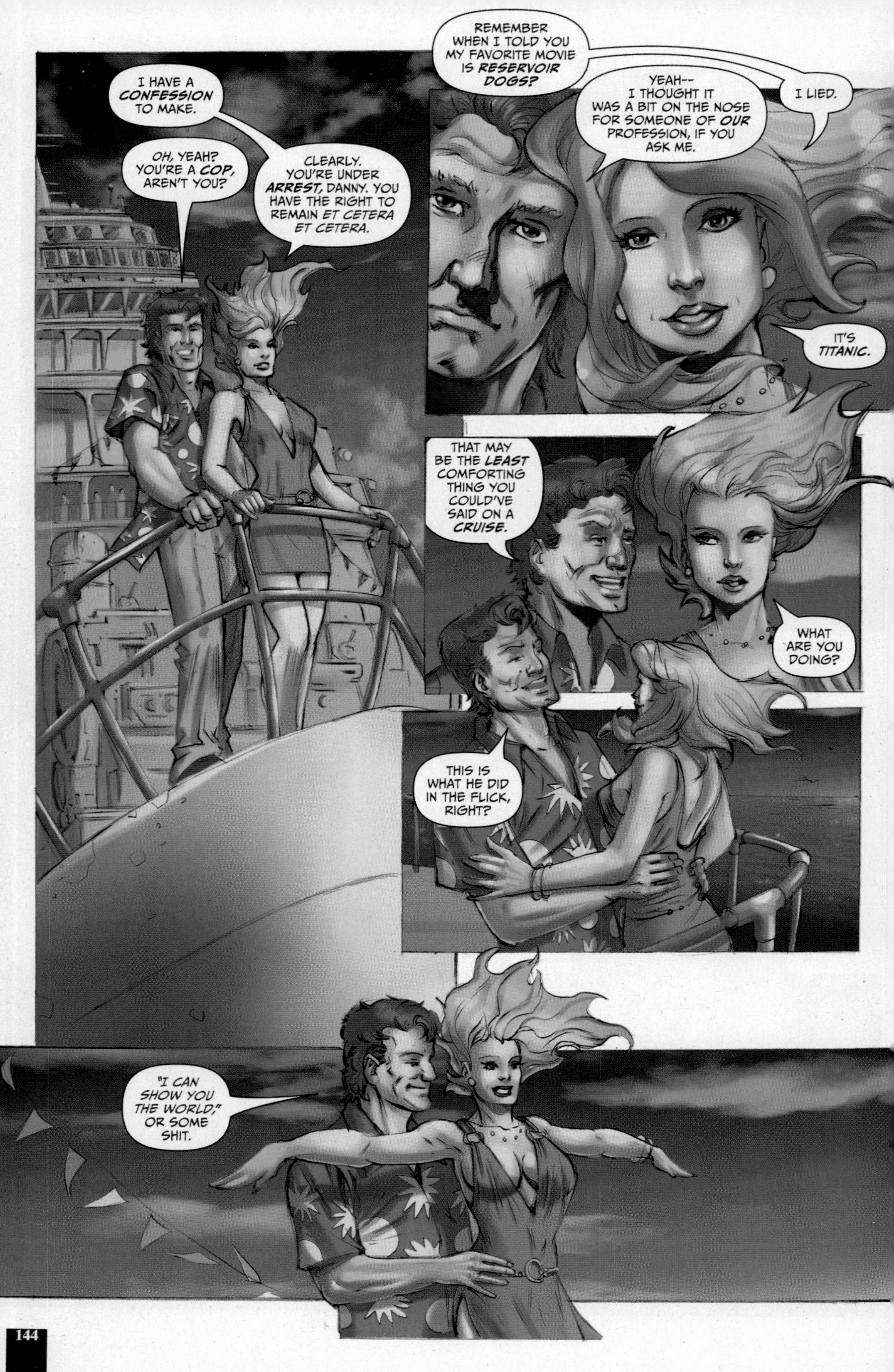
I HAVE A CONFESSION TO MAKE.
OH, YEAH? YOU'RE A COP, AREN'T YOU?
CLEARLY. YOU'RE UNDER ARREST, DANNY. YOU HAVE THE RIGHT TO REMAIN ET CETERA ET CETERA.
REMEMBER WHEN I TOLD YOU MY FAVORITE MOVIE IS RESERVOIR DOGS?
I LIED.
YEAH-- I THOUGHT IT WAS A BIT ON THE NOSE FOR SOMEONE OF OUR PROFESSION, IF YOU ASK ME.
IT'S TITANIC.
THAT MAY BE THE LEAST COMFORTING THING YOU COULD'VE SAID ON A CRUISE.
WHAT ARE YOU DOING?
THIS IS WHAT HE DID IN THE FLICK, RIGHT?
"I CAN SHOW YOU THE WORLD," OR SOME SHIT.

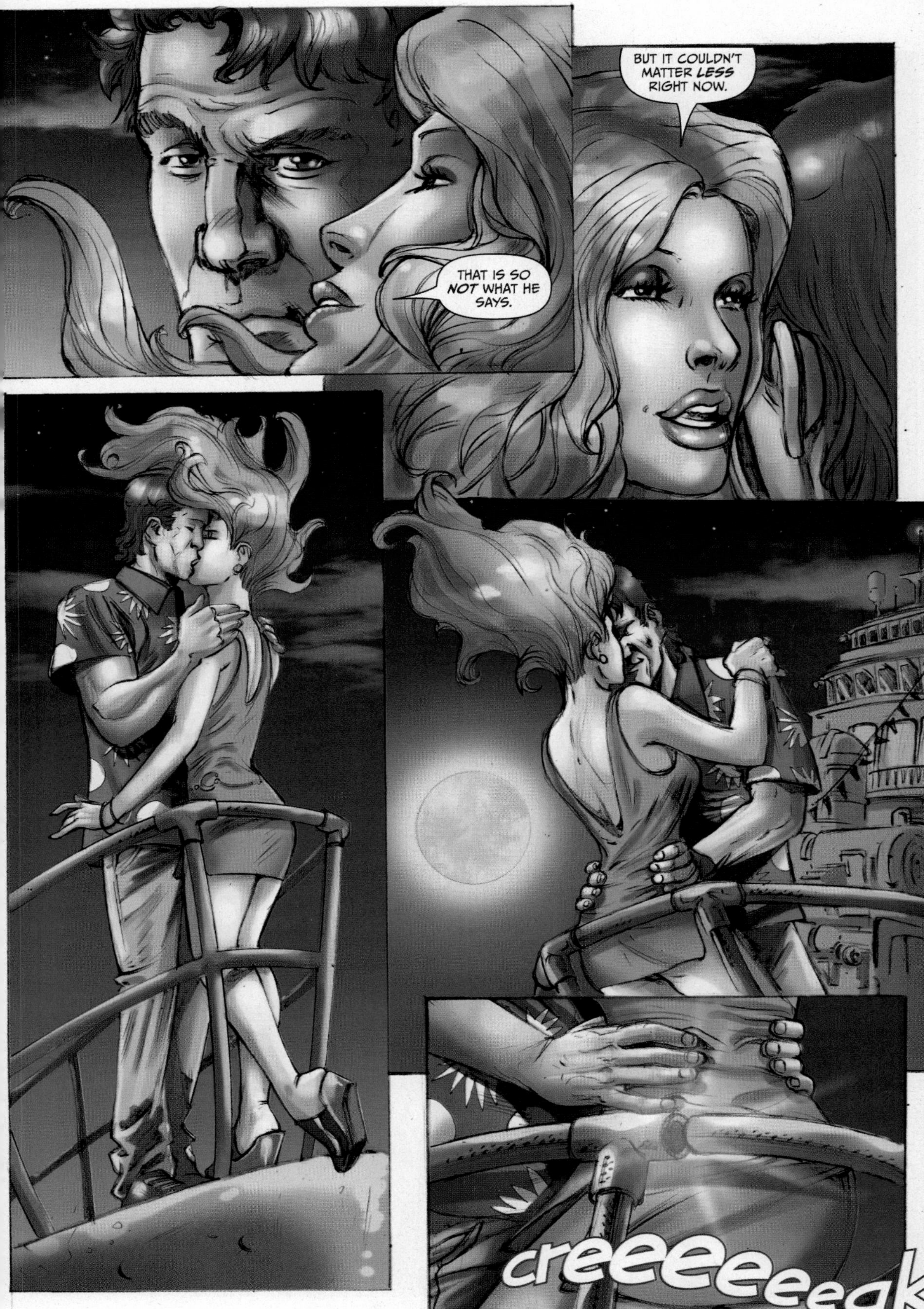
THAT IS SO NOT WHAT HE SAYS.
BUT IT COULDN'T MATTER LESS RIGHT NOW.
creeeeeeak

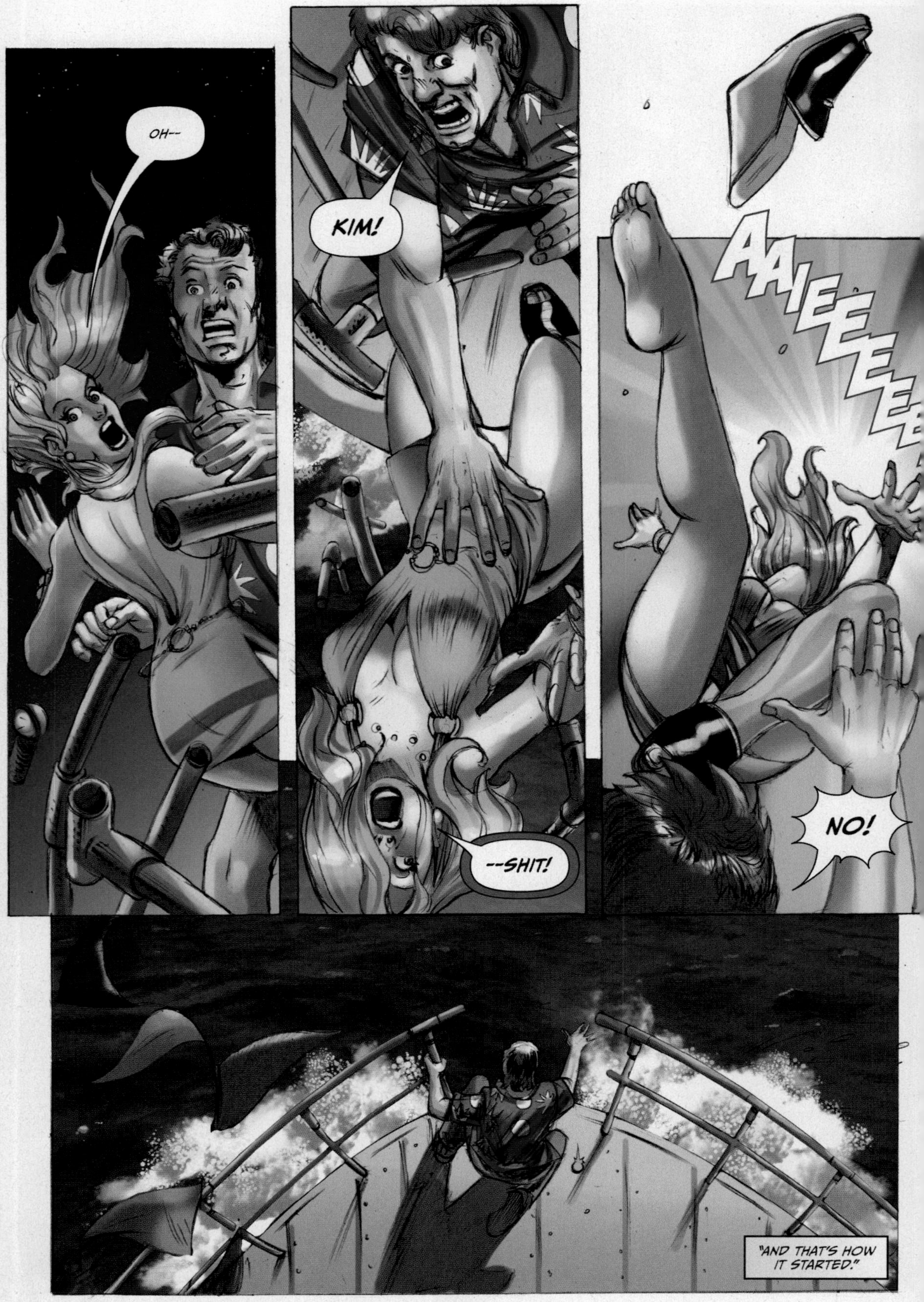
OH--
KIM!
--SHIT!
AAIEEEEEE
NO!
"AND THAT'S HOW IT STARTED."

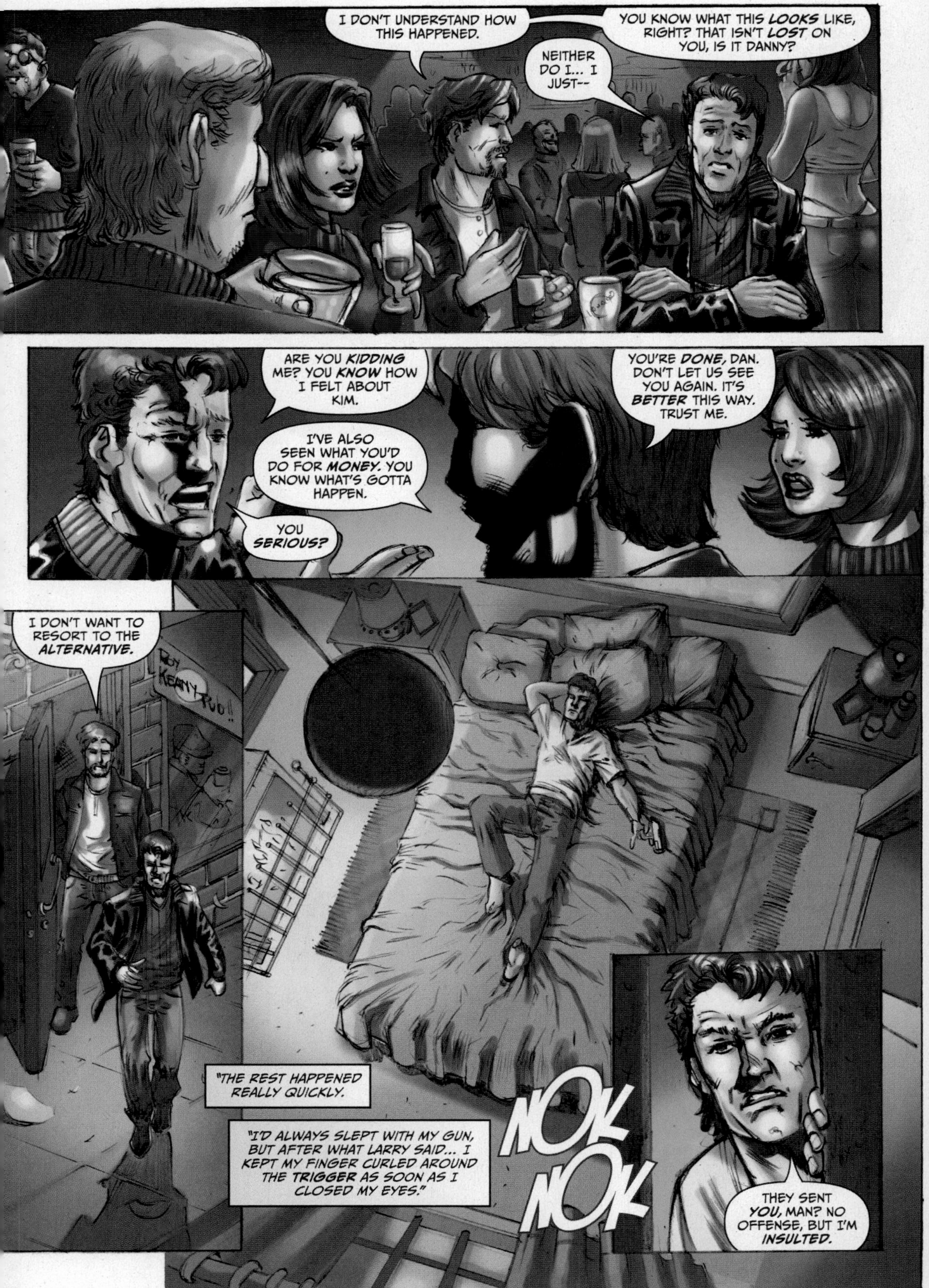
I DON'T UNDERSTAND HOW THIS HAPPENED.
YOU KNOW WHAT THIS LOOKS LIKE, RIGHT? THAT ISN'T LOST ON YOU, IS IT DANNY?
NEITHER DO I... I JUST--
ARE YOU KIDDING ME? YOU KNOW HOW I FELT ABOUT KIM.
I'VE ALSO SEEN WHAT YOU'D DO FOR MONEY. YOU KNOW WHAT'S GOTTA HAPPEN.
YOU SERIOUS?
YOU'RE DONE, DAN. DON'T LET US SEE YOU AGAIN. IT'S BETTER THIS WAY. TRUST ME.
I DON'T WANT TO RESORT TO THE ALTERNATIVE.
"THE REST HAPPENED REALLY QUICKLY.
"I'D ALWAYS SLEPT WITH MY GUN, BUT AFTER WHAT LARRY SAID... I KEPT MY FINGER CURLED AROUND THE TRIGGER AS SOON AS I CLOSED MY EYES."
NOK NOK
THEY SENT YOU, MAN? NO OFFENSE, BUT I'M INSULTED.

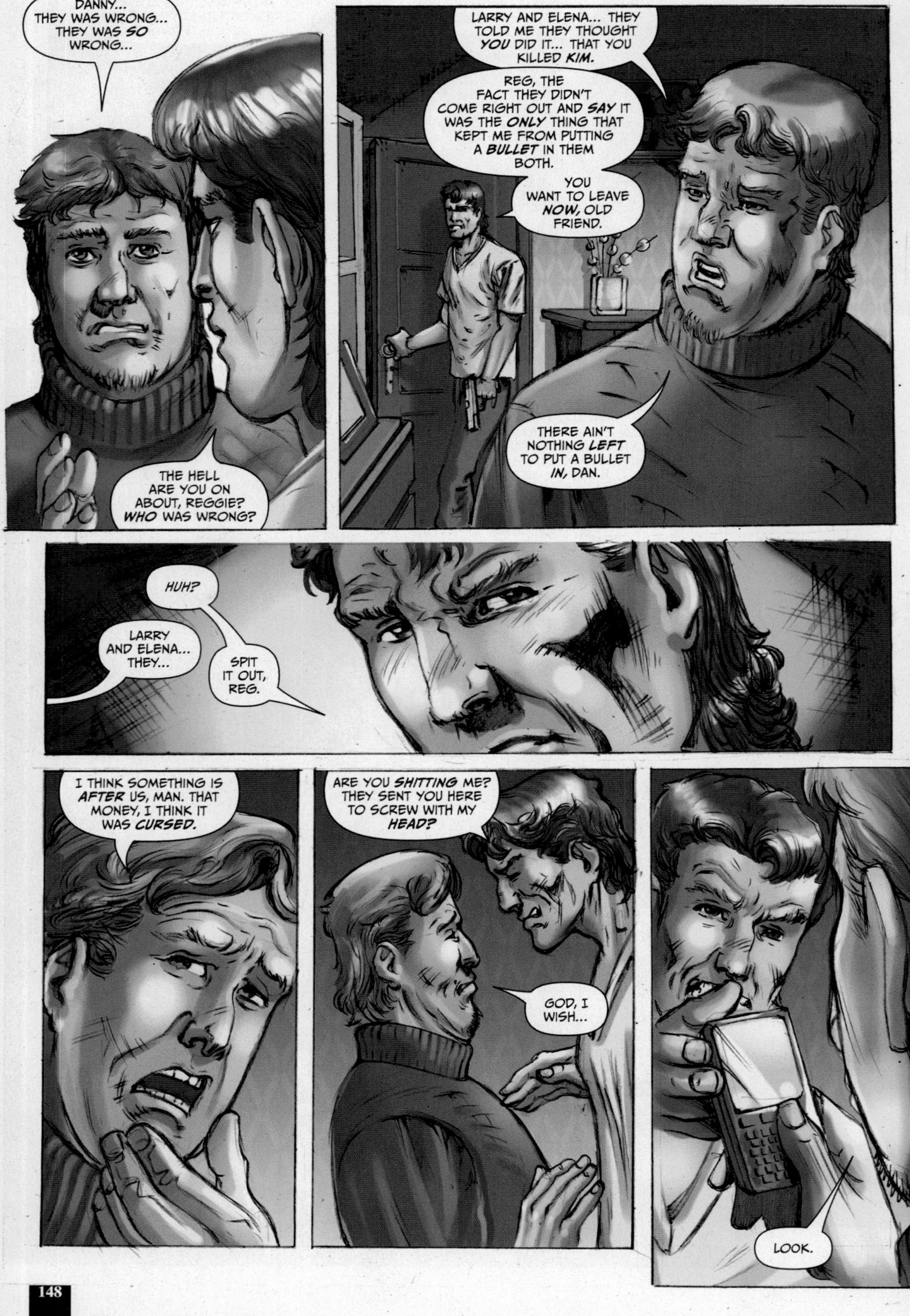
DANNY... THEY WAS WRONG... THEY WAS *SO* WRONG...
THE HELL ARE YOU ON ABOUT, REGGIE? *WHO* WAS WRONG?
LARRY AND ELENA... THEY TOLD ME THEY THOUGHT *YOU* DID IT... THAT YOU KILLED *KIM.*
REG, THE FACT THEY DIDN'T COME RIGHT OUT AND *SAY* IT WAS THE *ONLY* THING THAT KEPT ME FROM PUTTING A *BULLET* IN THEM BOTH.
YOU WANT TO LEAVE *NOW,* OLD FRIEND.
THERE AIN'T NOTHING *LEFT* TO PUT A BULLET *IN,* DAN.
HUH?
LARRY AND ELENA... THEY...
SPIT IT OUT, REG.
I THINK SOMETHING IS *AFTER* US, MAN. THAT MONEY, I THINK IT WAS *CURSED.*
ARE YOU *SHITTING* ME? THEY SENT YOU HERE TO SCREW WITH MY *HEAD?*
GOD, I WISH...
LOOK.

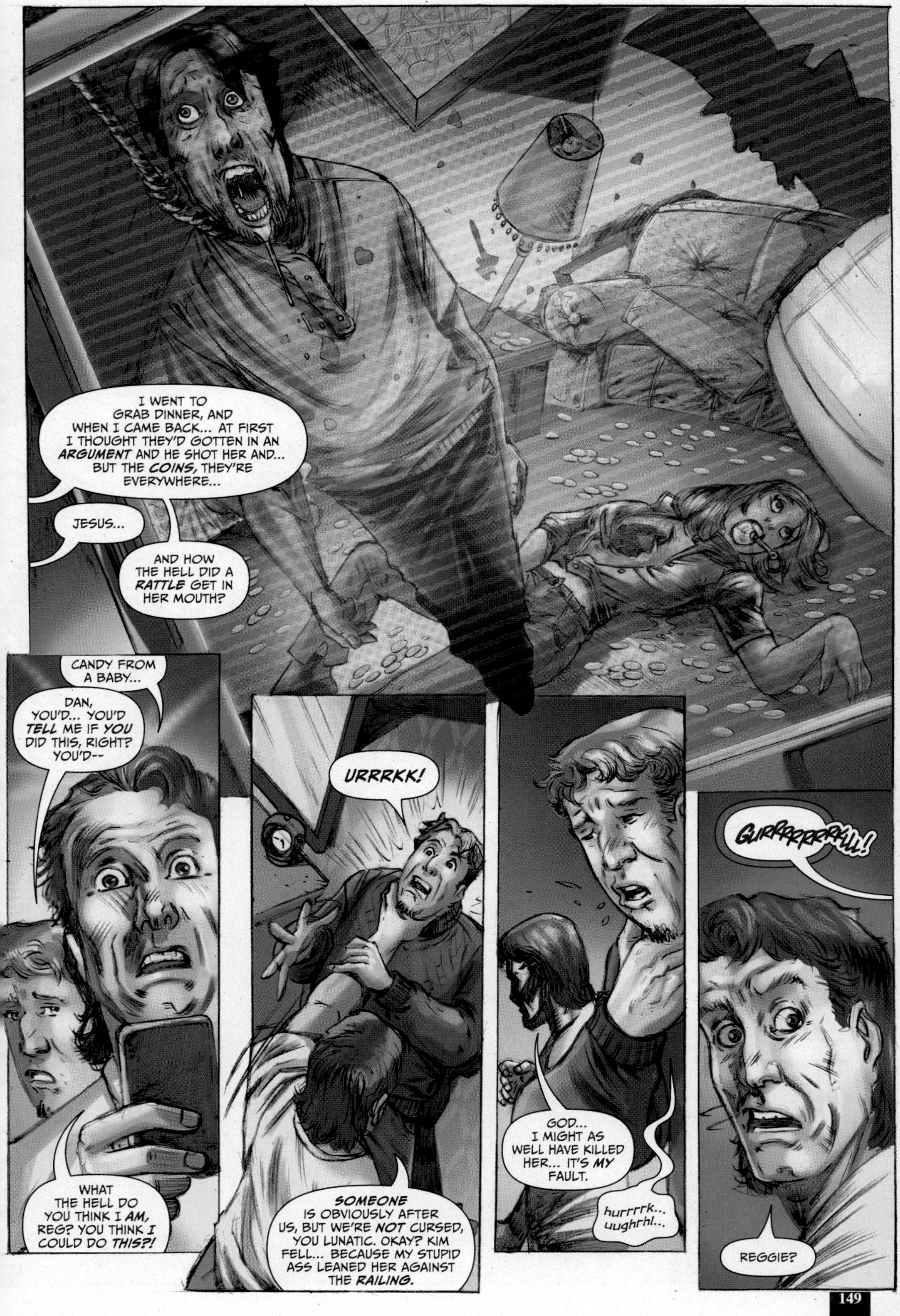
I WENT TO GRAB DINNER, AND WHEN I CAME BACK... AT FIRST I THOUGHT THEY'D GOTTEN IN AN *ARGUMENT* AND HE SHOT HER AND... BUT THE *COINS,* THEY'RE EVERYWHERE...
JESUS...
AND HOW THE HELL DID A *RATTLE* GET IN HER MOUTH?
CANDY FROM A BABY...
DAN, YOU'D... YOU'D *TELL* ME IF *YOU* DID THIS, RIGHT? YOU'D--
WHAT THE HELL DO YOU THINK I *AM,* REG? YOU THINK *I* COULD DO *THIS?!*
URRRKK!
SOMEONE IS OBVIOUSLY AFTER US, BUT WE'RE *NOT* CURSED, YOU LUNATIC. OKAY? KIM FELL... BECAUSE MY STUPID ASS LEANED HER AGAINST THE *RAILING.*
GOD... I MIGHT AS WELL HAVE KILLED HER... IT'S *MY* FAULT.
hurrrrk... uughrhl...
GURRRRRRRRAAALL!
REGGIE?

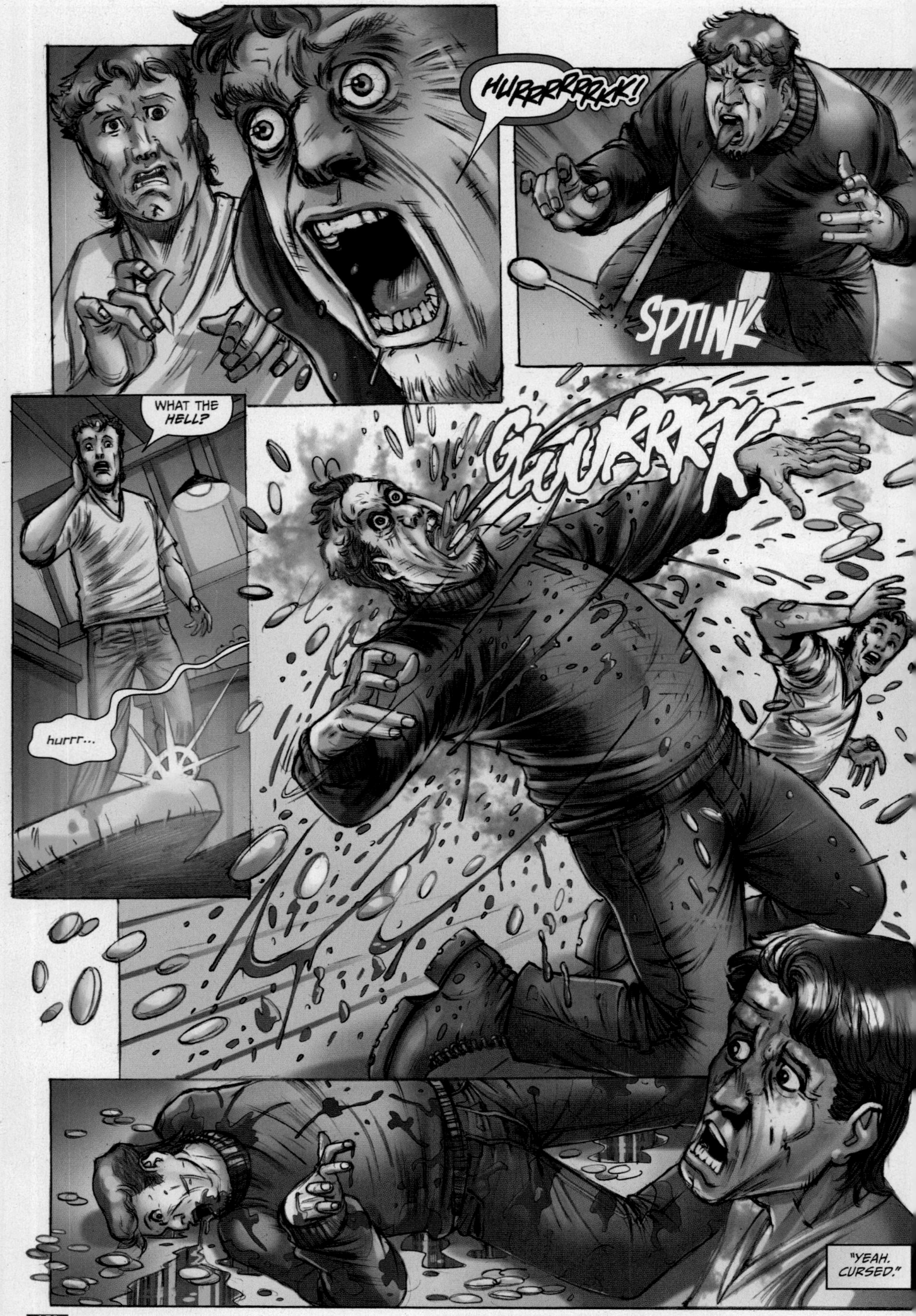
HURRRRRRRK!
SPTINK
WHAT THE HELL?
hurrr...
GLUURRRK
"YEAH. CURSED."

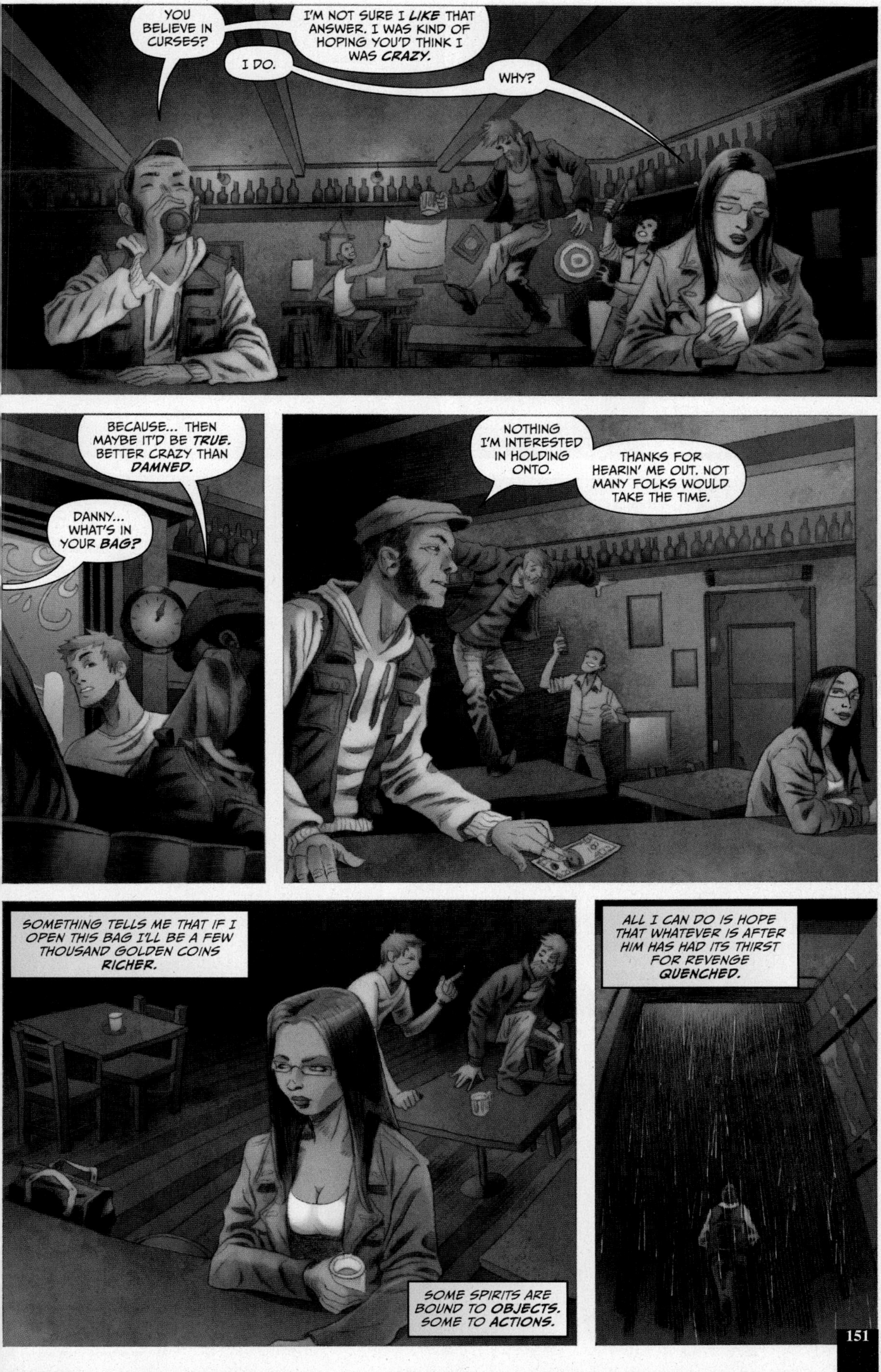
YOU BELIEVE IN CURSES?
I DO.
I'M NOT SURE I LIKE THAT ANSWER. I WAS KIND OF HOPING YOU'D THINK I WAS CRAZY.
WHY?
BECAUSE... THEN MAYBE IT'D BE TRUE. BETTER CRAZY THAN DAMNED.
DANNY... WHAT'S IN YOUR BAG?
NOTHING I'M INTERESTED IN HOLDING ONTO.
THANKS FOR HEARIN' ME OUT. NOT MANY FOLKS WOULD TAKE THE TIME.
SOMETHING TELLS ME THAT IF I OPEN THIS BAG I'LL BE A FEW THOUSAND GOLDEN COINS RICHER.
SOME SPIRITS ARE BOUND TO OBJECTS. SOME TO ACTIONS.
ALL I CAN DO IS HOPE THAT WHATEVER IS AFTER HIM HAS HAD ITS THIRST FOR REVENGE QUENCHED.

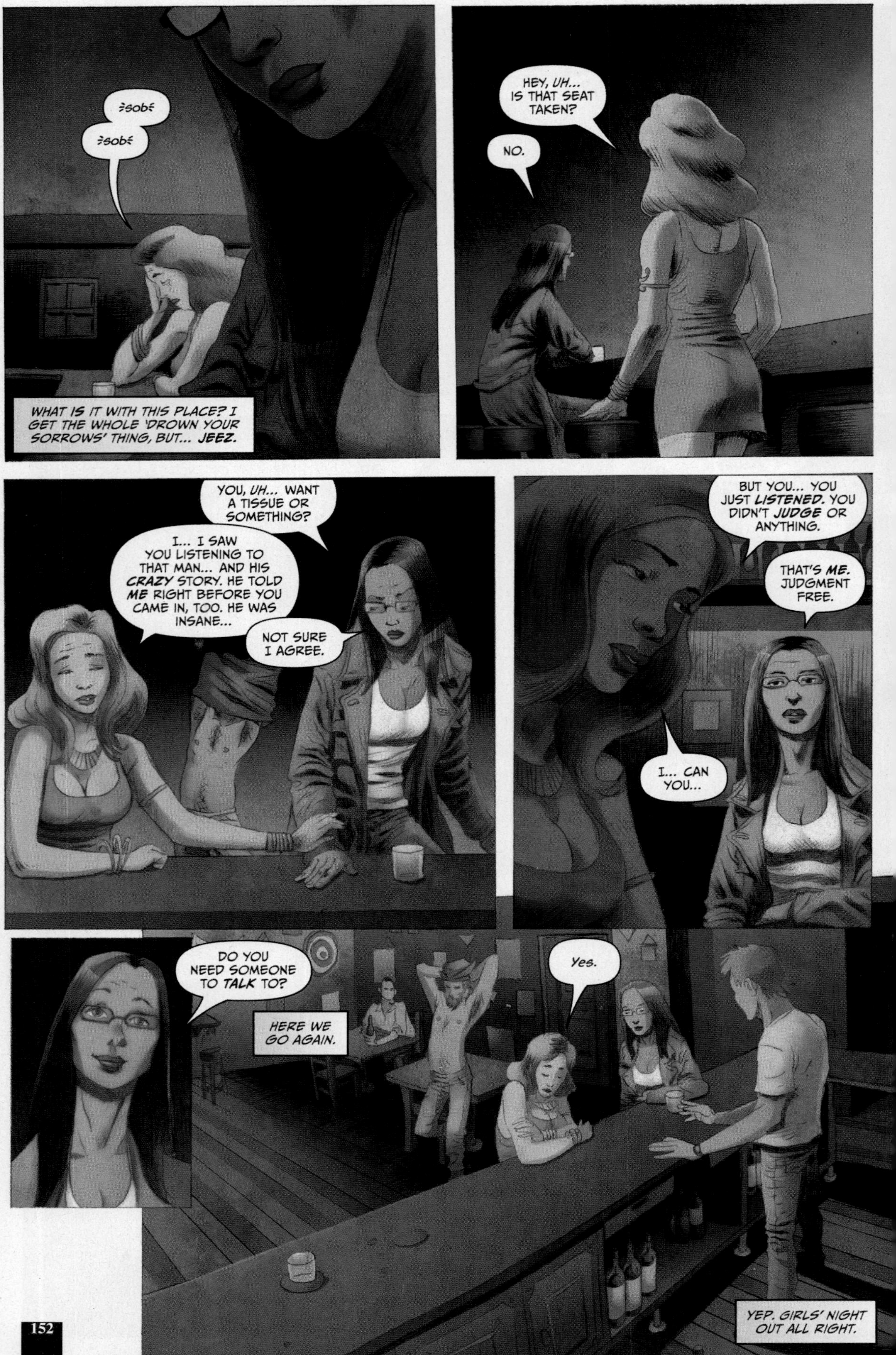

sob
sob
WHAT IS IT WITH THIS PLACE? I GET THE WHOLE 'DROWN YOUR SORROWS' THING, BUT... JEEZ.
HEY, UH... IS THAT SEAT TAKEN?
NO.
YOU, UH... WANT A TISSUE OR SOMETHING?
I... I SAW YOU LISTENING TO THAT MAN... AND HIS CRAZY STORY. HE TOLD ME RIGHT BEFORE YOU CAME IN, TOO. HE WAS INSANE...
NOT SURE I AGREE.
BUT YOU... YOU JUST LISTENED. YOU DIDN'T JUDGE OR ANYTHING.
THAT'S ME. JUDGMENT FREE.
I... CAN YOU...
DO YOU NEED SOMEONE TO TALK TO?
HERE WE GO AGAIN.
Yes.
YEP. GIRLS' NIGHT OUT ALL RIGHT.

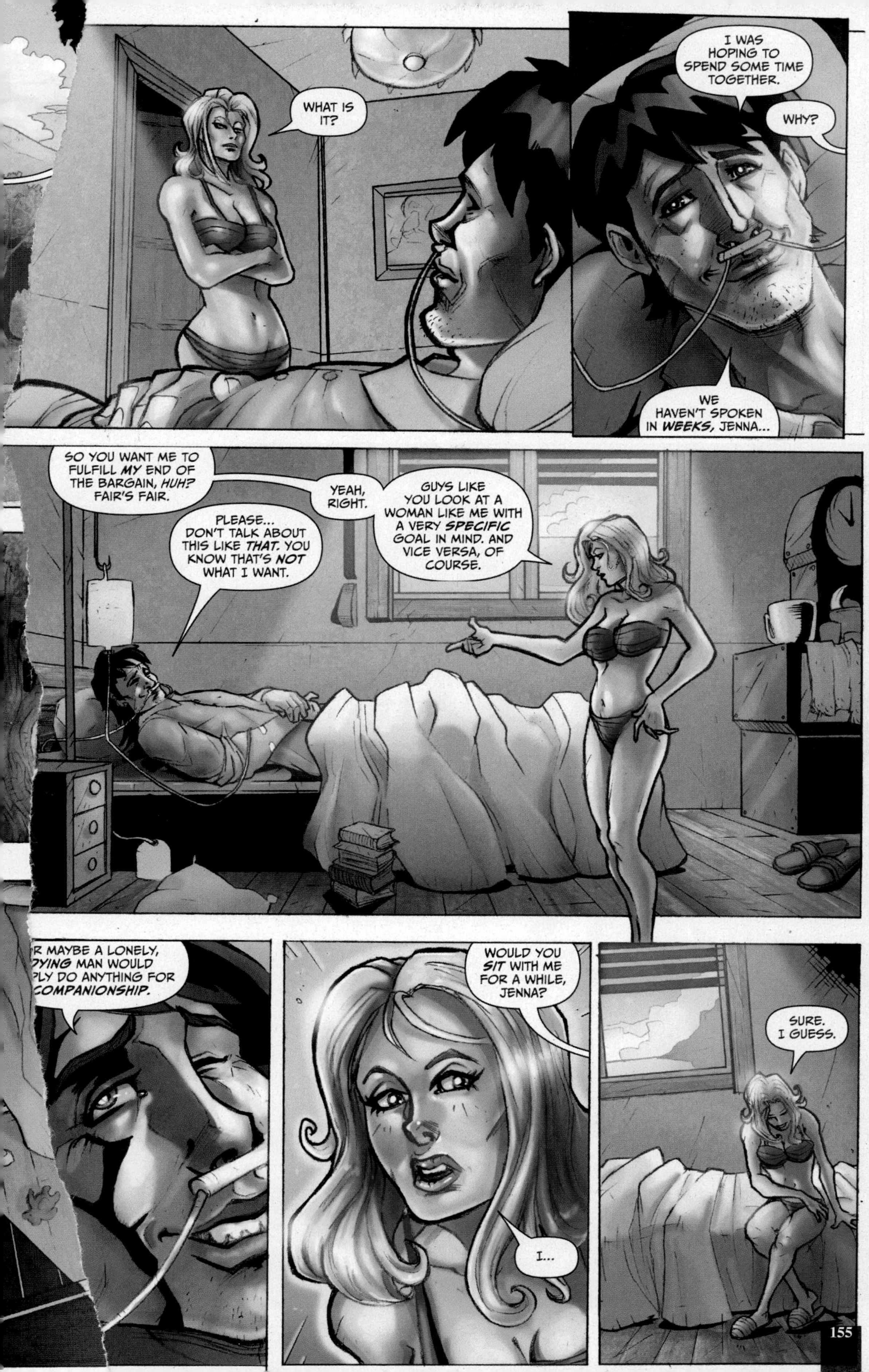
WHAT IS IT?
I WAS HOPING TO SPEND SOME TIME TOGETHER.
WHY?
WE HAVEN'T SPOKEN IN *WEEKS*, JENNA...
SO YOU WANT ME TO FULFILL *MY* END OF THE BARGAIN, *HUH?* FAIR'S FAIR.
PLEASE... DON'T TALK ABOUT THIS LIKE *THAT.* YOU KNOW THAT'S *NOT* WHAT I WANT.
YEAH, RIGHT.
GUYS LIKE YOU LOOK AT A WOMAN LIKE ME WITH A VERY *SPECIFIC* GOAL IN MIND. AND VICE VERSA, OF COURSE.
R MAYBE A LONELY, *DYING* MAN WOULD PLY DO ANYTHING FOR *COMPANIONSHIP.*
I...
WOULD YOU *SIT* WITH ME FOR A WHILE, JENNA?
SURE. I GUESS.

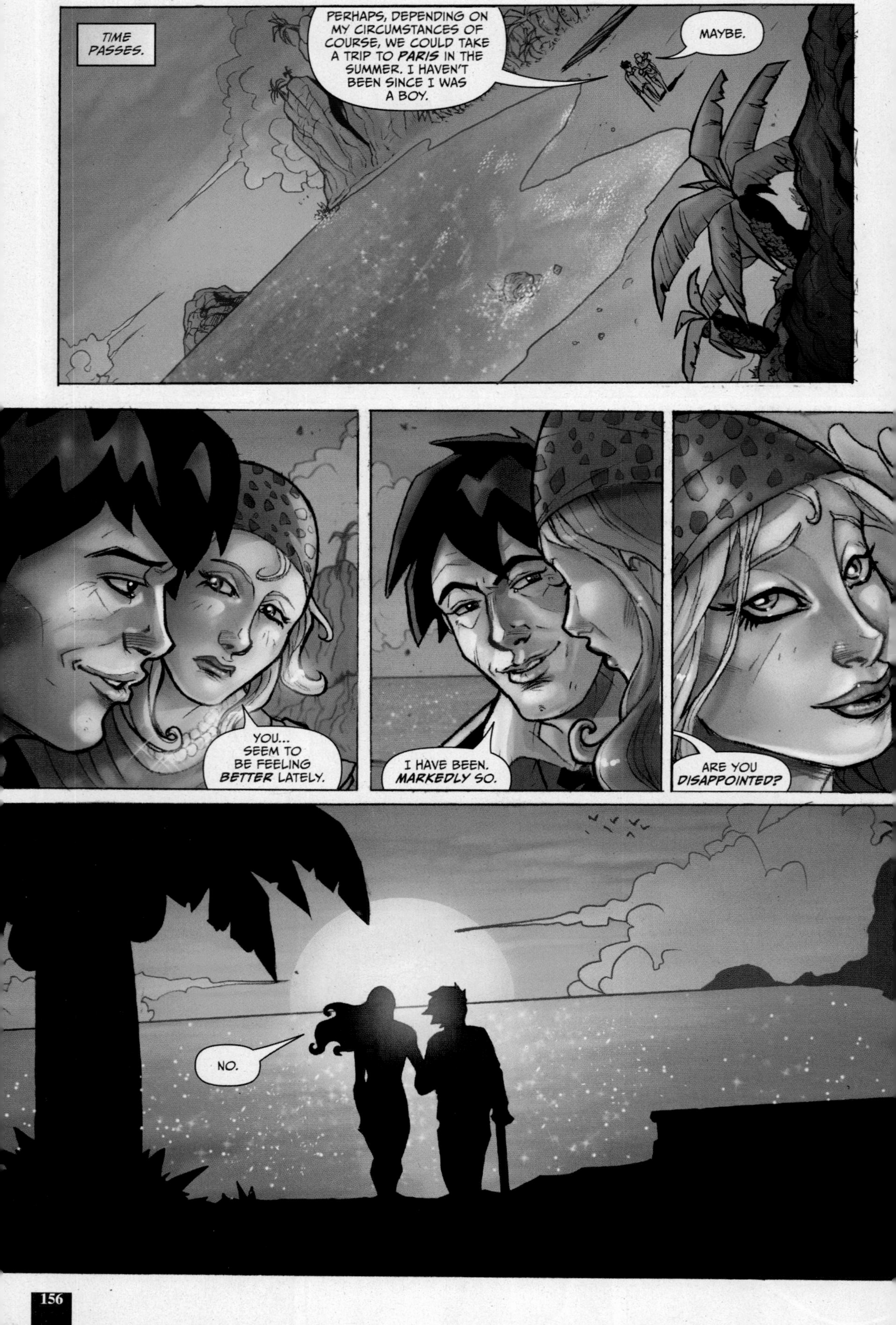
TIME PASSES.
PERHAPS, DEPENDING ON MY CIRCUMSTANCES OF COURSE, WE COULD TAKE A TRIP TO PARIS IN THE SUMMER. I HAVEN'T BEEN SINCE I WAS A BOY.
MAYBE.
YOU... SEEM TO BE FEELING BETTER LATELY.
I HAVE BEEN. MARKEDLY SO.
ARE YOU DISAPPOINTED?
NO.

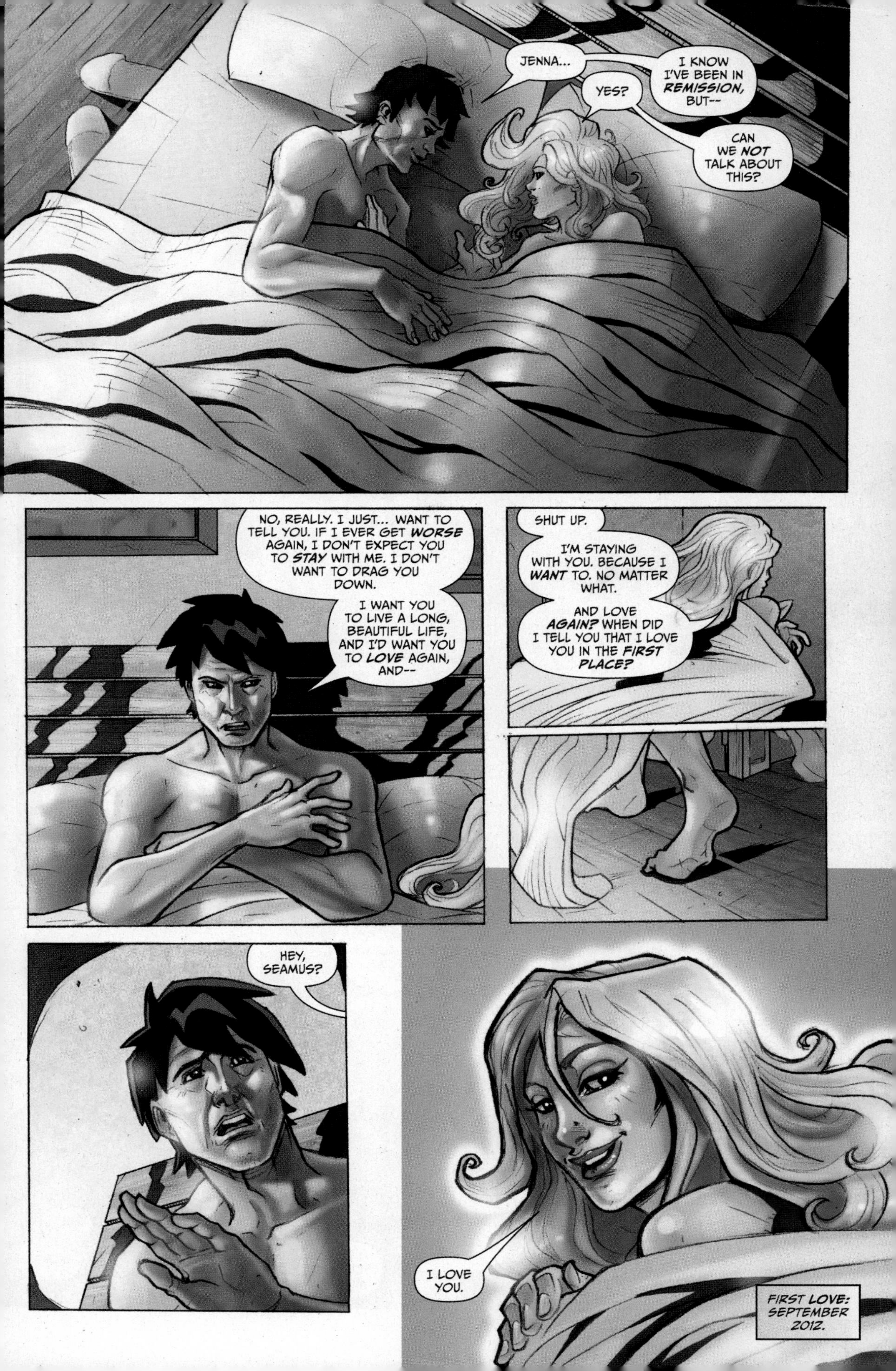
JENNA...
I KNOW I'VE BEEN IN REMISSION, BUT--
YES?
CAN WE NOT TALK ABOUT THIS?
NO, REALLY. I JUST... WANT TO TELL YOU. IF I EVER GET WORSE AGAIN, I DON'T EXPECT YOU TO STAY WITH ME. I DON'T WANT TO DRAG YOU DOWN.
I WANT YOU TO LIVE A LONG, BEAUTIFUL LIFE, AND I'D WANT YOU TO LOVE AGAIN, AND--
SHUT UP.
I'M STAYING WITH YOU. BECAUSE I WANT TO. NO MATTER WHAT.
AND LOVE AGAIN? WHEN DID I TELL YOU THAT I LOVE YOU IN THE FIRST PLACE?
HEY, SEAMUS?
I LOVE YOU.
FIRST LOVE: SEPTEMBER 2012.

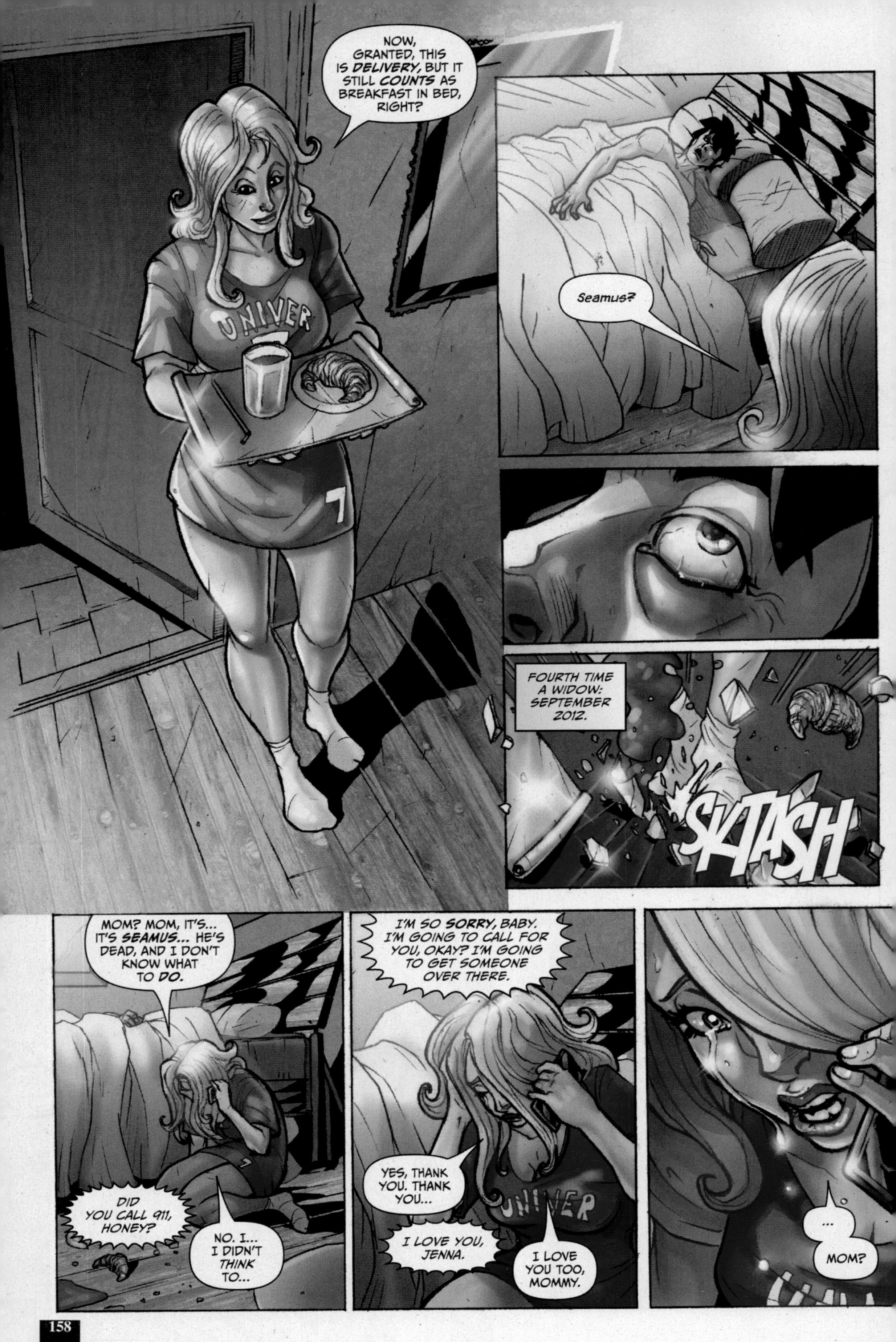
NOW, GRANTED, THIS IS *DELIVERY,* BUT IT STILL *COUNTS* AS BREAKFAST IN BED, RIGHT?
UNIVER
7
Seamus?
FOURTH TIME A WIDOW: SEPTEMBER 2012.
SKTASH
MOM? MOM, IT'S... IT'S *SEAMUS...* HE'S DEAD, AND I DON'T KNOW WHAT TO *DO.*
DID YOU CALL 911, HONEY?
NO. I... I DIDN'T *THINK* TO...
I'M SO *SORRY,* BABY. I'M GOING TO CALL FOR YOU, OKAY? I'M GOING TO GET SOMEONE OVER THERE.
YES, THANK YOU. THANK YOU...
I LOVE YOU, JENNA.
I LOVE YOU TOO, MOMMY.
UNIVER
...
MOM?

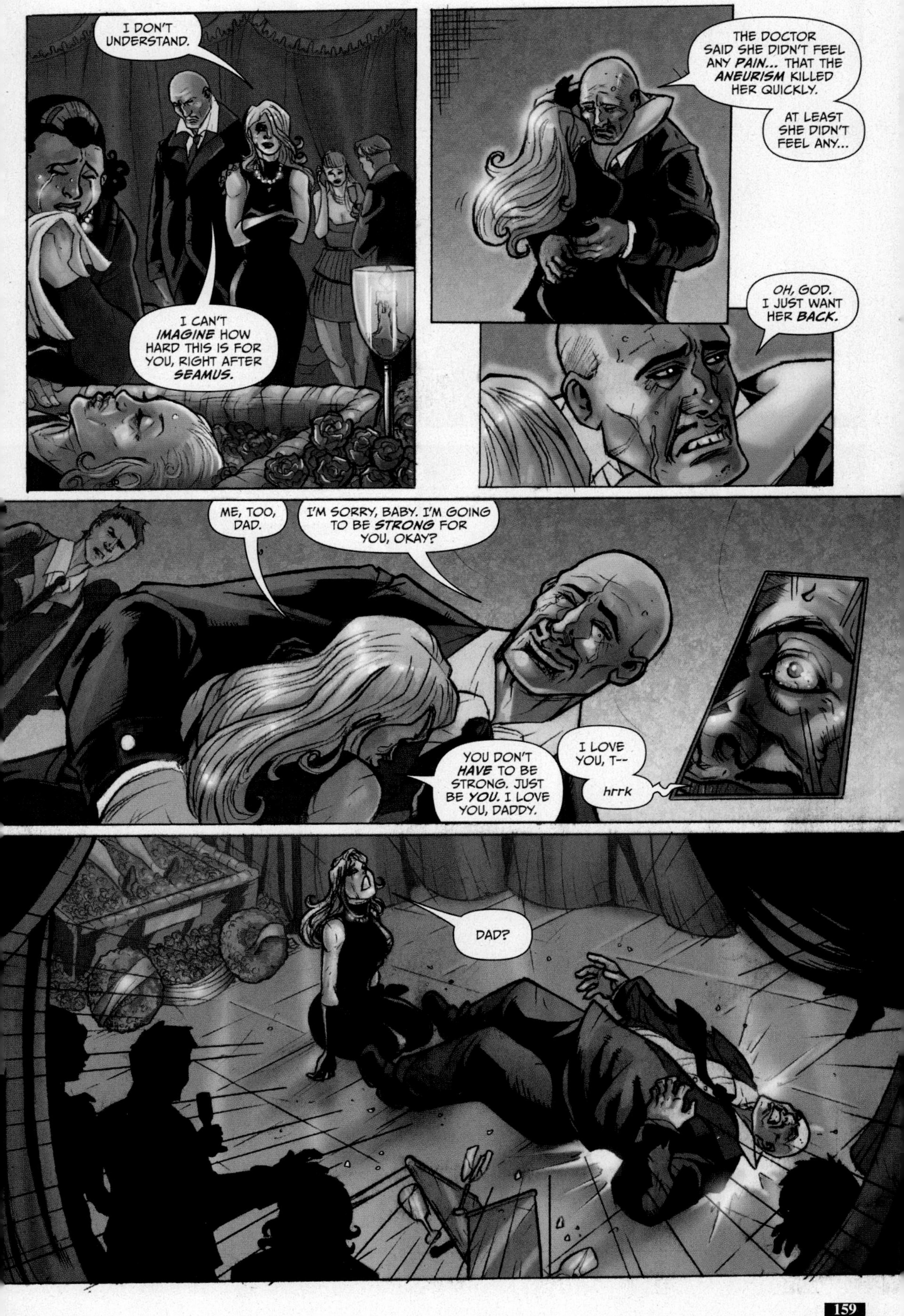
I DON'T UNDERSTAND.
I CAN'T IMAGINE HOW HARD THIS IS FOR YOU, RIGHT AFTER SEAMUS.
THE DOCTOR SAID SHE DIDN'T FEEL ANY PAIN... THAT THE ANEURISM KILLED HER QUICKLY.
AT LEAST SHE DIDN'T FEEL ANY...
OH, GOD. I JUST WANT HER BACK.
ME, TOO, DAD.
I'M SORRY, BABY. I'M GOING TO BE STRONG FOR YOU, OKAY?
YOU DON'T HAVE TO BE STRONG. JUST BE YOU. I LOVE YOU, DADDY.
I LOVE YOU, T--
hrrk
DAD?

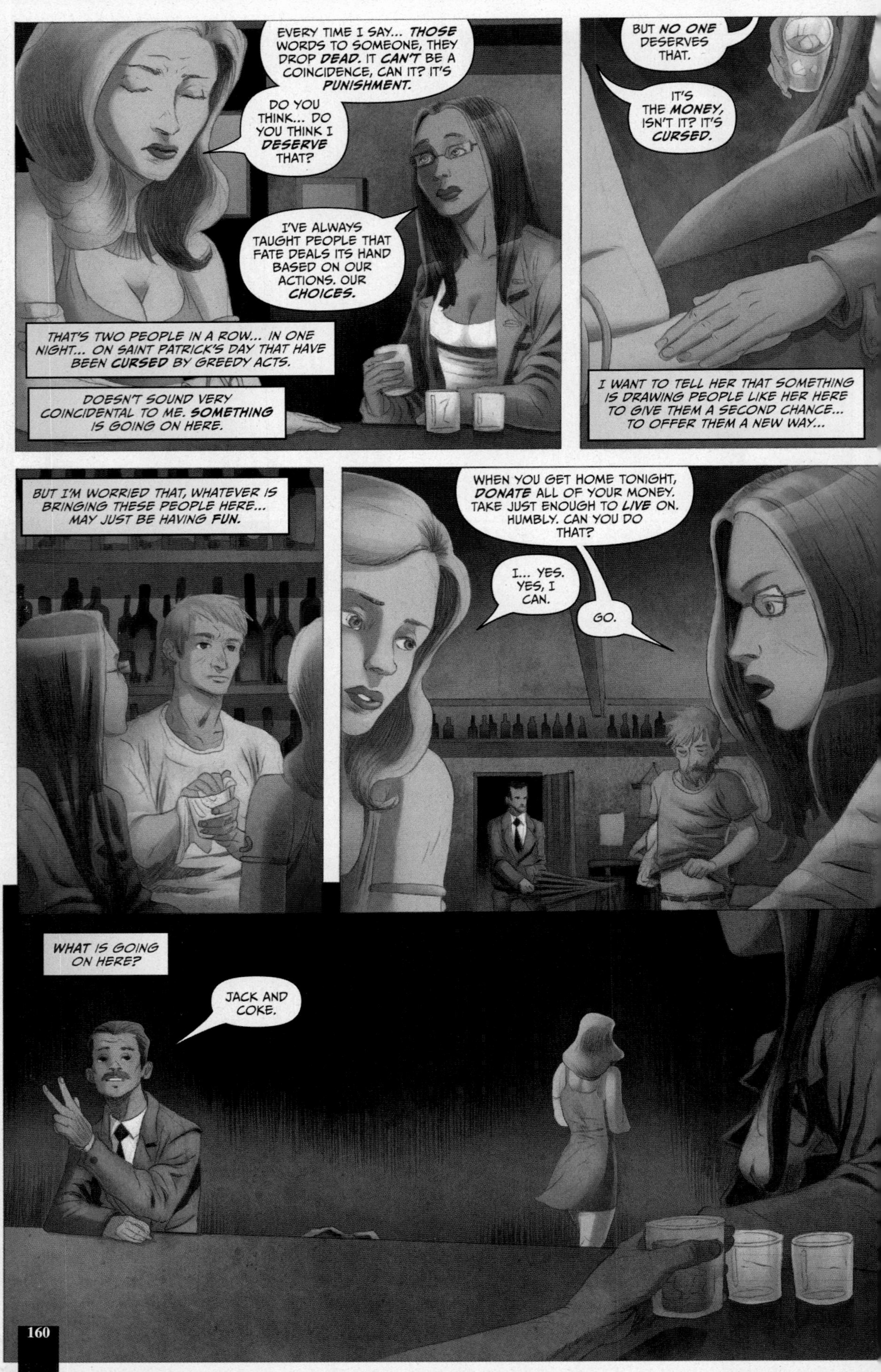
EVERY TIME I SAY... THOSE WORDS TO SOMEONE, THEY DROP DEAD. IT CAN'T BE A COINCIDENCE, CAN IT? IT'S PUNISHMENT.
DO YOU THINK... DO YOU THINK I DESERVE THAT?
I'VE ALWAYS TAUGHT PEOPLE THAT FATE DEALS ITS HAND BASED ON OUR ACTIONS. OUR CHOICES.
THAT'S TWO PEOPLE IN A ROW... IN ONE NIGHT... ON SAINT PATRICK'S DAY THAT HAVE BEEN CURSED BY GREEDY ACTS.
DOESN'T SOUND VERY COINCIDENTAL TO ME. SOMETHING IS GOING ON HERE.
BUT NO ONE DESERVES THAT.
IT'S THE MONEY, ISN'T IT? IT'S CURSED.
I WANT TO TELL HER THAT SOMETHING IS DRAWING PEOPLE LIKE HER HERE TO GIVE THEM A SECOND CHANCE... TO OFFER THEM A NEW WAY...
BUT I'M WORRIED THAT, WHATEVER IS BRINGING THESE PEOPLE HERE... MAY JUST BE HAVING FUN.
WHEN YOU GET HOME TONIGHT, DONATE ALL OF YOUR MONEY. TAKE JUST ENOUGH TO LIVE ON. HUMBLY. CAN YOU DO THAT?
I... YES. YES, I CAN.
GO.
WHAT IS GOING ON HERE?
JACK AND COKE.

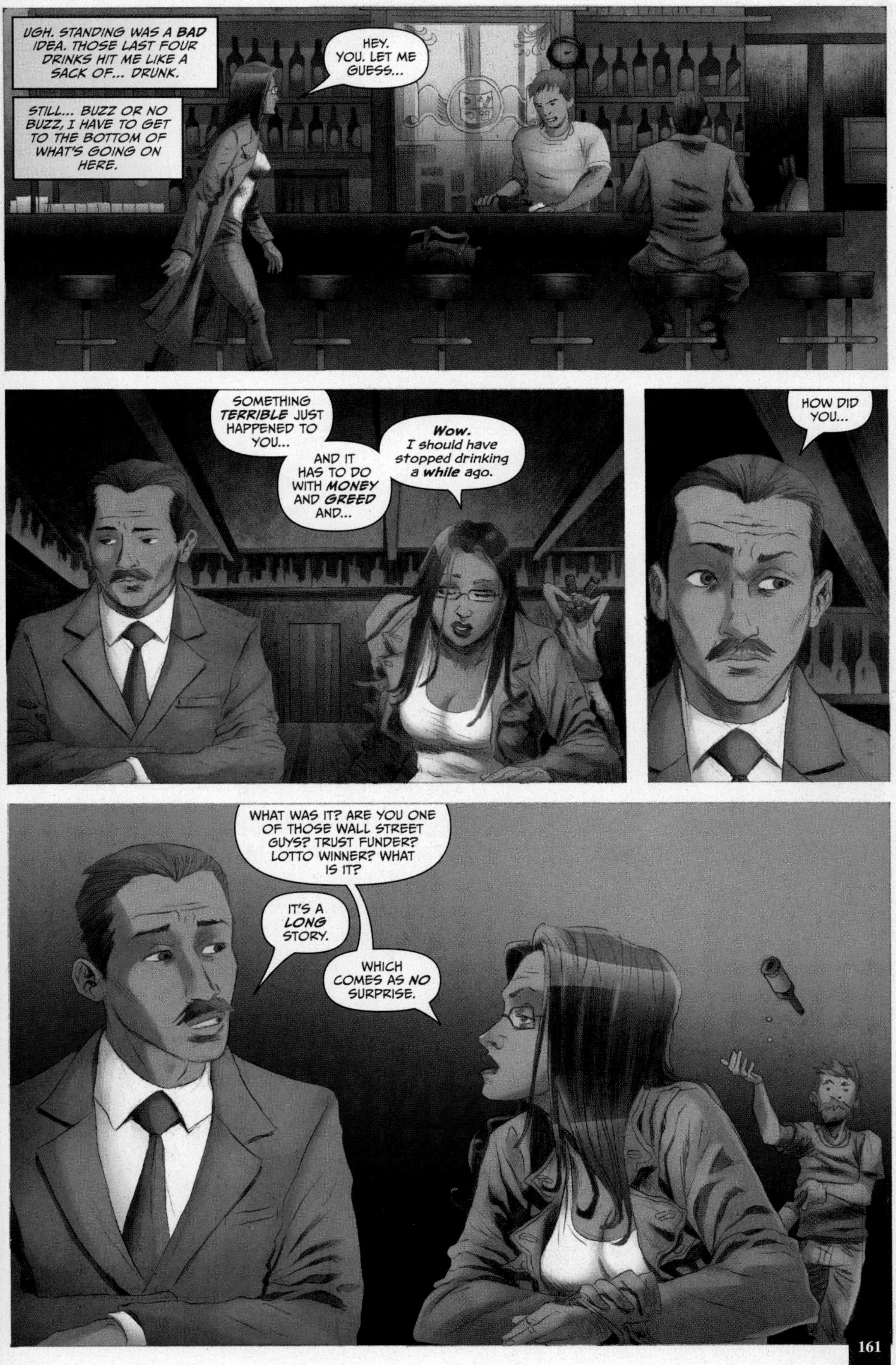
UGH. STANDING WAS A BAD IDEA. THOSE LAST FOUR DRINKS HIT ME LIKE A SACK OF... DRUNK.
STILL... BUZZ OR NO BUZZ, I HAVE TO GET TO THE BOTTOM OF WHAT'S GOING ON HERE.
HEY. YOU. LET ME GUESS...
SOMETHING TERRIBLE JUST HAPPENED TO YOU...
AND IT HAS TO DO WITH MONEY AND GREED AND...
Wow. I should have stopped drinking a while ago.
HOW DID YOU...
WHAT WAS IT? ARE YOU ONE OF THOSE WALL STREET GUYS? TRUST FUNDER? LOTTO WINNER? WHAT IS IT?
IT'S A LONG STORY.
WHICH COMES AS NO SURPRISE.

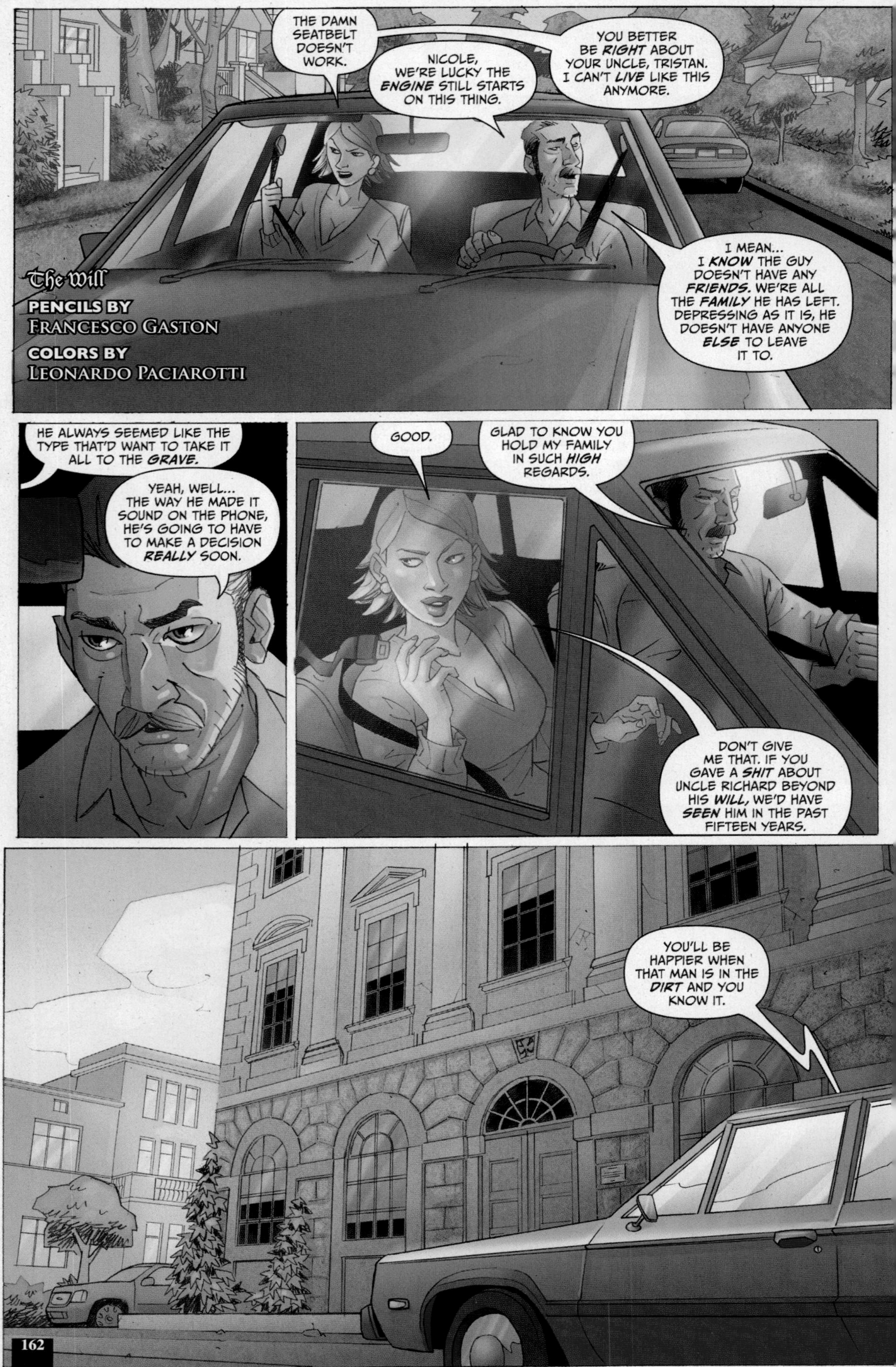
THE DAMN SEATBELT DOESN'T WORK.
NICOLE, WE'RE LUCKY THE ENGINE STILL STARTS ON THIS THING.
YOU BETTER BE RIGHT ABOUT YOUR UNCLE, TRISTAN. I CAN'T LIVE LIKE THIS ANYMORE.
The Will
PENCILS BY
FRANCESCO GASTON
COLORS BY
LEONARDO PACIAROTTI
I MEAN... I KNOW THE GUY DOESN'T HAVE ANY FRIENDS. WE'RE ALL THE FAMILY HE HAS LEFT. DEPRESSING AS IT IS, HE DOESN'T HAVE ANYONE ELSE TO LEAVE IT TO.
HE ALWAYS SEEMED LIKE THE TYPE THAT'D WANT TO TAKE IT ALL TO THE GRAVE.
YEAH, WELL... THE WAY HE MADE IT SOUND ON THE PHONE, HE'S GOING TO HAVE TO MAKE A DECISION REALLY SOON.
GOOD.
GLAD TO KNOW YOU HOLD MY FAMILY IN SUCH HIGH REGARDS.
DON'T GIVE ME THAT. IF YOU GAVE A SHIT ABOUT UNCLE RICHARD BEYOND HIS WILL, WE'D HAVE SEEN HIM IN THE PAST FIFTEEN YEARS.
YOU'LL BE HAPPIER WHEN THAT MAN IS IN THE DIRT AND YOU KNOW IT.

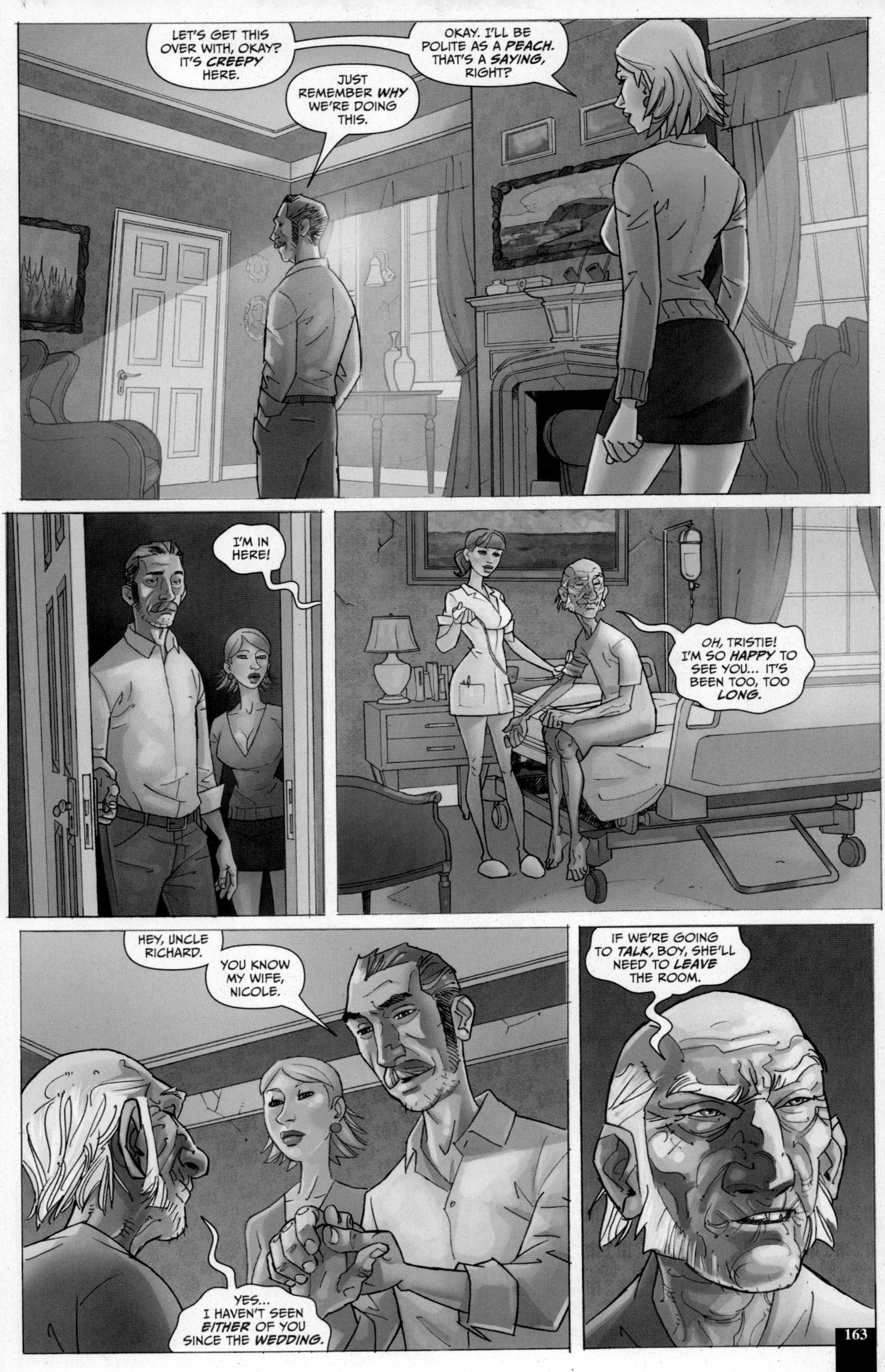
LET'S GET THIS OVER WITH, OKAY? IT'S CREEPY HERE.
OKAY. I'LL BE POLITE AS A PEACH. THAT'S A SAYING, RIGHT?
JUST REMEMBER WHY WE'RE DOING THIS.
I'M IN HERE!
OH, TRISTIE! I'M SO HAPPY TO SEE YOU... IT'S BEEN TOO, TOO LONG.
HEY, UNCLE RICHARD.
YOU KNOW MY WIFE, NICOLE.
YES... I HAVEN'T SEEN EITHER OF YOU SINCE THE WEDDING.
IF WE'RE GOING TO TALK, BOY, SHE'LL NEED TO LEAVE THE ROOM.

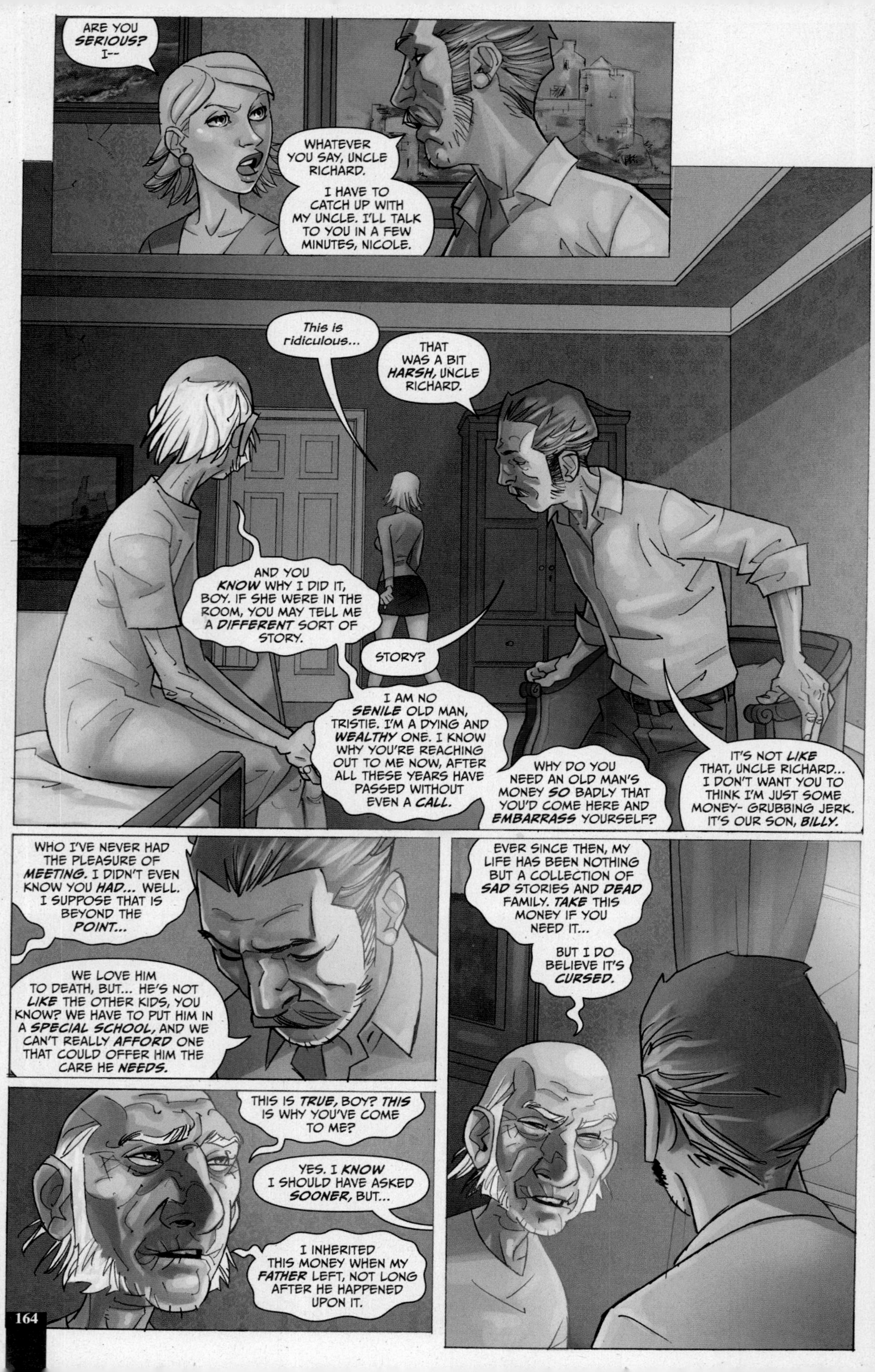
ARE YOU SERIOUS? I--
WHATEVER YOU SAY, UNCLE RICHARD.
I HAVE TO CATCH UP WITH MY UNCLE. I'LL TALK TO YOU IN A FEW MINUTES, NICOLE.
This is ridiculous...
THAT WAS A BIT HARSH, UNCLE RICHARD.
AND YOU KNOW WHY I DID IT, BOY. IF SHE WERE IN THE ROOM, YOU MAY TELL ME A DIFFERENT SORT OF STORY.
STORY?
I AM NO SENILE OLD MAN, TRISTIE. I'M A DYING AND WEALTHY ONE. I KNOW WHY YOU'RE REACHING OUT TO ME NOW, AFTER ALL THESE YEARS HAVE PASSED WITHOUT EVEN A CALL.
WHY DO YOU NEED AN OLD MAN'S MONEY SO BADLY THAT YOU'D COME HERE AND EMBARRASS YOURSELF?
IT'S NOT LIKE THAT, UNCLE RICHARD... I DON'T WANT YOU TO THINK I'M JUST SOME MONEY- GRUBBING JERK. IT'S OUR SON, BILLY.
WHO I'VE NEVER HAD THE PLEASURE OF MEETING. I DIDN'T EVEN KNOW YOU HAD... WELL. I SUPPOSE THAT IS BEYOND THE POINT...
WE LOVE HIM TO DEATH, BUT... HE'S NOT LIKE THE OTHER KIDS, YOU KNOW? WE HAVE TO PUT HIM IN A SPECIAL SCHOOL, AND WE CAN'T REALLY AFFORD ONE THAT COULD OFFER HIM THE CARE HE NEEDS.
THIS IS TRUE, BOY? THIS IS WHY YOU'VE COME TO ME?
YES. I KNOW I SHOULD HAVE ASKED SOONER, BUT...
I INHERITED THIS MONEY WHEN MY FATHER LEFT, NOT LONG AFTER HE HAPPENED UPON IT.
EVER SINCE THEN, MY LIFE HAS BEEN NOTHING BUT A COLLECTION OF SAD STORIES AND DEAD FAMILY. TAKE THIS MONEY IF YOU NEED IT...
BUT I DO BELIEVE IT'S CURSED.

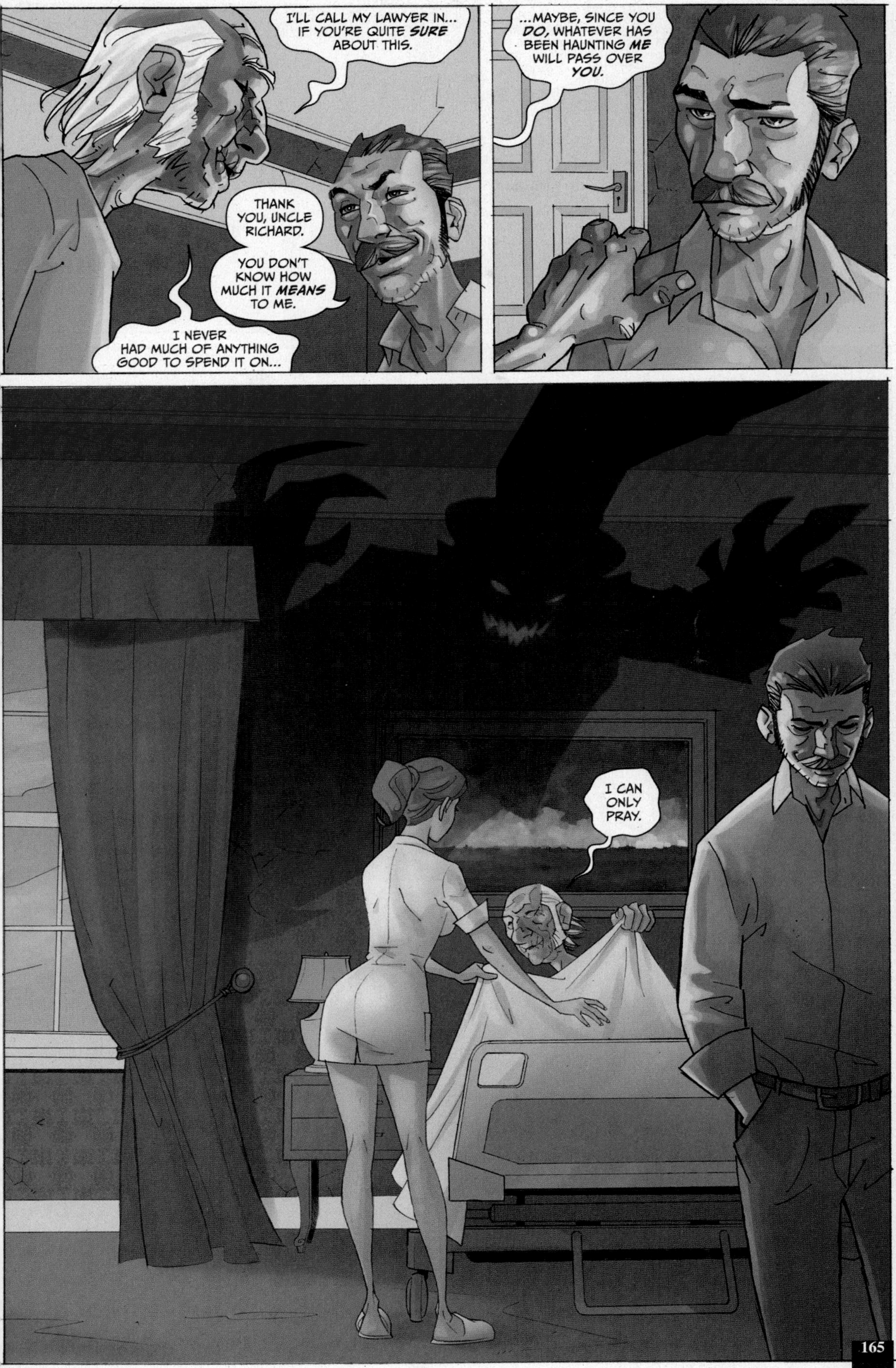
I'LL CALL MY LAWYER IN... IF YOU'RE QUITE SURE ABOUT THIS.
THANK YOU, UNCLE RICHARD.
YOU DON'T KNOW HOW MUCH IT MEANS TO ME.
I NEVER HAD MUCH OF ANYTHING GOOD TO SPEND IT ON...
...MAYBE, SINCE YOU DO, WHATEVER HAS BEEN HAUNTING ME WILL PASS OVER YOU.
I CAN ONLY PRAY.

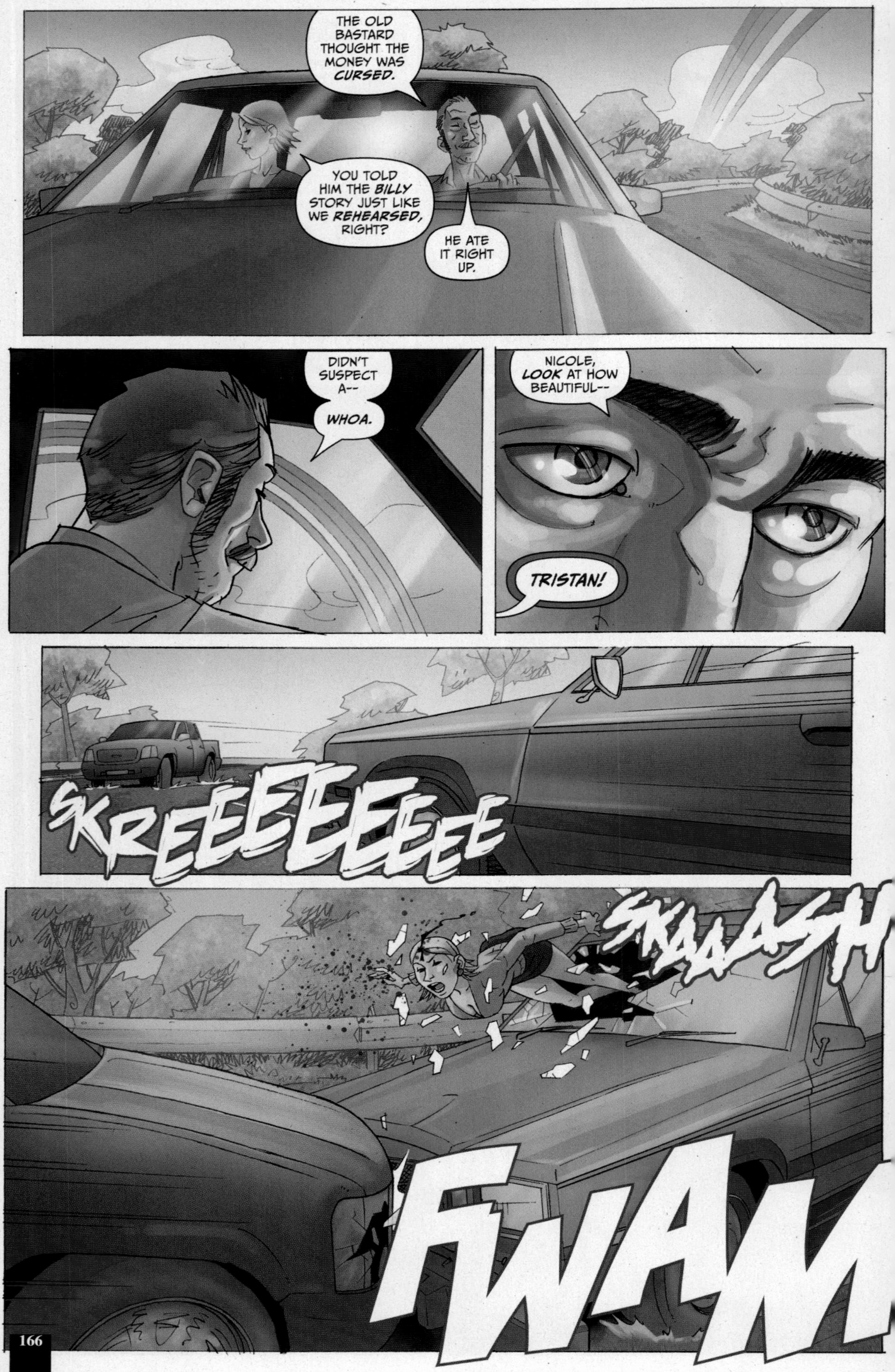
THE OLD BASTARD THOUGHT THE MONEY WAS CURSED.
YOU TOLD HIM THE BILLY STORY JUST LIKE WE REHEARSED, RIGHT?
HE ATE IT RIGHT UP.
DIDN'T SUSPECT A--
WHOA.
NICOLE, LOOK AT HOW BEAUTIFUL--
TRISTAN!
SKREEEEEEEEEEE
SKAAASH
FWAM

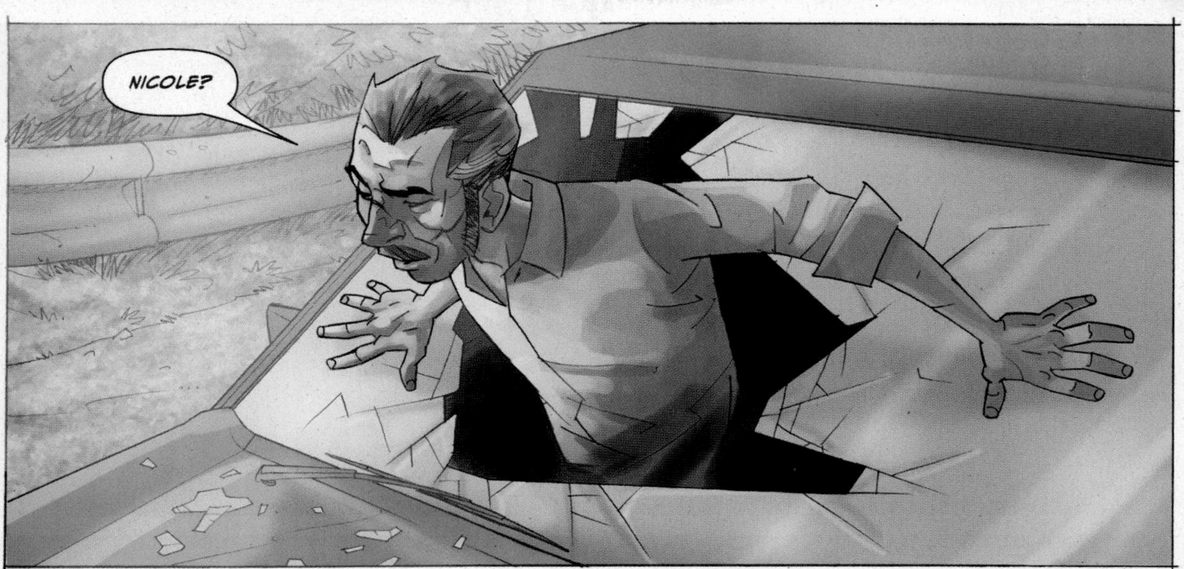
NICOLE?

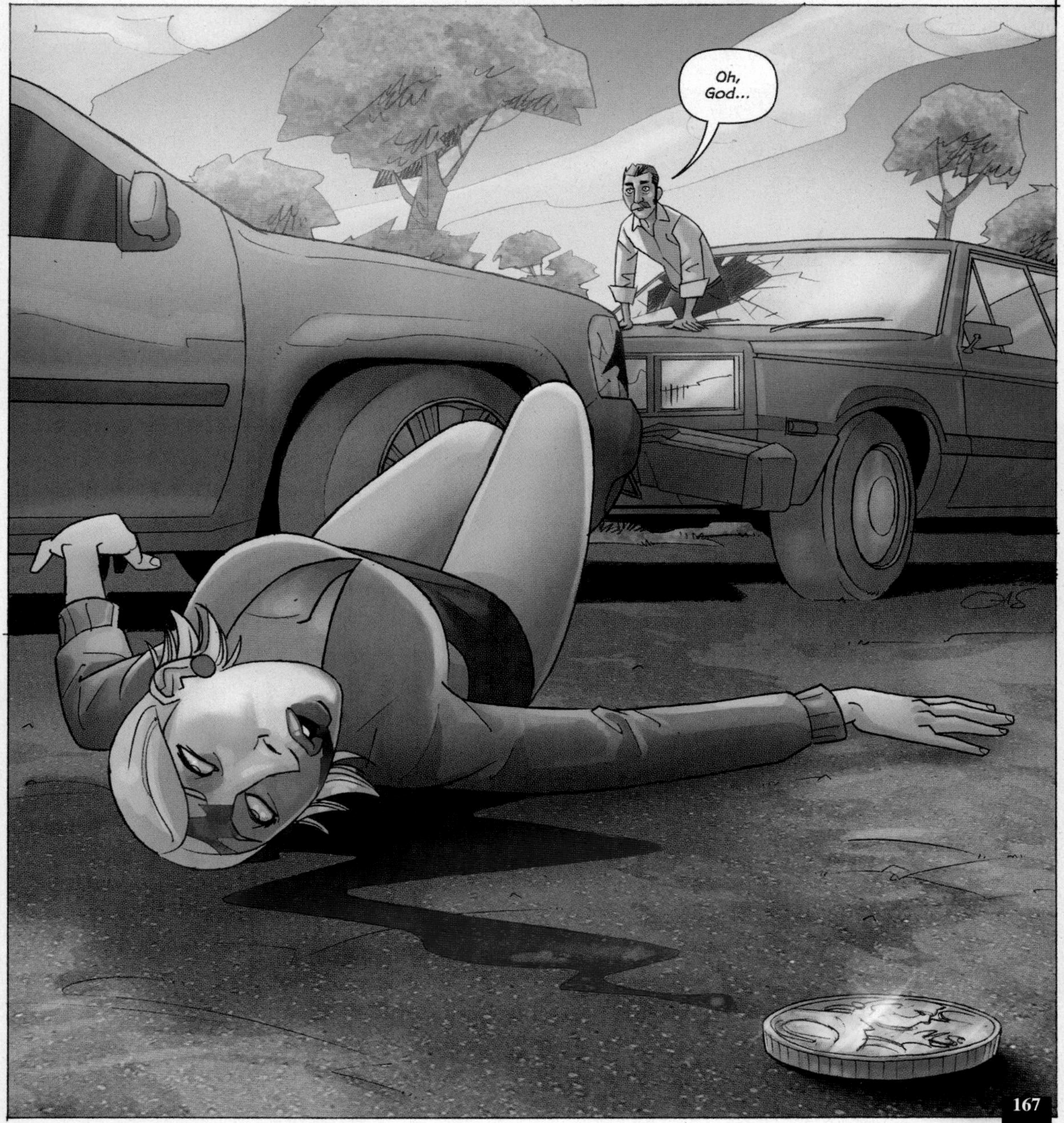
Oh, God...

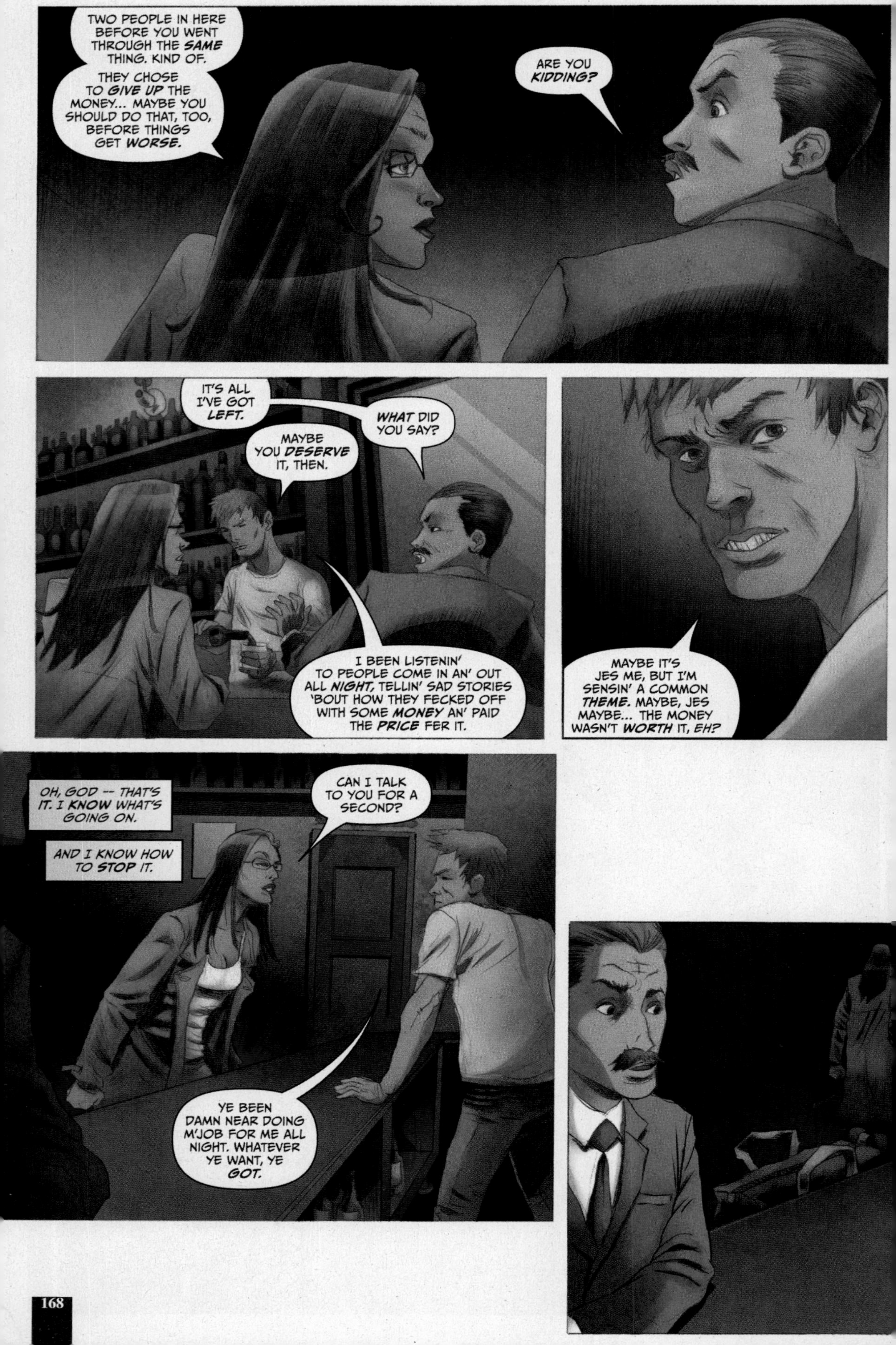
TWO PEOPLE IN HERE BEFORE YOU WENT THROUGH THE SAME THING. KIND OF.
THEY CHOSE TO GIVE UP THE MONEY... MAYBE YOU SHOULD DO THAT, TOO, BEFORE THINGS GET WORSE.
ARE YOU KIDDING?
IT'S ALL I'VE GOT LEFT.
MAYBE YOU DESERVE IT, THEN.
WHAT DID YOU SAY?
I BEEN LISTENIN' TO PEOPLE COME IN AN' OUT ALL NIGHT, TELLIN' SAD STORIES 'BOUT HOW THEY FECKED OFF WITH SOME MONEY AN' PAID THE PRICE FER IT.
MAYBE IT'S JES ME, BUT I'M SENSIN' A COMMON THEME. MAYBE, JES MAYBE... THE MONEY WASN'T WORTH IT, EH?
OH, GOD -- THAT'S IT. I KNOW WHAT'S GOING ON.
AND I KNOW HOW TO STOP IT.
CAN I TALK TO YOU FOR A SECOND?
YE BEEN DAMN NEAR DOING M'JOB FOR ME ALL NIGHT. WHATEVER YE WANT, YE GOT.

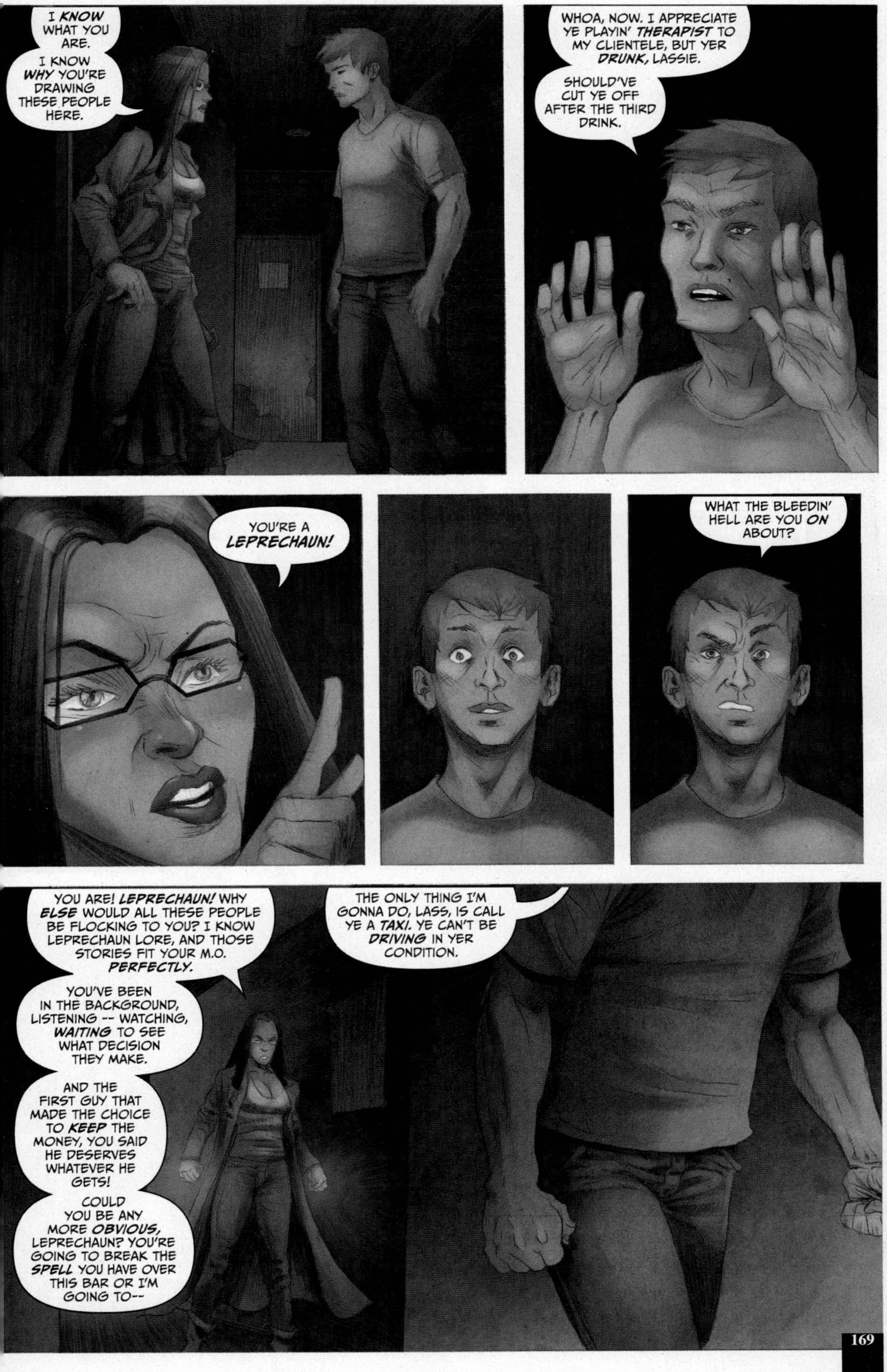
I KNOW WHAT YOU ARE.
I KNOW WHY YOU'RE DRAWING THESE PEOPLE HERE.
WHOA, NOW. I APPRECIATE YE PLAYIN' THERAPIST TO MY CLIENTELE, BUT YER DRUNK, LASSIE.
SHOULD'VE CUT YE OFF AFTER THE THIRD DRINK.
YOU'RE A LEPRECHAUN!
WHAT THE BLEEDIN' HELL ARE YOU ON ABOUT?
YOU ARE! LEPRECHAUN! WHY ELSE WOULD ALL THESE PEOPLE BE FLOCKING TO YOU? I KNOW LEPRECHAUN LORE, AND THOSE STORIES FIT YOUR M.O. PERFECTLY.
YOU'VE BEEN IN THE BACKGROUND, LISTENING -- WATCHING, WAITING TO SEE WHAT DECISION THEY MAKE.
AND THE FIRST GUY THAT MADE THE CHOICE TO KEEP THE MONEY, YOU SAID HE DESERVES WHATEVER HE GETS!
COULD YOU BE ANY MORE OBVIOUS, LEPRECHAUN? YOU'RE GOING TO BREAK THE SPELL YOU HAVE OVER THIS BAR OR I'M GOING TO--
THE ONLY THING I'M GONNA DO, LASS, IS CALL YE A TAXI. YE CAN'T BE DRIVING IN YER CONDITION.

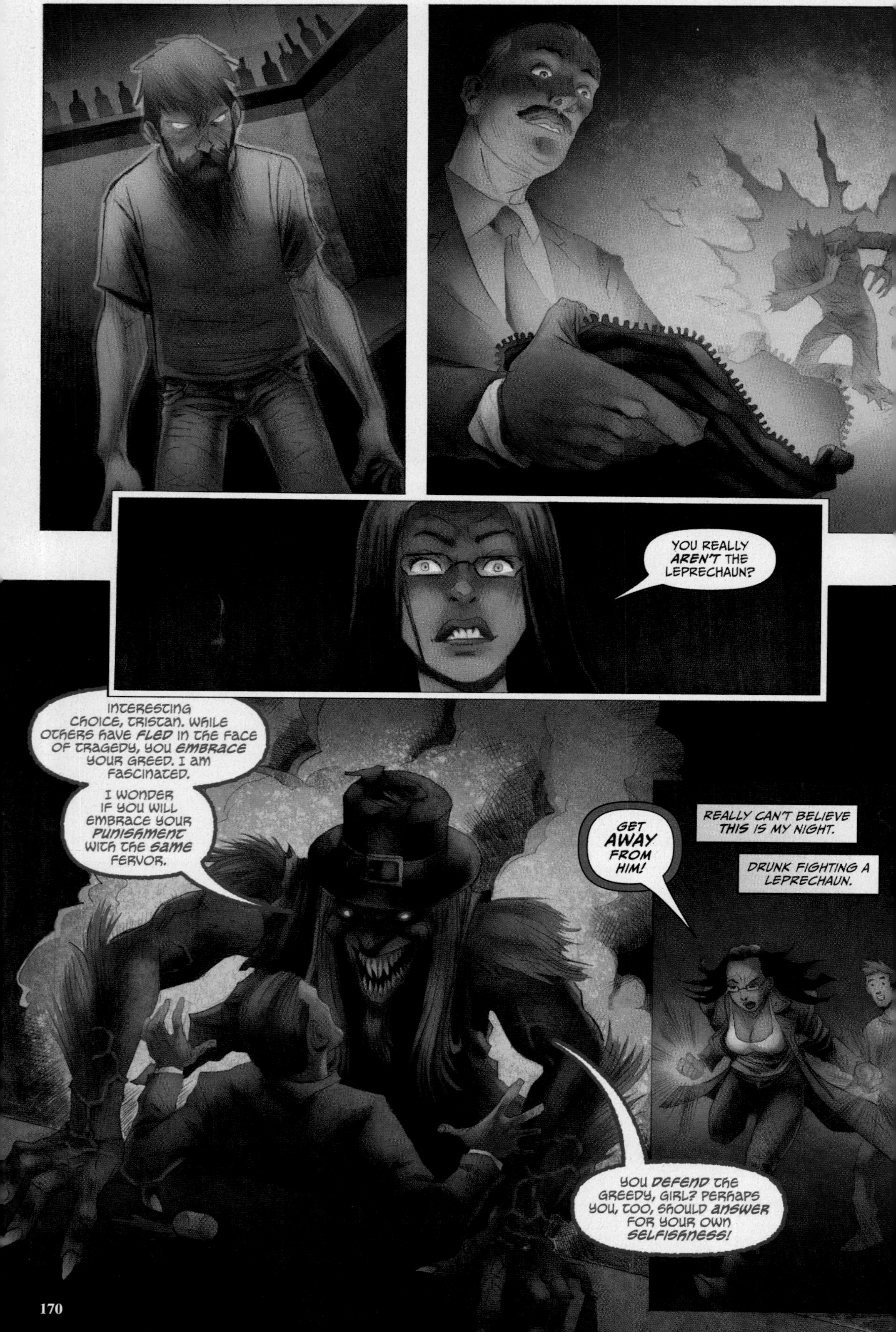
YOU REALLY AREN'T THE LEPRECHAUN?
INTERESTING CHOICE, TRISTAN. WHILE OTHERS HAVE FLED IN THE FACE OF TRAGEDY, YOU EMBRACE YOUR GREED. I AM FASCINATED.
I WONDER IF YOU WILL EMBRACE YOUR PUNISHMENT WITH THE SAME FERVOR.
GET AWAY FROM HIM!
REALLY CAN'T BELIEVE THIS IS MY NIGHT.
DRUNK FIGHTING A LEPRECHAUN.
YOU DEFEND THE GREEDY, GIRL? PERHAPS YOU, TOO, SHOULD ANSWER FOR YOUR OWN SELFISHNESS!

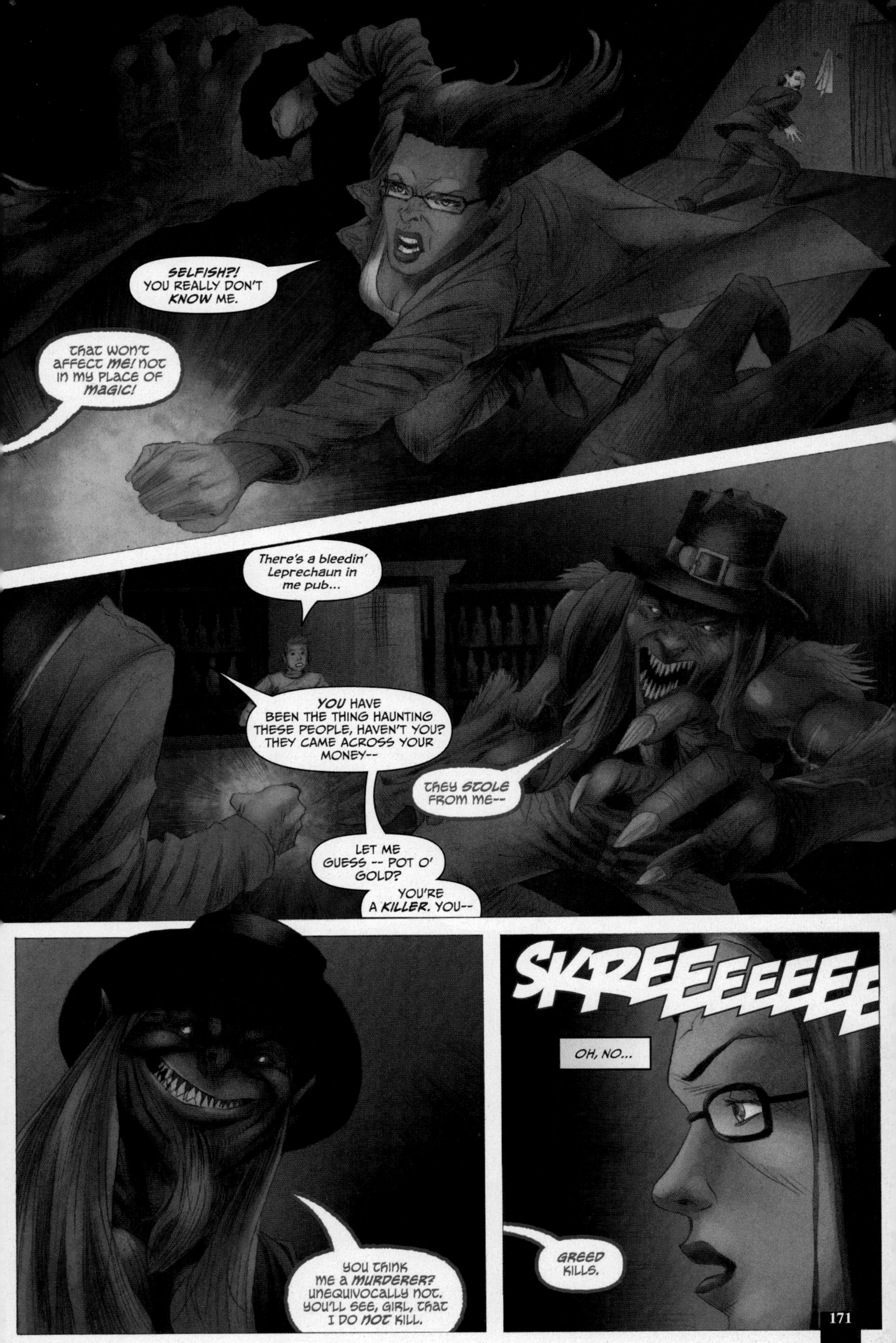
SELFISH?! YOU REALLY DON'T KNOW ME.
THAT WON'T AFFECT ME! NOT IN MY PLACE OF MAGIC!
There's a bleedin' Leprechaun in me pub...
YOU HAVE BEEN THE THING HAUNTING THESE PEOPLE, HAVEN'T YOU? THEY CAME ACROSS YOUR MONEY--
THEY STOLE FROM ME--
LET ME GUESS -- POT O' GOLD?
YOU'RE A KILLER. YOU--
YOU THINK ME A MURDERER? UNEQUIVOCALLY NOT. YOU'LL SEE, GIRL, THAT I DO NOT KILL.
SKREEEEEEEE
OH, NO...
GREED KILLS.

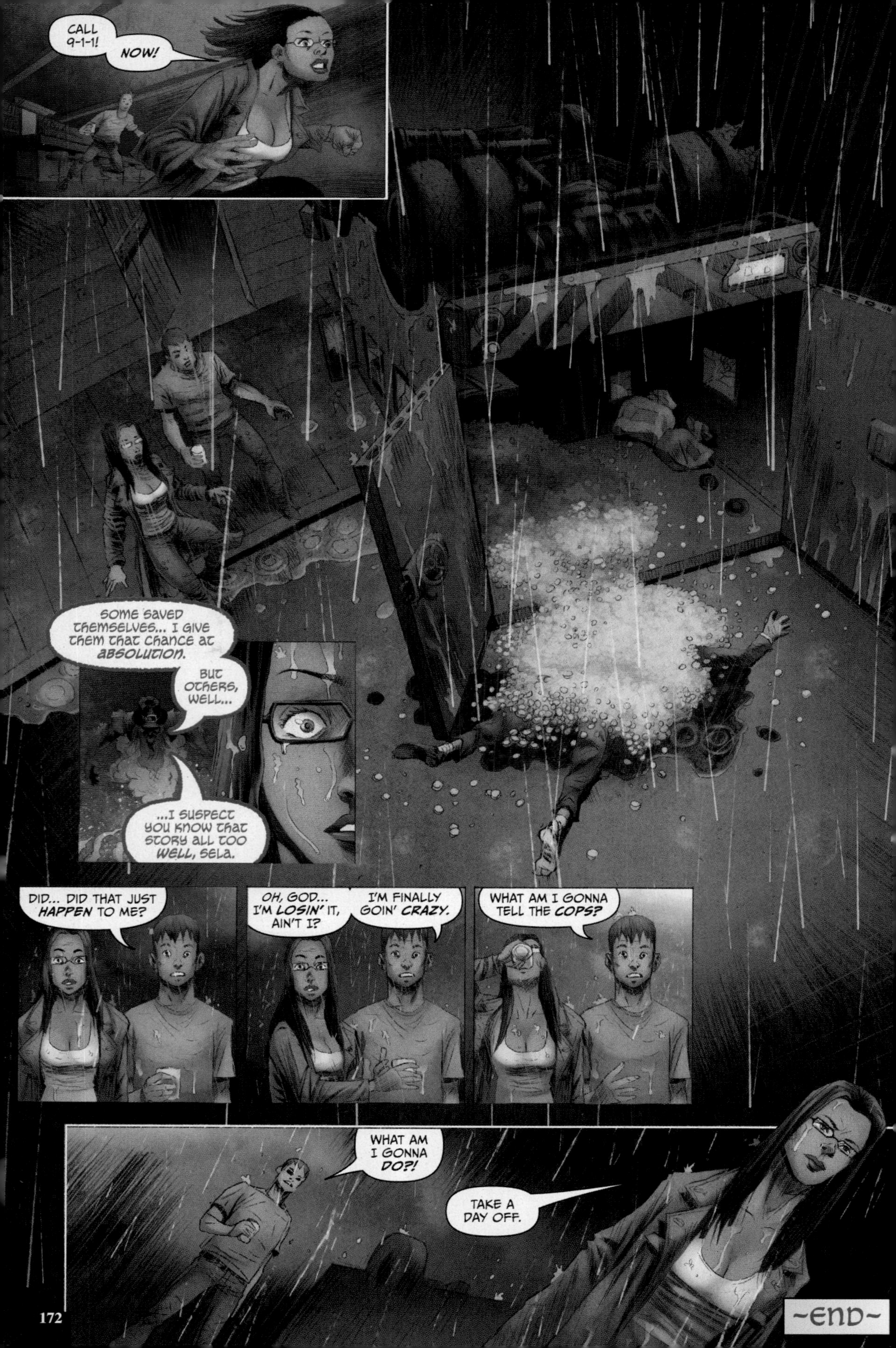
CALL 9-1-1! NOW!
SOME SAVED THEMSELVES... I GIVE THEM THAT CHANCE AT ABSOLUTION.
BUT OTHERS, WELL...
...I SUSPECT YOU KNOW THAT STORY ALL TOO WELL, SELA.
DID... DID THAT JUST HAPPEN TO ME?
OH, GOD... I'M LOSIN' IT, AIN'T I?
I'M FINALLY GOIN' CRAZY.
WHAT AM I GONNA TELL THE COPS?
WHAT AM I GONNA DO?!
TAKE A DAY OFF.
~END~

Grimm Fairy Tales

Different Seasons

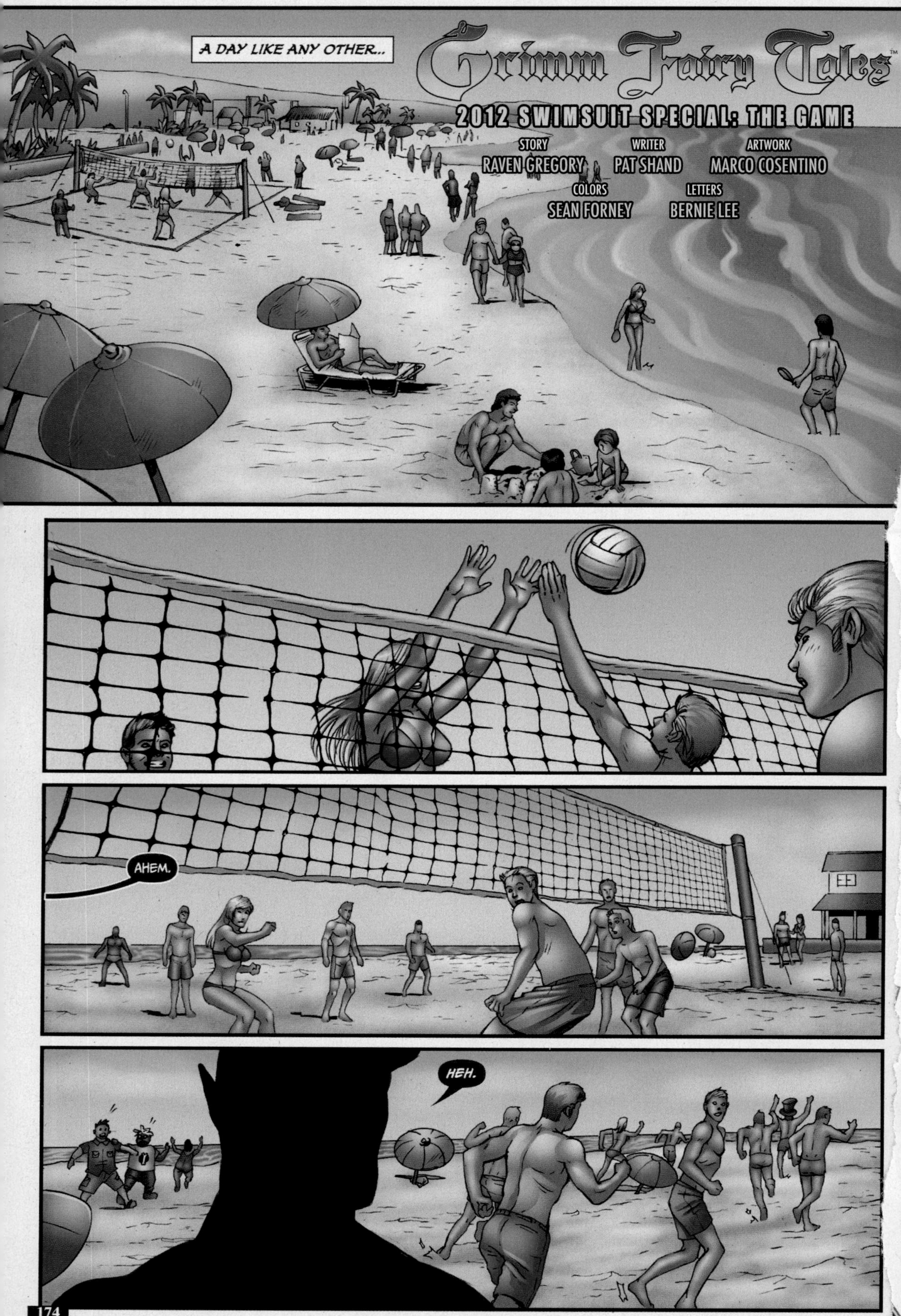
A DAY LIKE ANY OTHER...
Grimm Fairy Tales™
2012 SWIMSUIT SPECIAL: THE GAME
STORY
RAVEN GREGORY
WRITER
PAT SHAND
ARTWORK
MARCO COSENTINO
COLORS
SEAN FORNEY
LETTERS
BERNIE LEE
AHEM.
HEH.

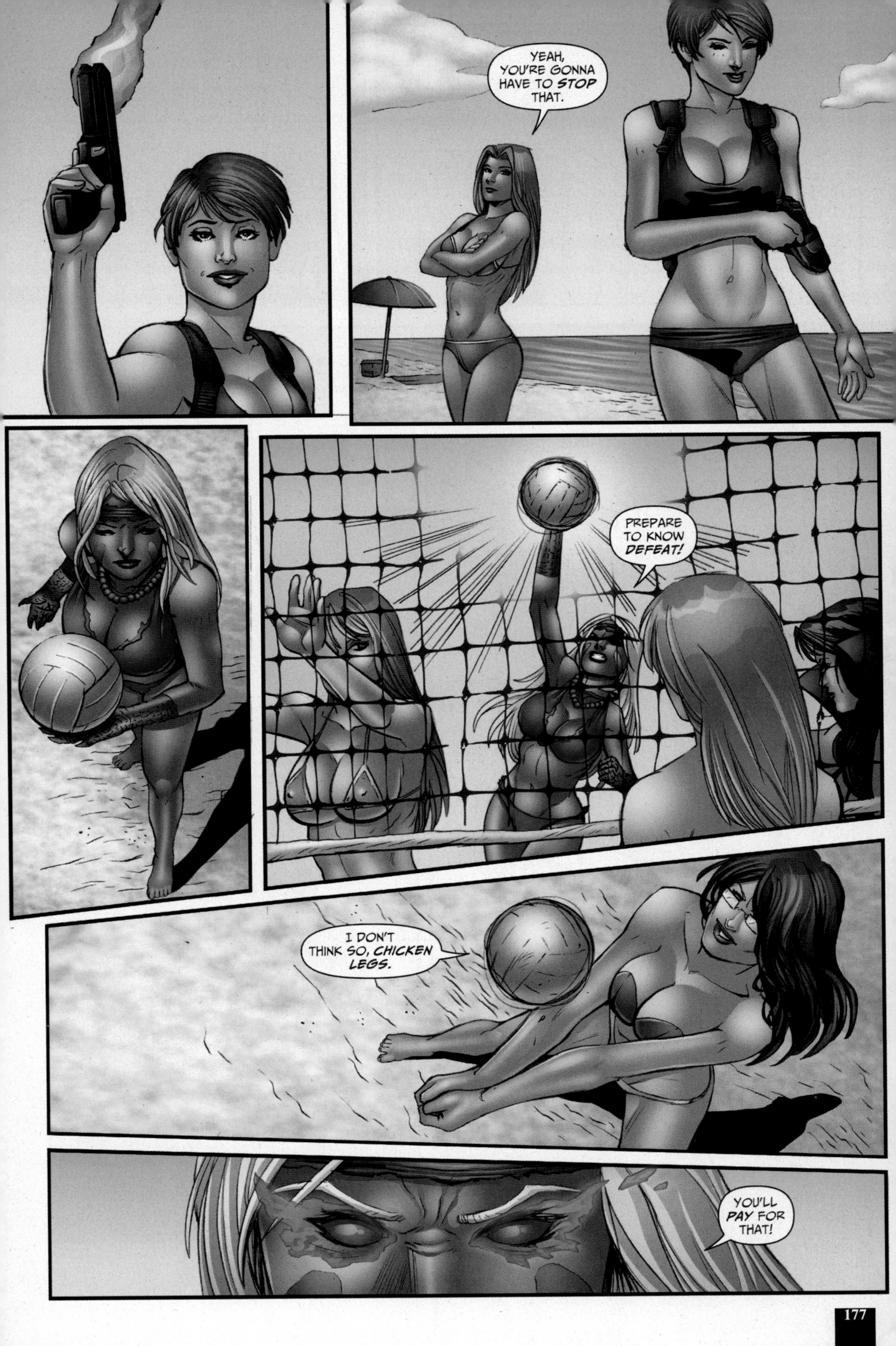
YEAH, YOU'RE GONNA HAVE TO STOP THAT.
PREPARE TO KNOW DEFEAT!
I DON'T THINK SO, CHICKEN LEGS.
YOU'LL PAY FOR THAT!

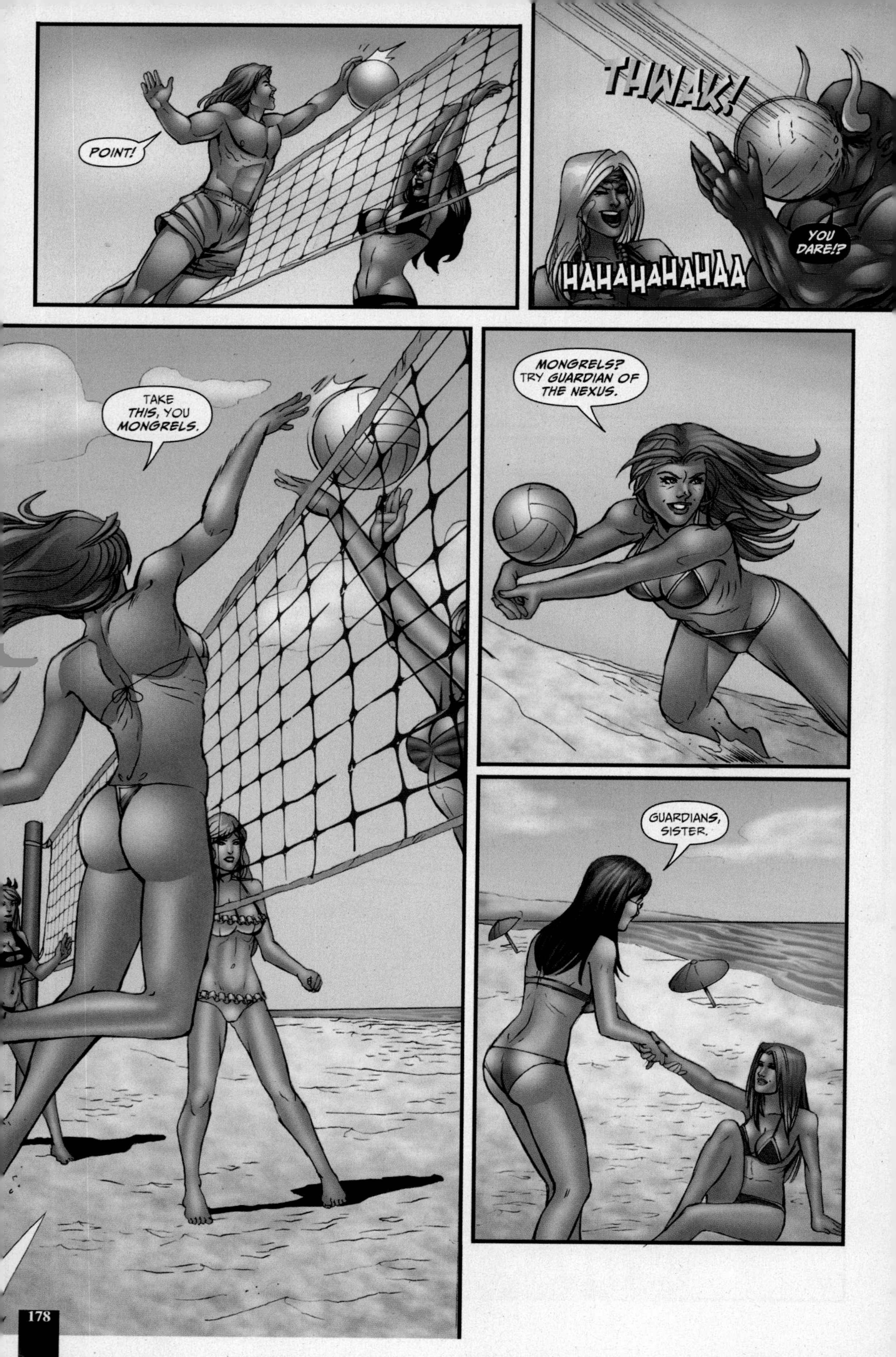
POINT!
THWAK!
HAHAHAHAHAA
YOU DARE!?
TAKE THIS, YOU MONGRELS.
MONGRELS? TRY GUARDIAN OF THE NEXUS.
GUARDIANS, SISTER.

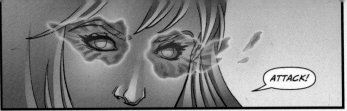

ATTACK!

TIME TO PUT AN END TO THIS.

GET BACK HERE YOU DIRTY WOLVES!

OOF!

WE'RE TIED NOW. LET'S FINISH THIS BY THE BOOKS. NO MORE MAGIC. AGREED?

AGREED. WE DON'T *NEED* TO CHEAT TO DEFEAT THE LIKES OF YOU.

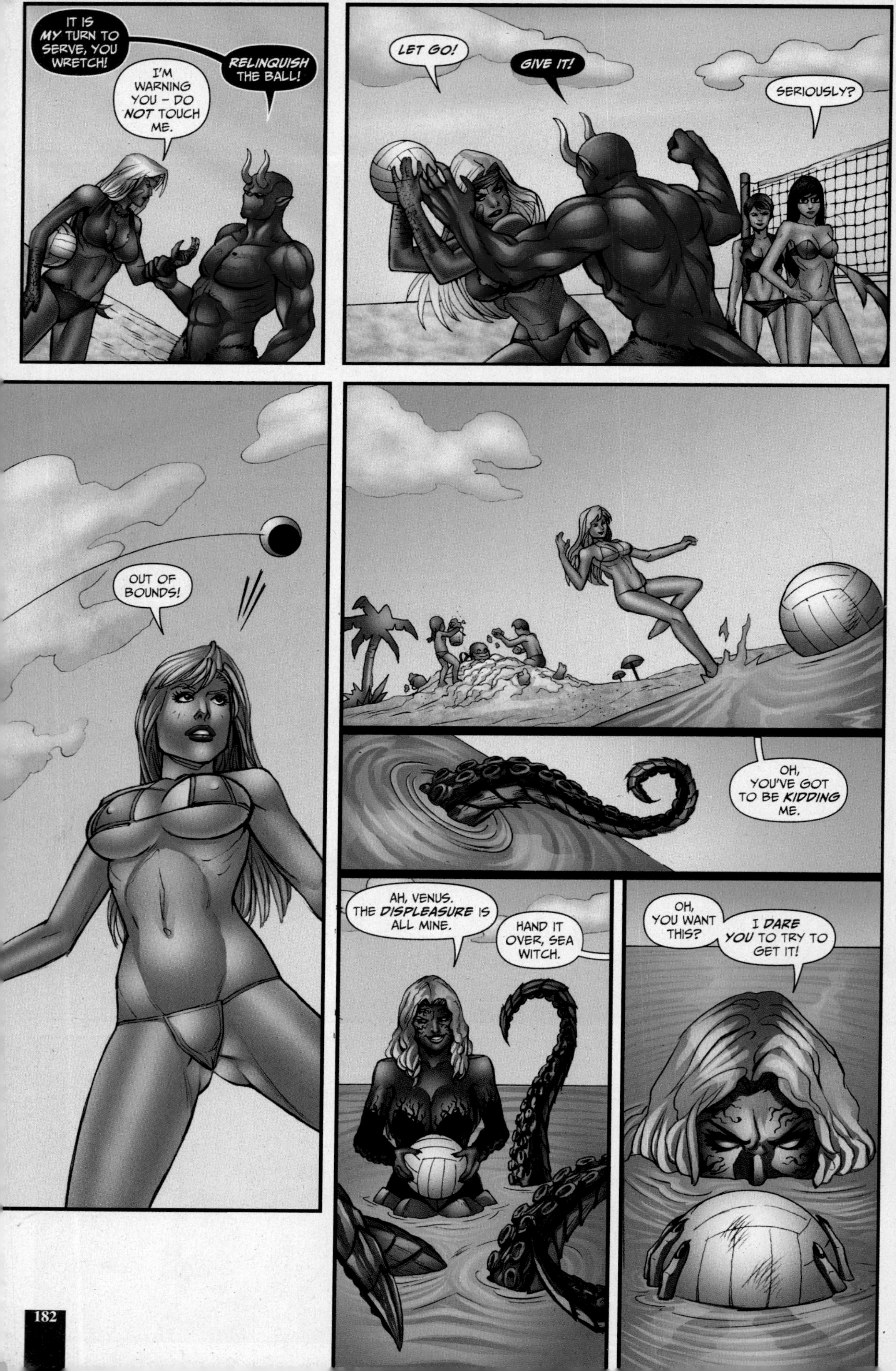
IT IS MY TURN TO SERVE, YOU WRETCH!
I'M WARNING YOU – DO NOT TOUCH ME.
RELINQUISH THE BALL!
LET GO!
GIVE IT!
SERIOUSLY?
OUT OF BOUNDS!
OH, YOU'VE GOT TO BE KIDDING ME.
AH, VENUS. THE DISPLEASURE IS ALL MINE.
HAND IT OVER, SEA WITCH.
OH, YOU WANT THIS?
I DARE YOU TO TRY TO GET IT!

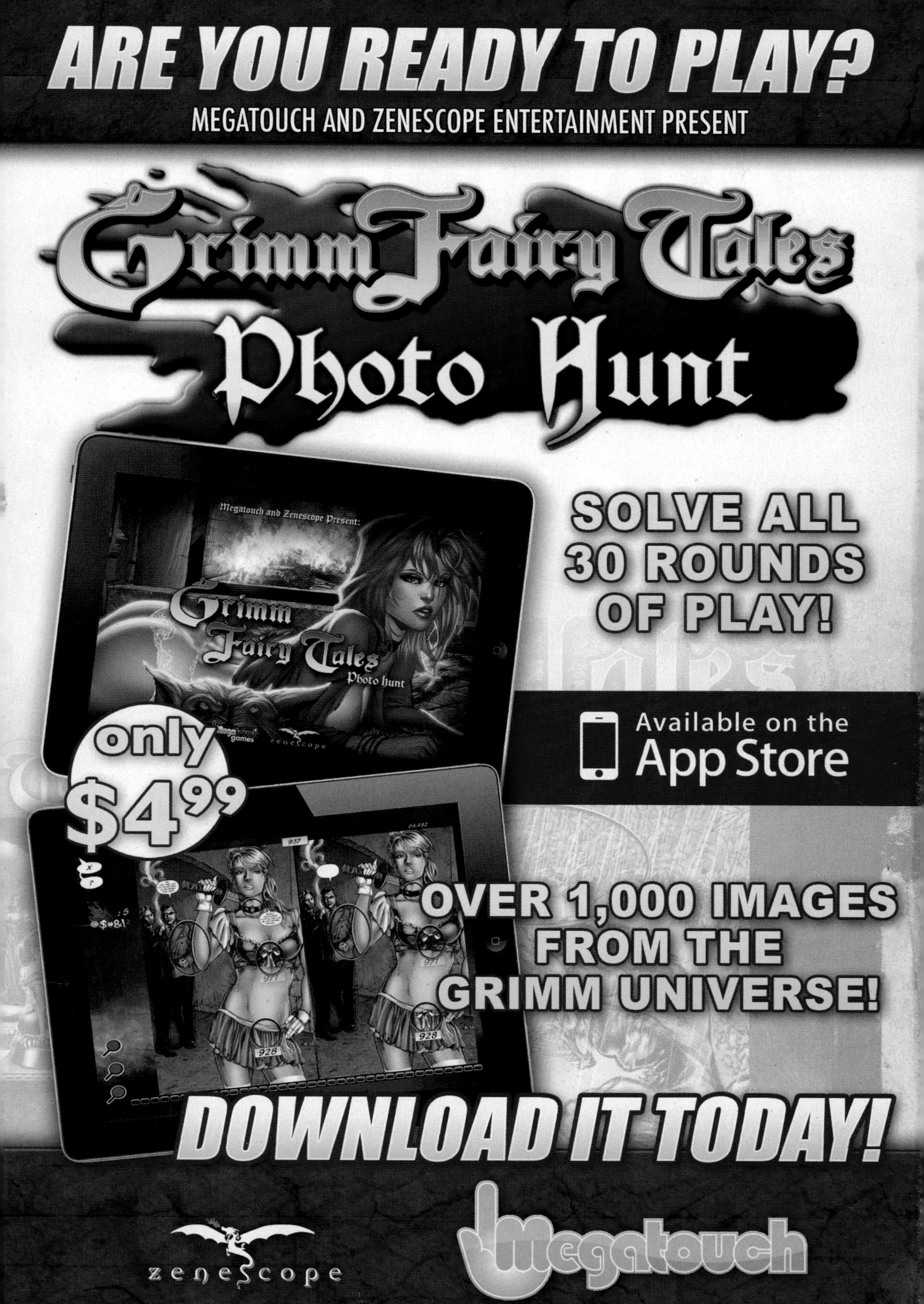
ARE YOU READY TO PLAY?
MEGATOUCH AND ZENESCOPE ENTERTAINMENT PRESENT
Grimm Fairy Tales
Photo Hunt
Megatouch and Zenescope Present:
Grimm Fairy Tales
Photo hunt
SOLVE ALL 30 ROUNDS OF PLAY!
Available on the App Store
only $4.99
OVER 1,000 IMAGES FROM THE GRIMM UNIVERSE!
DOWNLOAD IT TODAY!
zenescope
Megatouch

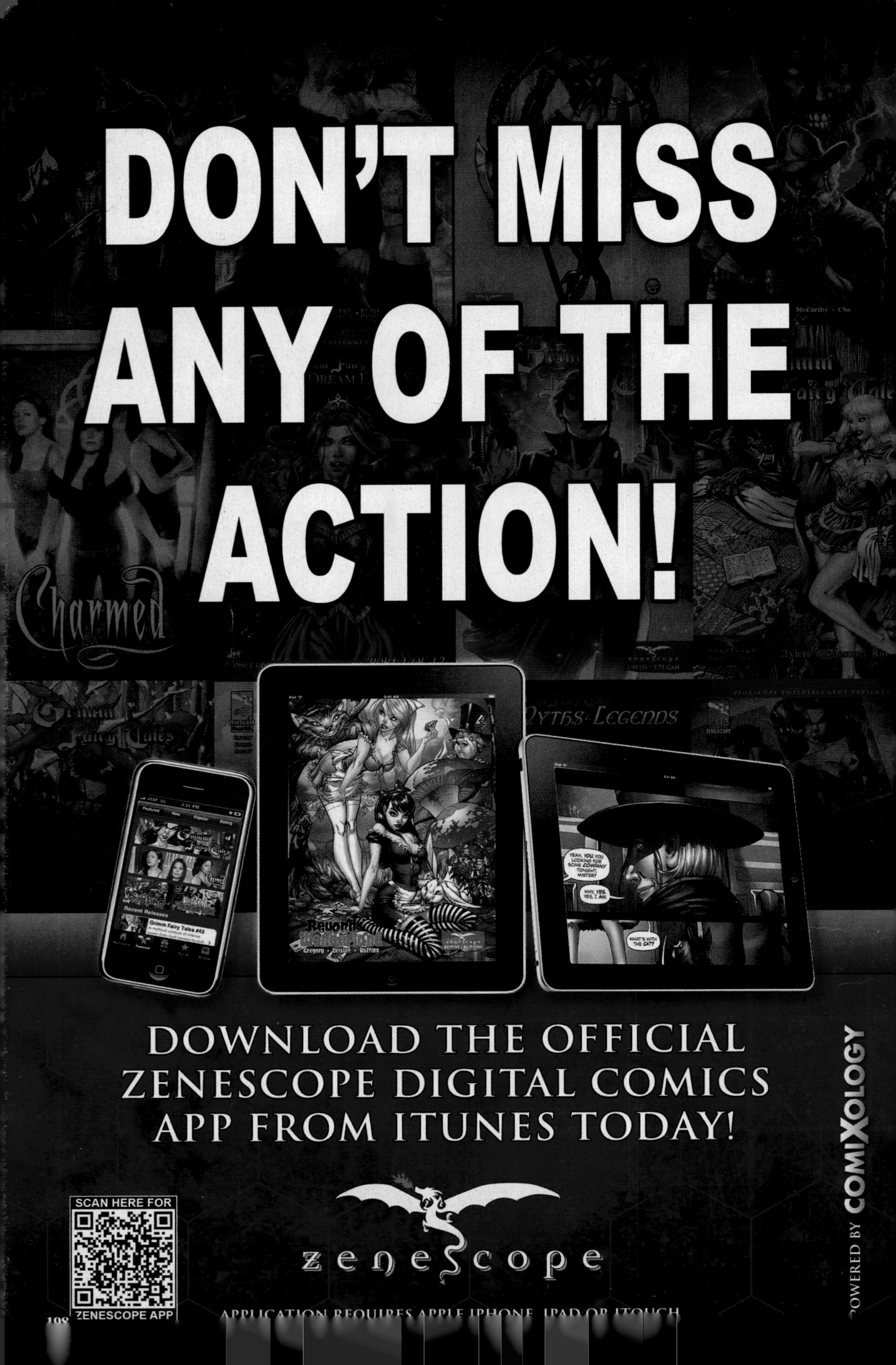
DON'T MISS
ANY OF THE
ACTION!
DOWNLOAD THE OFFICIAL
ZENESCOPE DIGITAL COMICS
APP FROM ITUNES TODAY!
SCAN HERE FOR
ZENESCOPE APP
zenescope
APPLICATION REQUIRES APPLE IPHONE, IPAD OR ITOUCH
POWERED BY COMIXOLOGY

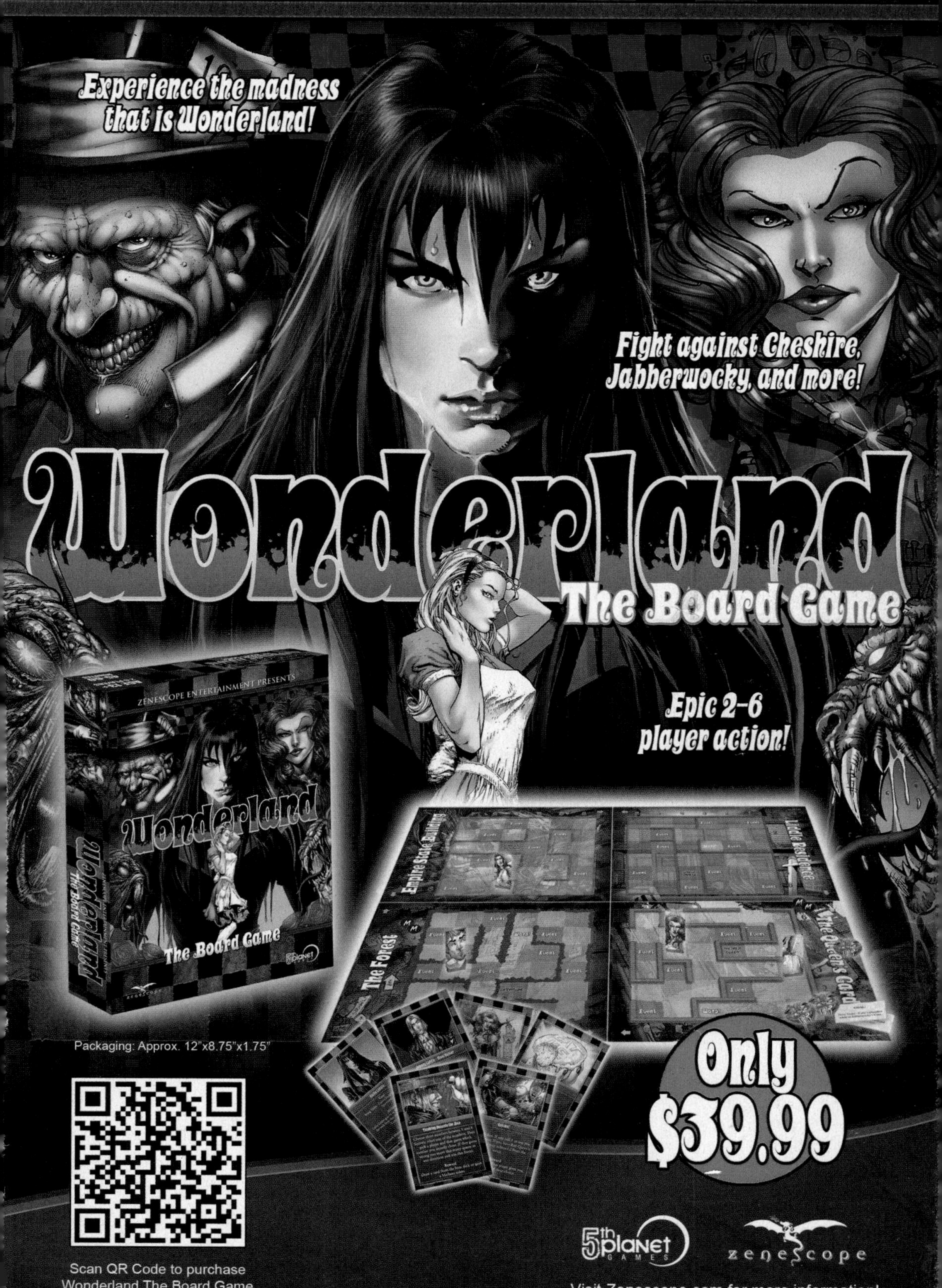
Experience the madness that is Wonderland!
Fight against Cheshire, Jabberwocky, and more!
Wonderland
The Board Game
Epic 2-6 player action!
ZENESCOPE ENTERTAINMENT PRESENTS
Wonderland
The Board Game
Empire State Building
The Forest
Packaging: Approx. 12"x8.75"x1.75"
Only $39.99
Scan QR Code to purchase Wonderland The Board Game
5th planet GAMES
zenescope
Visit Zenescope.com for more information!

Grimm Fairy Tales

Different Seasons Volume 3